PROTEST CAMPS IN INTERNATIONAL CONTEXT

Spaces, infrastructures and media of resistance

Edited by Gavin Brown, Anna Feigenbaum,
Fabian Frenzel and Patrick McCurdy

D1611176

P

First published in Great Britain in 2018 by

Policy Press
University of Bristol
1-9 Old Park Hill
Bristol
BS2 8BB
UK
t: +44 (0)117 954 5940
pp-info@bristol.ac.uk
www.policypress.co.uk

North America office:
Policy Press
c/o The University of Chicago Press
1427 East 60th Street
Chicago, IL 60637, USA
t: +1 773 702 7700
f: +1 773-702-9756
sales@press.uchicago.edu
www.press.uchicago.edu

© Policy Press 2018

British Library Cataloguing in Publication Data
A catalogue record for this book is available from the British Library

Library of Congress Cataloging-in-Publication Data
A catalog record for this book has been requested

ISBN 978-1-4473-2942-8 paperback
ISBN 978-1-4473-2941-1 hardcover
ISBN 978-1-4473-2944-2 ePub
ISBN 978-1-4473-2945-9 Mobi
ISBN 978-1-4473-2943-5 ePdf

The right of Gavin Brown, Anna Feigenbaum, Fabian Frenzel and Patrick McCurdy to be identified as editors of this work has been asserted by them in accordance with the Copyright, Designs and Patents Act 1988.

Cover design by Hayes Design
Front cover image kindly supplied by Darren Hynes
Printed and bound in Great Britain by CPI Group (UK) Ltd, Croydon, CR0 4YY
Policy Press uses environmentally responsible print partners

MIX
Paper from
responsible sources
FSC
www.fsc.org   FSC® C013604

This book is dedicated to all those, past,

present and future, who protest camp in

the name of justice.

Contents

List of figures   vii

Notes on contributors   ix

Acknowledgements   xvii

one   Introduction: past tents, present tents: on the importance of   1
studying protest camps
Gavin Brown, Anna Feigenbaum, Fabian Frenzel and
Patrick McCurdy

Part One: Assembling and materialising   **23**

two   Introduction: assembling and materialising   25
Patrick McCurdy, Anna Feigenbaum, Fabian Frenzel and
Gavin Brown

three   Textile geographies, plasticity as protest   35
Anders Rubing

four   Emergent infrastructures: solidarity, spontaneity   53
and encounter at Istanbul's Gezi Park uprising
Özge Yaka and Serhat Karakayali

five   Protest spaces online and offline: the Indignant movement   71
in Syntagma Square
Anastasia Kavada and Orsalia Dimitriou

six   Feeds from the square: live streaming, live tweeting and   91
the self-representation of protest camps
Paolo Gerbaudo

seven   Touching a nerve: a discussion on Hong Kong's Umbrella   109
Movement
Klavier Jieying Wang, Hope Reidun St John and Miu Yin Eliz Wong

Part Two: Occupying and colonising   **135**

eight   Introduction: occupying and colonising   137
Gavin Brown, Fabian Frenzel, Patrick McCurdy and
Anna Feigenbaum

nine   Carry on camping? The British Camp for Climate Action   147
as a political refrain
Bertie Russell, Raphael Schlembach and Ben Lear

ten   Losing space in Occupy London: fetishising the protest camp   163
Sam Halvorsen

eleven   Occupation, decolonisation and reciprocal violence,   179
or history responds to Occupy's anti-colonial critics
AK Thompson

twelve   Reoccupation and resurgence: indigenous protest camps   199
                in Canada
                Adam J Barker and Russell Myers Ross

thirteen   Democratic deficit in the Israeli Tent Protests: chronicle of a   221
                failed intervention
                Uri Gordon

fourteen   Euromaidan and the echoes of the Orange Revolution: 243
                comparing social infrastructures and resistance practices of
                protest camps in Kiev (Ukraine)
                Maryna Shevtsova

fifteen   Civil/political society, protest and fasting: the case of Anna   261
                Hazare and the 2011 anti-corruption campaign in India
                Andrew Davies

Part Three: Reproducing and re-creating   **277**

sixteen   Introduction: reproducing and re-creating   279
                Fabian Frenzel, Anna Feigenbaum, Patrick McCurdy and
                Gavin Brown

seventeen   From 'refugee population' to political community: 289
                the Mustapha Mahmoud refugee protest camp
                Elisa Pascucci

eighteen   The Marconi occupation in São Paulo, Brazil: a social   309
                laboratory of common life
                Marcella Arruda

nineteen   From protest camp to tent city: The 'Free Cuvry' camp   329
                in Berlin-Kreuzberg
                Niko Rollmann and Fabian Frenzel

twenty   Security is no accident: considering safe(r) spaces in the   353
                transnational Migrant Solidarity camps of Calais
                Claire English

twenty-one   Political education in protest camps: spatialising dissensus   371
                and reconfiguring places of youth activist ritual in Mexico City
                Nicholas Jon Crane

Part Four: Conclusion   **391**

twenty-two   Future tents: protest camps and social movement   393
                organisation
                Fabian Frenzel, Gavin Brown, Anna Feigenbaum and
                Patrick McCurdy

Index   403

List of figures

3.1 Protest Tent in centre of Silwan, Jerusalem 44

3.2 Protest Tent in centre of Silwan, Jerusalem 44

3.3 Protest Tent next to Oslo Cathedral 46

3.4 Palestinian protest camps in Oslo 47

7.1 Umbrella Movement occupation sites 112

7.2 Admiralty occupation site 114

7.3 The first umbrella fence built by protestors soon after the students 115
broke into the Civic Square, 27 September 2014

7.4 Yellow ribbons tied to the fence of the Civic Square, with a banner 118
stating 'We are crying because we are sad for HK, not because of the tear
gas',1 October 2014

7.5 Messages of solidarity from the Admiralty occupation site, 120
15 November 2014

7.6 Admiralty occupation site, 15 November 2014 122

7.7 'I want genuine universal suffrage' banner on top of Lion Rock, 127
24 October 2014

11.1 The Tennis Court Oath 181

11.2 OWS General Assembly, 2012 181

14.1 People gathering around a piano at Euromaidan Protest Camp, 250
2013/2014

14.2 Tires as barricades in Euromaidan, 2013/2014 253

18.1 Façade of the building occupied by MMPT 312

18.2 The sign reading 'I love my occupation' in a common room which 314
each inhabitant should clean once a week

18.3 Entry door of the building with the coexistence rules of 320
the occupation

18.4 Kindergarten and day care centre self-managed by the occupiers 322

19.1 View over the Free Cuvry protest camp from the river Spree 331

19.2 View over the Free Cuvry with Blu graffiti on the right 337

19.3 Activities on the Free Cuvry in summer 2014 343

19.4 & 19.5 After the eviction the buildings were bulldozed to the ground 345

21.1 Material infrastructure for political education in the July 2012 protest 375
camp of the *Movimiento de Liberación Nacional*

21.2 #YoSoy132 protest camp (the *Acampada Revolución*) at the 385
Monument to the Revolution, October 2012

Notes on contributors

Marcella Arruda studied architecture and urbanism in Escola da Cidade, São Paulo, Brazil and interactive media design at the Royal Academy of Arts, in Den Haag, Netherlands. Her interdisciplinary research focuses on the praxis of the commons, in urban interventions as means of contestation and resistance and in the construction of sense of belonging in self-managed social centres.

Adam Barker is an interdisciplinary scholar of social change, settler colonialism and decolonisation. He has recently published his first book (with Emma Battell Lowman) titled *Settler: Identity and Colonialism in 21st Century Canada* (Fernwood Press, 2015). Adam holds an MA in Indigenous Governance from the University of Victoria (Canada) and a PhD in Human Geography from the University of Leicester (UK).

Gavin Brown is an associate professor in human geography at the University of Leicester. He is a cultural, historical and political geographer with wide-ranging research interests. His recent research has recorded the history of a four-year long anti-apartheid 'protest camp' in London in the 1980s. He has a book (co-authored with Helen Yaffe) about *Youth Activism and Solidarity: The Non-Stop Picket Against Apartheid* forthcoming in 2018 with Ashgate. He is a co-editor (with Kath Browne) of *The Routledge Research Companion to Geographies of Sex and Sexualities* and is currently developing a new research project about the geopolitics of sexuality.

Nicholas Crane is an assistant professor in the Department of Geography at the University of Wyoming. Crane is currently working on: 1) an ethnographic study of the relay between youth protest in central Mexico and popular commemoration of the Mexican student movement of 1968, and 2) an action–research project with young racial and economic justice organisers in cities across Ohio. The latter project recently received financial support from the Institute for Human Geography. Crane's recent publications have focused on youth cultural politics, state formation and qualitative research design, among other themes.

Andrew Davies is a lecturer in human geography at the University of Liverpool. His work sits at the intersection of postcolonial and political geography, particularly as they relate to South Asia. This has previously included an examination of the global networks of Free Tibet activism, work on historical anti-colonial networks in India, and participatory work on political protests in contemporary and historical Liverpool.

Orsalia Dimitriou is a practicing architect (ARB) and a researcher. She holds a Diploma in Architecture Engineering from NTU Athens and an MA in Art and Architecture from UPC in Barcelona. She has recently completed her PhD in the Department of Visual Cultures at Goldsmiths University of London and her thesis focuses on public space, commons, democracy and social movements using as a research method both theory and visual media. Her research interests include design as a political tool, urban insurgencies and grassroots practices, theatrical and ephemeral interventions in urban space, participatory design and social sustainability. Orsalia has presented her research and films at numerous conferences (Princeton University, the Bartlett School of Architecture, UCL, Architectural Association, Oxford Brooks, Royal Geographers annual conference, among others). She is currently teaching design at Central Saint Martins and University of Westminster and is a founding member of multidisciplinary design Studio SYN.

Claire English is currently undertaking her PhD at the University of Leicester in the School of Management. She completed her MSc in Gender, Development and Globalisation at the London School of Economics and Political Science in 2010. She completed her BA in Australia at Griffith University where she studied International and Asian Studies majoring in Japanese Language. She is currently working as a researcher for the London School of Economics Gender Institute as part of the Commission in to Gender, Inequality and Power, specialising in the area of economic inequality. Claire's research explores the workings of gender and race within migrant solidarity organisations and activism in the UK and Europe, working particularly at the French/British border of Calais. In her life as both an activist and academic she is interested in the idea of collectivising vulnerabilities as an answer to troubling discourses of safety and security that permeate the left. She has been an active in No Borders, Calais Migrant Solidarity and Plan C. She is currently working with other members of Plan C writing about issues of safety and transformative justice in the left.

Anna Feigenbaum is a principal academic in digital storytelling at Bournemouth University. Her work focuses on communication and social justice. She is co-author of *Protest Camps* with Fabian Frenzel and Patrick McCurdy (Zed, 2013). Her current book project on the history of tear gas in policing will be published by Verso in 2017. Her research can be found in a variety of academic journals as well as in the *Guardian, The Atlantic, Al Jazeera America, The Financial Times, Vice and Waging Nonviolence,* among other outlets. Anna also runs community workshops on data storytelling and digital communications skills and provides consultancy to NGOs and cultural organisations, including Amnesty International and the Victoria and Albert Museum.

Fabian Frenzel is a lecturer in organisation studies at the University of Leicester. His research interest concerns the intersections of mobility, politics and organisation. He is the author of *Slumming It: Tourist Valorisation of Urban Poverty* (Zed, 2016) and co-author with Anna Feigenbaum and Patrick McCurdy of Protest Camps (Zed, 2013)

Paolo Gerbaudo is a researcher working on the transformation of social movements, political cultures and political organisations in a digital era, from a global perspective. He is the author of *Tweets and the Streets: Social Media and Contemporary Activism* (Pluto, 2012) and of the *Mask and the Flag: Anarcho-Populism and Global Protest* (Hurst/OUP, 2016).

Uri Gordon is assistant professor in politics at the University of Nottingham, and co-convenor of the Anarchist Studies Network. He holds a DPhil from the University of Oxford and has previously taught at Tel Aviv University and the Arava Institute for Environmental Studies. He is the author of *Anarchy Alive! Anti-authoritarian Politics from Practice to Theory* (Pluto Press, 2008) and has published in *Social Movement Studies, The Journal of Political Ideologies, Antipode* and *Peace and Change,* among others. His research involves participant observation in radical environmental, social justice and peace movements, and the application of analytical tools to the tensest debates within these activist networks. Gordon is also co-editor of the monograph series *Contemporary Anarchist Studies* (Manchester University Press) and the forthcoming *Routledge Handbook of Radical Politics.* His work has been translated into 13 languages.

Sam Halvorsen is a human geographer, currently a Leverhulme Trust Early Career Fellow at the University of Cambridge (co-sponsored by the Isaac Newton Trust). He is interested in the geography of contemporary forms of activism and social change, with a particular focus on the significance of territory and territoriality. His doctoral research examined the territorial practices of Occupy London and has been published widely in journals including: *Social Movement Studies, Antipode, Environment and Planning D: Society and Space* and *Area*. His current research examines the significance of territory to contemporary forms of political organising in Argentina and aims to open up greater dialogue between Latin American and Anglophone scholars of spatial politics.

Serhat Karakayali studied sociology and political science at the Johann Wolfgang Goethe University in Frankfurt/Main, where he also wrote his dissertation on the genealogy of illegal migration in Germany. He was researcher with the project 'Transit migration' (Institute for European Ethnology, University Frankfurt) and leader of the research project 'In the desert of modernity' (Haus der Kulturen der Welt, Berlin). He currently works as a researcher at the Berlin Institute for Migration Research at Humboldt University and at the ZHdK in Zürich.

Anastasia Kavada is senior lecturer in the Westminster School of Media, Arts and Design at the University of Westminster. She is co-leader of the MA in Media, Campaigning and Social Change and deputy director of the Communication and Media Research Institute (CAMRI). Her research focuses on the links between online tools and decentralised organising practices, democratic decision-making and the development of solidarity among participants in collective action. Anastasia's case studies include, among others, the Global Justice Movement, Avaaz and the Occupy movement. Her work has appeared in a variety of edited books and academic journals, including *Media, Culture and Society* and *Information, Communication and Society*.

Ben Lear is a political organiser and independent researcher based in Manchester. His research interests include social movements, environmental politics and the far right.

Patrick McCurdy (PhD, LSE) is an associate professor in the Department of Communication at the University of Ottawa, Canada. His research draws from media and communication, journalism as well as social movement studies to study media as a site and source of social struggle and contestation. Most recently, Patrick has been studying the evolution of campaigning around the Canadian oil/tar sands. Patrick's work has been published in several academic journals and he is the co-author of *Protest Camps* (with Anna Feigenbaum and

Fabian Frenzel; Zed, 2013) and the co-editor of two books *Beyond WikiLeaks: Implications for the Future of Communications, Journalism and Society* (edited with Arne Hintz and Benedetta Brevini, Palgrave, 2013) and *Mediation and Protest Movements* (edited with Bart Cammaerts and Alice Mattoni, Intellect, 2013).

Elisa Pascucci is Academy of Finland postdoctoral researcher at the University of Tampere, Finland. Her research interests involve the materialities and spatialities of humanitarian aid and theorisations of migrant and refugee political agency, including practices of transnational citizenship and collective mobilisation and protests. She has recently started a project on the impact of ICTs and private sector involvement on refugee aid. Elisa has a PhD in Human Geography (University of Sussex, UK, 2014), and a degree in Middle Eastern Studies (Ca' Foscari University of Venice, Italy, 2005). Her work focuses on North Africa and the Middle East.

Niko Rollmann is a historian working in adult education at the Robert-Tillmanns-Haus in Berlin, Germany. As an independent scholar he has published several books and articles about the city's subterranean architecture, for example 'Die Stadt unter der Stadt' (Jaron, 2006). His research interest extends to other 'underground' subjects, including the history of Jewish Berliners hiding in the city during the Nazi regime. He was closely involved with the 'Free Cuvry' protest camp and campaigns for the alternative 'Teepee Land' settlement.

Russell Myers Ross is from Yunesit'in, a community from the Tsilhqot'in Nation. After finishing a Masters of Indigenous Governance at the University of Victoria in 2010, he returned home to initially teach at Thompson Rivers University as a sessional instructor. Ross was later elected chief of his community for a four-year term in 2012 and has represented Yunesit'in to date.

Anders Rubing is an architect based in Bergen, Norway. Rubing received his MArch degree at Bergen School of Architecture (BAS) where he graduated with honours in 2012. His masters included a semester at Bergen Academy of Art and Design (KHIB). He teaches masters level courses at BAS and has lectured at both KHIB and BAS. Rubing's research focuses on the intersection between protest and security in architecture. He is co-editor of the book *The City Between Freedom and Security, Contested Public Spaces in the 21st Century*

(Birkhäuser, 2016) about the subject. His writing has appeared in Norwegian architecture magazines such as *Kote* and *Bytopia*. Rubing is currently practicing architecture at the office Asplan Viak in Bergen.

Bertie Russell is a research fellow in the Urban Institute, University of Sheffield. He has a PhD from the University of Leeds, exploring post-politics, environmentalism and climate justice activism. His current research is focused on alternative urban governance in the context of the UK devolution agenda, with a specific focus on Greater Manchester. He is also a member of the UK organisation Plan C (weareplanc.org). He has published in journals such as *Area*, *City*, and the *Journal for Aesthetics and Protest*.

Raphael Schlembach is a lecturer in the School of Applied Social Science at the University of Brighton and has published widely on social movement theory, climate action, far right politics and prefigurative protest. He has authored a book called *Against Old Europe: Critical Theory and Alter-Globalization Movements* (Ashgate, 2014) and published in journals such as *Citizenship Studies*, *Environmental Politics*, *Critical Social Policy* and *Sociology Compass*.

Maryna Shevtsova is a PhD student in Political Science at the Berlin Graduate School of Social Sciences. Her doctoral thesis aims to analyse the processes of Europeanisation and promotion of LGBTI rights as 'European' norms in the EU Neighbourhood. She also holds a PhD in Economics from Dnepropetrovsk National University, Ukraine and an MA in Gender Studies from Central European University, Budapest, Hungary. In 2014/2015 she was affiliated with Middle East Technical University and worked for the Center of Eurasian Studies (AVIM) in Ankara, Turkey.

Hope Reidun St John is a PhD student in Sociocultural Anthropology at the University of Washington. Her previous education includes an MA in Chinese Studies from the Chinese University of Hong Kong and a BA in Urban Studies and Global Studies from the University of Washington Tacoma. Her past research has concentrated on the spatial politics of protest space in Hong Kong, power and dissidence in the Chinese cybersphere, and cultural institutions and urban transformation in China. Her current research interests include the implications of urbanisation and urban development in Chinese cities electronic governance, and the exploration and utilisation of visual ethnography.

AK Thompson got kicked out of high school for publishing an underground newspaper called the *Agitator* and has been an activist, writer and social theorist ever since. His publications include *Keywords for Radicals: The Contested Vocabulary of Late Capitalist Struggle* (2016), *Black Bloc, White Riot: Anti-Globalization and the Genealogy of Dissent* (2010) and *Sociology for Changing the World: Social Movements/Social Research* (2006). Between 2005 and 2012, he served on the Editorial Committee of *Upping the Anti: A Journal of Theory and Action*.

Klavier Jieying Wang is a post-doctoral fellow in the Academy of Hong Kong Studies (AHKS), The Education University of Hong Kong. Established in July 2015, AHKS is the first academy dedicated to fostering Hong Kong studies within local tertiary institutions, adopting the strategic direction of "Focus on Hong Kong, Go beyond Hong Kong". She obtained her PhD in Communication from Hong Kong Baptist University and her masters degree from the Chinese University of Hong Kong. Her research interests include social movement studies, identity studies, popular culture and media. Her research papers (forthcoming) appear in the *International Journal of Cultural Studies*.

Miu Yin Eliz Wong is an MPhil candidate in Gender Studies at the University of Cambridge after she graduated, with an MPhil in Sociology, from the Chinese University of Hong Kong. Her major research areas are social movements, civil studies, gender and sexualities in Hong Kong, Mainland China and Taiwan. In her research, gendered perspectives in social movements and activism related to gender and LGBTIQ issues are her main concerns. Her studies, about LGBT participation and female activists in the Hong Kong Umbrella Movement, were presented at the twelfth Conference of the European Sociological Association 2015 and the 'Thinking Gender' Conference at UCLA respectively. She not only devotes her academic efforts to social movement and gender studies, she also participates in different movements in Hong Kong, including democratic movements and LGBT rights movements.

Özge Yaka received her PhD in Sociology from Lancaster University in 2011. She has held positions as an assistant professor at Ondokuz Mayis University in Turkey, as Einstein postdoctoral fellow and as a visiting professor at the Graduate School of North American Studies, JFKI – Freie Universität Berlin. She is currently based at Collège d'études mondiales, FMSH – Paris, as Gerda Henkel Research Fellow. Her research interests include critical social theory, social movement studies, global and environmental justice, gender, protest and subjectivity and the political ecologies of water commons. She has published her work in various journals and edited volumes in English and Turkish.

Acknowledgements

The editors would like to thank the chapter authors without whom this diverse and thought-provoking volume would have been impossible.

We also extend our thanks to our editors at Policy Press – and especially Emily Watt, Laura Vickers and Andy Chadwick – for their help and guidance throughout the process of producing the book.

Two events have been central to the development of this book – an initial workshop, held at the University of Leicester, to discuss protest camps; and a residential weekend where many of the contributors to the book came together to share their research. Funding for these events was provided by Department of Geography, the School of Management and by the College for Humanities and Social Sciences at the University of Leicester.

Gavin Brown would like to thank Anna, Fabian and Patrick for the intellectually and politically stimulating conversations over the years, and for the care with which we have all shared responsibilities and workloads to accommodate each other's competing priorities. I would like to thank two former colleagues, Jenny Pickerill and Peter Kraftl, for their on-going support and enthusiasm for my research. Thanks, too, to all those current colleagues who bring a certain levity to the absurdities of contemporary higher education over our regular 'herd lunches'. Finally, I would like to thank Joseph De Lappe for his love, care, cooking and critical mind – his support through this book and several parallel projects has been magnificent.

Anna Feigenbaum would like to thank her co-authors for bringing horizontal collaboration to life throughout the course of this project – and providing patient leadership when direction was much needed. I would also like to thank my colleagues and students at Bournemouth University, and the members of the Protest Camp Research Network who have provided enthusiasm and support throughout all of our protest camp projects. My appreciation also goes to all those who have hosted talks or provided feedback in a number of guises: Mehita Iqani and the fantastic folks at Wits University, University of Fine Arts Hamburg, SOME Seminars, the Institute for the Art and Practice of Dissent at Home, Icon magazine, Kheya Bag, Adam Bobbette, Mel Evans, Isa Fermeaux, Gavin Grindon, Paolo Gerbaudo, John Jordan, Rodrigo Nunes and the wonderful audience at her Waterstones Bradford book talk. Finally, for all the re-creation that makes writing possible, my love and thanks to Daniel Buchan.

Fabian Frenzel would like to thank Anna, Gavin and Patrick for being fantastic collaborators, critical thinkers, joyful writers and reviewers on this project. My colleagues in the School of Management at the University of Leicester deserve gratitude for the critical, intellectually stimulating environment and the healthy doses of cynicism and hope they share on a daily basis. I would also like to thank Thomas Swann, Konstantin Stoborod, Stephen Dunne, Liam Barrington-Bush, Christiane Leidinger, Susanne Lang, Simon Teune, Priska Daphi, Christoph Haug and Nils Wenk for their shared interest in protest camps, their willingness to engage with ideas and to set up spaces for discussions. Finally, to Merry Crowson, for the many ways in which she enriches my life.

Patrick McCurdy would like to thank his co-authors and co-editors for their inspiration, insight and persistence throughout this project. He would also like to the Faculty of Arts at the University of Ottawa for a grant which helped fund some of his work on this project. Thanks to Judith Forshaw for her keen editing skills as well as to friends and colleagues who have provided feedback on the protest camp project along the way. Last, but not least, to Katrina, Lachlan and Beatrice for filling my days with laughter and light.

We would all like to extend our thanks to our friend Anja Kanngieser who has been a fellow traveller through many of our (mis)adventures over the last few years.

ONE

Introduction: past tents, present tents: on the importance of studying protest camps

Gavin Brown, Anna Feigenbaum, Fabian Frenzel
and Patrick McCurdy

Present tents: Protest camps in the contemporary world

This book examines protest camps as a key expression of contemporary social movement politics. From Tahrir Square to Syntagma Square, from Wall Street to the London Stock Exchange, 2011 was not just the year of the protester, but also the year of the protest camp. From the squares of Spain to the streets of Hong Kong, protest camps are a tactic used around the world. Though their history is much longer, since 2011, protest camps have gained prominence in waves of contentious politics, deployed by movements with a wide array of demands for social change. Through a series of international and interdisciplinary case studies, this book focuses on protest camps as unique organisational forms that transcend particular social movements' contexts. Whether erected in a park in Istanbul or a street in Mexico City, the significance of political encampments rests in their position as distinctive material and mediated spaces where people come together to imagine alternative worlds and articulate contentious politics, often in confrontation with the state.

Despite protest camps' increasing role as an organisational form of protest, little scholarship has considered protest camps as their own domain of enquiry. Some of the earliest scholarship on protest camps tended to view camps as either merely functional to the specific movements in which they were created, or saw them as organisational forms with little significance for the aims and objectives of social movements (McKay, 1998; Duncombe, 2002; Crossley, 2003; Chesters and Welsh, 2004; Della Porta et al, 2006; Pickerill and Chatterton, 2006; Brodkin, 2007). In either case, the protest camp is regarded as just one site among many in the context of studying a specific social

1

movement, and often grouped together with other social movement tactics such as street parties, demonstrations, assemblies and direct actions.

In recent years, more scholarship on protest camps has appeared, mainly driven by reflections on the Arab Spring (Gerbaudo, 2012; Ramadan, 2013), 15M (Castañeda, 2012), and Occupy (Juris, 2012; Kidd, 2014; Pickerill and Krinsky, 2012), either individually, or as linked phenomena (Feigenbaum et al, 2013; Frenzel et al, 2014). There has also been work that draws comparisons between the strategic and tactical functions of past and present protest camps (Leidinger, 2011; 2015). This book aims to build on this emergent scholarship, providing a comprehensive collection of cases, but also identifying ways in which research in this field can be structured. Our argument that protest camps cut across movements is not a structuralist one; instead, it is as an orientation to an understudied practice enacted within many social movements. Our objective is to extract protest camps from their siloed location within specific movements and consider the relations, connections, similarities and differences in their forms across time and space.

In this introduction we take a long view on the history of this organisational form of protest, while also examining why protest camps may have become so prominent in recent years. Exodus from a given polity, or political status quo, and the setting up of alternative political space might be considered one of the oldest available strategies for dissenters. It is, thus, of little surprise to find evidence for camp-like protest already in nomadic cultures and then in the ancient Roman republic (Cowan, 2002). The setting up of alternative and utopian communities in medieval and modern Europe (Hardy, 1979), and in the colonisation of the Americans and the Middle East forms a further historical precedent in which dissenters resorted to exodus and the building of new communities to realise their political aspirations and/ or to escape political persecution (Booth, 1999).

The growth of protest camps throughout the twentieth century parallels the emergence of camping for leisure, and organised youth camps, from the late nineteenth century onwards. Within these twin histories, there is frequent tension between camps set up for 'alternative hedonism' (or 'voluntary simplicity') on the one hand and camps set up out of necessity on the other hand (McKay, 1998; Hailey, 2009). Whether they seek to build alternatives to the status quo voluntarily or are impelled to seek shelter from the status quo, different protest campers bring a variety of diverging experiences into camp communities. Despite this diversity, a fragile commonality can be found in a shared antagonism to the status quo. The production of a common political project also depends significantly on how campers work on their relationships with each other and enact a politicised notion of mutual care. This communitarian conceptualisation of politics challenges social movement theories that prioritise contentious repertoires, like demonstrations, meetings or online campaigns. Protest camps are contentious acts, but they are complex and contradictory spaces that highlight the limitations of politics founded solely in contention. In line with a view of protest movements as communities of resistance, protest camps prompt the consideration of the material, social and spatial infrastructures of political action. This introduction, therefore, will examine the genealogy of protest camps in relation to key approaches from social movement theory, but articulate why it is important to expand the analysis of protest camps beyond that conceptual vocabulary.

Past tents: protest camps in historical perspective

Contrary to much contemporary media reporting, protest camping did not begin in Egypt in early 2011. Resurrection City, one of the largest protest camps we have found in our research, dates back to the US Civil Rights movement of the late 1960s. Protest camps were also an important part of the transnational anti-nuclear movement of the 1980s (Roseneil, 1995; Feigenbaum, 2008; Leidinger, 2011), and the anti-roads movement in the UK in the 1990s (Routledge, 1997; Seel, 1997; Doherty, 1999). The counter-summit mobilisations of the global justice movement in the early 2000s were often based around protest camps (Juris, 2008; McCurdy, 2009; Frenzel, 2010). In the late 2000s a wave of climate camps emerged, first in Britain and then across the world (Schlembach et al, 2012; Saunders, 2012; Frenzel, 2011; 2014). If camping for change, political exodus and territorial political organisation all have long histories, for the purpose of this book it is also important to suggest a starting point for a more specific notion of protest camping.

We suggest to begin the history of the protest camp in 1932, when the shanty town villages of the United States Great Depression, nicknamed 'Hoovervilles' after the then president, were mixed with elements of military base sites during the protests of the Bonus Army. Set up in Washington, DC these camps sustained first world war veterans struggling through the recession, while serving as planning bases and sites for the reproduction of daily life during the Bonus Army's months'-long protests demanding payment of promised benefits for their time served in the military. It makes sense to start with the Bonus Army's camps, because these directly influenced Resurrection City, the Poor People's Campaign 1968 'shanty town' camp on Washington Mall. Martin Luther King Jr himself drew attention to the links between Resurrection City and the Bonus Army protests. Shortly before his death he explained to a radio reporter that the marching caravans of city dwellers would be patterned after the Bonus Army back in the 1930s. From May to June of 1968 Civil Rights and anti-poverty activists set up a highly-organised 'tent city' that ran along the grassland between the Lincoln Memorial and Washington Monument in the American capital. The plans for this protest camp city-in-a-city drew on the model of a base camp, serving as a site for rest, rejuvenation and recreation. Its strategic placement near the Capitol served to lodge a visible act of mass resistance and have easy access to government buildings for daily protests. While like previous tent cities, it offered temporary shelter and sustenance for the poor, unlike its predecessors, Resurrection City was devised primarily as an act of protest.

The camp served many functions. It was a symbolic site that made American poverty visible to the public by bringing the poor to the government's front door. At the same time, Resurrection City functioned as a base of action as residents went on daily protests inside and outside of government offices. 'Solidarity Day' brought over 50,000 to Washington, DC with a march that included civil rights campaigners, labour unions, students and radical protest groups like New York's Up Against the Wall. The protest camp also stood as an experiment in alternative living. Dozens of volunteers including social workers, health professionals and educators helped set up and run on-site healthcare centres and kitchens serving three healthy meals a day, more than many of the city's residents had in their home lives.

While it faced a number of challenges in the form of floods, federal officials and in-fighting, Resurrection City captured public imagination. Months after the camp's heavy-handed eviction, Reverend Jesse Jackson argued, 'Resurrection City cannot be seen as a mud hole in Washington, it is rather an idea unleashed in history.' Years later his words would ring true. To mark the 40th anniversary of the protest camp, organiser's at the 2008 Democratic National Convention set up 'Resurrection City Free University', paying homage to the city's impressive efforts to bring together the nation's ethnically diverse poor to protest economic injustice. In 2011 the Reverend Jesse Jackson again spoke toward the eradication of economic injustice, this time standing on the steps of St Paul's Cathedral to deliver a Christmas message: Jesus was an occupier who chased out the robbers and the thieves.

In contrast to the professionally planned encampment of Resurrection City, the Aboriginal Tent Embassy in Canberra, Australia began far more spontaneously – yet remains the longest running protest camp to date. On 27 January 1972, the day after Australia Day – the country's national holiday which commemorates the landing of British colonisers on Australian soil – a group of indigenous activists went to Old Parliament House in the nation's capital to set up an Aboriginal Embassy. Pitching a beach umbrella into the lawn outside Parliament House (because they couldn't afford a tent and were instead donated an umbrella), the men announced that they were a sovereign people. The action was a direct response to the then government's handling of Aboriginal land rights. While Australian police would normally clear such an act of protest quickly, the laws governing the use of the lawn allowed camping as long as there were fewer than 12 tents. Aboriginal activist Gary Foley, who was involved in the Tent Embassy, recalls how the visibility and exposure of the camp largely led to its success:

> The inability for the government to remove this embarrassing protest from in front of their Parliament House captured the imagination of not just Indigenous Australia. Within days the site had established an office tent and installed a letterbox in front. Tourist bus operators became aware of the new attraction in town and began bringing their busloads of tourists to the 'Aboriginal Embassy' before escorting them across the road to Parliament House. (Foley, 2001, 17)

The 1970s and early 1980s also saw the rise of the protest camp tactic in a number of countries. In Europe and North America, as well as in Japan and the South Pacific, protest camps of this decade were primarily associated with the anti-nuclear movement (both attempting to block the military deployment of nuclear weapons in the context of the late cold war, and to block the expansion of nuclear power on environmental grounds) (Downey, 1986; Bartlett, 2013). One of the most high-profile protest camps of the 1980s was the Greenham Common Women's Peace Camp set up outside the Greenham Common airbase in southern England in 1981 in protest at the decision to base US cruise missiles there from 1983 (Harford and Hopkins, 1984; Roseneil, 2000). In December 1982, approximately 35,000 women converged on Greenham Common to 'Embrace the Base'. At its height, the women's peace camp consisted of up to nine separate encampments around the perimeter of the USAF base on

Greenham Common (Fairhall, 2006). The main, and longest running camp, known as Yellow Gate was located outside the main entrance to the airbase (with the last women finally leaving that camp in 2000 – nine years after the last missiles were removed). Some camps existed on narrow strips of land beside the road, while others were tucked away in more secluded sites in the wooded common land surrounding part of the base. Although these different camps shared many features, each also attracted different groups of women and acquired distinctive atmospheres, modes of living and repertoires of action (Roseneil, 2000; Marshall et al, 2009). Greenham women frequently took imaginative and daring direct actions, trying to prevent construction work on the missile silos, frequently invading the base and compromising its security, and obstructing the missile launchers whenever they were taken off the base on military exercises. This repertoire of direct action, with its irreverence for the authority of the police and the courts, combined with the improvisation needed to sustain the camps in periods when they faced almost daily evictions, had a profound impact on challenging the preconceived gender roles of many of the women who spent time there (Roseneil, 2000). A changed understanding of what they were capable of doing (individually and collectively) was one of the most lasting legacies of Greenham for many of the women who lived and visited there.

Several of the chapters in this book actively seek to question the boundaries of what counts as a 'protest camp'. The Greenham Common Women's Peace Camp clearly fits within commonly accepted understandings of a protest camp – it was a long-term, site-specific protest where people lived, congregated and took action together. On the other hand, one of the other most iconic long-term protests to take place in England in the 1980s is not so simply defined as a 'protest camp'. For nearly four years, from 19 April 1986 until February 1990, anti-apartheid solidarity activists organised by the City of London Anti-Apartheid Group maintained a continuous protest outside the South African embassy in London. Despite being a continuous, long-term protest, nobody lived or slept outside the South African embassy. The protest's physical infrastructure consisted of little more than a fabric banner (in later years, engineered so that it could be freestanding) and a few crates of equipment (that doubled up as seats, occasionally). The Non-Stop Picket demanded the unconditional release of Nelson Mandela and all political prisoners in South Africa, as well as calling for Britain to sever all political, economic and cultural links with South Africa while apartheid existed. Positioned on the pavement directly in front of the main entrance to the embassy, the Non-Stop Picket was strategically located to draw attention to (and cause maximum embarrassment to) the apartheid regime's representatives in Britain (Brown and Yaffe, 2013; 2014).

The modest infrastructure of the Non-Stop Picket looked fragile against the large stone edifice of South Africa House, but it proved to be remarkably resilient. The Picket was a constant irritant to the 'peace and dignity' of South Africa's diplomatic mission; and successfully resisted every attempt that was made to remove it (Brown, 2013). With its ephemeral infrastructures, The Picket was able nevertheless to create a substantial antagonism to the Apartheid state and also enacted a transnational politics of solidarity with comparable protests taking place in front of South African embassies around the world (Metz, 1986).

Transnational protest camps emerged in the form of convergence spaces in the late 1990s and early 2000s around international summits of elite government officials, military and corporate leaders, such as WTO and G8 meetings (Routledge, 2003; Nunes, 2005; Juris, 2008). World Social Forums saw the construction of some of the largest protest camps to date. In 2001 the Intercontinental Youth Camp in Porto Alegre, Brazil emerged in response to the practical problem of finding somewhere for thousands of people to sleep. Started somewhat by accident, Left and student groups worked together to solve an ensuing housing crisis as youth protesters were set to descend on the city. The formulation of the youth protest camp drew inspiration from the Zapatista encuentros or Intercontinental Meeting Against Neoliberalism and for Humanity (Ruggiero, 1998) that brought together thousands of campaigners from movements around the world, including agricultural workers, trade unionists and mothers of the disappeared in Argentina. Meeting, as well as eating and living together, these diverse groups of people converged in the Chiapas. In its second year, the form of the Youth Camp became more explicit and more organised. Protesters set out to create a 'city within a city' complete with its own currency (Nunes, 2005). This design of the Porto Alegre youth camp drew inspiration from the Argentinean piqueteros that saw weekly assemblies, consensus-decision making and the construction of self-sustaining local enterprises. The third camp in 2003 brought 23,500 people together from all across the world in a makeshift city made up of self-managed neighbourhoods that included an eco-built media centre, cultural and workshop spaces (Nunes, 2005).

Learning from – and alongside – these South American movements, the 2002 European No Border camp in Strasburg marked a crucial point in European transnational organisation and the use of the protest camp as an organisational form. Strasburg was the culmination of over a decade of 'no-border' activism in Germany, which had organised camps since the mid-1990s: first, mainly on the German borders with Poland; and later, as the European border regime expanded, camps were organised at different sites along the external borders of the emergent Schengen zone. At the same time, Strasburg also stood at the end of a decade of mobile countercultures represented in the anti-roads movement in Britain, combining protest camps, alternative living and a vibrant party scene (McKay, 1998). Much of this was expressed in Britain in the Earth First! gathering, a protest camp and convergence space that has taken place annually since the mid-1990s, leading to the first instances of alter-globalisation protests like the J18 Carnival Against Capitalism in London in June 1999 (Hunt, 2013). In Strasburg these two histories came together, involving a number of anarchist and radical collectives from around Europe. The camp was large, with over 2000 participants, following on from earlier anti-summit mobilisations, and particularly the protests against the G8 in Genoa the previous year (Juris, 2005).

The Strasburg no borders camp showed the potential for pan-European mobilisations converging in mass protest camps, but it was also broadly considered to be a failure in organisational terms (Schneider and Lang, 2002). The camp's organisational structures were not able to coordinate the different groups. There was no planning collective to coordinate and organise different neighbourhoods within the camp, and this led to permanent frictions. Nevertheless, the perceived failings of this camp and its political ineffectiveness did not undermine the development of a series of Europe-wide mobilisations in the 2000s. Improved planning processes resulted in a number of pan-European camps, from the 2003 anti-G8 camp at Evian, to the HoriZone camp in Scotland in 2005, and three parallel camps, consisting of over 15,000 protesters from across Europe, against the G8 in Germany in 2006 (Frenzel, 2010).

The 2005 HoriZone protest camp was held in Stirling, Scotland between 1 and 9 July 2005. HoriZone was constructed as both a *base for* protests against the 2005 Gleneagles G8 Summit and a *place for* protest (Harvie, 2005). The camp, which could accommodate up to 5,000 people, bordered the site of a 20-year-old filled-in rubbish tip, was on land ordinarily used as a grazing pasture for cattle and bound by the River Forth with only one entrance and exit making it very easy to police. The site's controlled access was acknowledged by HoriZone organisers but dismissed in their relief to secure a location just days before people were due to arrive. The idea of the protest camp had been announced long before a location had been secured. However, this was not for lack of effort on behalf of HoriZone organisers who had previously secured alternate locations only to have them scuppered due to active police interference. Scotland's strict squatting laws which allow police to immediately evict squatters also weighed heavily on selecting a camp site. Having HoriZone evicted even before the Gleneagles Summit began would have been counterproductive. After all, one of the camp's primary functions was to operate as a base for global justice activist mobilising against the G8 Summit.

The camp was not just a base, however, but also a 'media stage' (Feigenbaum and McCurdy, 2016); a site intended to showcase and demonstrate alternative possibilities through the execution and exhibition of practical experiments in sustainable living. To this end, the camp purposefully used alternative energy sources such as solar panels and biodiesel generators, installed greywater and rainwater collection systems, and built on-site compost toilets. HoriZone was more than a base, it was a symbolic arena where campers sought to challenge the political power and practices of G8 leaders through the symbolic power embedded and interwoven into the practices put on show at the camp. Of course, there were tensions in HoriZone's dual purpose as a base for and a place for protest which were particularly evident in the camp's efforts to manage mainstream media interest. While a group known as the CounterSpin Collective (CSC) formed to manage mainstream media interest before and at HoriZone, CSC members were subjected to harassment from some fellow protest campers. Despite the often hostile environment that CSC members worked in, the media practices developed at the 2005 G8 Summit were refined and carried forward to future mobilisations and protest camps. From this perspective, the protest camp was also a laboratory; a place to reflexively develop, test and refine protest camp practices – in this case media practices – which could be added to activists' repertoires of contention at future protest camps. Indeed, the media strategy developed and deployed at HoriZone laid the foundation for the media practices and strategies at future protest camps in the UK such as Climate Camp which ran from 2006 to 2011 (see Russell et al, Chapter Nine). Moreover, as with HoriZone the issue of media interaction at Climate Camp was a contentious and divisive one. More broadly, the issue of media practices – how they are developed within and constrained by camp politics; how they innovate in differing material and mediated environments; how these practices vary across differing social, political, geographic and media contexts – is an avenue of scholarly inquiry opened up by studying protest camps.

Conceptual frameworks for thinking about protest camps

We intend that this book should not only offer an insight into the range of different forms of protest camping that have occurred in different locations across the world in recent decades, but should also outline a framework for analysing protest camps. We point to the importance of detailing the unique spaces of protest camps, the infrastructures and practices that sustain them, and the similarities and differences between protest camps across movements and locations. We also consider the lack of theory which conceptually develops the importance of the protest camp as a distinct entity. We introduce the key concepts of assemblage, materiality, spatiality and territoriality, and social reproduction through which the collection is structured and articulated. These ideas are then explained further in the section introductions which follow. Collectively, the editors and contributors to this book have pioneered new conceptual frameworks for exploring historical and contemporary protest camps (Brown and Pickerill, 2009; Feigenbaum et al, 2013).

The different interdependent operational functions that make up the protest camp can be clearly categorised and distinguished as infrastructures. By common definition, infrastructures refer to the organised services and facilities necessary for supporting a society or community. We therefore use the term 'infrastructure' in its basic meaning to capture how camps build interrelated, operational structures for daily living. These structures function together to disseminate information, distribute goods and provide services. In order to conduct our analysis and work to code the recurring sets of structured objects, practices and behaviours that make up protest camps, we build on the typology of four sets of infrastructures, conceptualised in Feigenbaum et al (2013).

The first of these infrastructures are the communication and media infrastructures within protest camps which are concerned with media strategies, distribution networks and production techniques. Second, there are action infrastructures comprised of direct action tactics, education, police negotiations, legal aid, medical support and transportation networks. Third, camps operate through governance and organisation infrastructures (formal and informal decision-making processes, rules and procedures, but also their spatial organisation). Finally, and sometimes, forgotten, there are re-creation infrastructures which provide food, shelter and sanitation to camps and campers, the maintenance of communal and private spaces, as well as providing care and safety for those living in and visiting protest camps. We initially thought of 're-creation' infrastructures as 'domestic' infrastructures (Frenzel et al, 2014). While it is a key characteristic of many protest camps that they develop into home places for those participating in them, we aimed at articulating a political reading of the 'domestic' as a sphere of social reproduction. Often the domestic sphere is read as separated from economic and political spheres and also gendered. But the politicisation of 'house work' and social reproduction in many protest camps aims to move beyond this separation.

As these set of infrastructures dynamically interact, they sometimes enable and sometimes hinder each other. In these processes conflicts arise which produce a dynamic in which protest camps change, take locally specific forms, succeed or fail. In charting the transformation of sets of infrastructures and their interactions, we can analyse and better understand these dynamics, understanding protest camps' power and powerlessness. Thus, in historical perspective, protest camps emerge as the result of learning processes as well as (dis-)continuities between social and political movements across the world.

Infrastructure should also be read as emergent (see Yaka and Karakayali, Chapter Four) in the sense that many camps are not planned but spontaneous. Little to no preparation goes into some camps and the ability to rationally steer and set up certain infrastructures is limited. Nevertheless, the political experience of some participants, as well as their access to certain resources, still means that even 'spontaneous' camps are shaped by previous mobilisations. Yaka and Karakayali show that in spontaneous camps, such as the one at Gezi Park in Istanbul in 2013, infrastructures emerge without a plan, often as a result of affective linkages that tie together new collectives. It is precisely these emergent socialities that seem to have dominated many of the more recent urban protest camps.

Protest camps, in all their many forms, also have very specific geographies. Academic geographers are keen to argue that all forms of protest and contentious politics are spatial (Miller et al, 2013), but this is most obvious in the case of protest camps. To fully understand protest camps, it is important to pay attention to the spatialities through which they operate. Protest camps have a physical form that is located in a particular place. That location is unlikely to be random (although occasionally, as was the case with the Occupy London camp in 2011, police action may mean that the camp takes form somewhere other than the activists' planned, primary target). The sites of protest camps are chosen because they are strategic – they draw attention to an injustice (or those with power who have perpetrated it); by taking form in that place they have the potential to prevent or delay a further injustice occurring; or, they may occupy a site of symbolic importance in the popular imagination that helps add credence to their cause through their association with that location. Where a protest camp comes into being can have a very significant impact on how it functions, who can participate in it, and how (and for how long) it can exist. Put simply, the more remote a site is, the more logistically challenging it will be for a large number of people to participate in it over an extended period of time. Urban camps can attract greater volumes of participants, but they are more likely to come and go with greater regularity, balancing time at the camp with the other aspects of their lives. Different locations facilitate different degrees of on-site infrastructure. In this respect, the location and physical form of a camp will have a significant impact in shaping how a camp functions and the ways in which people participate in it.

The diversity and specificity of this myriad of protest camps, means that it is important to take grounded approaches when researching them. While protest camp infrastructures are adopted and adapted across time, space and geographic place, it is important not to preclude the analysis of infrastructures by assuming any new protest camps will follow the patterns that have preceded it. With this caveat in mind, let us consider the dominant set of infrastructures in turn.

Media and communications infrastructures

As campaigns and protests, camps need to speak. They need to speak to outside audiences (members of the public, potential supporters, or politicians), but participants also need to speak among themselves. In the history of protest camps both dimensions are important, however classical social movement scholarship, drawing from traditional social movements has focused on the former, considering the mainstream media relations of protest movements, and their effectiveness in dominating media frames and representations. In protest camps relations with the media are of central importance. Protest camps have set up a number of ways of communicating with the outside; but, just as much, they have considered their own internal communications. While protest camps have often created media tents, sometimes outside the actual camp, for external media to address the camp, other specific ways of managing media have also been invented. Protest camps have sometimes 'embedded' journalists from outside media in order to control their media images. At the same time camps have developed infrastructures that enable onsite alternative media production.

Today this point seems self-evident as media production can swiftly be done using a mobile phone. But such a view underestimates the specific catalytic influence protest camps can have on autonomous and independent media production. Prior to social media saturation, protest camps created media production spaces, like media tents, pirate radio stations, video production suites and print shops on site, as places where participants could gather, exchange knowledge, and become media producers. The collective organisation of media is thus the prime character of autonomous media production in camps. This is also true in the realm of social media today, where collective media strategies, and the conscious use of collectively agreed approaches, can render social media use beyond its often atomistic nature. Media infrastructures in protest camps are not limited to content production, but also concern the medium and its autonomous production. In Tahrir Square protesters hacked the only remaining internet line to the world (the one of the Cairo stock exchange) to continue broadcasting to the outside (Feigenbaum et al, 2013). Whether live streaming or banner-making, the protest camp is a place of hybrid digital and analogue communications, the material and symbolic dimensions of communication are closely intertwined and scholars must pay close attention to these dynamics

Action infrastructures

The infrastructures of political action present at protest camps differ widely, starting from those tools directly needed to pursue certain activities. This includes the organisation of political action; training to prepare people for action; and, sometimes, the provision of care for people after actions have taken place (see also re-creation infrastructures, below). Action infrastructures also concern the more practical boundary work needed to make protest camps. As barricades rise up, the question of how to relate to the outside is often limited to defence and a (seemingly) clear 'us- versus-them' logic. The alternative world created in the camp needs to be protected. The camp provides a number of basic infrastructures to provide such functions. Due to being in place for a number of days, with routines other than action also occurring, the camp lends itself to the training of certain action techniques, including mass action, legal skills and first aid training. Such training can occur more formally, in the sense that particular workshops are set up and advertised in the camp communications; but, it also occurs more informally, when people catch up about experiences around the camp fire, or when they encounter each other after actions.

Action infrastructures provided in protest camps concern not only the actual teaching of certain techniques they also concern the establishment of spaces in which perceptions of action and activity can be questioned and destabilised. Direct action can be highly gendered and considered as the preserve of male activists (despite a long history of women taking direct action of many kinds). Direct action consists both of the defence of the camp against attack by police and other political opponents of the camp, but also the more offensive practices undertaken by protesters, such as blockades and trespasses. Protest camps provide spaces and infrastructures of training and action where gendered roles in relation to such action can be challenged. Certain perceptions of what constitutes legitimate action can also be challenged. For example, when the breaking of certain laws in civil disobedience is experienced for the first time, camps can provide spaces in which such experiences may be shared and reflected upon.

Governance infrastructures

The organisation and governance of protest camps is again based on the idea of the protest camp as an alternative world. In this context, protest camps have developed from rather hierarchically organised structures, akin to the Scouts' camping tradition, to utilise a number of innovative new approaches to governance and organisation, driven by the desire to not simply form a political force, but to create alternative political cultures. The rejection of traditional ways of decision-making, found in left-wing and counter-cultural movements, has been articulated strongly in many protest camps. By their very spatial and temporal character, they enable experimentation with self-organisation in more horizontal and anarchist inspired ways (even if these experiments often fail). In contrast to such organisational experimentations elsewhere, the spatial proximity of people within camps and their daily routines can serve to support and stabilise these experiments.

One example of this function of the protest camp relates to the development of spatialised organisational forms. In camps from Resurrection City to Tahrir Square, the shared opposition to the status quo is expressed territorially and this expression enables the formation of governance based on horizontal and shared decision-making. A further crucial innovation, visible in the history of South American, British and European camps in particular, is the development of decentralisation within the camp. The neighbourhood (or barrio) structure enables campers to self-organise in a very horizontal fashion, decentralising decision-making and linking it, at the same time, to social reproduction within the camp.

Re-creation infrastructures

Social reproduction, or what we have called re-creation infrastructures, is ultimately linked to the ability of the camp to function as an alternative world in that it provides safety, care, shelter and food for its participants. Tents and marquees form the basis of this provision, as do kitchens and medical tents. Re-creation infrastructures can emerge spontaneously, and they often do as people gather in protest, bringing together not just materials to help occupy a site, but the necessary equipment and provisions to allow them to stay there, safely, healthily and relatively comfortably, for a period of time. In more planned camps these infrastructures are often most sophisticated, and sometimes even provided by specialised teams, such as the Tat Collective in the UK which overlooks and supplies a stock of material needed to build a camp. There are also a number of kitchen collectives in several countries that cater specifically for protest camps, setting up large kitchens to sustain campers. The labour of preparing the food remains the responsibility of participants, organised in rotas to ensure that everybody participates. This was often the case in the protest camps of the alter-globalisation movement and in climate camps. In other protest camps like 15M, Tahrir and Occupy, such organisational forms developed quickly, while in others like the anti-roads movement and Greenham Common, day to day routines were more ad hoc. This points to the ways in which repertoires of social reproduction are also adapted over time, and can become institutionalised as social movement practice.

This is a paradox in so far as much of the motivation for the creation of autonomous protest camps lies in their ability to create exceptional political spaces and experiences that are separate and distinct from the status quo. The imagined and promised autonomy of protest camps is often performatively practised within them, in ways which produce an exceptional politics, in which conventional political processes and realities may (appear to) be suspended. When protest camps become more institutionalised forms of protest with established infrastructures, this exceptionality is arguably less evident. Indeed, the tension between the appeal of spontaneous assembly and the creation of protest camps seems to stem significantly from the ability to generate and express a collective antagonistic affect. The more professional protest camps infrastructures become in their planning and delivery, the less powerful the expression of this collective antagonistic affect may be.

But this is not the only tension to emerge in recent protest camps. The desire for alternative forms of organisation and autonomy often conflicts with the actual political expression adopted by given camps. Attending to social reproduction can take time away from many of the other potential activities that are more closely related to political action and expression (Halvorsen, 2015). Consequently, a frequent critique of camps is that they become self-absorbed and forget about the need to actually speak to the outside world about their political cause. Throughout this book, we pay attention to these and other contradictions within protest camps.

Aims and structure of the book

The structure of this book arises around these four sets of infrastructures. Organised into three sections, each one focuses on how particular practices and concerns emerged in specific protest sites. In Part One – *Assembling and Materialising* – the chapters examine how camp infrastructures are co-created. Chapters in Part Two – *Occupying and Colonising* – address questions around spatial politics and governance, particularly looking at questions of power and territorialisation. Finally, in Part Three – *Reproducing and Re-creating* – the chapters look at how different protest camps negotiate the day-to-day struggles of simultaneous resisting and living together. Throughout the collection, each individual chapter offers case studies of protest camps. They offer both new and original empirical accounts of protest camps across varied cultural, political and geographical landscapes of protest. Moreover, the collection draws on work across the fields of social movement studies, incorporating perspectives from geography, media and communication, architecture, anthropology, sociology and management studies.

Introduction to the book's themes

In Part One, on *Assembling and Materialising*, we consider the different elements that are brought together to create the material and social infrastructures of camps. We consider what material objects, technologies and social relations are brought together inside the space of a protest camp to make it function as a place-based site of protest and political contestation. Taking seriously the material and social infrastructures of camps, we examine the spatial division of labour within protest camps (as well as the ways in which they relate to publics 'outside' their physical boundaries). We also introduce how the architecture of the public squares and gardens that are occupied by protesters can shape the ways in which politics is practised within them. Protest camps are seldom spontaneous, and we need to understand better the processes by which camps are planned, and the ways in which political practices travel between camps over time, often entangled with the material histories of specific pieces of camping equipment. This includes the important role of media and communication infrastructure. We highlight the need to examine the relationship between the physical space of occupation and the mediated or virtual space. Of interest here are the media practices used to maintain and amplify spaces of protest with particular attention given to the role of media – and social media in particular – in maintaining and amplifying corporeal protest camp sites.

Part Two, *Occupying and Colonising*, addresses a different set of spatial politics posed by protest camps. We are concerned here with the politics of occupying (public) space for protest and the tensions that can arise from this. Urban protest camps, in particular, frequently seek to occupy public space in order to draw attention to the policies of political and economic elites; frequently, in doing so, they invade spaces that homeless and other vulnerable groups have previously made their own. We need to question how certain 'publics' are brought into being by protest camps, while the existence of others might be elided or erased. These are fundamental questions about the complex (and contradictory) ways in which camps position themselves in relation to what is outside them. This section addresses the constitutive power of the protest camps as a political and communicative space. Here the spatial character of the protest camp as its own sphere of life and communication creates a disposition between the two, something that leads to various relationships from clear-cut antagonism between 'the camp' and 'the outside' to more heterotopic overlaps, as well as more blurred boundaries in communication and action.

The title of Part Three is *Reproducing and Re-creating*. Considering camps as home places – places where people feed, care for and house each other, means to see them as sites where social reproduction takes place. This raises a number of questions, for example concerning the balance between social reproduction and more confrontational forms of political contestations (as well as the highly contested expectations about who should participate in each of these functions). Because they can become a temporary home for many people, questions of physical, psychological and symbolic safety (especially for women and minority groups) have frequently been the cause of tension within camps. How do campers struggle to realise some of their political hopes within the space of the camp – not just their 'big' hopes for a more just, equal and sustainable society; but their hopes for a transformation of everyday social relations between people? When protest camps become home places, we see the limits of conceptualisations of politics as rationalist speech acts: camps can create a space for participants to engage in deeper identity quests that seek life beyond the capitalist status quo. Precisely because protest camps prefiguratively embody alternative ways of being they can serve as powerful inspirations long after specific camps cease to exist.

By organising the book's material in this way, our focus is placed on specific thematic aspects of protest camps as seen through the lenses of varied academic traditions. This interdisciplinary approach allows for diverse and dynamic analyses of specific historically, culturally and spatially situated protest camps. Through the use of section introductions, we tease out key conceptual connections between the chapters' analyses of protest camps, navigating the reader through the different disciplinary approaches, explaining social movement contexts, and introducing key issues that the camps discussed in each section raise.

We trust that our approach reflects the scope of contemporary protest camp research and equally inspires academics – present and future – to explore further the practice of protest camping. Of course, it is not possible to cover all regions or types of protest camps. We have assembled case studies here that give a broad geographical range and cut across different kinds of social movements and a range of political issues. We have placed greater emphasis on recent and contemporary protest camps (in different parts of the world), while acknowledging their historical roots and associations. As protest camps – planned and spontaneous – continue to emerge around the world, our hope is that this collection will provide a basis for understanding them in all their political diversity and material complexity.

References

Bartlett, A. (2013) 'Feminist protest in the desert: researching the 1983 Pine Gap women's peace camp', *Gender, Place and Culture*, 20(7), 914–926.

Booth, M. (1999) 'Campe-toi! On the origins and definitions of camp', in F. Cleto (ed), *Camp: Queer Aesthetics and the Peforming Subject – A Reader*, Ann Arbor, MI: University of Michigan Press, pp 66–79.

Brodkin, K. (2007) *Making Democracy Matter: Identity and Activism in Los Angeles*. New Brunswick, NJ: Rutgers University Press.

Brown, G. (2013) 'Unruly bodies (standing against apartheid)', in A. W. G. Cameron, J. Dickinson and N. Smith (eds) *Body-states*. Aldershot: Ashgate, pp 145–157.

Brown, G. and Pickerill, J. (2009) 'Space for emotion in the spaces of activism', *Emotion, Space and Society*, 2(1), 24–35.

Brown, G. and Yaffe, H. (2013) 'Non-stop against Apartheid: practicing solidarity outside the South African embassy', *Social Movement Studies*, 12(2), 227–234.

Brown, G. and Yaffe, H. (2014) 'Practices of solidarity: opposing apartheid in the centre of London', *Antipode*, 46(1), 34–52.

Castañeda, E. (2012) 'The indignados of Spain: a precedent to occupy Wall Street', *Social Movement Studies*, 11(3–4), 309–319.

Chesters, G. and Welsh, I. (2004) 'Rebel colours: "framing" in global social movements', *The Sociological Review*, 52(3), 314–335.

Cowan, G. (2002) *Nomadology in Architecture Ephemerality, Movement and Collaboration*, MSc dissertation, Adelaide: University of Adelaide.

Crossley, N. (2003) 'Even newer social movements? Anti-corporate protests, capitalist crises and the remoralization of society', *Organization*, 10(2), 287–305.

Della Porta, D., Andretta, M., Mosca, L. and Reiter, H. (2006) 'Globalization from below', *Transnational Activists and Protest Networks*. Minneapolis, MN: University of Minnesota Press.

Doherty, B. (1999) 'Paving the way: the rise of direct action against road-building and the changing character of British environmentalism', *Political Studies*, 47(2), 275–291.

Downey, G. L. (1986) 'Ideology and the clamshell identity: organizational dilemmas in the anti-nuclear power movement', *Social Problems*, 357–373.

Duncombe, S. (2002) *Cultural Resistance Reader*. London: Verso.

Fairhall, D. (2005) *The Story of Greenham Common Ground*. London: IB Taurus.

Fairhall, D. (2006) *Common Ground: The Story of Greenham*, London: IB Tauris.

Feigenbaum, A. (2008) *Tactics and Technology: Creative Resistance at the Greenham Common Women's Peace Camp*, PhD thesis, Montreal: McGill University.

Feigenbaum, A. and McCurdy, P. (2016) 'Protest camps as media stages: a case study of activist media practices across three British social movements', in R. Figueiras and P. do Espirito Santo (eds) *Beyond the Internet: Unplugging the Protest Movement Wave*. London: Routledge, pp 31–52.

Feigenbaum, A., Frenzel, F. and McCurdy, P. (2013) *Protest Camps: Imagining Alternative Worlds*. London: Zed.

Foley, G. (2001) 'Black Power in Redfern 1968–1972', Koori History Website, http://kooriweb.org/foley/essays/essay_1.html.

Frenzel, F. (2010) *Politics in Motion: The Mobilities of Political Tourists*, PhD thesis, Leeds: Leeds Metropolitan University.

Frenzel, F. (2011) 'Entlegende Ort in der Mitte der Gesellschaft Die Geschichte der britischen Klimacamps', in A. Brunnengräber (ed), *Zivilisierung des Klimaregimes: NGOs und soziale Bewegungen in der nationalen, europäischen und internationalen Klimapolitik*, Wiesbaden: VS Verlag für Sozialwissenschaften, pp 163–186.

Frenzel, F. (2014) Exit the system? Anarchist organisation in the British climate camps', *Ephemera: Theory and Politics in Organization*, 14(4), 901–921, www.ephemerajournal.org/sites/default/files/pdfs/contribution/14-4frenzel_0.pdf

Frenzel, F., Feigenbaum, A. and McCurdy, P. (2014) 'Protest camps: an emerging field of social movement research', *The Sociological Review*, 62(3), 457–474.

Gerbaudo, P. (2012) *Tweets and the Streets: Social Media and Contemporary Activism*. London: Pluto Press.

Hailey, C. (2009) *Camps: A Guide to 21st-Century Space*. Cambridge, MA: MIT Press.

Halvorsen, S. (2015) 'Taking space: moments of rupture and everyday life in Occupy London', *Antipode*, 47(2), 401–417.

Hardy, D. (1979) *Alternative Communities in Nineteenth Century Britain*. London: Longman.

Harford, B. and Hopkins, S. (1984) *Greenham Common: Women at the Wire*. London: The Women's Press.

Harvie, D. (ed) (2005) *Shut Them Down!: The G8, Gleneagles 2005 and the Movement of Movements*. New York: Autonomedia.

Hunt, S. E. (2013) 'The echoing greens: the neo-romanticism of Earth First! and Reclaim the Streets in the UK', *Capitalism Nature Socialism*, 24(2), 83–101.

Juris, J. S. (2005) 'Violence performed and imagined militant action, the Black Bloc and the mass media in Genoa', *Critique of Anthropology*, 25(4), 413–432.

Juris, J. S. (2008) *Networking Futures: The Movements against Corporate Globalization*. Durham, NC: Duke University Press.

Juris, J. S. (2012) 'Reflections on # Occupy Everywhere: social media, public space, and emerging logics of aggregation', *American Ethnologist*, 39(2), 259–279.

Kidd, D. (2014) 'Social justice media: the case of occupy', *Mediaciones: Revista Academica de Comunicación*, Pre-publication version, 30 October, www.researchgate.net/publication/272170025_Social_Justice_Media_the_Case_of_Occupy.

Leidinger, C. (2011) 'Coalitions of contention in camps as political laboratories: antimilitarist and feminist alliances and coalition work as contingent social processes', *Osterreichische Zeitschrift fur Politikwissenschaft*, 40(3), 283–300.

Leidinger, C. (2015) *Zur Theorie Politischer Aktionen – Eine Einführung*. Berlin: Edition Assemblage.

McCurdy, P. (2009) *'I Predict a Riot' – Mediation and Political Contention: Dissent!'s Media Practices at the 2005 Gleneagles G8 Summit*, PhD thesis, London: London School of Economics and Political Science.

McKay, G. (1998) *DIY Culture: Party and Protest in Nineties Britain*. London: Verso.

Marshall, Y., Roseneil, S., Armstrong, K. (2009) 'Situating the Greenham archaeology: an autoethnography of a feminist project', *Public Archaeology*, 8(2–3), 225–245.

Metz, S, (1986) 'The anti-apartheid movement and the populist instinct in American politics', *Political Science Quarterly*, 101(3), 379–395

Miller, B., Beaumont, J. and Nicholls, W. (eds) (2013) *Spaces of Contention: Spatialities and Social Movements*. Aldershot: Ashgate

Nunes, R. (2005) 'The intercontinental youth camp as the unthought of the World Social Forum', *Ephemera: Theory and Politics in Organisation*, 5(2), 277–96.

Pickerill, J. and Chatterton, P. (2006) 'Notes towards autonomous geographies: creation, resistance and self-management as survival tactics', *Progress in Human Geography*, 30(6), 730–746.

Pickerill, J. and Krinsky, J. (2012) 'Why does occupy matter?', *Social Movement Studies*, 11(3–4), 279–287.

Ramadan, A. (2013) 'From Tahrir to the world: the camp as a political public space', *European Urban and Regional Studies*, 20(1), 145–149.

Roseneil, S. (1995) *Disarming Patriarchy: Feminism and Political Action at Greenham*. Buckingham: Open University Press.

Roseneil, S. (2000) *Common Women, Uncommon Practices: The Queer Feminisms of Greenham*. London: Cassell.

Routledge, P. (1997) 'The imagineering of resistance: Pollok Free State and the practice of postmodern politics', *Transactions of the Institute of British Geographers*, 359–376.

Routledge, P. (2003) 'Convergence space: process geographies of grassroots globalization networks', *Transactions of the Institute of British Geographers*, 28(3), 333–349.

Ruggiero, G. (1998) *Zapatista Encuentro: Documents from the First Intercontinental Encounter for Humanity and Against Neoliberalism*, New York: Seven Stories Press.

Saunders, C. (2012) 'Reformism and radicalism in the climate camp in Britain: benign coexistence, tensions and prospects for bridging', *Environmental Politics*, 21(5), 829–846.

Schlembach, R., Lear, B. and Bowman, A. (2012) 'Science and ethics in the post-political era: strategies within the Camp for Climate Action', *Environmental Politics*, 21(5), 811–828.

Schneider, F. and Lang, S. (2002) 'The dark side of camping', www.tacticalmediafiles.net/article.jsp?objectnumber=44087.

Seel, B. (1997) 'Strategies of resistance at the Pollok Free State road protest camp', *Environmental Politics*, 6(4), 108–139.

Part One
Assembling and materialising

TWO

Introduction: assembling and materialising

Patrick McCurdy, Anna Feigenbaum, Fabian Frenzel and Gavin Brown

Introduction

Convergence and assembly in physical space provides a protest camp's foundation. Yet a protest is not only comprised of bodies together in space. The dynamics and political trajectories of a protest camp are formed from the entanglements and interactions of material objects (canvas tents, city roads, bicycles, wooden pallets, tarps and tables), physical geographies (environments, built architectures, climate), mediated representations (from mainstream newspapers to twitter feeds), as well as local, provincial and national laws that shape how protesters navigate all of these conditions at once. It is these entanglements and adaptations that give rise to the emblematic symbols of protest camps – from the beach umbrella that first marked the Aboriginal Tent Embassy in Australia, to Occupy Wall Street's people's mic (Cowan, 2002; Costanza-Chock, 2012).

Drawing on a range of empirical cases across a wide geography of protest camps sites in cities including Athens, Berlin, Hong Kong, Istanbul, Jerusalem, Madrid, New York, Oslo and Ramallah, contributions in this section consider how the different elements assembled to create a protest camp are brought together in their specific temporal, social, cultural and political context to create the material and social infrastructures of protest camps. In what follows, this section's themes are discussed by way of Occupy Melbourne's 'tent monsters' phenomenon, which embodies, problematises and captures the limits of protest camps' processes of assembling and materialising. This is followed by a thematic and chapter-by-chapter review of this section.

Tent monsters

Section 2.11 of the Melbourne City Council Activities Local Law 2009 reads, 'Unless in accordance with a permit, a person must not camp in or on any public place in a vehicle, tent, caravan or any type of temporary or provisional form of accommodation' (City of Melbourne, 2009). While such laws may lie dormant, unnoticed by the public, in times of protest they may act as a legal wedge to intervene and shut down political contention. Occupy Melbourne protesters camped in Melbourne's city squares and parks between October and late December 2011. During this time the city issued approximately 150 'notices to comply' with the local law that prohibited camping in public places without a permit (Hunt and Hunt Lawyers, 2016). However, on 5 December 2011 a small collective of self-identified Occupy Melbourne activists assembled in Flagstaff Gardens in west Melbourne to playfully test the boundaries of the camping ban. The result was an action that attracted international media attention and produced the viral video: *Occupy Melbourne Tent Monsters* (see TheFreemanSmith, 2011).

Set against the soothing soundtrack of Haydn's Symphony No 94 in G Major, 'The Surprise', the YouTube video 'Tent Monsters' (TheFreemanSmith, 2011) opens with a shaky shot of a blue and grey nylon tent pitched in the lush, green grass of Flagstaff Gardens. In the distance, approximately a dozen uniformed city council and police officers in high visibility vests are filmed walking towards the department store-grade tent for a routine eviction. As the guards approach past lounging park goers, the tent springs to life. A head of thick, fiery red curls pops through the top, arms burst through the left and right side, while legs spring out the bottom. What was, seconds before, a static and prohibited object, is transformed into a playful costume worn by 'tent monster' Sara Louise Kerrison. The video then zooms in on Ms Kerrison as she is joined by two other 'tent monsters'. They frolic about and playfully taunt the police, who circle around them, seemingly befuddled by these human-tent assemblages. The camera then follows the officers as they make their way out of the park, with the tent monsters in close pursuit. In need of a new strategy, the authorities scrimmage beneath a tree on the park's boundaries. The video ends on a scene of Ms Kerrison and her fellow tents showing off their costumes, demonstrating flexibility and speed with skips and curtsies.

The stunt received international media attention. CNN's Jeanne Moss reported the confrontation under the headline 'Occupy's "tent monsters" cause flap' (CNN, 2011), portraying it as a playful and unconventional use of a tent, which ended in activist victory. However, what was not captured in the original Occupy Melbourne Tent Monsters video, or the original CNN news story, was the police action afterwards. Officers deemed that even though Ms Kerrison was wearing the tent as a piece of clothing, she was still in violation of Local Law 2.11 prohibiting camping and sought to seize the banned article. What happened next is captured in a disturbing collection of YouTube videos (see RynChristoph, 2011; sean bedlam, 2011a) which shows how the police engages in public husking of Ms Kerrison by ripping, pulling and cutting the tent costume, leaving Ms Kerrison in her underwear as she reportedly refused offers of clothing from police (AAP, 2014). Ms Kerrison is later shown rebuking the police for their treatment of her; wearing, as a makeshift robe, a vinyl Occupy banner which read 'Welcome to Occupy Melbourne: Welcome to direct democracy' (sean bedlam, 2011b). After the incident, Ms Kerrison and one other Occupy Melbourne member filed a challenge in Australian Federal Court against Melbourne City Council and the Victoria Police. They argued that Occupy Melbourne's aggressive eviction from city parks and the subsequent issuing of infringements violated their freedom of protest (AAP, 2014; Hunt and Hunt Lawyers, 2016). However, a Federal Court judge a ruled that the Council acted lawfully in evicting Occupy Melbourne, a ruling which was upheld by a subsequent appeals judge (AAP, 2014; Human Rights Law Centre, 2013).

The case of Occupy Melbourne's tent monsters embodies the themes of assembling and materialising which cut across contributions in this section, in particular, the rights and boundaries of political assembly, the creative use and appropriation of everyday objects, as well as the role of media and communications in the mediation of these images as they circulate within and beyond the space of the protest camp. While not erecting tents as temporary structures, the costumed activists were still treated by police as camping and therefore breaking city law. The persistence and vigour with which police issued infractions in this instance speaks to the wider symbolic power of the tent. Indeed, particularly in Occupy's wake, the tent has been transformed from a portable, pragmatic shelter to a potent symbol of resistance. The popularity of protest camps as a form of assembly has been met with legal challenges through the enforcement of local bylaws, and even through the drafting of specific new laws targeted at camping equipment. For example, in the shadow of Occupy London and in advance of the 2012 London Olympics, the British government passed legislation prohibiting tents from Olympic sites (Home Office, 2012).

Indeed as Wang et al's contribution (Chapter Seven) show in their discussion of Hong Kong's 2014 umbrella protests, laws, in tandem with the accompanying political culture, have a significant impact on the scope and shape of protest.

After the 2011 global wave of occupations, the symbolic power of the tent persists, amplified by the rise of activist 'mass self-communication' (Castells, 2009). Contributions in this section explore how activists' media and communication practices mediate and inform their material practices, from the real-time streaming of protest events, to debating protest tactics and strategies online, to the crafting and sharing of media content. Protest camping is increasingly both an attempt to occupy physical space and mediated space in efforts to capture and spark public imagination and imaginaries. Indeed, given the temporality of protest camps, some permanence may be found in the digital representation of protest camps. Long after a camp's physical site is removed – whether through forcible eviction or protesters' own volition – its material life lives on, archived in a variety of media forms.

Often the sites that are occupied by protesters are already rich in material history. Physical spaces rich with historical significance – often city squares – are transformed by protest camps as they reconfigure our understanding of, relationship to, and engagement with public space. Moreover, the impact of creating and engaging in a protest camp can generate impacts and bonds, which extend well beyond the temporality of the physical occupation. Contributions in this section consider what material objects, technologies and social relations are brought together inside the space of a protest camp to make it function as a place-based site of protest and political contestation. These contributions ask us to take objects seriously, to see protest camps from a perspective that views infrastructures and architectures as responsive and adaptable to their environments. The objects that form a protest camp can range from symbolically striking yet pragmatically (relatively) impotent barricades (like the umbrellas used by pro-democracy protesters in Hong Kong), to malleable and slapdash infrastructures (such as the street kitchens serving soup to the masses that were also established in Hong Kong). This responsive and adaptive nature of assembling and materialising suggests that the material culture of protest camps should therefore be analysed as a set of processes or practices, rather than as artefacts alone. Lastly, the material objects, which come to assemble a protest camp, need to be understood not just in terms of their pragmatic utility, but also for the politics infused in their portability, adaptability and durability as it reaches beyond the temporality and life of the protest encampment itself. It is often this adaptation and recirculation – via media – that gives objects of protest their symbolic power, forging transnational solidarities (Gillan and Pickerill, 2008).

Taking seriously the material and social infrastructures of protest camps also requires us to recognise the division of labour and space within protest camps (as well as the ways in which camps relate to publics 'outside' their physical boundaries). For example, Kavada and Dimitriou's contribution in this section (Chapter Five) examines how political divides at the 2011 Indignant ('Αγανακτισμένοι') movement's protest camp occupation of Syntagma Square were reinforced spatially at the camp. Thus, a focus on assembling and materialising requires a consideration of the arrangement of both material space and digital space, paying attention to how people and practices convergence, as well as where they diverge. The architecture of the public squares and gardens that are occupied by protesters, as well as the social media platforms they use, can shape how politics is practised within them. Consequently, we need to understand better the processes by which camps are planned, how they react to evolving political, legal and social contexts, and how political practices, or the tactical repertoires of protest camps (McCrudy et al, 2016), travel between camps over time. Likewise, attention needs to be paid to how the objects of protest camping are often entangled with the material histories of specific places, as well as specific pieces of camping equipment. This includes the important role media and communication infrastructures play in the transnational circulation of material practices. The purpose of this section then, is to highlight the need to examine the relationship between the physical space of occupation and the mediated or virtual spaces that are also involved in the shaping, circulating and archiving of material life. Of particular interest are the media practices used to maintain and amplify corporeal protest camp sites.

The chapters of Part One

Part One opens with architect Anders Rubing's exploration (Chapter Three) of the role of textiles – the fabric of tents – as central components of the materiality and organisational structure of protest camps. Within architectural discourse the role of textiles as an architectural material, medium and object has largely been neglected given its temporal and flexible qualities and, as a consequence, there is a lack of knowledge pertaining the function and political implications of textile as architecture. Drawing on fieldwork conducted in Oslo, Norway, Jerusalem, Israel and Ramallah, Palestine between 2010 and 2012, Rubing uses Weizman's (2007, 318) concept of 'political plastic' in an effort to move our understanding of architecture beyond static and completed objects towards an appreciation for how space is produced by adding or reshaping objects. Textile architecture such as the tents of protest camps, Rubing argues, allows for fluid political spaces to be constructed, which can adapt to the space, context and needs and thereby shift architecture from a static object to a malleable process. Given the textile architecture of protest camps is a central component of the materiality and organisational structure of protest camps, Rubing's application of 'political plastic' allows for built objects – their materials and the process of building and maintaining them – to be conceptualised as political objects, statements and tools, as well as resistant practices.

Chapter Four, written by Özge Yaka and Serhat Karakayali, examines the role of materiality in creating the political atmosphere at Istanbul's Gezi Park during the protests of June 2013. Drawing from participant observation, as well as the visual and textual analysis of movement documents produced around the Gezi Park protests, the authors argue that the material infrastructures of protest camps are context dependant – based on the actions, objects, spaces and affects that produce them. In the particular case of Gezi Park, the chapter argues that the materials, objects and accompanying infrastructures of Gezi Park were never intended as permanent spaces of protest. Instead, the protest camp was a temporary and spontaneous space, which forged relations and created bonds between individuals by intervening and interrupting the logic of urban public space. From this perspective, the authors view protest camps as specific political infrastructures that facilitate or enable certain modes of action and interaction during a protest event. The protest camp's strength, then, does not necessarily come from its permanence but from the links and social relations forged within and carried beyond these spaces. The very form of the camp implicates the organising of reproductive and everyday practices, albeit in a different mode than those shaped by market or state rationality. Consequently, protest camps must be understood as a form of protest situated between more classic forms of symbolic protest and the construction of alternative social relations and institutions.

Chapter Five, written by Anastasia Kavada and Orsalia Dimitriou, is the first of two chapters that critically examine how social movements navigate material and mediated space. Based on a case study of the 2011 Indignant ('Αγανακτισμένοι') movement's protest camp occupation of Syntagma Square in Athens in Greece, this chapter focuses on the movement's 'spatial agency' (Sewell, 2001) and how physical and virtual spaces informed and shaped the movement's spatial repertoire of contention (Tilly, 1978). The authors open with a conceptual discussion of space using Henri Lefebvre's (1991) distinction between *perceived*, *conceived* and *lived* space. Lefebvre's distinction, the authors argue, offers an important conceptual tool for politicising spatiality and the links between the physical and virtual environment. The case of Syntagma Square demonstrates how these dynamics work in practice by outlining how space and social movements co-constitute each other. Kavada and Dimitriou devote particular attention to how a divide in physical space within Syntagma Square between the Upper and Lower Square reflected a larger political cleavage and the uptake of differing repertoires of contention at the square itself as well as in mediated domains such as websites and Facebook pages. Despite, or perhaps in spite of these divisions, the authors acknowledge that Syntagma Square functioned as a central and singular gathering point which allowed for different movement factions to converge whereas online spaces were multiple and dispersed. The authors conclude that, taken together, the online and offline spaces of the movement facilitated the production of a public that followed the rules of critical democracy, empowering excluded voices in such a way as to directly challenge existing institutions without necessarily seeking to occupy a sovereign position. They allowed the movement to be diffuse but connected, to scale up but maintain a central focus, to be united in its indignation but divided in its practices.

Paulo Gerbaudo, in Chapter Six, extends Kavada and Dimitriou's exploration of the relationship between material and mediated space to focus on activists' practices of digital self-representation at protest camps. Gerbaudo is particularly interested in how social media practices dovetailed with the act of protest camping during the wave of protest movements in 2011 encompassing the Spanish indignados and New York's Occupy Wall Street. He explores how social media are utilised to amplify the experiences taking place in the protest camps, to wider groups of supporters who cannot attend physically. Gerbaudo documents how the activist practices of live-streaming and live-tweeting from protest camps construct a collective narrative of the events taking place at the protest camps and are subsequently made available to dispersed publics of supporters. Moreover, these activist practices contribute to casting protest camps as prefigurative spaces, whose doings contribute in creating the imaginary of an alternative and more equitable world.

The last chapter of this section, Chapter Seven, is the product of a conversation between three Hong Kong-based researchers, each of whom was active in the 2014 Umbrella Movement. The discussion opens by contextualising the political and legal environment created after Hong Kong was handed over by the United Kingdom to the People's Republic of China in 1997. Next, the authors briefly outline the challenges Hong Kongers continue to face in their desire for democratic rule. It is this desire, the authors argue, which lays the foundation for the Umbrella Movement. The discussion also covers the rise of the umbrella from an everyday object carried by Hong Kongers to cope with the city's weather, to a pragmatic and innovative solution for dealing with police tear gas and pepper spray. In so doing, the authors argue that the umbrella was transformed from a material object with no political legacy, to a culturally infused and internationally recognised symbol of democratic struggle in Hong Kong. The authors also contextualise the use of historically linked cultural symbols by democratic activists with the uptake of the colour yellow. The discussion reflects on how the protest camp was a material and mediated intervention in to every day.

As contributions in this section make clear, processes of assembling and materialising form the core of protest camping. However, the form and practice of protest camping is contingent on the social, political and economic context of a camp, together with the material and mediated resources and realities that campers inhabit. The chapters presented in this section offer a window into how context and circumstances can influence, modify and foster innovations in acts of protest camping and protest camp repertoires (McCurdy et al, 2016). In so doing they provide timely and multidisciplinary, empirical case studies, contributing to an understudied area of scholarship. They offer, as well, conceptual and methodological insights for studying the act of protest camping, along with the objects, processes and infrastructures that sustain it.

References

AAP (Australian Associated Press), (2014) 'News: Occupy Melbourne tent wearer loses appeal', *The Australian*, 3 October, www.theaustralian.com.au/news/latest-news/occupy-melbourne-tent-wearer-loses-appeal/news-story/dced3e30b4ee30cf76e9ad7fe2d9f174.

Castells, M. (2009) *Communication power*, Oxford: OUP.

City of Melbourne (2009) 'Activities Local Law 2009', www.melbourne.vic.gov.au/about-council/governance-transparency/acts-local-laws/pages/activities-local-law-2009.aspx

CNN (2011) 'Occupy's "tent monsters" cause flap', 5 December, www.cnn.com/videos/bestoftv/2011/12/05/pkg-moos-tent-monsters.cnn.

Costanza-Chock, S. (2012) 'Mic Check! Media cultures and the Occupy movement', *Social Movement Studies: Journal of Social, Cultural and Political Protest*, 11(3–4), 375–385, doi:10.1080/14742837.2012.71074.

Cowan, G. (2002) 'Nomadology in architecture ephemerality, movement and collaboration', MSc dissertation, University of Adelaide.

Gillan, K. and Pickerill, J. (2008) 'Transnational anti-war activism: solidarity, diversity and the internet in Australia, Britain and the United States after 9/11', *Australasian Political Studies Association*, 43(1), pp 59–78.

Home Office (2012) 'News story: tents banned from Olympic sites', 25 January, Home Office and The Rt Hon Theresa May MP, www.gov.uk/government/news/tents-banned-from-olympic-sites.

Human Rights Law Centre (2013) 'Ruling vindicates 'Occupy Melbourne' protesters but highlights lack of legal protections for free speech and protest rights', 1 October, http://hrlc.org.au/ruling-vindicates-occupy-melbourne-protesters-but-highlights-lack-of-legal-protections-for-free-speech-and-protest-rights/.

Hunt and Hunt Lawyers (2016) 'Occupy Melbourne – the rights of Councils to use Local Laws and Crown Land Regulations to protect public spaces from damage by protesters', www.hunthunt.com.au/news-and-publications/occupy-melbourne.

Jones, J. (2012) 'Occupying the Olympic Games: Resisting London 2012', *Sport and Society*, British Library: London, www.bl.uk/sportandsociety/exploresocsci/politics/articles/occupying.pdf.

Lefebvre, H. (1991) *The Production of Space*. Oxford: Blackwell.

McCurdy, P., Feigenbaum, A. and Frenzel, F. (2016) 'Protest camps and repertoires of contention', *Social Movement Studies*, 15(1): 97–104.

RynChristoph (2011) *Tent protest costume violently stripped from protester's body 061211.MOV (Concise version)* [YouTube Video], 5 December, www.youtube.com/watch?v=JAkUB7jRb2c.

sean bedlam (2011a) *Sara Tent Monster Brutal Vision*, 5 December, www.youtube.com/watch?v=MtwuGAOR9a4.

sean bedlam (2011b) *Sara Tent Monster Naked Outrage*, 5 December, www.youtube.com/watch?v=XSq6tPXJHZ4.

Sewell, W. H. Jr (2001) 'Space in contentious politics', in R. R. Aminzade, J. A. Goldstone, D. McAdam, E. J. Perry, W. H. J. Sewell, S. Tarrow and C. Tilly (eds) *Silence and Voice in the Study of Contentious Politics*, Cambridge: Cambridge University Press, pp 51–88.

TheFreemanSmith (2011) *Occupy Melbourne Tent Monsters* [YouTube Video], 3 December, www.youtube.com/watch?v=zKMwigI3mdM.

Tilly, C. (1978) *From Mobilization to Revolution*. Reading, MA: Addison-Wesley.

Tilly, C. (2000) 'Spaces of contention', *Mobilization: An International Journal*, 5(2), 135–159.

Weizman, E. (2007) *Hollow Land: Israel's Architecture of Occupation*. London: Verso.

THREE

Textile geographies, plasticity as protest

Anders Rubing

Introduction

Green, blue, red, domes, A-frames, collapsed, interlocked and freestanding: images of tents are central to the representation of protests at Tahrir, Zucotti Park, St Paul's and many other contemporary and historical protests. Tents play such a central role in them, because a sustained protest needs bodies, and the bodies need some type of protection. In a protest camp, this protection is partly provided by soft, flexible and moldable material, the textile. From clothes to banners, blankets and tents, textile simultaneously supports the protest as it provides bodies with a dry place to sleep, protects them from the elements, facilitates privacy within the public space, and promotes messages. In this chapter I will take a closer look at the geography and architecture of the textile constructions in camp – the tent.

The tent is only a thin membrane held in tension by poles and lines. A bullet, a knife or even a fist can easily penetrate the tent's membrane making vulnerable anything behind it. Either fire or force will quickly reduce a tent to a small pile. Simultaneously, the textile material can also work as a protection against certain threats. The material can expand to create space and provide a shield from sun, cold and water. All textiles have some common elements and universal qualities. The cheapest nylons as well as the finest silks and wools have qualities such as flexibility, portability and softness. These material qualities are employed in various ways in the different camps I have visited.

Within the discourse of protests and protest camps, materiality and the importance of materiality have been sparsely researched. This chapter is an introduction to my research on architectural materiality in political protest, a field that could benefit from further research. Some architectural discussions claim that the impoverished appearance of protest camps forms an intentional contrast to the cityscape representing wealth, or that the 'unplanned' camp marks a conscious critique of the planned city (for example, Hosey, 2000; Cresswell, 1996). In this chapter I argue that the function of textile is instrumental for reasons other than just appearance. I explore the tent's protective functions by examining the unique qualities of the tent as both symbolic and infrastructural elements of protest camps. Textile and other support infrastructure are fundamental in sustaining protests, camps and especially in supporting protest bodies. Today, textile shelters are as much an urban phenomenon as a rural one. The juxtaposition between the nomadic and flexible textile of the camp, and the fixed permanent infrastructure of the city, is worth examining further.

The chapter examines the textile as geopolitical agent by referencing both Butler (2011) and Weizman (2007). I will examine Occupy LA and propose how it may be read as a new layer of geography on top of the existing one. This new layer of geography will be compared to the term 'political plastic' coined by Weizman (2007). Further, I will discuss textile as an extension of the body, and how bodies are essential to both protests and politics according to Butler (2011). In doing so, I will look at how the presence or absence of bodies can produce politics and how textile can be political through both spatial and non-spatial examples.

Can tents be read as producers of geopolitics? Can tents in protest camps function both as infrastructure and protection *in support of protests* and simultaneously as a *manifestation of a geopolitical agenda*? Historic examples such as the Resurrection City, Greenham Common and the Aboriginal Tent Embassy show how textile as a material can be used within a political struggle and simultaneously as support for protest in protest camps (see, for example, Feigenbaum et al, 2013; Cowan, 2001; Hosey, 2000) . Two more cases of protest camps will be examined. First, I turn to a protest tent in Silwan, East Jerusalem, Israel Palestine where Palestinians protest against the occupation. From Israel I then move on to Norway to examine a protest camp set up by Palestinian refugees. I show how the history of protest camps made by indigenous minorities has informed the struggle of today's threatened minorities and how protesters employ gray areas of the law in order to protect the camps. Finally, I introduce plasticity politics as a frame of understanding, arguing that textiles/tents can be considered producers of, or expanding forces for, politics.

Textile as protection

> If the nature of architecture is the grounded, the fixed, the permanent, then textiles are its very antithesis. (Albers, 1957, 44)

Typically, textiles are associated with interior decorations and soft surfaces, while materials such as steel, rock, concrete, glass and wood are associated with the exterior materialisation of architecture. Looking at architecture and urban history, we find that textiles always had functions beyond decorative ones. Indeed, textile as dwelling has a long tradition. The first tents were either made of wool or hide adapted to the local environments. The traditional black wool tent is used by nomadic Bedouin tribes in the Middle East and North Africa to this day. The tent is made up of a large cloth that is held up by a few poles and suspended in tension from two sides. In Northern Europe and the North of America indigenous tribes traditionally employ a tent structure called 'tipi', with its characteristic cone shape, while groups in Northeast Asia used the Yurt, a cylinder form with a cone roof (Kuusisto, 2010). Another important textile element of these traditional structures is the rug, which serves not only as a floor cover but also as a room divider. In this way the rug occupies two opposing functions: it expands privatised space on the floor and/or divides interior space. Nineteenth-century architect and theorist Gottfried Semper confirms the deep connection between architecture and textile. According to Semper (2010, 255), architecture is an emergence of textile arts.

> Woven fabrics almost everywhere and especially in the southern and warm countries carry out their ancient, original function as conspicuous spatial dividers; even where solid walls become necessary, they remain only the inner and unseen structure for the true and legitimate representations for the spatial idea; namely, the more or less artificially woven and seamed-together, textile walls.

Semper describes the spatial idea of the firm wall, separating private and public as a transposed rug. This idea is also found in modernism. Schindler thus describes his house on Kings Road, Los Angeles as a translation of tent fabric in to concrete (Hailey, 2009). I argue that the materiality gives the textile other qualities than the function of a spatial division.

In camps textile can be the sole divider between private and public, safe and unsafe. In urban contexts, textile operates both as an independent element and in combination with several other materials (for example, a tent supported by a building). The protective function and the relationship between tent, textile, private and public have changed through time. Prefabricated military tents project a strict order where the private is concealed, but self-made structures of trees and plastic such as those used in the protest camp at Greenham Common made private space possible (but also visible through the textile) (Roseneil, 2000). Similar tendencies can be found in the anti-road protests in Britain (Feigenbaum et al, 2013). By adding tents or personal belongings, protestors 'privatised' existing infrastructure of trees, dwellings or fences, changing their appearance and perceived functions to protest support infrastructure.

Textiles are still being used as space dividers between private and public but also between safe and unsafe spaces, and between diplomatic zones. The late dictator of Libya, Muahammar Gaddafi, used an extravagant Bedouin tent as his diplomatic quarters when visiting other countries (*Guardian*, 2009; Bohlen, 2007). When travelling, the President of the United States, Barack Obama, holds meetings in a tent inside rooms as protection against potential eavesdropping with cameras or lasers (Schmidt and Schmitt, 2013).

Extension of bodies, body geography

> For politics to take place, the body must appear. I appear to others, and they appear to me, which means that some space between us allows each to appear. (Butler, 2011, 3–4)

Butler describes the relationship between bodies, protest and the political, relating public space to bodies and to the theories of Arendt (1958) and Agamben (1998). According to Butler, *bodies in public space* is the first condition that needs to be fulfilled in order define a situation as *a protest*. The presence of the bodies transforms this space into a political space. After occupying the public space, the politicisation can extend outward to the more private streets, and the protest can politicise the private as well. Significantly, politics is dependent on bodies, not only for the occupation of public space, but also to create different categories of spaces between bodies. One is the perceived visual space, another, as important, is the relational space (Butler, 2011).

Architecture, in one way or another, relates to bodies through living, working, congregating, separating, and so on. We occupy and experience space with our own bodies. Bodies are the human connection to space. Even in a time when the technology of social media provides us with numerous ways of communicating discontent or a political standpoint, we have seen, over the last couple of years, that bodies are still an important factor for protests.

Textile is intimately connected to the body either as clothes or as architecture. In the theory of textile and architecture, there is a recurrent discussion on textile as an extension of the body, or as a secondary skin. Albers (2000) suggests that skin makes us independent from or less dependent on the environment. She writes: 'prototypes of fabric and it is their use as our secondary skin, either in their Paleolithic or their transposed form, that has made us independent of place, hour, and season, in the remote past as today' (Albers, 2000, 44)

Butler (2011) suggests that the movement of this protection or extension of the body also moves the private in to the public. The protesting body makes public spaces both private and public at the same time. Hundertwasser adds that clothes are a part of how humans relate to space and present their identity in space (Hundertwasser and Scmied, 2003). Clothes are not only protecting and connecting the body to the environment but are also a literal expansion of the body.

The position of the textile as an extension of the body could also be understood as a strict pragmatic, spatial and temporal framework. A body occupies physical space, and with a layer of textile around it, the body occupies more space. These layers have further functions as well, as we will see in the rest of the chapter. Clothes are the first layer and the tent occupied by the body could be the second layer. With a tent you have suddenly expanded your ability to occupy much more space. In contrast to clothes, the tent is not attached to the body; it is less flexible and therefore more permanent. By considering textile constructions like the tent as an extension of the body, the body's restricted mobility leads to its more permanent occupation of space. Consequently, one could see protest camp tents as occupation through the extension of bodies. The tent extends the body both in time and in space: 100 bodies could fit into 25–50 square metres while 100 tents could occupy an area of almost 400 square metres in tent floors alone. Looking at the different camps I examine in this chapter, one can postulate that these types of occupations were as dependent on tents as they were on bodies occupying both space and space in time. In Occupy London Stock Exchange, for example, there were not always enough bodies in the space to occupy it. The media highlighted this dependency on the presence of bodies. The police checked tents for inhabitants with an infrared camera and the uninhabited tents became a news story (Kelly, 2012). Another news story both showing the potential of spatial extension as well as the extension of private space in the public sphere is from the Occupy Melbourne camp. A woman dressed in a tent, as a humorous last resistance against the ban against tents in a park, was undressed by the police and left in her underwear on the lawn. (Flower, 2011).

Textile, city, landscape and camp

Los Angeles

The Los Angeles City Hall, a 28-floor high-rise and architectural symbol of civic power, has been an important landmark for the city of Los Angeles. It is situated in the grid structure of LA, surrounded by roads on all four sides, with a green lawn and a park between the roads and the building (Clancy, nd). In 2011 hundreds of dome shaped tents appeared on the lawn as Occupy LA settled down following the example of Occupy Wall Street in New York. People and banners were moving along the roads, on sidewalks and on new paths between the tents. The symbolic building had become a backdrop for another type of urbanism that emerged: a camp urbanism. Moving on the paths between the tents, I experienced one particular scale of architecture and urbanity punctuated by the sounds and smell of people using the space and living there. This urbanism is not only of a different scale but also different in its permanence and movability. I experienced urbanism at two scales simultaneously; the temporary camp urbanism and the permanent City Hall complex.

The temporary urbanism created by the tent architecture is a new layer of architecture, a flexible spatial layer that can be read as the result of a political intent by the people creating it. A geography of soft constructions that could potentially move from one open space to another open space in the city. This architecture is contested, it is moving into parts of the city that are often confined to public space and public functions. It is an architecture that is dependent on being temporary and on interacting with the surrounding, more fixed architecture.

Occupy LA, as with the rest of the Occupy camps popping up around the globe in 2011, was a protest against economic inequalities and, similarly, used the prolonged occupation of public space as one of the main means of protest. At the same time as the camp was erected in LA, there was another camp emerging in Oslo. In Silwan, Jerusalem, a single tent had stood as a protest for some time. Reading the three cases of camp urbanism in contrast they reveal an understanding of the textile architecture in relation to a more conflicted, controlled and secured city that is the city today (see, for example, Sorking, 2008; Graham, 2010).

Architecture as a 'political plastic'

In order to describe the conflict in Israel and Palestine, Eyal Weizman formulates a new term and develops a new description of a function for architecture and urbanism, the function of a 'political plastic'. With the term 'political plastic', Weizman suggests a reading of space as a result of exterior impact. He refers to how the space produced by these exterior impacts can be read as a map of political intent formed by the relationship of all the forces that shaped it. The term does not imply that only forces in space create politics, but that architecture often can be read as an image of politics. By 'plastic' he means that maps and spaces are fluid. Plasticity both in the architecture and urbanism points to the importance of studying their process character: what is built, how things move in space, what is erased in this process (Weizman, 2007). This does not necessarily imply that the architecture is the soft, pliable, 'plastic', rather, the softness lies in the reorganisation of architecture. Describing the frontier between Israel and the West Bank, and the strategies of the Israeli settlers and military he writes:

> The elastic nature of the frontier does not imply that Israeli trailers, homes, roads or indeed the concrete wall are in themselves soft and yielding but that the continuous spatial reorganisation of the political borders they mark out respond to and reflects political and military conflicts. The various inhabitants of this frontier do not operate within the fixed envelope of space – space is not the background for their actions, an abstract grid on which events take place – but rather the medium that of a rigid container to 'soft' performance. Political action is fully absorbed in the organisation, transformation, erasure and subversion of space. (Weizman, 2007, 5)

Weizman put into words how the changing nature of a non-fixed border, or the fluidity in space, can be of political consequence. He suggests that this fluidity is deliberately kept non-fixed so the Israeli can continuously change the space to their political advantage.

The point of departure for Weizman's theories is the extreme environment in the conflict between Palestine and Israel, and the spatial instruments Israel uses as a part of the conflict and the occupation. Transferring this term to other conflicted spaces like the protest camp, and the textile nature of the camp, is not meant as a comparison to how the political plastic can work, but rather an interpretation of how to see the protest camp and the tent as a political plastic. Examining the Occupy LA camp as a 'political plastic' I would argue that the nature of the camp and its various elements confirm its geopolitical function. The plasticity lies in the changing geography, the extension and expansion of the camp both adapting and breaking the external boundaries of the site: simultaneously altering its density to the number of protesters present. The camp is also formed by politics, in its relation to city planning. In Los Angeles' car-based infrastructure the camp adapts to use the sidewalks as a billboard with the official building as a backdrop. Here the infrastructural politics of car as transport influence the space and the architecture of the camp.

Textile as politics

Silwan, East Jerusalem

Textile can be a political tool, used against colonisation and colonising empires. Mahatma Gandhi in his traditional Indian clothing, the Kahdi, serves an important example (Bean, 2012; Maharaj, 1991). The cloth was in itself a protest against the English rule and a symbol of economic nationalism. In the beginning of the twentieth century, the cotton harvested in India was exported to England and made into fabric, and then sold back to India. In order to make his Kahdi, Gandhi learned how to weave and thus reintroduced weaving as an Indian industry independent of the English. The item of clothing thus gained a political character expressing protest against English colonialism.

Textile as politics also takes on a spatial form that fulfills not only the support and protection for bodies but also functions as a geopolitical object in and of itself. In 1968 the Poor People's Campaign organised a large protest in Washington, DC of which the protest camp 'Resurrection City' played an important role (Feigenbaum et al, 2013). In contrast to the ad hoc Occupy movement, Resurrection City was planned out and designed beforehand, making use of military tents. The camp was divided into various blocks of tent. The camp occupied Washington Mall, one of the most important political spaces in Washington. Lance Hosey describes the camp as contrasting to the symbolic buildings of the mall: a relocated slum within the organised representational architecture. Both visually and experientially, the camp contrasted the portrayal of power and wealth that the civic buildings of the capital were made to represent (Hosey, 2000).

The Aboriginal Tent Embassy in Canberra, Australia was a protest by a minority indigenous group and simultaneously functioned to relate textile back to the origins of shelter. Gregory Cowan (2001) describes the protest not only as a non-western way of protesting, but also as a non-western way of looking at space. He further claims that the aboriginal use of space and shelters can be directly linked to the protest. The protest started with the erection of a beach umbrella outside the Provisional Parliament House in Canberra. Later, this umbrella constituted the point of departure for a camp with different kinds of ad hoc structures, such as tents and shelters made from various materials including textile. The protest was a reaction to laws defining land rights, but through its physical location, the protest also made a statement about how land can be used. If the camp had been a more permanent construction it would have been considered illegal, but, since it was more akin to camping, it was neither illegal nor fully legal. For Cowan it is the ephemerality and temporality of the tent that make up the politics of the protest.

In contrast to Hosey's claim that the Resurrection City was political in the way the tents and other constructions displayed an impoverished marginalised existence, the Australian Tent Embassy operated by adopting ephemerality as its geopolitical 'weapon'. The foldable, temporal ephemeral architecture was not only the protest's political tool, it also emphasised the difference to the Australian settler culture urbanism (Cowan, 2001). Cowan's focus on the ephemerality can be compared to Weizman's argument of constant change as a creator of politics. They both discuss changeability, but it differs in the timeframe and how it is conceived. For Cowan it is a visually apparent flexibility and appearance, whereas for Weizman it is as much the changes that are not necessarily obvious at first sight (Weizman, 2007).

I would like to introduce the third contemporary example. In the old Palestinian village of Silwan, now a part of East Jerusalem, one tent stands in a central plot. The tent is located next to the old city in East Jerusalem even though the protest has now ended. What is especially interesting here is that the tent cannot be read as protection since the conflicting parties ignored the protective function. Instead it can only be read as a geopolitical object. Walking down from the old city to the center of Silwan, you see the tent next to the road.

It is made of various textiles and supported by a wooden structure. It was erected to protest against a proposed demolition of some houses to make way for a new park. The protesters read this proposal as a strategy

Figure 3.1: Protest Tent in centre of Silwan, Jerusalem

Figure 3.2: Protest Tent in centre of Silwan, Jerusalem

by the Israeli government to remove Palestinians from East Jerusalem and push them into the Occupied West Bank. The tent served as the focal point for the protest as well as the primary meeting place for people involved in the protest (de Vries, personal communication, 9 May 2011; Acri, personal communication, 10 October 2013). Unlike the temporality of movement and deployment seen in the Occupy movement, or the legal temporality of the Aboriginal Temporal Embassy, the structure's strength was its resilience to temporal change; when the structure was torn down by the Israeli police, it could be rebuilt in a couple of hours. The tent's main political value was not, as with the Resurrection City, its appearance and contrast to the existing built structure. It was the structure of the tent itself that made it politically loaded. As in the Resurrection Camp or the Aboriginal tent embassy, the structures still played on appearance, however its main strength was its ability to contrast the very buildings the protest attempted to save: the tent was a built structure that refused to be demolished. The possibility of this resistance was not in hardening the structure, but rather in softening it. If the structure can give in to pressure without collapsing, it can also later be expanded or easily rebuilt. Weizman addresses the changing geographies in Israel by highlighting the external forces creating politics. With the Silwan example we see another way of dealing with these external forces: the structure demolished by the Israeli Police shrinks to almost nothing and then regains its presence in a new form. The vulnerability of the textile is as symbolic as it is practical.

Norwegian textiles, Norwegian camps

A protest camp of Palestinian refugees emerged in Oslo in 2011. Around 20 Palestinians lived in three military tents and protested through the rough Norwegian winter. The Palestinian Camp in Oslo stands in close relation to previous protest camps in Norway. In the 1970s eight activists erected a traditional Sami tent 100 metres from the parliament to protest against a hydroelectric dam in the far north of Norway, and more generally for the rights of the indigenous Sami minorities (Helgegren, 2012). The camp was raided after five days, and the eight activists and hundreds of their supporters were removed from the site. The protest, like the Aboriginal Tent Embassy or the Resurrection City, was a demonstration of a physical, material opposition (Nango, 2010).

In the last ten years there have been three major protests by other, new minorities in Norway. In 2006, a group of Afghani immigrants started the first of the three protests. The immigrants were not given political or humanitarian asylum and were threatened with deportation back to Afghanistan. The protest was a hunger strike with about 100 Afghans in a tent camp outside the Oslo Cathedral. The camp was sustained for 26 days (Iraki, 2006; Klungtveit, 2006).

Five years later Ethiopian refugees set up a tent and conducted a hunger strike in the same location outside the cathedral. They were also protesting the government's refusal to provide asylum as well as for the right to live in Norway. The same year, the Oslo Palestinian Camp

Figure 3.3: Protest tent next to Oslo Cathedral

was erected. It was first located outside the Norwegian parliament where it was allowed to stay for one night, and later next to a smaller church in the city centre. The protesters stayed on the church's ground located next to the Norwegian immigration authorities.

To understand the context of these later camps it is important to discuss the concept of church asylum in Norway. Refugees can receive asylum in a church or sanctuary space if the Norwegian state does not grant them asylum, but since the church is also owned by the state, the question of who should give the asylum is contested. Even though the concept of church asylum is not sanctioned in any Norwegian law (nor will it be), the Ministry of Justice has concluded that the immigration police should not enter churches due to the historical value of the church asylum. The administration of the State church defined staying in the church room as being protected by God in 'God's house' (domus Dei).

There is also an unwritten rule that even if the church, as consisting of the pastor or the congregation, do not agree to protect the persons seeking asylum, the asylum seekers are still protected in 'God's house' and the church must adapt (Andresen, 2013; Harris-Christensen, 2006). Even though none of the camps were actually located inside a church, I would argue that the concept of church asylum was still partly present in the examples listed above. The tents became extensions of the churches. During the camp's existence none of the refugees were arrested while staying in the Palestinian camp. However, the

Figure 3.4: Palestinian protest camps in Oslo

immigration police arrested several of its inhabitants while they were outside the camp. (Normann, 2011; Palestinerleir, 2011).

All these camps could be considered extensions of the church asylum rules. But, the Palestinian camp differed from the other two camps in several ways. It labelled itself not only as a protest camp, but as a refugee camp; the only Palestinian refugee camp outside the Middle East. After the first night outside the parliament, it applied for and was granted a permit to be located outside the church. The camp and the church were also located 100 metres away from the longest squatted building in Oslo. They supplied the camp with water and shower facilities while the church provided the camp with electricity.

The case of the Oslo Palestinian camp is interesting because of the different legal statuses it had and its relationship to the city. Both in theory and in practice, it was as ephemeral as all the other camps described above, but at the same time it obtained and used a permit to stay for one year in one place. The strength of the Occupy camp in LA came, in part, from the camp's ability to move. In this example, an important strength was the length of time the camp stayed in the same location always occupied by bodies. The textile worked in several ways: as protection for bodies, as extension of the church and as demarcation of the protest. Going back to Butler (2011), and in contrast to Silwan, here again the number of bodies was the important factor. The geopolitical plasticity of the tent allowed the textile to simultaneously expand the church asylum and facilitate the existence of bodies there. The camp plugged into a number of other spatial networks, such as the cooperation with the squatted house, of which other camps could not take advantage. Significantly it reinterpreted the concept of refugee camp by turning it into a protest camp while simultaneously reinterpreting the safe space of the church.

Plasticity politics

When Semper wrote about textile in the 1850s he thought about how the material was a predecessor to solid architecture, how the architectural elements we see in buildings had a textile origin. In the beginning of the twenty-first century Cowan (2001) and Hosey (2000) describe the textile as a symbolic protest by contrasting it to either the structure, the wealth or the permanence of the existing architecture. Albers (2000) and Hundertwasser (Hundertwasser and Schmied, 2003) read textile as an extension of the body.

Apart from these readings of textile as protest material and protest architecture, it is possible to add new readings that my research has begun to examine. Textile's physical properties make it vulnerable but, I argue, these vulnerabilities can be both reimagined and reinterpreted as strengths rather than weakness. The two examples of Palestinian protest camps, the tent in Silwan in East Jerusalem and the camp in Oslo, Norway, supported this view, providing different examples of textile's plasticity and importance as a geopolitical power.

The first is the plasticity in geography related to what Weizman (2007) refers to as 'political plastic'. In the Oslo example, both its inhabitants and the police acknowledge the church as a safe space and this safe space is expanded through the use of the tent, the textile and the camp. The Palestinian camp in Oslo, as well as the Afghan and Ethiopian camps before it, exploit the inconsistent directives, or the lack of legal status, of the church asylum. The textile expands not only the protest bodies, but also the safe space protecting these bodies against the immigration police.

Transposing the concept of plasticity into the architecture of protest, we can consider several qualities of textile. The plasticity we see in Silwan is not a flexible, moveable geographical movement that can be produced by a light and moldable material (as we saw in Oslo and LA). The plasticity is inherent in the fact that textile can be reattached, rebuilt and reconfigured. The police tear it down and it is rebuilt again. Such plasticity is not restricted to the textile, but in the Israeli–Palestinian conflict, also concerns concrete architecture: in the attack on the refugee camp outside Jenin, the Israeli Defense Force (IDF) entered not through the streets, but through buildings. Blowing holes through walls and slabs of concrete and stone, the military moved through the built fabric: a permanent molded stone and concrete maze that the IDF had mapped to the last detail. Stone and concrete, previously considered invulnerable, proved to be just as vulnerable as fabric; making the body, yet again, more vulnerable both to weapons and to the flying debris from the hard material (Graham, 2004; Weizman, 2007).

Butler (2011) defines bodies as the central part of making politics in public space. The tent could be seen as a temporal and spatial extension, an extension to the body and we can therefore consider textile extending the possibility of creating politics. Butler describes the body as vulnerable to outer forces, but at the same time it is this vulnerability that makes the bodies political. Textile is both vulnerable and resilient. This is what makes it capable of both extending and reinforcing the body while simultaneously creating politics.

Acknowledgements

I would like to express my deepest gratitude to Kari Anne K Drangsland and Simone Ghetti for their input on the text and to Borghild for all her support and for making it possible to be a father of two and a writer at the same time.

References

Agamben, G. (1998) *Homo Sacer: Sovereign Power and Bare Life*, Stanford University Press.

Albers, A. (2000) 'The pliable plane: textiles in architecture', in *Anni Albers: Selected Writings on Design*, Middletown, CT: Wesleyan University Press, pp 44–51.

Andresen, K. (2013) *Kirkehuset og lovgivningen* [*The Church Building and the Legislation*], Kirkebyggutredningen: Kirkerådet, Den Norske Kirke

Arendt, H. (1958) *The Human Condition*, Chicago, IL: University of Chicago Press.

Bean, S. S. (2012) 'Gandhi and khadi, the fabric of indian independence', in J. Hemmings (ed) *The Textile Reader*, New York: Berg Publishers, pp 234–247.

Bohlen, C. (2007) *Qaddafi Pitches Tent in Paris for Sarkozy Summit – Bloomberg*. (10 December), www.bloomberg.com/apps/news?pid=n ewsarchive&sid=ayiM8VKQC1X4.

Butler, J. (2011) *Bodies in Alliance and the Politics of the Street* (Vol 2013). Vienna: European Institute for Progressive Cultural Policies.

Clancy, L. (nd) *Los Angeles City Hall*, http://studentreader.com/la-city-hall/.

Cowan, G. (2001) 'Collapsing Australian Architecture: The Aboriginal Tent Embassy', *Journal of Australian Studies*, 25(67), 30–36, doi:10.1080/14443050109387636.

Cresswell, T. (1996) *In Place – Out of Place: Geography, Ideology, and Transgression*. Minneapolis, MN: University of Minnesota Press.

Feigenbaum, A., Frenzel, F. and McCurdy, P. (2013) *Protest Camps*. London: Zed.

Flower, W. (2011) 'Police conduct under investigation after "tent" dress torn from protester', *Herald Sun*, 7 December, www.heraldsun. com.au/news/police-criticised-after-tent-dress-torn-off-occupy-protester/story-e6frf7jo-1226215099340.

Graham, S. (2004) 'Constructing urbicide by bulldozer in the Occupied Territories', in S. Graham (ed) *Cities, War, and terrorism: Towards an Urban Geopolitics*. Malden, MA: Blackwell Publishing.

Graham, S. (2010) *Cities under Siege: The New Military Urbanism*. London: Verso.

Guardian (2009) 'Muammar Gaddafi and his travelling tent', *World News*, 23 September, www.theguardian.com/world/gallery/2009/sep/23/muammar-gaddafi-libya-united-nations

Hailey, C. (2009) *Camps: A Guide to 21st-Century Space*. Cambridge, MA: MIT Press.

Harris-Christensen, H. (2006) *Kirkeasyl i grenseland*, [*The Altra Conflict from civil disobedience to sapmi terrorism*], University in Bergen, https://bora.uib.no/bitstream/handle/1956/1475/Master-HarrisChristensen.pdf?sequence=1.

Helgegren, C.-M. (2012) 'Alta-konflikten, Från Civil Olydnad Till Samisk Terrorism, P3 Dokumentär', *Sveriges Radio*, 15 July, http://sverigesradio.se/sida/avsnitt/44486?programid=2519#

Hosey, L. (2000) 'Slumming in Utopia: Protest Construction and the Iconography of Urban America', *Journal of Architectural Education (1984-)*, 53(3), 146–158.

Hundertwasser, F. and Schmied, W. (2003) 'On the second skin', in *Hundertwasser 1928–2000, catalogue raisonné, Vol II*, Cologne: Taschen, pp 955–958.

Iraki, R. (2006) *VG Sultestreikende Afghanere Nekter Å Gi Seg – Asyl-debatten – VG*, [*Afghans on hunger strike refuses to give up*] 15 June, www.vg.no/nyheter/innenriks/asyl-debatten/sultestreikende-afghanere-nekter-aa-gi-seg/a/119792/.

Kelly, T. (2012) *Occupy London: 9 Out of 10 Tents Remain Empty Overnight at St Paul's Camp | Daily Mail Online*, 20 March, www.dailymail.co.uk/news/article-2053068/Occupy-London-9-10-tents-remain-overnight-St-Pauls-camp.html.

Klungtveit, H. S. (2006) *Dagbladet, Sultestreiken Er Over – Innenriks – Dagbladet.no*, 20 June, www.dagbladet.no/nyheter/2006/06/20/469457.html.

Kuusisto, T. K. (2010) *Textile in Architecture*, Tampere University of Technology, https://dspace.cc.tut.fi/dpub/bitstream/handle/123456789/6619/kuusisto.pdf?sequence=3.

Maharaj, S. (1991) 'Arachne's genre: towards inter-cultural studies in textiles', *Journal of Design History*, 4(2) 75–96.

Nango, J. (2010) 'Goalmmát ávus - det tredje rommet', [*Goalmmát ávus - the third room*] *Arkitetkur N*, 2010(7), 22–25.

Normann, C. (2011) *Palestinerne Ved Akerselva Nekter Å Flytte – TV2.no*, [*Palestinians by Akerselva Refuse to Move*] 23 October, www.tv2.no/nyheter/innenriks/palestinerne-ved-akerselva-nekter-aa-flytte-3618760.html.

Palestinerleir (2011) 'Pressemelding: Mohammad Fra Palestinerleiren Arrestert På Vei Til LOs Markering Mot Rasisme', [*Mohammad from the Palestinian Camp arrested on his way to the worker unions manifestation against racism*] *Palestinerleir*, 30 November, www.palestinerleir. no/2011/11/30/pressemelding-mohammad-fra-palestinerleiren-arrestert-pa-vei-til-los-markering-mot-rasisme/.

Roseneil, S. (2000) *Common Women, Uncommon Practices: The Queer Feminisms of Greenham*. London: Cassell.

Schmidt, M. C. and Schmitt, E. (2013) *Obama's Portable Zone of Secrecy (Some Assembly Required)*, 9 November, www.nytimes. com/2013/11/10/us/politics/obamas-portable-zone-of-secrecy-some-assembly-required.html?pagewanted=2&_r=3&hp&

Semper, G. (2010) *The Four Elements of Architecture and Other Writings*. Cambridge and New York: Cambridge University Press.

Sorkin, M. (2008) *Indefensible Space: The Architecture of the National Insecurity State*. Abingdon: Routledge.

Weizman, E. (2007) *Hollow Land: Israel's Architecture of Occupation*. London: Verso.

FOUR

Emergent infrastructures: solidarity, spontaneity and encounter at Istanbul's Gezi Park uprising

Özge Yaka and Serhat Karakayali

Introduction

Encampments have become a highly visible and frequently utilised protest practice in the repertoire of contemporary social movements. While the practice of protest camping spans the globe, academics have only recently begun to study the spatial and performative dimensions of protest practice. In their pioneering study Feigenbaum, Frenzel and McCurdy (2013) pay special attention to the infrastructures of protest camps, which enable them to produce unique experiences of 'participation, collaboration, collectivity and mutuality'. Following up on their focus on infrastructures, this chapter analyses the role of materiality in the formation of a specific political atmosphere and space in Istanbul's Gezi Park during the protests of June 2013. The research question driving this chapter asks: why do the similar infrastructures of protest camps not engender similar political atmospheres? Answering this question requires a deeper engagement with the specific infrastructures of the protest camp under study, in our case Gezi Park. Moreover, it also requires an analytical approach which focuses not only on a camp's different types of infrastructures, but also on how these emerge and evolve over time, what functions they serve as well as how they communicate with the protestors and resonate with the broader political environment. Lastly, developing an analysis of infrastructures with this perspective – one that pays attention to how infrastructures either facilitate or enable certain modes of action and interaction during a protest – also requires examining the relationship between specific material and spatial forms and practices and the political atmosphere created in and through those forms and practices.

Our analysis of the Gezi Park protest camp suggests that the materials, objects and infrastructures of a camp might not primarily serve to build a sustainable space of protest or to support a community of resistance, as they are often conceptualised. Instead, they allow for individuals to relate to each other in a certain way, create bonds and affects between participants and enable a process of emergence and recomposition. These functions are not inscribed in the instrumental use of the materials used to assemble the camps but were produced within the specific political and affective atmosphere of Gezi Park itself. To this end, our main argument throughout this chapter is that the conventional topology of infrastructures and practices, in which infrastructures enable certain types of actions was, in fact, inverted at Gezi Park. To advance this line of argumentation the chapter pays special attention to the spontaneity of the emergence of the infrastructures in Gezi Park. Moreover, it also examines the intensified temporality of the camp (which lasted two weeks until police brutally evicted the park on 15 June 2013) as a means to explain the particular functions the material infrastructures inhabited.

Our analysis is based on our participatory observation in and around Gezi Park between 2 and 6 June 2013, as well as the use of visual, audio and written material produced by various sources during and after these Gezi Park protests.

From a tree to an uprising: a short overview

We do not intend to discuss the reasons and dynamics that gave rise to the Gezi Uprising in detail (see Özkırımlı, 2014; Gürcan and Peker, 2014; Kuymulu, 2013; Karakayali and Yaka, 2014). However, before going deeper into our analysis of the protest camp, we feel the need to define the wider context of the protests in which the camp was situated.

Taksim Square, including the Gezi Park, encompasses several layers of historical meaning and has been a space for political contestations as well as contesting urban imaginaries from the late Ottoman Empire to this day. The 2013 conflict was initiated by the AKP (Justice and Development Party) government's plan to build a shopping mall at Taksim Square, which was supposed to resemble the Artillery Barracks, built in 1806, and regarded as a significant element of the urban memory of modern Islamism. In the early republican period the Artillery Barracks were demolished and Taksim Square was re-constructed as 'the republican ideological showcase of modernisation' (Gül et al, 2014). Traditionalists and Islamists, who conceived the demolition of the barracks as a signifier of the destruction of the Ottoman heritage, coming to power in 2002, strived to roll back.[1] The AKP's project to 'erase the republican memory of the place' (Gül et al, 2014) has started with the closure of the Atatürk Cultural Centre in 2008, and continued with the 'Taksim Pedestrianisation Project', which involved the reconstruction of the former Artillery Barracks to be used as a shopping mall. The whole project was criticised severely by professional organisations, NGOs and community networks that established Taksim Solidarity Platform in 2012 to prevent the destruction of Gezi Park and Taksim area through the Taksim Pedestrianisation Project. The AKP government insisted on the project, though, ignoring criticisms.

Taksim Solidarity organised a campaign, which involved demos, public petitions, lawsuits and various conscious-raising activities against the project. However, bulldozers started to uproot the trees to demolish the park on 27 May, even though the lawsuits against the government plan had not been concluded yet. Around 100 people gathered in Gezi Park on 27 May, responding to a call of Taksim Solidarity. The next day the protestors were attacked by the police – it was here that one of the most shared images of civil resistance against police violence came into existence: the so-called 'woman in red'.[2] On the day, the destruction was prevented as people – including Sırrı Süreyya Önder, a prominent director and a member of the Parliament – stood in front of the trees to stop the diggers and decided to keep guard in the park against any further attempts of demolition. This decision was the rationale of the protest camp as people brought their tents to sleep in at night. In the early morning of 31 May, the police attacked the people in the tents again, this time more brutally.

Images of the burning tents at twilight and videos of police brutality circulated rapidly through social media,[3] creating a widespread reaction and mobilising people to come to the Park. The day and night of 31 May was experienced and narrated by all participants as a miraculous rebellion, especially around the Taksim area, with the numbers continuously rising as the police violence intensified. As one of our activist friends recounts, to the ordinary leftist urban activist it seemed, in the beginning, to be an ordinary protest event – as even massive police violence is quite normalised in Turkey. Everybody expected the dispersion of people in the face of police violence as experienced hundreds of times before. Instead something unusual happened. People refused to retreat, hiding in the side streets of Beyoğlu to recover and reassemble, again and again, only to get together, face the police violence and take Gezi Park on 1 June.

Emergence of the protest camp in Gezi Park

When Gezi Park was taken around 3 pm, a feeling of victory and solidarity was in the air. Many people's first reaction was to gather in the park, shout, sing and dance. But since the victory was very surprising people did not have a clear sense of what to do with the space they took over. Our interactions with people from Taksim Solidarity on 2 June clearly showed that they didn't expect to incite an uprising with their modest call to prevent the government's plan to destroy Gezi Park. They were very happy and excited but unprepared as also seen from the interviews made with the activists of Taksim Solidarity (in Uluğ and Acar, 2014, 457–478). Thus, the protest camp was not planned at all: tents had been set up gradually but there were also a lot of people who spent the night awake, in the Park or around the barricades.

It is essential to keep in mind here that the protest camp represents only a limited dimension of what was happening in Gezi Park and all around Turkey. The Turkish Ministry of Internal Affairs stated that two and a half million people participated in the protests in 79 cities of Turkey and some estimates were as high as eight million according to independent sources. Only a few hundred people stayed in the tents of Gezi Park each night, up to a few thousand in total as people took turns to stay at nights. The convention was to take turns to go to work, to school, to exams or home to take a shower and get some rest. The population in the Park regularly grew during the evening hours from a few thousand to more than 100,000 people, when workers arrived from their offices and workplaces (Uluğ and Acar, 2014).

Even though the encampment was only a limited part of the whole event, it had a central importance. Not only because the whole protest wave started with the police attack on the initially small number of tents built in the park, it was also the locus and the symbol of the wider movement. The space of the camp enabled the building of an alternative space of living, which in turn came to symbolise how the protestors wanted to act politically, live together and socialise with each other. It is not a coincidence that recent uprisings had a dimension of encampment nearly everywhere from North Africa to North America and Europe. The occupied space provides a spatial plane in which the encounters of the protest could be developed and sustained into the composition of new collective subjectivities.

Gezi Park and not Taksim Square

Taksim Square is loaded with historical and political memories and meanings. It has been a site of spatial, ideological and semiotic struggles. The Gezi Park movement in a sense represents a new layer, a reassembly of elements of the former political projects (since it included socialist, Kemalist, Muslim, and liberal elements, among others). We want to point out a largely ignored issue here: the relation between Taksim and Gezi Park. While in this sense Taksim itself is highly contested symbolically, there is also a significant difference between the two spaces Gezi Park and Taksim Square. 'Everywhere is Taksim' for example rather connects to a universalist stance of politics, in which the singular practice of resistance claims to represent the political space in general. It is no coincidence that the term 'Spirit of Gezi' – meaning a specific practice of political 'care', solidarity and heterogeneity connects rather to the very space of Gezi Park. What is expressed here by the term 'spirit' can also be framed in the concept of 'affective atmospheres' understood as a 'shared ground from which subjective states and their attendant feelings and emotions emerge' (Anderson, 2009, 78).

This is precisely what we felt, when we arrived at Taksim Square on 2 June 2013. Our initial response, when we saw the scene at Taksim Square was utter disappointment. There were groups of people, each holding their party's or organisation's flags and banners, occasionally chanting slogans and mostly sticking to their own group. Classical slogans like 'shoulder to shoulder against fascism' were chanted as if to form a block for a march. When we eventually entered the neighbouring park of Gezi we immediately realised that we were facing two very different sites and that the actual event we were looking for was taking place in Gezi Park. The scene here was composed of people who jumped and sang, who rallied in small groups to chant funny slogans (particularly the LGBT groups), who performed concerts, lectures, yoga classes, cooked, or sat together in little assemblages to discuss their issues and demands. In short, people related to each other in a mixture of political, social and cultural practices so that political identities became challengeable. It was the act of subversion more than affirmation that enabled the deviant, minor and heterodox subjectivity of the park, as reflected in a famous graffiti: 'Shoulder to Leg against Fascism'.

Spontaneous and heterogeneous: Gezi Park as an open and inclusive political space

Being in the very centre of Istanbul, the space of Taksim Square and Gezi Park both practically and symbolically reflects the pace and density of urban capitalism. This aspect of location is also important in terms of its relation to the movement of urban bodies, which normally is governed by the rhythm of work and consumption. It is both a specific mode and speed of movement, and also a certain type of interaction between individuals, an anonymous 'non-relation', as paradigmatically theorised by Simmel (1971). The transformation of Gezi Park into a space of the camp, shaped as an 'open' space, not a coded one (as in some camps, which are immediately identifiable as 'radical' spaces), affected this movement and deployment of urban bodies and initiated a transformation of the modes of interaction (from ignorance to attention).

This openness of Gezi was emphasised very often in the various accounts of people who participated. It was partly a consequence of the spontaneity and heterogeneity of the uprising. The fact that *no one* 'owned' the event – and *everyone* resisted together against the police brutality beforehand[4] not only paved the ground for a process of recomposition (see Karakayali and Yaka, 2014) but also equalised all in his or her capacity and right to appropriate the park as their social and political habitat. The emphasis on the openness of Gezi relates both to heterogeneity of the participants, from Kemalists to Kurdish and leftist activists, from feminists and LGBT groups to football ultras, from marginalised youth to middle-class professionals and to the inclusive character of the space,[5] as people from very different backgrounds find it equally easy to become a part of it.

It is often stressed that Gezi was a political space dominated by educated youth. It is true that the majority of the people who spent considerable time in the park were between 15 and 30 years of age, most of them high school and university students (see KONDA, 2014). However, young workers from the margins of the city also joined, housewives and retired people kept commuting from their homes in far away residential areas, telling us 'these kids' gave them hope and joy to live. We came across moving stories of 'street children' who settled in the park from the first day and started to take part in it from the second and third day, distributing free food and attending the children's workshops organised within the park. Some of them wanted to keep guard at the barricades but were sent back to the park by grown-ups (Iplikci, 2013, 21–50 and 167–194). Participants of the protest express how sad they were, as they lost their new home on 15 June, when the police evicted people from the camp.

It was also a common experience that people didn't want to return home (see interviews in Iplikci, 2013 and Uluğ and Acar, 2014, see also Halvorsen, Chapter Ten). We saw high school kids, who were studying for university exams in the park. As a strong division of labour was never established, no one was 'responsible' for the camp apart from a few representatives of Taksim Solidarity, who felt a certain responsibility. Of course the participation in organised/planned camps is also voluntary but there is a clear dividing line between the organisational team and ordinary participants, which might lead to a hierarchical conduct, discourage ordinary participants to take part in the formation of novel infrastructures and practices, and create a sense that some 'own' the event more than others. In Gezi, this was not the case. From democratic infrastructures (people's assemblies, workshops, forums and so on) to life-enhancing practices (organisation of cleaning and cooking, library, free food stances or 'revolution markets', and a wall of needs where people put food, drinks and medicine, health point, kids club and so on) materialities of Gezi emerged spontaneously within the park. Of course, the ideas and knowledge of more experienced activists were instrumental in the creation of an open and inclusive living/political space as well as the forms and gestures of square movements that travelled across borders. However, as the infrastructures of the park had not been designed beforehand and the space of the park was open to everyone to create new forms and to contribute the formation of the *space-to-come* in various ways, in relation to their capacities but irrespective of the positions and professions they assumed beforehand.

The emergent forms of division of labour were based entirely on voluntary participation and were flexible to include 'non-experts'. Of course, medics build infirmaries within the park or the football ultras and radical left activists went to build barricades on the roads surrounding the park. However, established roles were increasingly negotiated by 'non-experts' assuming new roles. Non-doctors providing basic medical care was a common example. Another interesting example was Demet Evgar, a famous actress without any credentials in pedagogy, who decided to establish a children's atelier noticing the number of children in the park. The result was amazing in terms of giving children a venue to express how they understood, felt and experienced what was happening.[6] Also negotiated were the gender roles as women refused to remain behind and stayed on the front at the barricades and during the violent clashes with the police. As a women protestor told us, young men stopped trying to 'protect' women by sending them behind and increasingly accepted the fact that more than half of the protestors were women, who claimed pioneering positions everywhere, including the barricades (see also Iplikci, 2013, 317–334).

So, not having a professional, organisational body to orchestrate infrastructures and practices did not result in chaos but encouraged people to participate and take initiative. A broadly shared feeling emerged of not only being a part, but also being a subject, of a big historical event. We argue that this was a consequence of this spontaneous nature of organisation and egalitarian dispersion of initiative in forming, creating, organising and maintaining new practices and institutions. This particular organisation of things engendered a new understanding of the park as a public space, which challenged the established codes of behaviour, such as throwing rubbish around in the Turkish case. Cleaning the park has emerged as a central and collective practice, and as some protestors state, Gezi Park had never been cleaner, as people collected even the old rubbish, such as three-month's old fag-ends (Iplikci, 2013, 93).

The aspect of spontaneity also conduced to some quite unexpected incidents such as the suspension of the money economy within the park. Remarkably suspending the money economy and making everything free emerged out of smaller and spontaneous decisions (such as taking first the alcohol and then the food sellers out of the park, as drinking makes people vulnerable to police attacks and the stench of meatball disturbed people) (see interviews with Taksim Solidarity activists in Uluğ and Acar, 2014, 458–459) and the fact that bringing or sending food, medicine, water, tents and blankets had become a sign of solidarity (as we will discuss later). These factors led to an abundance of food and other resources and made it possible to distribute everything for free. Only after some time this spontaneously emerging alternative economy was coined as 'commune' and framed accordingly. There indeed was a tangible atmosphere of communism, also depicted in banners like 'Revolution has blinked' or 'To the Taksim Commune' and graffiti such as 'Wow, this is really the revolution' (Ay resmen devrim!).

Radical infrastructures

It is a commonplace in social theory, that social structures function as entities which stabilise individual action so as to reproduce the overall makeup of the social body. Although the structuralist paradigm in theory was brought to an end with the events of 1968 (Dosse, 1997), there is still a widespread assumption that social behaviour or action has to be moulded in non-individual social and cultural patterns. Our first assumption, as researchers and participants of the events in Gezi Park and Taksim Square, was that there would have to be a kind of facilitating structure, which made the unbelievable sequence of events in the two weeks of the uprising possible in the first place. Something must have been 'behind' the event, of course not a secret organisation, but structures, which might have been developed beforehand by the communities or groups involved in the struggle, and which then have circulated within the masses. But a closer look at the ways in which the different 'modules' of the encampment functioned, reveals that objects, infrastructures and even certain codified practices can have different impacts and functions. What has been an 'infrastructure' in a camp, such as, for example, the different 'no border' camps from Strasbourg to Lesbos, became a different thing at Gezi Park. Things, as could be said in a Latourian terminology, have become parts of a different network. To reason that human beings together with objects form a 'network', in which neither determines the other means to assess the plane of indeterminacy so much so that material infrastructures, understood in this way, do not bring about a particular and predetermined subjective reaction (Latour, 2005).

The notion of infrastructure is associated with the paradigm of materialism (both 'historical materialism' and the so-called 'New Materialism' (Coole and Frost, 2010). Marx (1977), who introduced the metaphor of infrastructure into the study of historical social formations, was not only concerned with a critique of the hegemonic idealism of his time. He was similarly critical of contemporary versions of materialism, which seemed to simply invert idealism by putting 'matter', where idealism had placed the 'spirit'.

In more recent debates scholars such as Bruno Latour (2005), Jane Bennett (2010), Karen Barad (2012), Brian Massumi (2002) and many others made the case that social theory should reconsider the linguistic turn and look at the role of objects, things and matter – including 'infrastructures' – independent from procedures of signification. One current in the recent materialist literature often approaches matter as a productive or creative principle, resembling the inverted idealism mentioned above. As an alternative we want to draw on a different understanding of materialism, which rather rejects any notion of a pre-existing order, essence, beginning or finality (and even a subject) and favours disorder, dissemination (as Althusser writes with reference to Derrida) and processes (without subjects) (Althusser, 2006).

In Althusser's account materialism represents the idea that there is no determination of an essence of an entity that is pre-inscribed in the essence of the encountering elements. Such an essence only emerges out of the 'seizure' of the encounter. In this sense, infrastructures should be seen as (partly objective) elements, which 'encounter' actions and behaviours, significations and other social and cultural entities. The importance of the material infrastructure in the case of Gezi Park can only be understood in this way, which exceeds a purely instrumental, 'facilitating' function. We want to demonstrate this point with a few examples, each showing the radical decoupling of the practices from their conventional functions.

Food, barricades and teargas

Our claim that material infrastructures and practices emerged from 'encounters' rather than having been set up as 'facilitating' functions generally ascribed to them can be evidenced with a few examples. One of them is the people's assemblies and forums, the main political infrastructures of the square's movements, that functioned in Gezi mainly as instruments of expression, encounter and recomposition,[7] more than as technologies of decision making. Here, though, we want to focus on less discussed materialities, such as food, barricades and teargas.

The Gezi Park camp shared many features with other camps around the world from the reproductive elements to the small meetings and the horizontal communication structures. One of these elements is the supply of food. Usually, organisers of a camp will consider the preparation and distribution of food (as well as sanitation and shelter) as one of the basic things that have to be provided to participants. Not only because food is essential for the sheer physical reproduction, but also because it has a profoundly symbolic function. To produce food at the site of the camp is part of the public performance of 'self-organisation'. As a 'heterotopian performance' it presents to the general public notions of self-organisation and autonomy. At the same time it not only allows for members of the camp to be addressed as (responsible) producers, who cooperatively govern their own life, it also helps to keep the participants 'on site', which is often a central concern of organisers of political and cultural events.

Since Gezi Park emerged spontaneously no such organisational structure was set up. Food was mainly brought to the park by sympathisers and then redistributed. Additionally, thousands of people around Turkey (and from abroad) have sent food through delivery services both online and through phone orders (*Milliyet*, 2013). Thus, food supply never became a real issue. While in planned camps the food, its preparation and distribution can become a means of negotiating the modes of commonality within a camp, including struggles over the division of labour, food did not play such a role in Gezi Park. What was at stake here can be illustrated by the experience of a protestor who, to his surprise, ate stuffed zucchini flowers (a sophisticated, hard to make type of food) from a stand (Uluğ and Acar, 2014, 228). Another protestor likens his experience to *Alice in Wonderland*: 'You say water and water drops from the sky, you say you are hungry and someone immediately gives you pastries and cakes, just like Alice in Wonderland' (Iplikci, 2013, 92–93).

Another story is told by a young woman, who was giving out sandwiches to people during the first days of the encampment in June. When someone said that she didn't need to walk around to distribute them, that she instead could put them to the 'wall of needs' she replied that she had prepared the sandwiches all night for the protestors and wanted to give them to people herself. Apparently, giving away food was a means for her to relate to people, to show solidarity and to become a part of the event. As for many others – like the high school students we come across in Gezi Park, who told us that they bought simit (Turkish bagels) with their small amount of pocket money and distributed them in the park or the flight attendants who supplied us with sandwiches from the airplane's stock, when they heard we were on the way to Gezi Park – sharing and giving food is less about supply, but an act of symbolic care, a way to connect to strangers and create a social bond.

While in both planned and spontaneous camps providing food has a symbolic function, in the latter this social or symbolic function prevails. A very similar observation can be made about the barricades, which very often were not quite functional in the sense of providing efficient protection against police vehicles. Rather, barricades become spaces of encounter, the symbolic borders of the utopia and hybrid artefacts people constantly rebuild, keep guard at and construct small communities around (see Ertür, 2014).[8] In the case of the barricades in Ankara's Dikmen neighbourhood or Istanbul's Gazi Mahallesi, people donated all kinds of objects to barricades (from washing machines to cars) as their personal contribution to the event itself. The objects, more than serving a purely technical aim (like blocking a street), become means of communication in a double sense. By donating objects one enters the Gezi community. It is a way of demonstrating or communicating one's willingness to sacrifice (even if only a sandwich) and this gift at the same time constitutes the community. All kinds of objects, which maintain their conventional and technical functions (like gas masks, cigarettes, medicine, Wi-Fi passwords), are predominantly assessed from the perspective of their bonding-function.

In an almost paradoxical manner, this relationship between objects, social interaction and the formation of a collective subjectivity even holds for 'hostile' objects such as water cannons and teargas. Much graffiti, as well as slogans and jokes centred on the bonding impacts of objects, whose actual function is to hurt or damage protesters. A graffiti at Istiklal Caddesi, close to Taksim Square read 'Tear gas beautifies the skin' (written on the shutters of a well-known cosmetic shop), another one addresses water cannons as romantic interest.

One could argue that these utterances must be seen as ironically inflected, but when we consider the accounts of people who went through the initial battles with the police which lasted approximately two days before the space of the park was occupied, the relationship particularly to teargas becomes quite ambivalent: on the one hand, people experienced tear gas as something extremely painful, an experience which is actually supposed to make people surrender. However, because people helped each other during these first two days, whenever someone was in distress, and also because the vast majority of those people were not experienced street fighters, the tear gas succinctly transformed into a hybrid object. Inhaling the gas, one could say, began to represent both the violence of the state apparatus as it was connected with the bond of care that it brought with it (see interviews in Arman, 2013, 44–49 and 148–157).

Conclusion

From the perspective of its genealogy, the Gezi Park protest camp, as noted above, was not meant to be an infrastructure. It emerged more or less 'accidentally' out of the spontaneous practices of the people involved in the uprising. This is one of the reasons, we assume, that the camp has been able to support the exceptional nature of the event itself. The practices connected to the camp neither prescribed the modes nor the range of participants involved, as it might have been the case with a thoroughly prepared and well-thought-out protest camp.

It was the particular condition of a spontaneously emerged camp that brought about a dimension of enchantment accompanying every activity – from cleaning up to inhaling tear gas. Because of this, different from the observations of Halvorsen (2015) on the Occupy London protest camp(s), people in Gezi were eager to contribute, and often the supply of helping hands exceeded the demand. Also, the radical openness of the protest space at Gezi encouraged people to take part in the formation of reproductive, political and communication infrastructures without establishing a hierarchy among them. However, one should also consider that in comparison to the four and a half months of camping in St Paul's courtyard in London, Gezi lasted only two weeks and tens of thousands of people – up to half a million – spent time each and every day in Gezi Park and the Taksim area. Thus, the timespan and the volume of circulation prevented the accumulation of feelings of burnout or the establishment of any patterns, roles or a rigid division of labour. And because of the sheer amount of people, the reproductive function was not at the centre of the event.

In this sense, we could say that only specific elements or dimensions of the camp served as infrastructures in a conventional sense during the two weeks. As we have outlined, infrastructures should not be mistaken as structures, which determine actions or behaviour (as in the crude version of the infrastructure/superstructure model), but rather as things that have different impacts according to the specificity of the encounter between them and actions, feelings, objects or narrations. We found the Gezi Park case to be an ideal instance to make this case. The heterotopian moment of camps, Feigenbaum et al (2013) emphasised, seemed to be located in our case not so much on the level of the practical organisation of alternative daily routines. The heterotopian moment was rather carried by the spirit or atmosphere of care and solidarity, which was transferred to the park and could be kept alive there through the 'institutions' of the camp. If there should be a lesson drawn for the future of social protest, we would suggest considering that camps do not necessarily have to be planned in advance – that they can just as well emerge as the consequence of an event. Our analysis of Gezi Park's emergent infrastructures contributes to the growing literature of protest camps showing that specific formation of infrastructures enable specific modes of action and interaction and specific political atmospheres to emerge. Our approach also speaks to the broader field of social movements, in which structures, as well as models of opportunity, framing and organisation, are usually understood as fixed and static, leaving no room to understand the dimension of emergence and recomposition.

Of course, some of the practices performed in Gezi Park were developed elsewhere, that is, more precisely in planned camps, while many other practices were just improvised. That is to say that even in the state of exception, in the extraordinary moment of the event, people rely on established and tested practices. What our analysis shows is that these kinds of practices, and particularly infrastructural practices bring about 'maintenance'. They support or facilitate a mode of being together or being in common. But the very quality of the social bond they support seems to be related to something beyond the mere infrastructures. It is this living experience of the extraordinary, or what Walter Benjamin called the 'real state of exception' (Benjamin, 1968, 257), which succinctly generated practices of commoning and 'infrastructures'.

Notes

[1] Taksim has also been a site of the socialist movement since the 1970s. It has a historical meaning due to the memories of important May Days of the 1970s, especially of the bloody May Day of 1977 in which 37 people were killed and hundreds were injured by snipers. This event retained as a symbol of state and fascist terror against the rising socialist workers' movement of the 1970s. The military regime of the early 1980s and the following civilian governments strictly banned the May Day celebrations at Taksim. From 1990s onwards Taksim Square has been a space of dispute between the state and trade unions, workers' organisations and socialist groups. Several attempts to organise a demo at Taksim have resulted in injuries and deaths due to violent attacks of the police.

[2] www.theguardian.com/world/2013/jun/05/turkey-lady-red-dress-ceyda-sungur

[3] Especially Twitter was important in disseminating the news and images of police brutality from the streets of İstanbul and Ankara (as mainsteam media censored the mass protests in the first few days of the uprisings) and connecting the protestors in the rush of police attacks. Only on 1 June, two million tweets sent before 4 pm, mentioning hashtags related to the protest (see http://smapp.nyu.edu/reports/turkey_data_report.pdf). The twitter bird has become one of the popular symbols of the uprising, too.

[4] There are countless accounts of 'solidarity of strangers' in the narrations about 30 and 31 May. Nearly everyone has been 'saved' from water cannons and tear gas bullets, 'treated' by Talcid solutions (one of the first discoveries of the protests was that a heartburn medicine called Talcid provides fast recovery from the severe symptoms of tear gas) or helped in various ways (sharing the gas mask is a common act of solidarity and care, for example). The vital importance of this care and solidarity practices can be appreciated better if one considers the intensity of police violence which led to several deaths and more than 8,000 injuries within two weeks of protests (see Amnesty International, 2013).

[5] This inclusive character involved the rejection of closing the event to the 'other side' – the supporters of the government and even to the police. The police officer, who died falling down from a bridge during the protests, Mustafa Sarı, was commemorated within the park, in spite of the brutal police violence the protestors experienced. AKP supporters were called to join, and some actually did.

[6] See the video of Children's Atelier of Gezi with English subtitles (Aykanat, 2013).

[7] See (Istanbulda neoluyor, 2013) for an impressive example. Other political infrastructures of encounter and recomposition were the informal discussions and workshops, as the one done by feminists and LGBTQ activists to formulate new non-sexist slogans against the sexist ones used frequently by football ultras. In that

workshop they decided to correct those slogans, both when they were being chanted and written on the walls – the corrections were so popular that the legendary ultra group, Çarşı of Beşiktaş, have apologised for their sexist and homophobic slogans and agreed to change them (see the interview with a LGBTQ activist in Uluğ and Acar, 2014, 147–164).

8 See *There is a Wonderful World Behind*, a photo album of Gezi's barricades by a young talented activist photographer, Cem Ersavci, who died in a motorcycle accident in the summer of 2014 (Ersavci, 2013).

References

Althusser, L. (2006) *Philosophy of the Encounter: Later Writings, 1978–87.* London: Verso.

Amnesty International (2013) *Gezi Park Protests: Brutal Denial of the Peaceful Assembly in Turkey,* www.amnestyusa.org/research/reports/gezi-park-protests-brutal-denial-of-the-right-to-peaceful-assembly-in-turkey.

Anderson, B. (2009) 'Affective atmospheres', *Emotion, Space, Society* 2(2009), 77–81.

Arman, A. (2013) *Gezi'nin güzel insanları* [*Beautiful people of Gezi*](4th edn). İstanbul: Doğan Kitap.

Aykanat, A. (2013) Çocuklarımızın Gözünden Gezi Parkı (video file), [Gezi Park from the eyes of our children] 15 June, www.youtube.com/watch?v=HVx0dOse6yY.

Barad, K. (2012) *Agentieller Realismus* [*Agential Realism*] Berlin: Suhrkamp.

Benjamin, W. (1968) *Illuminations* (ed. by Hanna Arendt). New York: Schocken Books.

Bennett, J. (2010) *Vibrant Matter: A Political Ecology of Things.* Durham, NC: Duke University Press.

Coole, D. H. and Frost, S. (2010) *New Materialisms: Ontology, Agency, and Politics.* Durham, NC: Duke University Press.

Dosse, F. (1997) *History of Structuralism.* Minneapolis, MN: University of Minnesota Press.

Ersavci, C. (2013) *There's a Wonderful World Behind (Photo Album),* www.cemersavci.com/arkada-ok-gzel-bir-dnya-var.

Ertür, B. (2014) *Haydi Barikata!?* ("*To the Barricade!?*") in *#Diren Direniş, Ajanda 2014 (#Resist Resistance, Diary 2014)* . İstanbul: Metis.

Feigenbaum, A., Frenzel, F. and McCurdy, P. (2013) *Protest Camps.* London: Zed.

Goodwin, J., Jasper, J. M. and Polletta, F. (2001) *Passionate Politics: Emotions and Social Movements.* Chicago, IL: University of Chicago Press.

Gül, M., Dee, J. and Cünük, C. N. (2014) 'Istanbul's Taksim Square and Gezi Park: the place of protest and the ideology of place', *Journal of Architecture and Urbanism*, 38(1), 63–72.

Gürcan, E. C. and Peker, E. (2014) 'Turkey's Gezi Park demonstrations of 2013: a Marxian analysis of a political movement', *Socialism and Democracy*, 28(1), 70–89.

Halvorsen, S. (2015) 'Taking space: moments of rupture and everyday life in Occupy London', *Antipode*, 47(2), 401–417.

Iplikci, M. (2013) *Biz Orada Mutluyduk: Gezi Parkı Direnişindeki Gençler Anlatıyor* [*We were happy there: Youth of the Gezi Park Resistance Speak*] Istanbul: Doğan Kitap.

Istanbulda neoluyor (2013) 'Gezi Park People's Assembly/Halk Meclisi – 6 June 2013/6 Haziran 2013' (video file), www.youtube.com/watch?v=VQ1UKAyVqZI.

Karakayalí, S. & Yaka, Ö. (2014) The spirit of Gezi: the recomposition of political subjectivities in Turkey, *New Formations*, 83, 117–38.

KONDA (2014) *Gezi Report: Public Perception of 'Gezi Protests', Who Were the People at Gezi Park?*, http://konda.com.tr/en/raporlar/KONDA_Gezi_Report.pdf.

Kuymulu, M. B. (2013) 'Reclaiming the right to the city: reflections on the urban uprisings in Turkey', *City: Analysis of Urban Trends, Culture, Theory, Policy, Action*, 17(3), 274–278.

Latour, B. (1993) *We Have Never Been Modern*. Cambridge, MA: Harvard University Press.

Latour, B. (2005) *Reassembling the Social an Introduction to Actor-Network-Theory*. Oxford: Oxford University Press, http://site.ebrary.com/id/10233636.

Law, J. and Hassard, J. (1999) *Actor Network Theory and After*. Oxford: Blackwell/Sociological Review.

Marx, K. (1977) *A Contribution to the Critique of Political Economy*. Moscow: Progress Publishers.

Massumi, B. (2002) *Parables for the Virtual: Movement, Affect, Sensation*. Durham, NC: Duke University Press.

Milliyet (2013) 'Dünyanın her yerinden Gezi parkı için sipariş yağdı', [Meal orders amassed from all over the world for Gezi Park] 9 June. www.milliyet.com.tr/dunyanin-her-yerinden-gezi-parki/gundem/detay/1720586/default.htm.

Özkırımlı, U. (2014) *The Making of a Protest Movement in Turkey: #Occupy Gezi*. Hampshire and New York: Palgrave Macmillan.

Simmel, G. (1971) 'The metropolis of modern life', in D. Levine (ed) *Simmel: On Individuality and Social Forms*. Chicago, IL: Chicago University Press.

Uluğ, Ö. M. and Acar, Y. G. (2014) *Bir olmadan biz olmak: Farklı gruplardan aktivistlerin gözüyle Gezi direnişi [Being us without being one: Gezi Resistance from the eyes of activists from different groups]*. Ankara: Dipnot.

FIVE

Protest spaces online and offline: the Indignant movement in Syntagma Square

Anastasia Kavada and Orsalia Dimitriou

Introduction

The summer of 2011 saw the largest occupation of public space in Greece in recent memory. Enraged by the government's austerity measures and following the example of the square occupations in Spain, thousands of people flooded Syntagma Square in the centre of Athens on 25 May 2011. Calling themselves 'Αγανακτισμένοι', meaning 'Indignants' in Greek, protesters stayed in the square for nearly two months, turning it into a stage of dissent and a place of political fermentation. This chapter explores the characteristics, practices and agency of the movement by focusing on space, both online and offline. We examine the Indignants' repertoire of contention (Tilly, 1978) – the tactics that they employed to challenge the government, express their anger and construct alternatives – with an eye on the spatial aspects of this repertoire. In so doing, we provide a sense of the movement's 'spatial agency' (Sewell, 2001), of the ways in which the movement altered the physical arrangements and symbolic associations of space. At the same time, our inquiry also looks at how spaces – online, offline and hybrid – shape patterns of mobilisation and social movement activity. To provide a basis for this research, we begin with a framework for understanding both physical and mediated space and its relation with contentious politics.

Defining space

Space is often perceived as a 'container' of social life, a structure that restricts the activity unfolding within it, as something separate both from the meaning people give to it and of the actual uses and practices taking place 'in space' (Lehtovuori, 2010). However, such perspectives disregard the cultural aspects of space: how space is invested with particular symbolic meanings, rules and norms. Consequently, this view also fails to acknowledge that space both shapes and is itself constituted through the social relationships of the actors associated with its design, use and regulation (Martin and Miller, 2003).

Lefebvre's (1991) analysis of space as 'produced' by material practices of representation and everyday practices of appropriation helps to address this gap. Lefebvre identifies three types of space that together make a triad: *perceived*, *conceived* and *lived*. *Perceived* space refers to the concrete space that people encounter in their everyday life (for example, shops, houses, parks). *Conceived* space designates the mental constructions, creative ideas about and representations of space. *Lived* space is the complex combination of perceived and conceived space and represents a person's actual experience of space in everyday life (Lefebvre, 1991, 39). Space and social relations are mutually constituted and for Lefebvre, space is the product of triadic interrelations; always under construction and always in a process of becoming.

Lefebvre's triad provides a framework for studying the spatiality and overlaps between physical and mediated environments. The relationship between physical and mediated space is an issue that has always occupied the study of media. For Scannell (1996), the media lead to a 'doubling of space' as mediated events 'now occur, simultaneously, in two different places: the place of the event itself and that in which it is watched and heard' (p 76). Other scholars have talked about the creation of a hybrid space that is both mediated and physical, either in relation to mobile internet technology (Gordon and de Souza e Silva, 2011) or to the current 'hybrid media system' (Chadwick, 2013) more generally where the dichotomies between online and offline are blurred. In a similar vein, Meyrowitz (1985) discusses the media's effect on our sense of place and how media can change the 'situational geographies' of space by altering its boundaries, publicness and visibility, as well as the norms of its operation and the nature of interaction. The media also modify our perceptions of proximity through 'time–space compression' (Harvey, 1989) by increasing the speed with which information can travel around the world.

Furthermore, we can think of mediated contexts as places with their own spatiality. This is particularly the case for the internet whose initial conception as 'cyberspace' generated serious reflection on whether and to what extent we can consider it as a space (Saco, 2002). In this respect, Saco (2002) notes two divergent responses, one rejecting the view of cyberspace as a space because '"it is only virtual" (read: not physical)', the other emphasising 'the radical implications of viewing cyberspace as a space: namely, that this perspective could foreground for us that all space is in a sense virtual because it discursively constructed' (p 23). Following Lefebvre's triad of space, (Saco, 2002) considers the internet as made up of the physical components, infrastructures and devices that allow us to 'go online'. The spatiality of the online realm is also constructed through practices of networking that in turn depend on the operation of different rules and internet protocols. These are combined with 'spatial discourses about what that networking space is and how it should be ordered' (p 27), as well as the lived practices that define our cultural experience of the internet and the metaphors that we use to perceive what we do online as a movement in space, such as referring 'to *going online, surfing,* and the various *welcome-to* "home pages" on the Web that signify an arrival somewhere' (p 28).

Therefore, the imaginations of the space and the metaphors or objects that represent it, the actual practices of using the space, as well as its physical components are all equally important elements of spatiality. This view of view of space and social relations as mutually constituting provides a framework for conceptualising both mediated and physical spaces and the interplay between the two.

Space and contentious politics

The nuanced view of space presented above is largely absent within sociological and political science approaches to contentious politics. Instead, the literature largely treats 'space as an assumed and unproblematized background' (Sewell, 2001, 51–52), while the social constructivist understanding of space 'only very slowly seems to find its way in empirical research' (Daphi, 2014, 170). Research in contentious politics also tends to focus on the physical environment at the expense of the mediated aspects of space.[1] When they are taken into account, the media are considered mainly for their capacity to connect physically distant spaces but not as contexts with their own spatiality. Yet, the idea that space and contentious politics co-constitute each other as space is both an outcome *and* a medium of contentious politics (Sewell, 2001, 55).

Space shapes the interactions that give rise to social movements as it affects co-presence and proximity. The ability of potential movement participants to communicate with each other depends on physical distance, but also on *time-distance* defined as 'the length of time required for persons, objects or mediated messages to get from one place to another' (Sewell, 2001, 60). Time-distance is a function of both modes of transportation and the activists' communication media. Spatial routines, meaning the 'known and transposable formulae for particular kinds of occupation and use of space' (Sewell, 2001, 46) also influence social movement activity. Co-presence, proximity and routines affect patterns of mobilisation. For instance, Tilly (2000) calls our attention to the different mobilisation processes of 'workers who gather daily in the same workplace and revolutionary conspirators who improvise new meeting places day by day' (p 138).

Contentious activity also needs 'safe' or 'free' spaces where alternative ideas and relationships can be nurtured. Although the literature lacks a common definition, 'free spaces' often 'refer to small-scale settings within a community or movement that are removed from the direct control of dominant groups, are voluntarily participated in, and generate the cultural challenge that precedes or accompanies political mobilization' (Polletta, 1999, 1). These can be both real and conceptual spaces (Polletta, 1999) that facilitate the development of alternative codes and visions and the practice of different forms of organising and decision-making. Protest camps can be considered as a particular form of 'free space' as they are both 'a place of ongoing protest and a site of nurturing, a community of resistance' (Feigenbaum et al, 2013, 43).

As the history of protest illustrates, space can be at the core of grievances giving rise to social movements and of claims around which people rally to defend their interests. Discussions around the 'right to the city' best exemplify this function of space (Harvey, 2013; Lefebvre, 1996). Space also influences the tactics of public claim-making in which social movements engage (Tilly, 2000). Thus, we can think of movements and their tactics as 'produc[ing] the spatiality that permits exercising [the] right [to speak]' (Swyngedouw cited in Kaika and Karaliotas, 2014, 4). The movements' repertoire of contention can therefore be perceived in spatial terms, in terms of the manipulation, occupation or engineering of space. Tactics may include the disruption of spatial routines, for instance through the blocking of streets or entry points to specific meetings. They may also involve the 'physical assembling of large numbers of people into limited spaces' (Sewell, 2001, 58) such as in demonstrations or large gatherings. The symbolic meaning of specific places is also crucial in this respect, as '[p]rotesters typically attempt to mount demonstrations or rallies in places with politically salient meanings' (Sewell, 2001, 65). Other tactics include efforts to gain access to the space, physical or symbolic, of targets, for instance by attending meetings that are only open to political insiders. Movements can also attempt to establish relations between previously unconnected social sites by building infrastructures of flexible territorial control that allow the coordination of activities and the diffusion of contentious activity. Prefiguration is another tactic here, which consists of the creation of utopian spaces where activists can practice the world they would like to see (Tormey, 2005). Whether physical or mediated, these are spaces whose design and operation embody the values of the movement and serve as tangible illustrations of its vision.

Thus, the outcomes of social movements and the changes that they effect are also expressed as transformations of space. Sewell (2001) calls this 'spatial agency', meaning both 'the ways that spatial constraints are turned to advantage in political and social struggles and the ways that such struggles can restructure the meanings, uses, and strategic valence of space' (p 55). This brings us to the notion of power which can also be perceived in spatial terms, as control over the routines, symbolic associations, design, regulation and access to space (Lefebvre, 1991). What we refer to as a movement's 'spatial repertoire of contention' thus outlines the tactics employed by movements as they strive to gain power over other actors. Focusing on the spatial repertoire of contention also helps us to identify more clearly the obstacles that social movements may encounter, as well as the power that other actors, such as the state or the police, can wield on social movements. At the same time, this 'spatial' view of power can help to analyse the internal power relations within social movements and to unravel their hidden hierarchies.

In what follows, we examine how space and social movements co-constitute each other by focusing on the case study of the Indignant movement in Syntagma Square. Our focus rests on the movement's spatial repertoire of contention and on how the movement was shaped by the online and offline spaces in which it unfolded. We also examine the processes of centralisation and decentralisation with regards to space, and the advantages and limitations of privileging one location over others. Our empirical results derive from in-depth interviews with 18 'Indignant' activists, three of whom belonged to the press/multimedia team. The interviews were conducted in Greece between September 2011 and March 2013. Interviewees were asked in Greek about the movement's organising and decision-making processes, media use, interactions with authorities, as well as the governance, management and regulation of the square. Interviews were complemented with a 'features analysis' of three Indignados websites (www.real-democracy. gr, amesi-dimokratia.org and aganaktismenoi.com) which focused on the design, conditions of access and communication services on offer.

The Indignant movement in Syntagma Square

Occupying a space of symbolic significance

Syntagma Square is the main statutory public space of Athens, a spatial expression of the relationship between state and public. The square was named after the constitution ('syntagma' in Greek) that King Otto, the first king of Greece, was forced to grant after the popular and military uprising of 1843 (Melembianaki, 2006). The most prominent building, and the one that dictates the character of the square, is the former royal palace and current parliament building. Constructed in 1836, the palace was designed in a way that bestows 'an air of power and permanence on the capital and its institutions' (Bastéa, 2000). The location of the palace rendered Syntagma Square the ideal residential area for the upcoming Athenian bourgeoisie and by 1860 it was the centre of political and social life. The royal palace was turned into a parliament building in 1924 and the square maintained its pluralistic character until 1938. It was surrounded by numerous cafes, restaurants and places of social gathering for the upper and middle class, a promenade for the low class, a site for performing artists and a place for national celebrations and parades, political rallies and discussions, as well as demonstrations and riots (Melembianaki, 2006). However, by the 1950s, the majority of the residences were replaced by hotels, commercial and governmental buildings, while the increasing vehicle traffic cut off the main square block from its surroundings. The function of the cafes as a space of everyday political discussions was also diminished and finally completely abolished during the military dictatorship that ruled Greece from 1967 to 1974. The contemporary square is mainly an extended and beautified street junction. It is also home to one of the main metro stations in Athens which reinforces its transitory character as most of the users meet in the square but do not remain there. Thus, in its current form, Syntagma Square has completely lost its initial character as a social and political forum, even though its location in front of the parliament means that it sometimes hosts political events (Dimitriou, 2014).

Still, the symbolic significance of the square and its central location in front of the Greek parliament offered a prime site of protest for the Indignant movement. As one interviewee put it, 'The parliament is there, the ex-palace is there, even if you are unaware of the history of the place, it has great importance in the collective imaginary and what you perceive that is happening there. It would be hard for these events to take place in Propylaia, even though the space is more political for a small percentage of the population' (Apostolis, personal communication, 11 September 2011). Therefore, in terms of the spatial repertoire of contention, the Indignant movement employed the long established tactic of gathering large numbers of people in spaces of symbolic importance.

Most interesting in spatial terms was that this assembling of people did not involve a temporary movement between two points, like in a demonstration, but a long-term presence in the square. As a participant in the movement mentioned

> The first gatherings were all about presence. And this presence was related to time: staying at the space for as long as we can. These gatherings were not like typical protests – there is a big difference. In protests we usually gather and then we march through the city, we follow banners and there is a certain route, a beginning and an end. In this case, at the time it all started, there was just a beginning without a visible end. (Nikos, personal communication, 15 September 2011)

It was, therefore, not only the location itself, but its open-ended occupation that defined the claims of the movement, stating in no uncertain terms its willingness to remain in the square, to continue discussing the problems until they were addressed. This crowd of people also served to unify, albeit temporarily, the space of the square with that of the parliament and the surrounding commercial streets. As the same interviewee put it, 'There was for the first time an extensive spatial presence of people...that covers the square...This brings about traffic adjustments...there is a first unification of the parliament space with Syntagma Square through the presence of this crowd' (Nikos, personal communication, 15 September 2011).

Upper and Lower Square: the Dionysian and the Apollonian

This heterogeneous gathering soon split into two broad groups, each one occupying a different part of Syntagma Square and employing a different spatial repertoire of contention. The upper square, the part that is in front of the Parliament, included a disparate assortment of mostly nationalistic and some right-wing elements. Nikos K (personal communication, 10 July 2013), one of our interviewees who belonged to the press/multimedia group, noted that the upper square consisted of groups such as the '300 Greeks' which emphasised nationalism and patriotism and the 'Autonomous Nationalists', a grouping that is loosely associated with a strand of neo-Nazism inspired by groups like CasaPound. It was also frequented by the 'Greek Mothers' who were demanding jobs for their children and blamed immigrants for the problem of youth unemployment (Kaika and Karaliotas, 2014). Yet, the upper square also included leftist elements, such as the far-left nationalist 'Spitha', as well as Maoists and some members of the Marxist-Leninist Communist Party. But mostly, according to Nikos K (personal communication, 10 July 2013), the upper square involved fewer political people who wanted to express their blind indignation towards traditional political authority.

In this respect, the location and '[t]he direct visual contact that this part of the square has with the entrance level of the parliament building made it the perfect stage for those who wanted to launch direct verbal abuse and obscene gesticulations against Members of Parliament' (Kaika and Karaliotas, 2014, 5). Thus, in terms of its repertoire of contention, the Upper Square exhibited a more carnivalesque character that emphasised direct action and conflict with government. Tactics included the closure of the street in front of the parliament that both disrupted the vehicle traffic in one of the main street of Athens, and managed to connect the main block of the square with the parliament in a single continuous space. They also comprised the expression of disrespect towards the parliament through gestures like the 'mountza'[2] and sounds made by whistles, which soon started to be sold on the square by various vendors. Some interviewees called the upper square Dionysian, referring to its more disruptive, emotional and unruly nature (Nikos, personal communication, 15 September 2011; Thanos, personal communication, 4 September 2011).

This was opposed to the Apollonian character of the lower square, which revolved around a process of participatory democracy based on consensus, open assembly and equality. The lower square sought to transform the angry protest into a movement that was demanding Direct Democracy Now, 'asking for a radical restructuring of politics in the country and the way the country operates' (Ilias, personal communication, 11 September 2011). But this long-term presence on the square also transformed it, according to Nikos, 'into a space of continuous habitation' (personal communication, 15 September 2011). Working groups and teams dealing with specific tasks, such the media, the organisation of the assembly, or the logistics of the camp, started to appear, each one establishing a physical location in the square. There was also a designated space for assembly meetings, situated 'in the lower part of the square after the fountain' (personal communication,

15 September 2011). In other words, the differentiation between the various functions of the movement and the development of a makeshift structure also occurs in spatial terms as it is a process that involves both specialisation and spatialisation.

The assembly of the lower square developed its norms and rules of decision-making through open procedures, some of which are documented below. As Nikos explained, 'the main idea was to allow for as many voices as possible to be heard during the assembly and to discuss different topics as this would help the gradual formulation of claims and the fermentation of opinions' (personal communication, 15 September 2011). Because of the high number of participants, the secretariat devised a system where each attendee was issued, on a first come first served basis, with a little paper indicating their number in the queue of speakers. The agenda was formulated every day by compiling and summarising the items proposed by the working groups of the lower square (Ntina, personal communication, 10 July 2013). The assemblies were livestreamed and the minutes were uploaded online, as well as printed and photocopied to be distributed on the square. In contrast, the lower square focused on creating a utopian space of prefiguration where participants could practice and experiment with different forms of democratic participation.

Some of our interviewees felt that more could have been done to join the two parts of the square. Kiki (personal communication, 8 September 2011) noted that moving the assembly to the steps dividing the upper from the lower square would have solved the problem. Another solution would have been to unify the square in a common soundscape through the positioning of the lower square loudspeakers, by turning them to face the upper part of the square (Kiki, personal communication, 8 September 2011; Ntina, personal communication, 10 July 2013).

Yet, despite the lack of unity between upper and lower square, being physically present in the same space meant that the diverse occupants of the square were still in each other's line of vision and had to enter into some sort of negotiation around how they were using the space. The two parts of the square also came together during days of intense protest when the police descended on the square in order to quell dissent (Nikos K, personal communication, 10 July 2013). Moreover, the square was unified through the spatial practices of casual supporters and interested bystanders who would promenade and pass by the whole square (Ntina, personal communication, 10 July 2013).

Therefore, the upper and lower squares both expressed their criticism towards parliamentary politics through a different set of tactics.

Participants in the upper square employed disruption and carnivalesque resistance, while those in the lower square put together a system of decision-making whose values and operation constituted an implicit critique of the parliamentary process.

The Indignant movement online

The Indignant movement was also online and their presence in virtual space augmented their presence in the physical space of the square. The mobilisation actually started on Facebook, when, inspired by the Spanish 15M movement, a page was set up calling for a similar gathering in Athens (Nikos K, personal communication, 10 July 2013). The website real-democracy.gr was already set up to facilitate the protest of a group against austerity (and in solidarity with the Spanish 15-M movement) that decided to converge with other groups in Syntagma Square on the 25 May 2011. Real-democracy.gr was created by a group of Linux enthusiasts who volunteered their time and resources to running it.

Conflicts soon arose, however, over the administration rights of the website. The management of the site came under the newly formed press/multimedia team. Counting up to 90 people in its heyday (Nikos K, personal communication, 10 July 2013), the team was tasked with shooting videos and photographs, and maintaining the website and social media channels of the movement. They were also liaising with the press, both domestic and international. The three members of the press/multimedia team who were interviewed all commented on the difficulty of dealing with the main person who had set up the real-democracy website and who was unwilling to provide access and administration rights to the rest of the team. He would sometimes change the passwords without notifying them, a vexing problem during large events when the press/multimedia team urgently needed to upload content (Loukia, personal communication, 31 March 2013). Such conflicts are a frequent occurrence in recent movements (compare Kavada, 2015) as the internet allows activists to easily set up online spaces, which are then owned and controlled by the individuals who created them, rather than by the collective. The rather organic and chaotic manner in which movements arise means that such mobilisations rarely operate with a clear plan for the establishment and governance of the movement's online properties in advance. Rules and guidelines are often worked out along the way, but by the time issues arise, specific activists may already hold significant power over specific online spaces (compare Gerbaudo, 2012; Kavada, 2015).

To overcome this conflict, the press/multimedia team soon set up another website, amesi-dimokratia.org (the title means 'direct democracy' in Greek) which became the official online space of the lower square. In contrast to real-democracy.gr, the new website (amesi-dimokratia.org) was created in consultation with the working groups of the movement and was run by the 'website' sub-group of the press/multimedia team. It however appeared at a time when the occupation of the square was on the wane and despite the efforts of the team to raise awareness about the new site, it garnered a smaller audience than real-democracy (Ntina, personal communication, 10 July 2013).

The design of the two websites reflects the values of the lower square and demonstrates the designers' intention for the online space to serve the tactic of prefiguration embraced by the assembly. Both websites were thus built on values of openness and equality. Information was public and users needed to register only for posting on forums. The sites included pages with the minutes and decisions of past meetings and the agenda of future ones. However, it was only real-democracy that allowed interaction between users, either asynchronously in the forum, or real-time in the 'kafeneio' (meaning 'café' in Greek) where users could log in with their Facebook account and start conversations with others logged in at the same time. Lack of resources for moderation was posited as one of the reasons why the design of amesi-dimokratia.org did not comprise any fora or discussion groups (Nikos K, personal communication, 10 July 2013). It was also that participants could cover their needs for interaction through Facebook (Loukia, personal communication, 31 March 2013).

While the two websites complemented the activity of the assembly, the internet was not used to allow those online to have a say in the assembly. This was due mainly to practical issues, such as the time it would take to include internet users in the discussion, or the difficulty of ascertaining someone's identity in online voting (Nikos K, personal communication, 10 July 2013). There were, however, discussions about incorporating the internet more fully into the decision-making process of the movement. The administrators of real-democracy proposed that those watching the assembly on live-stream should have their questions read and discussed. They also suggested integrating a 'voting up/down' feature in the forum and for the two top topics to be added to the agenda. However, the assembly rejected these suggestions as they were thought to be too complicated.

Another website, that was already up and running at the end of May, was aganaktismenoi.com, which seemed to belong to the upper square, even though it brought news and live-streams from other occupied squares in Greece. The website had a rather more nationalist bent and focused more on criticising and ridiculing the government and the then Prime Minister George Papandreou. This was partly evident in the imagery of the site and its associated Facebook page. In its January 2013 iteration, the site included the word 'Hellas' written with large letters on the top of the page, while the Greek flag featured prominently in the Facebook page. It was also obvious in the modes of address (the audience is often addressed as 'Greeks'), as well as the opinions expressed on some key topics like immigration. Aganaktismenoi.com did not seem that interested in the methods of decision-making of the assembly, but mainly in providing information, news and critique.

Each website had links to a dedicated page on Facebook, although there was not a single official page for the whole movement. Instead, there were numerous Facebook pages with the words Αγανακτισμένοι, Athens or Syntagma or real democracy in their title. A study by Lu, Cheliotis, Cao, Song and Bressan (2012) put the initial number of Facebook pages, groups and events at 178. Yet the same study found that Facebook users converged to a smaller number of publics very quickly, within the first three days of the mobilisations, and this unequal distribution of users remained constant throughout the sampling period between May 2011 and January 2012.

These three websites and their dedicated Facebook pages did not link to each other and, instead functioned like isolated internet islands. To an extent, this replicated the spatial organisation of Syntagma Square and particularly the division between the upper and lower square. However, online it was much easier for the disparate parts of the movement to ignore and avoid each other. This was also evident in the interviews as the three interviewees from the press/multimedia group were not aware of the existence of aganaktismenoi.com. Thus, compared to the physical space of the square, the online realm was characterised by greater division and dispersion.

Syntagma Square as a centre of mediation and contentious activity

The physical space of Syntagma Square therefore emerged as the central point of the movement. It was the space that defined who the movement was and constituted the centre of its mediation. In this respect, Feigenbaum, Frenzel and McCurdy (2013) highlight the dual nature of protest camps, which 'function simultaneously as a "staged" and symbolic protest for the media and the public, and as "activist spaces" where protesters plan, organise and live' (p 74). As with other movements of the squares, Αγανακτισμένοι did not believe in central leadership or official spokespeople. Those liaising with the media did so in a personal capacity and not as formal representatives of the movement. Since the collective became manifest in the activity of the assembly, the press/multimedia team focused mainly on remediating the square. They also covered the major protests to ensure that information about what was happening in the streets was available online.

The media team, however, refrained as much as possible from writing news stories, from editorialising and thus speaking for the movement. Instead, their press releases and the content uploaded on the website mainly referred to the decisions of the assembly (Nikos K, personal communication, 10 July 2013). For Ntina, a professional journalist and member of the press/multimedia team, the media team's editorial guidelines made for quite 'boring' content: 'the information that we uploaded was always decisions, nothing else, let's say that…I wanted to learn…what happened today in Syntagma square: Did they dance? Was there violence?…We didn't have such a text' (personal communication, 10 July 2013). Moreover, the website design of amesi-dimokratia.org lacked a blog element that would facilitated the team to provide live news updates (Ntina, personal communication, 10 July 2013).

Activists of the lower square insisted on maintaining control of the movement's media coverage not only by developing alternative media operations, but also by limiting the access of journalists from the mainstream media to the square.[3] The press/multimedia team attempted multiple times to have the assembly agree to opening up the lower square to professional journalists but the proposals were always rejected (Ntina, personal communication, 10 July 2013). The distrust towards the mainstream media was such that professional-looking journalists were often questioned and forcibly ejected from the square (Anna, personal communication, 10 September 2011; Ntina, personal communication, 10 July 2013). To counter this distrust towards professional journalists, members of the press/media team would often accompany them in the square to signal that the presence of these specific journalists was sanctioned by the movement (Ntina, personal communication, 10 July 2013). This effort to limit the presence of professional journalists on the square was part of the movement's struggle to provide its own interpretation of reality and to challenge the dominant view provided by the mainstream media which are owned and controlled by a small set of organised interests (Apostolis personal communication, 11 September 2011). Yet restricting the access of professional journalists to the lower part of the square meant that mainstream media coverage focused instead on the happenings on the upper square where their presence encountered less resistance (Ntina, personal communication,10 July 2013). Nikos K (personal communication, 10 July 2013) attributed this to the dynamic and carnivalesque nature of the upper square which made for more compelling news content than the decision-making assemblies of the lower square whose more nuanced politics were difficult to explain to a lay audience.

The centrality of Syntagma Square in the movement's existence, both mediated and physical, meant that remaining in the square was viewed as crucial for maintaining the movement in public consciousness (Loukia, personal communication, 31 March 2013). However, the long term presence on the square and the difficulties of maintaining and regulating the camp shifted discussions in the assembly towards the practicalities of camping rather than the discussion of broader issues. As Isa put it, 'we were making decisions only on problems arising from the fact that we were camping. So enough with the camping, we should be concentrating on the most important issues, which were the memorandum, the euro agreement, things like that' (personal communication,8 September 2011). This continuous presence on the square was also linked to the development of internal hierarchies, with those who have camped the longest claiming more power in the assembly. Isa playfully called this phenomenon 'culocracy' (or 'ass-o-cracy') as 'those who sit on the square for the longest time have the right to say what they want, the others not'.

Keeping Syntagma Square as the main space of the movement also led to bureaucratisation. This constrained the organic character of the movement and limited its diffusion to other neighbourhoods of Athens. As Kiki noted,

> even from a spatial point of view, [Syntagma Square] creates a hierarchy, a leadership, such as the 'Central Committee'... it is *the* central space of Syntagma Square. So if you basically use this as a centre and you don't alternate [to other neighbourhoods], you are already – because of this spatiality – creating in essence the same authoritarian elements that you want to abolish. (personal communication, 8 September 2011)

Ntina concurred:

> I was one of those, from the side who was saying 'Enough with Syntagma, this will become a camping and nothing

else, instead…it should disperse in the neighbourhoods so other people learn about it because Syntagma is a transit station, not a space where you can remain, there is nothing to take care of like in your neighbourhood, there's only hotels and shops around it, there are no residents that can start talking to each other.' (personal communication, 10 July 2013)[4]

A further issue with the centrality of Syntagma Square concerned the vulnerability of the space to police repression. Although it is a public space, and thus should be *of* the public, it is actually the government, and its disciplinary mechanism, the police, who dominate the structure. This became evident in the worst case of police violence that occurred during the protests of 28–29 June 2011. On June 28 and during a general 48-hour strike the demonstrations turned violent as protestors clashed with police in front of the Greek parliament and other areas of central Athens. Violence continued during the night and on 29 June, the day when a new package of deeply unpopular austerity measures was passed. The police attempted to evacuate Syntagma Square and other key protest points in Athens by driving through the crowds on motorbikes and throwing 10,000 stun grenades and 8,000 units of tear gas, destroying the tents and sending 650 people to hospital, 99 of whom were seriously injured. The violence was so extreme that 'Amnesty International (2011) as well as the medical and hospital associations, called the Greek state to restrain police repression' (Kousis, 2016, 162-63). Having a central space that is open to attack means that a movement can be easily taken out by adversaries. In this respect, one could argue that it was easier for the movement to escape repression online as it was more dispersed and arguably more anonymous.

Nevertheless, the online and the offline are not that clearly divided. The physical location of the press/multimedia team was in the square. This left it vulnerable to police repression during the major protests. Recognising that danger and the need to maintain a continuous coverage of the events in the streets, the media team relocated to a more secure space on these occasions. They established a press office in the building of one of the largest trade unions that had offered the space for free and used three other locations around Syntagma Square as makeshift media centres from where activists could upload visual and audio material. The team had runners who would take the material to assigned locations and then return the empty cards to those covering the protests in the streets. The exact location of these four centres was not known to other protesters to ensure maximum security.

Therefore, the centrality of Syntagma Square in the movement's activity and mediation was due to both to the location and the symbolic significance of the space. It had, however, both advantages and limitations in terms of the movement's mediation, as well as its operation and its vulnerability to police repression.

Conclusion

Space and contentious politics mutually constitute each other. Following Lefebvre (1991), we consider space as the product of metaphors, designs, and practices, as made up of both physical and mediated components. Space affects protest movements as it shapes, in different ways, the interactions that give rise to them or the grievances around which they rally. At the same time, movements possess spatial agency as activists manipulate and engineer space to achieve their goals. A movement's repertoire of contention can thus be viewed in spatial terms, as consisting of tactics that make public claims through the management of space.

Our analysis of the Indignant movement online and offline provided a case study of how these dynamics work in practice. The political and social history of Syntagma Square renders it a meeting point of symbolic significance, while its location in front of the parliament makes it a prime setting for voicing opposition to political authority. Syntagma Square was split into two groups, each one employing a different spatial repertoire of contention and occupying a different part of the square. The upper square focused on ridicule, disruption and the expression of anger, while the lower square opted instead for prefigurative politics by setting up a popular assembly based on the values of equality and direct participation. The principles of the lower square informed the design of the two websites created by activists of the lower square and were reflected in their spatiality. The divide between upper and lower square was echoed online, in the absence of links between the internet spaces serving each part of the movement.

Yet, Syntagma Square remained 'one' in the movement's collective imaginary, even for those activists who participated more in the lower or the upper square. As a single space, Syntagma Square served as a central gathering point, as the embodiment of the movement, and as the stage from which it was mediated. The representation of the movement centred on what was happening in the square, the main space where the movement made itself visible to itself and to others. This centralisation prevented the dispersion of the movement in the neighbourhoods of Athens, while the long-term stay in the square focused the assembly's attention on the protection and regulation of the space rather than on broader political visions.

Space is also connected to power struggles both within the movement and between the movement and its adversaries. The capacity to control, regulate or access specific spaces of the movement, both online and offline, afforded certain activists more power within the collective. This was the case for the administrators of websites who could bar others from publishing information online, as well as for the long-term campers in the square who felt that their voices should be heard more loudly in the assembly. Struggles over space are also evident in the relationship between the movement and the mainstream media, with movement activists determined to retain control of the media representation of the movement by restricting the access of professional journalists to the space of the square. It is also visible in police repression, which focused more on the central space of the movement, Syntagma square, than on its online presence. In this respect, centralisation limits the capacity of the movement to evade state repression as the movement can be eradicated by removing its centre. Thus, taken together, the online/offline spaces of the movement facilitated the production of a heterogeneous movement that employed a diversity of tactics, mounting a more multifaceted challenge to political authorities and their implementation of austerity. They allowed the movement to be dispersed but connected, to scale up yet maintain a central focus, to be united in its indignation while divided in its practices.

Following the eviction of the movement, the space of Syntagma Square returned to its 'regular' condition, as the main public square of the official state. Some digital traces of the movement remain visible, even though both real-democracy.gr and amesi-dimokratia.org are no longer active. However, the effects of the Indignant movement are still felt in the civic education which it provided to its participants that was, in part, a spatial lesson. As one of our interviewees put it, 'What we learned from this experience is how to use our squares. We were always only in the streets, in demonstrations, always on the go…So only the fact that we started using the squares is a revolution for Greece' (Kiki, personal communication, 8 September 2011). The revolutionary spirit of the square and the practices of the assembly were diffused in the local neighbourhoods where grassroots initiatives, such as community clinics, kitchens and pharmacies, have started to flourish. Yet part of the spatial agency of the Indignant movement was also to revitalise the political character of Syntagma square. This coincides with what Kousis (2016, 169) calls the 'parliamentarisation of contention' in Greece after 2010, when parliament, rather than actors such as the Troika, becomes the primary target of protest. In the minds of many participants, Syntagma 'emerged as a space of freedom' (Nikos, personal communication, 15 September 2011) and its reverberations are still felt today in the practices, cultures and tactics of contentious politics in Greece.

Notes

[1] This is the case for instance in Harvey's analysis of contentious politics in his book *Rebel Cities* (2013).

[2] This is an open palm gesture that signifies disrespect in Greece.

[3] The activists' experience with the Greek media system, which is profoundly corrupt and beholden to political and business interests, was also at the core of the movement's initial reluctance to even set up a press/multimedia team (Loukia, personal communication, 31 March 2013).

[4] Furthermore, some interviewees noted the failure to create broader networks between the occupied squares in Greece. The press/multimedia team tried to do this, mainly by republishing news from other occupation on the website. However, the team could not make proposals to the assembly with regards of appropriating ideas from other squares or co-organising events with them (Ntina, personal communication, 10 July 2013). Nevertheless, there was one weekend when delegates from different occupations around Greece gathered in Syntagma Square to exchange experiences. In terms of networking with movements around Europe, the lower square also had some live video links with some other movements of the squares, like those in Madrid or Barcelona.

References

Bastéa, E. (2000) *The Creation of Modern Athens: Planning the Myth.* Cambridge: Cambridge University Press.

Chadwick, A. (2013) *The Hybrid Media System: Politics and Power,* Oxford and New York: Oxford University Press.

Daphi, P. (2014) 'Movement space: a cultural approach', in B. Baumgarten, P. Daphi and P. Ulrich (eds) *Conceptualizing Culture in Social Movement Research* (pp 165–185). Basingstoke and New York: Palgrave Macmillan.

Dimitriou, O. (2014) 'Six acts in/for Syntagma square and the emergence of new publics', in M. Tsillibounidi and A. Welsh (eds) *Re-mapping 'Crisis'.* London: Zero Books.

Feigenbaum, A., Frenzel, F. and McCurdy, P. (2013) *Protest Camps.* London and New York: Zed.

Gerbaudo, P. (2012) *Tweets and the Streets: Social Media and Contemporary Activism,* London: Pluto Press.

Gordon, E. and de Souza e Silva, A. (2011) *Net Locality: Why Location Matters in a Networked World.* Chichester: Wiley-Blackwell.

Harvey, D. (1989) *The Condition of Postmodernity.* Oxford: Blackwell.

Harvey, D. (2008) 'The right to the city', *New Left Review*, 53, 23–40.

Harvey, D. (2013) *Rebel Cities: From the Right to the City to Urban Revolutions*. London: Verso.

Kaika, M. and Karaliotas, L. (2014) 'The spatialization of democratic politics: insights from Indignant squares', *European Urban and Regional Studies*, doi: 10.1177/0969776414528928.

Kavada, A. (2015) 'Creating the collective: social media, the Occupy movement and its constitution as a collective actor', *Information, Communication and Society*, 18(8), 872–886, doi: 10.1080/1369118X.2015.1043318.

Kousis, M. (2016) 'The spatial dimensions of the Greek Protest Campaign against Troika's Memoranda and Austerity Measures, 2010–2013', in M. Ancelovici, P. Dufour and H. Nez (eds) *Street Politics in the Age of Austerity: From the Indignados to Occupy*. Amsterdam: Amsterdam University Press, pp 147–73.

Lefebvre, H. (1991) *The Production of Space*. Oxford: Blackwell.

Lefebvre, H. (1996) *Writings on cities/Henri Lefebvre* (selected, translated and introduced by E. Kofman and E. Lebas). Oxford: Blackwell Publishers.

Lehtovuori, P. (2010) *Experience and Conflict: The Production of Urban Space*. Farnham: Ashgate.

Lu, X., Cheliotis, G., Cao, X., Song, Y. and Bressan, S. (2012) 'The configuration of networked publics on the web: evidence from the Greek Indignados movement', *Proceedings of the 4th Annual ACM Web Science Conference*, pp 185-94, New York: ACM.

Martin, D. G. and Miller, B. (2003) 'Space and contentious politics', *Mobilization: An International Journal*, 8(2), 143–156.

Massey, D. (2005) *For Space*. London: Sage Publications.

Melembianaki, E. (2006) Οι πλατείες της Αθήνας: *1834–1945: Διαδικασία διαμόρφωσης, λειτουργία, πολεοδομική σημασία* [The squares of Athens:1834-1945: Planning, function, urban significance], PhD thesis, Athens: National Technical University of Athens.

Meyrowitz, J. (1985) *No Sense of Place: The Impact of Electronic Media on Social Behaviour*. New York and Oxford: Oxford University Press.

Polletta, F. (1999) '"Free spaces" in collective action', *Theory and Society*, 28(1), 1–38.

Saco, D. (2002) *Cybering Democracy: Public Space and the Internet*. Minneapolis, MN and London: University of Minnesota Press.

Scannell, P. (1996) *Radio, Television and Modern Life: A Phenomenological Approach*. Oxford: Blackwell.

Sewell, W. H. Jr (2001) 'Space in contentious politics', in R. R. Aminzade, J. A. Goldstone, D. McAdam, E. J. Perry, W. H. J. Sewell, S. Tarrow and C. Tilly (eds) *Silence and Voice in the Study of Contentious Politics*. Cambridge: Cambridge University Press, pp 51–88.

Tilly, C. (1978) *From Mobilization to Revolution*, Reading, MA: Addison Wesley.

Tilly, C. (2000) 'Spaces of contention', *Mobilization: An International Journal*, 5(2), 135–159.

Tormey, S. (2005) 'From utopian worlds to utopian spaces: reflections on the contemporary radical imaginary and the social forum process', *Ephemera: Theory and Politics in Organization*, 5(20), 394–408.

SIX

Feeds from the square: live streaming, live tweeting and the self-representation of protest camps

Paolo Gerbaudo

Introduction

'Have you seen what is going on in Madrid?' The phone call came in mid May 2011 from a Spanish friend living in the UK at a time when names such as Indignados or 15M, still had to become established as the identifiers of the emerging 'movement of the squares'. She had spent entire days watching the live video feed transmitted by Sol.tv. Making up for the initial silence of Spanish mainstream news media on the protests, this self-managed live-streaming service had for days broadcasted the events unfolding in Puerta del Sol in central Madrid, what would soon become one of the main icons of the so-called movements of the squares of 2011, the wave of grassroots mobilisation spanning from the Arab Spring revolution to Occupy Wall Street in the US, that used square occupations as its key protest tactic. The live feed that attracted 10 million visits during the first seven days of occupation (Monterde and Postill, 2013), was often flickering and pixelated. Yet, it still managed to convey the enthusiasm experienced by the people occupying the square. 'You have to watch it. It's incredible!' – my friend told me emphatically.

Many supporters of the 2011 wave of protest, like my Spanish friend, have found in live feeds 'radiating' from protest camps, either in the form of video feeds, transmitted via various live streaming services such as Livestream,[1] Bambuser[2] and so on, or in the form of text-based feeds transmitted via Twitter, a powerful way to connect from a distance with protest movements. Live feeds have provided movement sympathisers and supporters with the opportunity to follow the life of the protest camp, without relying solely the mediation of the often scorned 'mainstream media', in a way that is unprecedented in both intensity and extent when compared with previous protest movements starting from the anti-globalisation movement. Yet, so far, little discussion has been dedicated specifically to video live streaming (Thorburn, 2014), as well as to live tweeting, and the motivations that underlie them. Why have live feeds become such an important component to the protest camps of 2011? What does this host of practices tell us about their meaning?

Exploring these questions, this chapter proposes a cultural analysis of live feeds and their role within the protest communications of the movements of the squares of 2011. Drawing on 50 interviews with activists, on observations of protest camps and on analysis of social media material, in the Spanish Indignados, and Occupy Wall Street in the US, I want to explore two key aspects of live feeds: 1) their contribution to the symbolic construction of the protest camp; and 2) the connection between core activists and their dispersed publics of supporters and sympathisers. First, practices such as live streaming and live tweeting contribute to the activist representation of protest camps, complementing and competing with the representation conducted through mainstream news media. Second, live feeds facilitate connections with the diverse and diffuse support base of these movements, including the so-called 'internet occupiers' (Julian, interview, New York, November 2011) people who never attended protest physically, yet strongly identify with the movement. Looking at these two aspects we will come to appreciate the considerable differences in worldview and attitude between the media operations of the 2011 protest wave and of the anti-globalisation movement.

Live feeds have not only played an important role in constructing the public image of the 2011 wave of protest, but were also one of the main media innovations of this cycle of struggle. They have been instrumental in expressing – in content and practice – the populist character of this protest wave, its appeal to people power and its ambition to capture the support of the '99 per cent' of the population. The populist nature of live feeds has been manifested in their underlying intention of turning protest camps into a radically transparent mediated agora, open for everyone to see. Counter, to what happened in many anti-globalisation camps, which were often disseminated with warning messages instructing people not to film or photograph (McCurdy, 2010), out of fear for police repression, the camps of the movements of the squares have seen a friendlier attitude towards by-standers and the public. They have often displayed invitations for people to film and photograph, and have thus become the most popular theme in the social media content of this protest wave. The populist orientation of live feeds has also been manifested in their attempt to target a highly diverse range of publics, and to reach well beyond the narrow confines of the activist community, including what some of my interviewees described as 'internet occupiers': people who followed movement doings from a distance without ever participating directly, as distinct from 'physical occupiers', those participating 24/7, by living in protest camps for the duration of the mobilisation.

Live feeds turn our attention to the complex forms of grassroots mediation that surround the physical presence of specific protest sites, and are ultimately crucial in the symbolic power of these sites. In this light protest camps can be seen not just a physical site occupied by activists, but that also as a 'mediated ritual' (Couldry, 2003), a heavily symbolically laden event, whose mission revolves around acting as a unifying role for distant and dispersed publics. Live feeds have contributed to the protest camps of 2011 attracting the attention of millions of people and involving them in a process of collective reflection about the root causes of the economic crisis and possible solutions. Furthermore, they have facilitated the construction of bonds of solidarity, between the people 'who are there' and those 'who cannot be there', between the core activist communities and the various rings of support of the movement of the squares. In so doing live feeds have become an important channel to express the new political ethos of these protest movements, with their attempt to construct a popular protest culture and reach people who were previously at the margins of protest politics.

Protest camps between location and mediation

Protest camps such as the ones in Tahrir square in Egypt, Puerta del Sol in Spain, Syntagma square in Athens and Zuccotti Park in New York possess a double nature: a material and a symbolic one, location and mediation. The first and most evident is their nature as a 'place': a physical location in which protestors gather, set up tents, and create their own occupied and self-managed space. Protest camps involve the physical occupation of a specific geographic location: a site where to erect the tents and establish various activist services, kitchens, toilets, workshops that allows for their existence and persistence. Location matters a lot in protest camps (Feigenbaum et al, 2013, 76), since they derive their identity from the place they occupy. This has been clearly seen in the movements of the squares of 2011, with the occupation of such iconic places as Tahrir square in Cairo, and Puerta del Sol in Madrid (Ramadan, 2013), or in the case of ecological protests with camps erected next to various sources of evil as airports or coal power stations.

The second, no less important, nature of the protest camp is as the stage of a 'media ritual' (Couldry, 2003) or of a 'media spectacle' (Kellner, 2012), that transcends the narrow geographic limits of the protest camp and involves the addressing of various publics of supporters and sympathisers, who are at a distance from the camp. This process has been traditionally channelled through the representation of protest camps by mainstream news media, but is also increasingly conveyed through various forms of grassroots 'self-representation', in the era of social media and 'user-generated content'. Protest camps are places that stand there to *represent* to those who are not physically *present* what activists are campaigning against and why. They are stages of 'mediation' (Cammaerts et al, 2013) as much as sites of location. Thus for example as Feigenbaum and McCurdy (2015) argue, 'protest camps offer a ready-made stage, a site to which journalists and photographers can go to get a story'. Restated, protest camps provide protest movements with an effective and economic strategy to secure media coverage, but also increasingly a space for self-representation, through various forms of grassroots communication channelled via social media.

An illustration of this mediated character of protest camps can be found in the case of the queer feminist and anti-war camp of Greenham Common. Greenham Common, the site of a large protest by a committed group of feminist against an RAF base (Roseneil, 2000). While the camp was small and hosted only few dozens of women at any time, it soon made ripples in the UK media and inspired a diffuse community of supporters who identified with its practices and demands (Couldry, 1999). Similar is the case with the anti-road protests in the UK in the 1990s (Seel, 1997; Rootes, 2000). Because of their resort to the occupation of often geographically remote locations these protests called for '24/7 participation' from a close-knit community of hard-core activists, free from work or family commitments. Yet, they became widely known nationally because of the intense news media reporting on them, attracted by the picturesque forms of protest adopted by activists. This is exemplified by the celebrity status acquired by 'Swampy' a young activist who participated in the protest against the extension of the A30 road in Fairmile, Devon, the last to be evicted by police from a complex network of tunnels activists had dug to prevent the road being built – hence his namesake – in front of rolling TV cameras.

Already at the time of Greenham Common and the anti-road movement, activists were not just objects of media representation channelled through the images broadcasted by TV or the articles written in the press – but also its subjects (Couldry, 1999). Activists, in fact, do not only attempt to capture the attention of mainstream news media, they also create their own forms of self-representation engaging in what Feigenbaum and McCurdy (2016) describe as 'reflexive media practices'. In pre-digital movements this effort of self-representation was manifested in various analogue radical media (Downing, 2000) such as fanzines and pirate radio. These forms of alternative communication were, however, seriously limited in reach due the high costs and narrow scope of distribution for radical media in an analogue environment. It was only with the popularisation of the web in the late 1990s and the slashing of information distribution costs, that activists started to progressively expand their audiences. Part of this effort revolved precisely around the provision of live coverage of protest events, as exemplified by the live reports produced by the alternative news site Indymedia that was used during large anti-globalisation protest events starting from the November 1999 protests in Seattle (Kahn and Kellner, 2004).

The effort of self-representation of protest movements has evolved substantially in recent years as a consequence of the development of web 2.0 and of corporate social network sites, such as Facebook and Twitter enthusiastically adopted by the new generation of activists. The 'new media ecology' navigated by contemporary activists is underscored by a profound political and ethical contradiction. Social media are not just a commercial but more so a corporate space, owned by companies quoted in the stock exchange as Facebook (NASDAQ: FB) and Twitter (NYSE: TWTR). Furthermore, they are platforms that have been utilised by the American government as a channel for intelligence gathering as revealed by information analyst turned whistle-blower Edward Snowden starting in 2013. Despite these elements that seem to define social media as a 'space of the enemy', much alike what mainstream news media as TV and the press constituted for previous protest movements, activists in the 2011 wave of protest have found in these platforms a highly fertile space to develop their protest communications, as seen in the emergence of popular activist Twitter feeds, political Facebook pages, and video streaming channels on websites as Bambuser and Livestream, and the way in which they have provided a space of 'mass self-communication' (Castells, 2007), allowing activist messages to reach large internet user bases.

One of the most important functionalities introduced by platforms as Facebook, Twitter, Tumblr, LiveStream and so on, has been their provision of textual and video live feeds.[3] These services are not altogether new. They can be seen a popularisation of functionalities that existed in an embryonic form in the open publishing system of Indymedia (Pickard, 2006), and it is notable that some engineers of both Twitter and YouTube came from Indymedia (Pablo Ortellado, phone interview, 13 October 2013). The novelty is the unprecedented reach they have offered activists, unlocking an audience of hundreds of thousands people, one or two order of magnitudes above the reach enjoyed via self-managed activist websites as Indymedia. The remainder of this chapter is driven by two, interrelated question: What kind of representation of the protest camp was constructed through live feeds on Twitter or livestreaming services? And what kind of relationship do these live feeds construct with various audiences of supporters and sympathisers?

Methodology

To approach these questions, I draw on data gathered as part of a research conducted between 2011 and 2014, about the 2011 wave of 'movements of the squares', so-called because of their occupation of public spaces, through the erection of protest camps. For the purpose of this chapter I concentrate on the case of the Indignados in Spain and of Occupy Wall Street in the US, and utilise 50 interviews with activists and participants, as well as observations of protest camps and protest events and of select social media material connected with these movements. My approach to the analysis of this data follows the blueprint of discursive analysis. I am interested in identifying the different themes that emerge out of interviews and other data gathered as part of the present project, to understand the way activists understand their media operations and the way they use live feeds present themselves to the world. In this case the two main themes are:

1. the role of live feeds as an instrument of publicness and transparency in these movements and their construction of a 'mediated agora';
2. the role of live feeds in facilitating a connection between the core activist community and their dispersed publics of supporters.

These themes are connected by a common interpretive narrative that revolves around the assertion of the populist nature of live feeds, the way in which they reflect these movements' ambition of representing the popular will of the '99 per cent'.

The meaning of live feeds

During the 2011 wave of protest video and Twitter live feeds have come in overwhelming quantity, as seen in the presence of dozens of video streaming channels, and an equal number of dedicated Twitter accounts providing minute-by-minute reporting of protest movements and of protest camps in particular. Matching a period of intense voluntarism, fuelled by a generous outpouring of grassroots energy, many protestors improvised themselves as journalists, reporters, cameramen and social media bloggers.

To understand the meaning of this intense activist effort in the production of live feeds it is important to delve into its root motivations, which stems from a discontent with the dominant system of representation. Activist investment in producing protest live feeds is rooted in a profound mistrust towards corporate news media which is seen as partisan, complicit with power-holders and having a tendency to portray protestors as mindless and violent. This critical perspective which was suspicious of corporate news media was shared by many of my interviewees. Linnea, a 28 year Occupy activist argued that 'the problem with news media is that they are so biased against us' (interview, New York, 10 November 2011). Similar is the experience of Anna an Indignados protestor in Barcelona who laments that 'mainstream news media have no interest in representing the movement fairly' (interview, Barcelona, 29 May 2011) and goes on to describe the connection of various news outlets in Catalunya with the governing Convergència i Unió (CiU) party.

Trying to by-pass mainstream news media, accused of anti-protestor bias, activists have found in video live streams, and live tweeting, the means to produce an instantaneous and intimate account of protest camps. Live feeds have covered virtually all the aspects of these movements' lives: from specific events as assemblies, and meetings, to the everyday life of the camp and its big and small hurdles, as well as of more contentious events, such as the repressive action of police forces, and the evictions of specific protest camps and other occupations. A review of various live feeds in Spain and the US testifies to the breadth of these media practices, and the centrality they have acquired in the 2011 wave of protest.

Live feeds in the Indignados and Occupy Wall Street

Since the beginning of the occupation of Puerta del Sol in Madrid, the Spanish Indignados movement made ample use of video and

Twitter live feeds to report on its protest activity in all its diverse manifestations. A great number of activist teams were set up in order to produce live feeds from the protest camps in Madrid, in Barcelona, and tens of other cities. The most remarkable example of video live feeds was undoubtedly Sol.tv, the live streaming service, mentioned in the introduction, that broadcasted live for over a week the activities conducted in Puerta del Sol. The service, set up by two journalists Pepa González and Kike Álvarez, registered thousands of accesses at the height of the Indignados protest, and it made up for the initial lack of media coverage about the protests. Besides Sol.tv, many others live streaming services were created in the course of the protests including those hosted by the websites Toma La Plaza[4] (Take the Square), and Toma la Tele[5] (Take the TV). Furthermore, most protest camps had their own local streaming service. Besides video streaming, Twitter was widely used to provide live reporting by both individuals and dedicated activist communication teams. One of the most famous cases was 'Difusion de red' (network outreach), a collective tasked with running various activist social media accounts such as @acampadasol. This was the account that sent one of the first tweets from the occupied Puerta del Sol and covered the events from the square during the entirety of the occupation rapidly becoming one of the most visible political Twitter accounts in Spain with tens of thousands of followers.

Occupy Wall Street made a similar intense use of video and textual live feeds from the various protest camps erected around the US starting from its most iconic occupation: the one in Zuccotti Park few metres away from the New York Stock Exchange. Among the most prominent video livestream channels featured Global Revolution,[6] the livestream of the counter-information blog Truth Out,[7] as well as the website 'Occupy Streams',[8] which hosted video streams from protest camps all over the US and the World, including Occupy Oakland and Occupy Toronto. Besides video livestreams, also in the US Twitter proved a highly popular means for live reporting on the last minute events of protest camps. Among the most popular account featured the movements' two main official ones, @OccupyWallStreet and @OccupyWallStreetNYC alongside the accounts of local camps, and of specific working groups. Furthermore, individual activists and small groups often took the initiative to provide live coverage about specific activities. For example, Tim Fitzgerald, an Occupy activist in New York used his twitter account @diceytroop, to provide a 'live minuting of all meetings' (phone interview, 12 October 2014), to allow supporters to follow the movement's decision-making process, thus contributing in turning the General Assembly, into a public event followed from a distance by thousands of people.

To explore the role of live feeds as means of self-representation of the movements of 2011, the continuation of the empirical section is divided in two parts. The first analyses the political orientation of live feeds, highlighting how their emphasis on publicness and transparency was conducive to the populist character of these movements. I compare and contrast this strategy with the restrictions on the representation of protest camps prevalent during the anti-globalisation period, out of security considerations. In the second part I move to discussing the ways in which live feeds constructed a relationship between the movement 'core', to be understood as composed of those activists dedicating themselves 24/7 to the movement, or at least more than half of their time at the height of the mobilisation, and less committed participants, including part-time supporters and sympathisers. This reach-out function of live feeds was particularly important due to the populist ambition of the movements of the squares of 2011, to gain the consensus of the majority of the population, of the '99 per cent', for whom they purported to fight.

Please do post me: live feeds and the new culture of transparency

'This is the people's stage' – proclaimed a handwritten sign hung on a tent in the Occupy Wall Street protest camp in Zuccotti Park, when I visited it in early November 2011, just few days before the wave of eviction that targeted Occupy in New York and many other cities across the US. The message provides a lead to understand the meaning of live feeds within the culture of the movements of the squares, and their protest camps. Live feeds in textual or video form were a manifestation of attempt of protest camps in the 2011 wave to constitute a stage for the display of a popular, or in a positive sense populist, politics, uniting the people in criticism of both the business class and the political class. Through the ongoing activist coverage of events and activities taking place in the camp, live feeds contributed in framing the protest camp as a truly public space, open and transparent to the entire citizenry, in a way that was radically different from the image of protest camps in previous protest movements and in particular in the anti-globalisation protests around the turn of the millennium.

Indicative of the divergence between anti-globalisation camps and camps in the 2011 wave was their starkly different external appearance and its policies regarding the mediation of the camp. In the anti-globalisation movement, protest camps were far more militant places than it was the case with movements of 2011. They often appeared from the outside as something akin to guerrilla bivouacs at short distance from the battlefield, quasi-military spaces often defended by heavy barricades to counter police attacks and displaying aggressive visual messages (Gerbaudo, 2016). And what matters most for the purpose of this discussion is that this militancy was also expressed in the attitude towards the mediation of protest camps, with customary prohibitions to photographing and filming often encountered in those spaces, out of legitimate fears of police attempts to identify protestors and prosecute them. Within many anti-globalisation camps 'no photographs' signs abounded, conjuring an impression of strong militancy, and strong and sometimes exaggerated fears about the presence of police infiltrators.

The protest camps of 2011 adopted a profoundly different attitude to the ones of the anti-globalisation movement. In line with of the value of radical transparency derived from hacker ethic (Levy, 2001), and the idea that 'information wants to be free' it seemed as if every moment, every activity, and every participant had to be recorded, filmed, or tweeted. Invitations to film, photograph, post, were sometimes almost as explicit as it was with prohibitions in anti-globalisation camps. This was seen in the quantity of messages hanging all over camps inviting photographing and video recording, or in the presence of protestors holding cardboard signs for the benefit of passers-by, a common sight in Zuccotti Park. Matching these insistent invitations to mediation, the camps I visited in Spain and the US, were overflowing with digital devices, iPads, iPhones, handheld cameras, constantly documenting everything that was happening in the camp, for the benefit of friends, family members and anonymous internet users who could not make it there.

This openness to mediation angered some activists, especially those with a longer history of militancy. Since the decline of the Indignados and Occupy Wall Street, there has been lot talking within the activist community about the fact that livestreaming has become a form of self-imposed surveillance, which – besides serving to denounce various episodes of police violence – can also be used by police to gather intelligence about the movement and prosecute some participants. These risks are obviously to be taken very seriously. However, they need to be understood in a context of protest movements, that have made a firm commitment to non-violent protests, and have avoided whenever possible illegal actions, and which therefore were not as liable as more militant movements, to police attempts to incriminate participants, also using self-produced video material. Reflecting their commitment to a politics of radical citizenship, aiming at rescuing basic democratic rights rather than challenging the state, live feeds have served the purpose of turning protest camps into a citizen space, virtually opened to the view of the entire citizenry; not just a movement or activist space, but a truly civic space of collective reflection, deliberation and action.

Feeds for our 'closet supporters'

In tandem with the effort to open up protest camps and make them as much as possible 'transparent spaces', whose activities should be visible to all those sympathising with the movement live feeds have targeted a diverse range of audiences, not limited to the activist community. Among the different audiences they have addressed we can identify a) core activists, highly involved participants committing more than half of their time to protest action, who look at these feeds to keep abreast of what is going on, either when they are not 'on site', or when they are but they still feel the need for further information; b) less committed participants, who use live feeds to make up for the impossibility of their being constantly present on site, or to verify the situation on the ground before a visit; c) journalists and other professionals covering or analysing the movement; d) movement sympathisers: people who sympathise with the movement and its cause but cannot participate directly because of a number of reasons including work and family commitments, or the fear of exposing themselves and endangering their career or social status; and e) 'plain curious' people, who do not necessarily support the movement but are eager to follow its action. Of these five categories, it is arguably the last the one the audience has been the real novelty of this protest wave, due to its ambition to reach out to people outside of the activist community, as seen in the way in which activists have coined new terms such as 'internet occupiers' (Julian, interview, New York, 9 November 2011) in order to describe these supporters at a distance.

While the movements of 2011 have been characterised by impressive levels of physical participation in public space, even more remarkable has been the breadth of public support as demonstrated by various opinion polls, pointing to the majoritarian backing won by most of these movements (Gerbaudo, 2014; 2016). Live coverage of protest events on the internet has played a significant role in building and maintaining this base of support. Jorge, a participant in the protest camp in Barcelona argues that these movements in utilising social media have managed to 'occupy' a space that is much larger than the physical space they occupy by taking the public square.

We have recovered the physical space, and the physical space is two thousand people. But the Facebook page has received two million hits in 15 days by people from all over the country, who are there connecting and sharing and thanking. When there was the police charge [in late May 2011] there were many people who were very worried about what was going on. Before it was impossible. Unless *la Vanguardia* [the largest news media in Catalunya] or *el Pais* told you, you would not know. Now the movement can by-pass all these media, *Publico, el Pais, la Sexta* [a TV channel]. Because if you have a person who puts a video on YouTube and the video is good, it can get 100,000 hits. Our Facebook page has 2 million visits! This is a very new thing. (Interview, Barcelona, 30 May 2011)

As Jorge notices the popularity of live feeds in the Indignados reflected the restructuring of the communication ecology of protest movements at the time of web 2.0. Whereas previously social movements had to rely on the coverage of mainstream news media, be they more right-wing or left-wing, in order to reach a mass public, the 'mass self-communication' (Castells, 2007) affordances of social media allowed protestors to reach sympathisers directly, without the filter and bias associated with mainstream news media.

Live feeds have been crucial in allowing protest movements to establish a connection with sections of the population that, while mostly unlikely to participate physically in protest action, such as by living and sleeping in a protest camp, were nonetheless keen to know more about these movements and be kept abreast of its actions. Julian a participant in Occupy Wall Street in New York, who recounts about a colleague of his, who she describes as an 'internet occupier', who while never attending physically protest activity was keenly following the activity of the movement.

I know a colleague [at this school] who has not yet ever been to the park, but has watched the live feed for hours and hours and hours, and knows everything that is going on now. And it's funny because I go in and she says. 'Oh my God! Do you know what happened in Oakland?' and I say 'No'. Then I go on my email and I say 'Oh shit!' Then she sends me an email saying that Zuccotti may be shut down any day now. And I ask myself 'How do you know about all this shit?' (Interview, New York, 9 November 2011)

Live feeds become, in this context, the vector of a vicarious experience of 'tele-participation', as participation from a distance that becomes increasingly available for movement supporters in this digital age. This is what Caiti a participant in Occupy Wall Street in New York describes as a form of connection as 'voyeurism':

> The internet has allowed people to watch the movement from afar and even to keep track of it daily without having to be in person. Therefore I assume that there are a lot of people who are closet supporters of Occupy Wall Street. You know we have police officers who get off duty and come to the park and show us their badges and say 'Hey guys, I support you!' There are a number of people who work at Wall Street who come there and give money and say 'Hey, I know this is a problem! You know this is my job, I am part of the problem but I don't like it.' A lot of them are in support of what we are doing but cannot say it out loud because otherwise they get fired. (Interview, New York, 7 November 2011)

Caiti's testimony highlights how for some sympathisers live feeds constitute the only reasonable means of engagement with the movement, due to the forms of reprisal people can be subject to if they demonstrate publicly their support for the movement. Thus live feeds provide an unprecedented way of partly overcoming the fear associated with participation in protest movements.

Some people might counter that live feeds are a manifestation of the internet trend towards 'slacktivism' (Morozov, 2009), that is the construction of forms of online participation that have no 'real world' effect. Live feeds are however not necessarily a substitution or compensation for actual participation in protest action. Rather they need to be understood as part of a complex texture of participation which encompasses both face-to-face and mediated forms of interaction, and of an array of levels of engagement available to participants, ranging from the ideal-type of full-time '24/7' participation which entails spending all the time in protest camps and sleeping there every night, to the ideal-type of mere 'internet occupation', people following the movement deeds from afar through live feeds and related news without ever joining it physically, with many in-between cases along this continuum.

Live feeds have in fact played an important role also in the experience of many 'physical participants', who often found in them a motivation to join the protests, or to re-join them after a temporary absence. Asun a Spanish protestor recounts how in the aftermath of the 15 May day of protest it was precisely a live feed from Puerta del Sol that alerted her about the beginning of the occupation and motivated her to travel back to Madrid. 'I had just got back home after the protest, when I watched on Facebook a live update and got to know that a group of people had taken the square. And I told myself, I need to catch this opportunity' (phone interview, 14 October 2011). Similarly James, a 22-years-old US Occupy participant, recounts how before going to New York to join the occupation in Zuccotti Park he had been following for days live streams from assemblies and other protest events in the area, and that this experience 'convinced me that it was worth travelling all the way from California because I realised that something was really happening' (interview, New York, 6 November 2011). Thus, while live feeds are indeed for certain category of supporters a substitute for physical participation in public space, for other they constitute a motivational channel that eventually leads them to join or to re-join the movement. They are part of a texture of participation in which mediated and direct participation are intertwined and in which the protest camp is both a physical and symbolic centre around which collective action is organised.

The activist self-representation of protest space

Reflecting this new populist and majoritarian approach of the 2011 protest wave (Gerbaudo, 2016), live feeds aimed at making the activities of the movements and the internal doings of protest camps, available also to those who could not participate in them directly. This effort of opening protest space through digital media is resonant to the value of transparency that constitutes a key element in the 'hacker ethic' (Levy, 2001), with its idea that information should be free, that as much information as possible should be made publicly available, to allow people to make their mind up about various issues without any filtering. It signals a shift away from the secretiveness and often conspiratorial attitude that imbued many protest camps in the previous protest movements, as seen in messages asking people not to take pictures or videos, because of fear of police surveillance. This leads to a framing of the protest camp as a 'people's stage', a sort of 'mediated agora', a public space whose symbolic actions are continuously broadcast to internet publics, allowing also those who – for various reasons – cannot or do not intend to participate physically in its actions. Live feeds are addressed not just at the core of committed activists who participate daily in the activity of protest camps, but also to various outer rings of support. In so doing live feeds have contributed in this protest wave's effort to win the hearts and minds of wide sectors of the population affected by the economic crisis and identifying itself with a '99 per cent' of citizens oppressed by political and economic oligarchies.

Live feeds project an image of protest camps that is radically different from the view of the protest camp as a self-standing territory, an autonomous and self-governed community, as sometimes proposed by anarchist activists. Rather they suggest the need to approach protest camps as a ritual centre, attracting the attention of thousands of people who might well be far away from it, but become symbolically and emotionally connected with it. Thanks to live feeds protest camps becomes a centre of attention and a point of identification for thousands of people who share common grievances and who find in protest camps a powerful dramatisation of their common desire, fears, and demands. While the camp can only exist through the physical occupation of a specific location, its ultimate significance relies in the processes of mediation that develops around it, and unifies thousands of dispersed internet users around a common event.

Obviously questions can be asked about the risks involved in the forms of 'tele-participation' facilitated by live feeds and similar forms of communication, that allow people to maintain connection to the movement, at a distance and at minimum cost. There is a risk that these practices can act as a mere 'spectacularisation' of protest action and a compensation, rather than a complement for actual participation in protest action. Yet, it cannot be denied that live feeds have played an important role in protest communications. They have provided activists with an effective way to counter the monopoly of corporate mainstream news media over the representation of protest events, and to channel different and more positive narratives of collective action. Furthermore, they have contributed in constructing bonds of solidarity within these movements and across the various rings of support they have attracted. Without live feeds, and similar practices involved in making the protest camps a public space, the square occupations would have risked falling prey to the same tendency towards self-ghettoisation seen in previous protest movements, in which camps were strongly marked as a militant spaces, available only to those directly participating in it. Thanks to live feeds and similar practices protest camps have become pulsing hearts of these movements, mediated ritual centres in which unifying symbolic practices were celebrated, and towards which hundreds of thousands of eyes and ears were constantly pointed, in search of a common source of meaning to mobilise against a social condition of rising inequality and political disenfranchisement.

Notes

[1] https://livestream.com/

[2] http://bambuser.com/

[3] It is important to highlight that since the movements discussed in this chapter new services as Meerkat (http://meerkatapp.co/) and Periscope (www.periscope.tv/) have emerged, which try precisely to integrate video feeds and Twitter.

[4] http://madrid.tomalaplaza.net/

[5] www.tomalatele.tv/web/

[6] http://globalrevolution.tv/

[7] www.truth-out.org/

[8] http://occupystreams.org/

References

Cammaerts, B., Mattoni, A., and McCurdy, P. (eds) (2013) *Mediation and Protest Movements*. Bristol: Intellect Books.

Castells, M. (2007) Communication, power and counter-power in the network society, *International Journal of Communication*, 1(1), 238–66.

Costanza-Chock, S. (2012) 'Mic check! Media cultures and the Occupy movement', *Social Movement Studies*, 11(3–4), 375–385, doi: 10.1080/14742837.2012.71074.

Couldry, N. (1999) 'Disrupting the media frame at Greenham Common: a new chapter in the history of mediations?', *Media, Culture and Society*, 21(3), 337–358.

Couldry, N. (2003) *Media Rituals: A Critical Approach*. London: Psychology Press.

Downing, J. D. (2000) *Radical Media: Rebellious Communication and Social Movements*. London: Sage Publications.

Feigenbaum, A. and McCurdy, P. (2015) Protest camps as media stages: A case study of Activist Media Practices across Three British Social Movements.' in Figueiras, R. & do Espírito Santo, P. (eds). *Beyond the Internet: Unplugging the Protest Movement Wave*. Routledge.

Feigenbaum, A. and McCurdy, P. (2016) 'Protest camps as media stages: a case study of activist media practices across three British social movements', in R. Figueiras and P. do Espírito Santo (eds) *Beyond the Internet: Unplugging the Protest Movement Wave*. London: Routledge, pp 31–52.

Feigenbaum, A., Frenzel, F., and McCurdy, P. (2013) *Protest Camps*. London: Zed.

Gerbaudo, P. (2012) *Tweets and the Streets: Social Media and Contemporary Activism*. London: Pluto Press.

Gerbaudo, P. (2016) *The Mask and the Flag: Anarcho-Populism and Global Protest*. London: Hurst/Oxford University Press.

Kahn, R. and Kellner, D. (2004) New media and internet activism: From the'Battle of Seattle'to blogging, *New Media & Society*, 6(1), 87–95.

Kellner, D. (2012) *Media Spectacle and Insurrection, 2011: From the Arab Uprisings to Occupy Everywhere*. Edinburgh: A&C Black.

Levy, S. (2001) *Hackers: Heroes of the Computer Revolution* (Vol 4). New York: Penguin Books.

McCurdy, P. (2010) 'Breaking the spiral of silence – unpacking the "media debate" within global justice movements: a case study of Dissent! and the 2005 Gleneagles G8 Summit', *Interface: A Journal for and About Social Movements*, 2(2), 42–67.

McKay, G. (1998) *DIY Culture: Party and Protest in Nineties Britain*. London: Verso.

Mattoni, A. (2012) *Media Practices and Protest Politics: How Precarious Workers Mobilise*. Farnham: Ashgate.

Mercea, D. (2012) 'Digital prefigurative participation: the entwinement of online communication and offline participation in protest events', *New Media and Society*, 14(1), 153–169.

Monterde, A. and Postill, J. (2013) 'Mobile ensembles: the uses of mobile phones for social protest by Spain's indignados', in G. Goggin and L. Hjorth (eds) *Routledge Companion to Mobile Media*. London: Routledge.

Morozov, E. (2009) 'The brave new world of slacktivism', *Foreign Policy*, 19(5), http://www.foreignpolicy.com/posts/2009/05/19/the_brave_new_world_of_slacktivism (Last accessed 5 November 2016).

Pickard, V. W. (2006) 'Assessing the radical democracy of Indymedia: discursive, technical, and institutional constructions', *Critical Studies in Media Communication*, 23(01), 19–38.

Ramadan, A. (2013) 'From Tahrir to the world: the camp as a political public space', *European Urban and Regional Studies*, 20(1), 145–149.

Reed, T. V. (2005) *The Art of Protest: Culture and Activism from the Civil Rights Movement to the Streets of Seattle*. Minneapolis, MN: University of Minnesota Press.

Rodriguez, C. (2001) *Fissures in the Mediascape: An International Study of Citizens' Media*. Cresskill, NJ: Hampton Press.

Rootes, C. (2000) 'Environmental protest in Britain 1988–1997', *Direct Action in British Environmentalism*, London: Routledge, 26–61.

Roseneil, S. (2000) *Common Women, Uncommon Practices: The Queer Feminisms of Greenham*. London: Cassell.

Seel, B. (1997) 'Strategies of resistance at the Pollok Free State road protest camp', *Environmental Politics*, 6(4), 108–139.

Thorburn, E. D. (2014) 'Social media, subjectivity, and surveillance: moving on from Occupy, the rise of live streaming video', *Communication and Critical/Cultural Studies*, 11(1), 52–63.

SEVEN

Touching a nerve: a discussion on Hong Kong's Umbrella Movement

*Klavier Jieying Wang, Hope Reidun St John and
Miu Yin Eliz Wong*

Introduction

This chapter is based on a round-table discussion of Hong Kong's 2014 suffrage-based pro-democracy movement, known as the Umbrella Movement. The Umbrella Movement was the largest social movement in Hong Kong for several decades and its bold defiance took the city, its governors and observers by surprise. As first-hand witnesses to the movement, we observed the movement from different physical and analytical vantage points. In this discussion, we aim to bring our different disciplinary perspectives, including communications, gender studies and sociocultural anthropology, into conversation with one another to compose a more comprehensive picture of how the Umbrella Movement unfolded. In doing so, we aim to contextualise the Umbrella Movement within its own unique social, political and historical context, as well as within the broader scope of occupation-based protest.

The roundtable table format of this chapter allows the authors to address, discuss and reflect upon a number aspects of the Umbrella Movement as if in conversation. With this format we hope to highlight our different perspectives and also, by avoiding the requirement of a standard research paper to reach conclusions, we aim to maintain the open character of the on-going movement and the interpretation of its meaning(s). We begin by introducing the Umbrella Movement through the frame of Hong Kong's geopolitical history. We subsequently explore several aspects of the movement within the camps and outside their borders including issues of presentation, inclusion, the production of protest, envisioning everyday life, the proliferation of support. Finally, we conclude by turning our attention to the legacy of the Umbrella Movement and the question this legacy raises.

Background

In 1997, after over 100 years of British colonial rule, Hong Kong was handed over to the sovereignty of the People's Republic of China (PRC, or China hereafter) and became special administrative region (HKSAR) of China. Governed by a mini constitution called the Basic Law, Hong Kong still operates using the social system adopted during British colonial rule, including a capitalistic economy, the common law system and freedom of speech. This makes Hong Kong distinct from the rest of mainland China.

Article 45 of the Basic Law clearly states that, 'The ultimate aim is the selection of the Chief Executive by universal suffrage upon nomination by a broadly representative nominating committee in accordance with democratic procedures'.[1] During the colonial age, Hong Kongers did not have the right to choose their governors until the late 1980s when a proportion of legislative seats were opened to popular election. Nearly 20 years after the handover, Hong Kongers continue to fight for democracy, specifically, the election of the Chief Executive (CE) and the Legislative Council (LegCo) based on universal suffrage. In 2013, an advocacy group called 'Occupy Central with Love and Peace' (OCLP) was founded by two university professors and a pastor – the OCLP trio. Holding a belief in non-violent civil disobedience, the OCLP advocated for citizen occupation of Central – Hong Kong's busiest commercial district – should the government fail to establish a democratic method for electing the CE. The OCLP members suggested a 2017 CE election method based on a year of popular consultation, deliberation and voting. A key component of OCLP's method was a process of 'civic nomination'. However, on 31 August 2014, China's People's Congress announced a framework (the 831 framework) to govern Hong Kong's CE election in 2017 whereby all eligible CE candidates would be pre-screened by a 1,200-member committee before the popular vote.

The Hong Kong Federation of Students (HKFS), a decades-old organisation of college students, regarded PRC's 831 framework as 'fake' universal suffrage and initiated a week-long boycott of classes which began on 22 September 2014. The class boycott was accompanied by series of 'public lectures' held near the government headquarters in the district of Admiralty. On the night of Friday 26 September, the last night of the class boycott, a group of students broke into the forecourt of a government building called 'Civic Square'. The unanticipated protest, widely reported via different online platforms, inspired citizens to flood to Admiralty which amplified the movement's visibility.

On 28 September (Sunday), an even larger crowd of citizens gathered, blocking the main avenues and demanding the release of the students arrested after the Civic Square action. At around 5 pm, the police began firing tear gas to disperse the enlarging crowds. However, after 87 rounds of tear gas, the crowds remained on the roads. In order to sustain the volleys of tear gas and pepper spray, citizens established medical supply stations to tend to protestors and receive public donations of supplies. Echoing events in Admiralty, citizens soon occupied the main crossroads at Mong Kok and Causeway Bay, Hong Kong's two primary commercial districts (see Figure 7.1).

Each occupation site had a distinctive style. Due to limitations of manpower and time, this chapter will focus on Admiralty and Mong Kok – the two sites with the largest occupant population. While the Admiralty occupation was initiated by a group of college students and as something of a continuation of the OCLP, the Mong Kok area was first taken by members of the working class such as freight drivers. In comparison to the Admiralty, Mong Kok revealed a grassroot 'battlefield', with skirmishes between groups of people for and against the movement. In contrast, the Admiralty occupation site was perceived as a utopia, filled with protesters chanting slogans and singing songs with mobile phones waved in hands, and a large variety of cultural activities. However, the Admiralty site also witnessed chaotic scenes, such as the conflicts between activists holding different opinions regarding how the movement should proceed, and unavoidably, violent confrontations between police and activists.

After 79 days of occupation, all three road occupations were cleared by police beginning in Mong Kok (26 and 27 November), Admiralty (11 December), and Causeway Bay (15 December). These sites were cleared through court-ordered injunctions filed by companies claiming that the occupations had negatively affected their business. However, after the clearance of the road occupations, a small camp remained in Admiralty outside the legislative building complex until the '831 framework' was officially voted down by the LegCo in June 2015.

The terminology of the 2014 pro-democracy movement remains controversial. In this chapter, we will refer to it as the 'Umbrella Movement' rather than the 'Umbrella Revolution,' another common name for the movement. After the protests, the CE election method will remain the same in 2017, with only 1,200 election committee members having the right to vote. This election is far from universal suffrage, 'fake' or otherwise. Bearing this result in mind, we refer to these events as a movement as opposed to a revolution.

Figure 7.1: Umbrella Movement occupation sites. Map by Hope Reidun St John

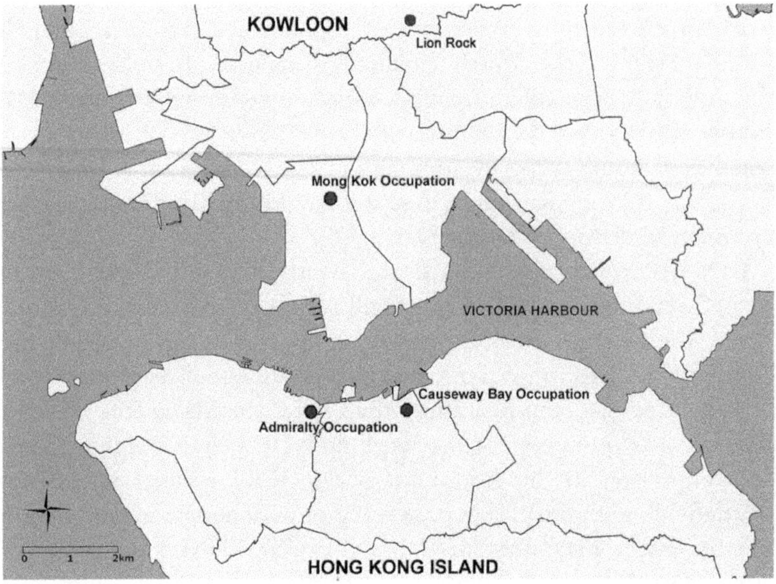

Producing protest

The Hong Kong police force's use of 87 canisters of tear gas on 28 September caught worldwide attention. Shortly thereafter, international journalists turned their cameras to the Admiralty occupation zone, watching day and night from a footbridge over Connaught Road. The use of tear gas simultaneously marked the beginning and the peak of the Umbrella Movement. However, it was rarely explained to international readers why and how this crucial moment took shape and led to the 79-day protest camp occupation.

Furthermore, the umbrella has been widely recognised as the symbol of the movement, yet it was also the subject of debate. Pro-government lawmakers claimed it was a more aggressive weapon than the tear gas itself,[2] while movement supporters deemed it representative of the humble and non-violent characteristics of Hong Kong's protestors.[3] How and why did the umbrella become the symbol of the movement?

Klavier Wang

First, it is necessary to explain why such a large population of people took to the streets to support the student protestors even though the students illegally broke into a government space. For decades, Hong Kong has been well known for its 'rule and order' protest style, characterised by people's orderly manners and ritualised actions (for example, chanting slogans and singing songs) during protest activities (Ku, 2007). For example, every year since 2003, on 1 July, tens of thousands citizens joined the annual '7.1 pro-democracy parade', walking along a police approved route and dispersing peacefully once the parade ended. However, on the night of 26 September 2014, Hong Kongers voluntarily flooded to Admiralty chanting the slogan 'protect the students'. This fierce reaction by the people can understood through the events of the previous week.

Beginning on 22 September, the HKFS held a week-long class boycott during which a series of open lectures with a variety of themes were given in Tamar Park and other sites near government headquarters. Throughout the week, the class boycott was consistent with exactly the 'rule and order' style. 'Students' (in this context) applied to virtually anyone: parents with kids, high schoolers, college students, even the elderly, who sat and listened to lectures on civil rights, human rights and political philosophy, among many others. From day to night, intellectual discussion and opinions regarding the future of Hong Kong filled Tamar Park. The class boycott reached far beyond the scope of college students, touching the hearts of many Hong Kongers.

The orderly, planned class boycott maintained support over the course of the week, escalating on 26 September. The original protest location, Tamar Park, was allocated to a patriotic organisation for China's National Day celebration. Subsequently, the class boycott could only be held on a narrow pedestrian path next to the LegCo complex. Despite the change of location, people kept coming to public lectures, including secondary and high school students, who came after school and still wearing their school uniforms. At night, more and more people came to the boycott site, packing the pedestrian path and roads nearby so that police had to stop vehicle traffic. This restriction of protest space and the escalating volume of protesting crowds made the scene so enormously tense that, when student leader Joshua Wong proclaimed 'let's reclaim our Civic Square', demonstrators immediately rushed to the square's gate (for the location of the significant spots, refer to Figure 7.2).

Seeing a group of youngsters held overnight by police after they broke into the Civic Square, supporters were touched by students' actions and enraged by the perception of police cruelty (for example, police did not allow the trapped protestors to go to the restroom). The crowds gathering in Admiralty grew larger and larger, from the night of 26 to the morning of 28 (Sunday), eventually leading to the eruption of the tear gas and the 79-day occupation movement.

Civic Square is steeped in symbolism. Once an open space available for public assembly, it was later fenced off after a number of large-scale protests were held there. Among others, the space witnessed the successful anti-moral-and-national education movement in 2012, when Hong Kong residents pushed the government to withdraw a perceived patriotic-driven school subject. During this 2012 movement, the Civic Square was occupied by activists for one week. This previous successful occupation made the Civic Square a cultural symbol signifying the power of citizens, and now had become an unexpected prelude to the 2014 Umbrella Movement.

Figure 7.2: Admiralty occupation site. Map by Hope Reidun St John

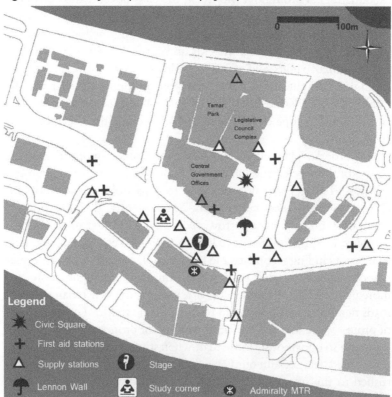

Though the name 'Umbrella Movement' is well known, the appearance of the symbolic umbrella is nothing but an accident. After protestors broke into Civic Square, the gate was soon closed and the protestors inside were surrounded by police. In order to stop more police from entering the square, other protestors built human chains outside the square's gate. Shortly after this the police began to use violent tactics such as pepper spray to disband the human chains. Facing the pepper spray, people grabbed whatever was on hand to protect their bodies and faces. The umbrella, an everyday object people carried in their bags during Hong Kong's humid summers became the 'most powerful' and convenient shield.

According to social movement scholars, movement participants tend to adopt some cultural elements from their movement precursors. Swidler's (1995) 'cultural toolbox' metaphor states that some stories, values and norms of behaviours are inherited, modified or recreated during particular movements. However, in the Umbrella Movement, the icon of this movement appeared naturally. Facing the immediate danger of pepper spray and riot police armed with shields and batons, a wall stacked with colourful umbrellas became the people's fence (see Figure 7.3).

Figure 7.3: The first umbrella fence built by protestors soon after the students broke into the Civic Square, 27 September 2014. Photo by Klavier Wang

On 28 September, known as '928 tear gas day', more umbrellas were donated to the protest site by thousands of citizens flooding to Admiralty. Hong Kongers soon adopted the name of the 'Umbrella Movement', signifying the characteristics of people's active involvement in the movement – vulnerable, but flexible and strongly determined.

Hope St John

I think Klavier makes an interesting point here about the symbolic significance of the umbrella. Unlike Taiwan's Sunflower Movement (an occupation-based movement in the spring of 2014), which gained its name and affiliation with the colour yellow as a result of a spontaneous and coincidental expression of support (Harrison, 2014), the Umbrella Movement linked into a vocabulary of existing images and symbols both political and otherwise. Although umbrellas retained no political significance in Hong Kong prior to the Umbrella Movement, they are omnipresent fixtures of everyday life in the city, as well as in other parts of East Asia. As a practical tool of protection from both weather and teargas, the umbrella appeared to represent the common person. As such, its potency as a cultural symbol of Hong Kong's suffrage movement derived its emergent status as quotidian object rather than a spectacular one.

(Re)presenting the movement

In September 2015, during the commemoration of the one-year anniversary of the birth of the Umbrella Movement, a group of artists, from an organisation called 'Umbrella Movement Visual Archive' showcased a series of artworks collected during the protest. This gallery of the Umbrella Movement brought to mind memories of the 79-day road occupations and triggered much reflection about these events. In addition to the umbrella, what were the other images that characterised these moments of protest? How did the movement – often referred to as a blossom field of creativity – as well as the social context as a whole, provide the raw materials for protestors to express their voices?

Hope St John

While the events of 26 and 28 September made umbrellas (spontaneously) iconic, the Umbrella Movement also featured another potent visual component – the colour yellow. Prior to the catalysation of the Umbrella Movement, pro-democracy suffrage demonstrations utilised the colour black to show its chromatic solemnity. Even in the early days of the road occupations, demonstrators and occupiers showed their solidarity by turning out in black clothes with yellow ribbons pinned to them. However, over time, the colour yellow eclipsed black, becoming synonymous with Umbrella Movement as the central colour of movement itself. Embedded within this colour shift is also a multitude of symbolic associations both near and far.

While the symbol of the umbrella was spontaneously appropriated, the integration of the colour yellow built on decades of intersecting political, historical and cultural legacies. Previously described as a 'symbol of hope' and representative of 'brightness and hope' in the pursuit of universal suffrage, the origin of yellow ribbons in association with democracy and suffrage remains somewhat ambiguous (Civic Party, n.d; Hong Kong Digital Photovision, 2005; Eagleton, 2014). Although global media outlets such as CNN and BBC tend to concentrate on the distant roots of the yellow ribbon in western suffrage movements and expressions of remembrance, closer inspection reveals that the colour has configured subtle, localised meanings within Hong Kong that predate the Umbrella Movement by several years (Crook, 2014; Coleman, 2014; Hume and Park, 2014). One example of this is the artwork of Pak Sheung Chuen, whose 2004 performance piece *The Yellow Ribbons: A Present for the Central Government*, which took the footprints of demonstrators participating in the annual 7.1 pro-democracy march on a strip of yellow cloth and created ribbons subsequently tied in Beijing's Tiananmen Square (Krischer, 2009; Cartier, 2009; 2010). This final action pulled directly from the marches themselves, which culminated in 'tying yellow ribbons to the iron gates of the Hong Kong government offices as an act of peaceful yet visible dissent' (Krischer, 2009, para 5; see also Cartier, 2010). The work and the practices it draws upon renders visible the contextualisation of the symbol of the yellow ribbon and the colour yellow itself into local contestations of political power and governance between post-colonial Hong Kong and mainland China (see Krischer, 2009; Cartier, 2009; 2010). As such, it is possible to see the colour yellow and the yellow ribbons as more than a remote reference to a distant past, but rather as the continuation of an at times tense exchange (see Figure 7.4).

In addition to its omnipresence within the occupation zones, the yellow colour palette was continually repeated and reproduced in a large variety of artefacts from the movement, such as hand-crafted paper umbrellas, stickers, stamps, pins, ribbons, and all of their variations, including necklaces made of yellow leather ribbons stamped with personal names or bracelets emblazoned with an umbrella. These

Figure 7.4: Yellow ribbons tied to the fence of the Civic Square, with a banner stating 'We are crying because we are sad for HK, not because of the tear gas', 1 October 2014. Photo by Klavier Wang

artefacts served as smaller, more mobile variations on visual motifs and themes within the occupation sites that, through their capacity for personalisation, allowed owners to enmesh themselves as social and political participants. This resonates with Bennet and Segerberg's (2013) conceptualisation of the 'personalisation of contentious politics', which has characterised many contemporary mass demonstration events. Onsite, prominent images included large sculptures depicting or utilising umbrellas; banners displaying quotes or opinions; and depictions of critical moments within the Umbrella Movement's chronology.

Emblematic examples of movement-characterising images include two less literal, but much discussed objects at the Admiralty camp, a sculpture known as Umbrella Man by the artist MILK, and a plush bear in a yellow hat and rain coat (see Figure 7.5). The former, constructed from small wooden boards, echoed the photos circulated in the media of resilient protestors brandishing their umbrellas in the midst of clouds of teargas and valorised the protest. The latter, a furry plush bear carrying the sign 'We all love Hong Kong, please don't hurt me', represented protestors and occupiers as wide-eyed dreamers. Although different from one another, both reflected existing perceptions of the movement and reproduced them in highly visible ways, helping to solidify both characterisations. These images joined a host of other banners, posters, drawings and sculptures that blanketed the occupation sites. In combination, these created a continuum of expression and (re)articulations rooted in common undercurrents of righteousness, innocence and perseverance, whether invested in critique (of the government, politicians, or mainland China), self-representation of the movement, or moral encouragement.

Among the symbols circulating in the occupation zones, however, were texts, motifs and images with specific cultural and historical legacies. These were deployed to make symbolic associations between the Umbrella Movement and protests from the past. Although quotes could be found throughout the occupation sites from figures such as Mahatma Gandhi, and Martin Luther King Jr, this historical referencing was at its most pronounced and most pointed in relation to mainland China, the PRC's history of revolution and China's 1989 democracy movement. One of the most striking illustrations of such historical interplay occurred in the form of 'tanks' constructed at the Admiralty site (out of tents and recycled water bottles) by a former student protestor from China's 1989 movement. The tanks invoked images of the 1989 movement, and were not the only references made to that historic protest movement throughout the occupation zones.

Eliz Wong

Besides utilising artistic objects to reveal mass resistance in the protest site, the body can also be a site of protest. Outraged by the sexual violence occurring in Mong Kok, two artists created a serial of visual artworks by writing slogans on nude female bodies. With the theme 'Resistance, Female Bodies, Future',[4] they wanted to empower female bodies as more than vulnerable targets for sexism. Photos were uploaded daily, in response to the movement's progress and dynamics. For example, rainbow paintings on lips and nude bodies were shown in the Pride Parade in November, while anti-harassment photos were posted when sexual violence was reported in the occupied zones.

'HeHe culture', another interesting trend, was created and developed quickly in this movement. Under the influence of Boy's Love (BL) subcultures, a netizen on Facebook framed two male student leaders in the HKFS, Alex and Lester, as a romantic couple. Surprisingly, the *Alexter* (the combined names of the two student leaders) Facebook page gained massive popularity among young participants.[5] Based on fantasies of romantic love between the two student leaders, hundreds of creations, from artworks and comics to novels, were shared online.

The 'HeHe' images of the student leaders can be treated as the collaborative creations of thousands of netizens. Challenging the traditional masculinity of social movement leadership, the student leaders wore the 'HeHe' labels proudly and used this popularity to help raise awareness of LGBT equality issues among the general public, including endorsing the Pride Parade 2014.

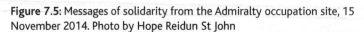

Figure 7.5: Messages of solidarity from the Admiralty occupation site, 15 November 2014. Photo by Hope Reidun St John

(Re)constructing everyday life in protest camps

When we consider occupation movements in other parts of the world, one of the key components that emerges is the process of turning the protest site into a living space – creating an alternative life space with an alternative logic of living in order to counter mainstream values (Castells, 2012). In the context of the Umbrella Movement, how did Hong Kong protestors transform the contentious protest zone into a living space for long-term occupation? How did they arrange their everyday camp life? What is implied in their spatial practice?

Hope St John

All three occupation sites were noteworthy in their relative longevity and individuality. Initially sites of spontaneous gathering, they rapidly developed into 'long-term' camps with the support of sympathetic donors. They helped build them in both the figurative and literal senses through the contribution of supplies, sustenance and skilled labour. One of the most visible examples of this occurred in the transformation of living arrangements in the occupation zones. During the first few days of occupation, participants often slept on the pavement. However, as occupiers began to extend their stays, tents became an increasingly conspicuous part of the landscape. At its height, the Admiralty occupation site was home to more than 2,300 tents, while Mong Kok retained more than 300 according to data collected by the Umbrella Movement Tent Population Census (雨傘運動營口普查).[6] As tent-living became an increasingly important part of the day-to-day occupation, living arrangements and living spaces also developed, equipped with basic furniture and 'housewares' (such as, rugs, cushions and mats), produced on site as well as purchased for use there. In the meantime, basic necessities such as food and water – distributed by volunteers and small, manned supply stations in the early days of the occupation – were consolidated in central, self-service style locations. By the time the sites were cleared, all of the occupation camps had developed some degree of semi-permanence through the establishment of distinctive spaces and clearly defined borders as well as distinct social sensibilities.

The protest camps in Hong Kong were particularly interesting in the ways that they unsettled the city's status quo. New social dynamics emerged within occupation zones, seemingly based on a sense of community and solidarity in which spaces and resources were shared with individuals stepping forward to help provide services such as charging cell phones or making snacks – a protest utopian community. This sense of bonding together was epitomised by one story in particular that circulated about $200 HKD (about $25 USD) of lost cash found in Admiralty during the height of the occupation. Under 'normal' circumstances, this might have simply been picked up and pocketed by a passer-by. However, the cash was instead taped to the ground where it was found and left with a note, awaiting the owner's return. In the context of the occupations as a whole, the story appears indicative of a heightened sense of care and awareness rooted in participants' broader concerns over the governance of their city and their shared identity as 'Hong Kongers'.

Figure 7.6: Admiralty occupation site, 15 November 2014. Photo by Hope Reidun St John

Klavier Wang

Besides the utopian practices in the occupation camps, I would also point out another cultural aspect that was revealed in the protest sites. In the Mong Kok occupation site, with a seemingly more grassroots atmosphere compared to the Admiralty area, people witnessed the erection of Guan Yu statues in the middle of the occupied road. This symbolic gesture brought into view another facet of Hong Kong people – the embodiment of traditional Chinese culture in everyday life. Guan Yu is a masculine martial guardian in ancient Chinese legend. In the contemporary age, it is usually placed at front doors in every police station, as an intimidation tactic. Gangsters worship Guan Yu in their community. By placing Guan Yu statues on the street of Mong Kok, the protestors created an interesting cultural parody in three aspects: presenting Guan Yu as a guardian of the occupation site; Guan Yu intimidating the police; and, by putting Guan Yu, and later a Christian altar, on the street, echoing the mixed cultures of Hong Kong. These small religious venues became a part of establishing a specific internal culture grounded within the site that simultaneously linked up with external institutions and integrated the diverse combination of belief systems of participants.

Hope St John

We shouldn't overlook the importance of 'student' as an iconic status in the whole movement. Although the Umbrella Movement attracted a wide array of participants, it was often perceived as a student movement. We could see 'students' not only as a defining aspect of the movement's identity, but also manifested in the material form of the camps. This was reflected in the development of 'study corners', where demonstrating students could keep up with their coursework. The largest such study area developed in Admiralty. This 'corner' started as a small niche, but developed into a large, tented study space complete with desks, lights, power supply and roving tutors. This became a highlight of media portrayals of the occupation, which applauded the dedication of the students to both their political mission and their education (see Crane, Chapter Twenty-one).

Klavier Wang

Regarding the study corner, I conducted an interview with a few study corner 'administrators' who were actively engaged in this sector. The corner was originally founded by a few high school students who brought their homework to the Occupy site after school. Recognising that other students might also have this need, they began to assemble simple desks and chairs. Soon, the study corner evolved, with university alumni groups and many individual teachers forming a teaching team. Arranging the voluntary teachers' schedules became one of the most important tasks. A large white board was set up with time slots stated. Anyone who wished to join could write their names in the time slots. If they regularly came to the study corner and started to get familiar with other teachers, they would be then added to existing WhatsApp groups or Google co-working teams to manage the task distribution together with other voluntary teachers.

During November and December, however, when the movement came to a deadlock, the number of teachers dropped dramatically. Those who remained were primarily rooted in certain alumni groups and existing circles of voluntary teachers. Here a common problem remained: how to sustain the momentum? Even with the ubiquity of convenient communication tools in people's lives, the efficacy of mobilisation is never guaranteed. After the initial excitement (with thousands of people facing the tear gas), the question of how to sustain people's morale and participation remained an important issue.

Eliz Wong

I would like to add a gender perspective to this discussion of everyday life in the occupation zones. The division of labour there tended to be gendered. For example, construction and building tended to be gendered male, while cleaning, cooking and delivering food and drink tended to be gendered female. These divisions were constructed not only based on individual's choices, but also on others' expectations, which once violated would trigger a disapproving response. A female activist I met mentioned that she would like to help in building the roadblocks, however when she tried to assist, a few men yelled at her saying, 'We are not men if women need to do this kind of building work', taking away the fence she held and asking her to step back. Masculinities were constructed and performed through the division of labour in protest camps, and especially on the contested front of the movement.

Many women were willing to confront the police on the frontline, although men were hesitant and shared a sense of protectiveness. Many female activists I met during or after the movement mentioned that they were asked to leave the risky frontlines by other male activists. Some male activists on the frontlines even directly pulled some female protestors backward, shouting 'Girls stay at the back!' Movement co-ordinators (usually the ones taking the microphone) even asked male activists to take care of the female activists around them. There was even an axiom, saying, 'Women go to Admiralty' (as mentioned, a more peaceful occupying zone), 'and men go to Mong Kok'. Mass media emphasised the masculinity of male activists protecting women. Later, protecting women was perceived as male's responsibility and thus became a symbolic performance of masculinity. With the slogan, 'Protect students and protect women', men from different walks of life were mobilised to occupy Mong Kok in order to protect women and children from police violence.

Embracing dissent

The significance of the Umbrella Movement extended far beyond what was happening in the occupation zones, reaching into other aspects of residents' social lives. Castells (2012) has observed a rhizomatic trend in today's networked social movements, with networked individuals carrying out actions from within their personalised frameworks – a personalisation of politics (Bennett and Segerberg, 2013). Was this also a feature of Hong Kong's Umbrella Movement? What notable characteristics emerged here?

Klavier Wang

Among all sorts of movement cultural artefacts, as a Hong Konger, I felt the action of hanging a huge 'I want genuine universal suffrage' banner on Lion Rock brought the movement to another peak alongside the '928 tear gas day' (see Figure 7.5). For Hong Kongers, Lion Rock is associated with 'Lion Rock spirit', signifying generations of Hong Kongers working diligently under Lion Rock to build Hong Kong into a world-class city. During the Umbrella Movement, nine rock-climbers utilised their expertise to make their voice heard, not in the protest camp sites, but on this natural landmark in the city. After hanging the banner, the nine climbers posted a statement online saying that they want to re-define the 'Lion Rock spirit' by highlighting Hong Kongers' quest for the right to choose their CE.[7] Deeply embedded in the social legacies and collective beliefs of residents, this banner touched a nerve for many Hong Kongers. The banner was quickly removed by the police for safety reasons. However, in the occupation sites, different sizes of yellow banners were soon designed, printed and distributed by different organisations and protesters, as a way to reproduce the banner hanging action in diverse forms.

Hope St John

During the period of the road occupations especially, campuses were dotted with movement slogans in the form of large yellow banners hung from campus buildings. In some cases, these lingered long after the roadways were cleared. Within the Umbrella Movement, occupation zones were critical sites of demonstration. However, outside the camps, universities also represented important centres of support and discussion. Although the movement was by no means limited to being a student movement, university campuses such as those of the University of Hong Kong and the Chinese University of Hong Kong provided external nodes of activism where individuals and groups could voice their political sentiments. Already key arenas for political discussion in the weeks prior to the galvanisation of the Umbrella Movement, universities became arenas for visual representations of support, including hanging large banners from campus buildings and pasting posters inside outward facing windows. Although these banners became less prevalent over the course of the movement, several managed to outlive the roadway occupations themselves, serving as both a timely message of support and a tribute to the cause, respectively. In this way, universities became linked into a network of political action that transformed already prominent urban spaces into foci of dissent.

Eliz Wong

Instead of focusing on solely democratic issues, universities were also sites within which a wide array of other social issues were expressed. Instead of the more typical large-scale yellow banner with a slogan, at the Chinese University of Hong Kong campus a (5 metres long) rainbow flag with the slogan, 'We want universal suffrage' was displayed. This flag symbolically connected LGBT issues with the democratic movement. The banner was originally held before Hong Kong Pride Parade 2014, which was organised across two occupation sites (Admiralty and Causeway Bay). Under the slogan, 'No democracy, no equality', around 8,900 participants turned out with their rainbow umbrellas to participate in Hong Kong Pride Parade to fight for both democracy and equality.

Klavier Wang

I must add that, besides hanging banners in the universities, ordinary citizens also took part in this collective action by hanging banners at home. In Manuel Castells' *Networks of Outrage and Hope* (2012), he pointed out that a rhizomatic form of movement can blossom around the world through contemporary network society. A movement could be actualised and evolved through a large number of nodes and hubs constituted by individuals and groups, anywhere and anytime. The Umbrella Movement vividly revealed this rhizomatic form of movement, with lots of ordinary citizens taking part by their own means and specialties. During this wave of 'banner hanging', a news story drew our attention in which a housewife placed the 'I want genuine universal suffrage' yellow banner in the window of her apartment. She soon received warnings from the estate management unit, saying the banner affected the building's exterior appearance.[8] Despite this kind of case, Hong Kongers continued posting banners, reiterating, 'You can't kill us all'. As such, yellow banners were distributed at the protest sites, universities and (supportive) legislative councillors' offices.

Figure 7.7: 'I want genuine universal suffrage' banner on top of Lion Rock, 24 October 2014. Photo by Klavier Wang

Communications and conflicts

In a network society, it is impossible to ignore communications among the networked population. The social movement setting is without exception. On the one hand, social media tools have been exalted in terms of drawing people to take to the street through 'Facebook revolution'. On the other hand, an increasing number of scholars have sought to revisit the issue of 'technology in movements' by taking a cautious view of the role of media and emphasising the importance of how human agents use communicative devices within their immediate context.

How was communication configured among Hong Kong protestors during the Umbrella Movement? If we call the Umbrella Movement a pro-democracy movement, do we imply the presence of an internal democracy within the movement itself? To what extent were different voices and political stances communicated among protestors during the movement?

Klavier Wang

Starting from '928', rumours flooded in regarding whether the People's Liberation Army would join Hong Kong police forces to control the crowd, whether the police would escalate the violence, and so on. After the police fired the tear gas, rumours about them shooting live bullets and imposing a curfew spread rapidly, causing an extremely chaotic situation. Rumours came from unclear sources, such as 'an anonymous public servant', 'an NGO volunteer' and so on. Seeing the tear gas and increasing numbers of the police force, people were afraid of any negative consequences similar to the 1989 Tiananmen tragedy. However, there was no way to verify the large number of messages coming from different mediums.

Despite the fact that Hong Kong people's everyday life has been largely integrated with information communication technologies (ICTs), at that crucial moment (and facing huge uncertainty and anxiety), people's information acquisition via ICTs was very cautiously embedded. It was said that people should try to avoid using China Mobile (a telecommunication operator based in mainland China) to exchange information, because there was a possibility that the signal could be intercepted. In this context, people experimented with shifting their mobile communication mode from 3G/4G to SMS and blue-tooth based channels, to avoid the 3G/4G data traffic jam. A blue-tooth-based information exchange system called 'Fire Chat' quickly became popular. Via blue-tooth, people within the range of transmission (approximately 8–10 metres) could exchange information through Fire Chat. On 28 September, the crowds occupied the main avenues across a number of blocks. When the police fired the first tear gas, protestors standing only two blocks away had difficulty getting the latest information via 3G/4G based news channel due to the user density, until they smelled the gas. In such a case, it seemed Fire Chat could provide an alternative medium. However, since anybody could set up a Fire Chat group and spread information to users nearby, the medium's greatest strength was also its biggest drawback. The anonymity facilitated the spreading of false rumours. Some protestors shifted back to the traditional SMS, asking those not in the protest sites send the latest news gained from mass media.

Another noteworthy mode of communication was called a 'station', resembling an information exchange centre. A 'station' was a friendship based community, wherein people set up a 'station' to facilitate the exchange the first-hand information anytime, anywhere between 'station members' (who were also known as pigeons). For instance, member A at Admiralty and member B at Mong Kok could exchange first-hand information via this platform. In the 'station', sometimes there were 'station coordinators', responsible for collecting and sorting out the latest news from mass media, which had 24-hour live reporting from the three occupation sites. By regularly integrating the news and sharing on the 'station', the 'station' could provide a relatively full picture to the 'station members'. To tackle the problematic circulation of rumours, some 'station members' set up Facebook pages called 'OCMK myth-killer'.[9] For example, a rumour said that the footbridge near the Mong Kok train station was already occupied. By providing the first-hand photos taken by other 'station members', the page administrators verified that the claimed area was empty without any hints of occupation.[10]

Klavier Wang

In the Umbrella Movement, besides the skirmishes occurring from time to time in the Mong Kok occupation site, the online world seemed another open site for verbal confrontation. A Facebook group established in 2013, called 'Silent Majority' had over 100,000 followers. During the Umbrella Movement, whenever anti-movement images or news reports were posted, they received over 100 comments, usually bombarding the movement with vulgar language. For instance, 'Silent Majority' followers often referred to student protestors as 'trouble-makers sabotaging Hong Kong's public order' and accused pro-democracy politicians of being 'traitors'.

After the '928 tear gas day,' a group of anti-Umbrella Movement demonstrators took the blue ribbon as their symbol, in contrast to the pro-democracy yellow ribbons. While yellow ribbon activists criticised the police's over-use of violence, the blue ribbon group applauded the police's tolerance and loyalty (for example, a group called 'Support HK Police' was established with blue ribbon as their icon). As more and more people took to the streets, many Facebook users changed their profile pictures into a yellow ribbon, while others posted blue ribbons. Conflicts between these two groups escalated as the movement proceeded. These happened not only in actual protest sites, such as in the skirmishes at Mong Kok where anti-movement citizens confronted activists, telling them to go home, but also in acrimonious verbal conflicts online. A picture was widely circulated online by 'blue ribboners' showing a 'policeman' with blood flowing from his face. Blue ribboners used this picture as evidence of Umbrella Movement activists' violence. However, it was soon discovered that this was actually a staged photo featuring a television actor. Facing accusations of violence, yellow ribbon activists in turn condemned the blue ribboners for failing to verify their 'evidence'.[11] A popular song called, 'If I Call You a Stupid Dick, I'm Afraid You'd Be Mad' (話你戇鳩怕你嬲), composed by pro-movement netizens humorously and straightforwardly expressed how the activists felt about the blue ribboners' perceived stubbornness and stupidity.

Eliz Wong

I cannot agree more with Klavier that we cannot overlook the chaos, not only between the yellow and blue ribboners, but also within the yellow ribbon circle. Although sharing a belief in democracy, many internet discussions descended into personal attacks between activists from various backgrounds and ideologies. Sexuality became one of the key targets for attack. Online cyber-bullying of female activists through criticising their faces and bodies was not rare during conflicts between different parties. Mocking and insulting female protestors of different political stances as 'hookers' or 'bitches' clearly showed the gendered nature of attacks in cyberspace. There were also constant rumours spread that women in the protest camps were promiscuous and these stigmas were used to discredit their participation.

Other than sexual harassment of female protestors, unfriendliness toward the LGBT community was even more serious in internet discussions. With the frequent usage of terms like 'faggots' and 'pussy-suckers' to attack opponents, LGBT protestors felt hurt and excluded from the movement. Triggered by the student leaders' endorsement of the Hong Kong Pride Parade, thousands of disapproving and spiteful comments appeared online, such as advocating that 'Homosexuality is sinful! Go to Hell'. Reflecting the patriarchy and heterosexism in Hong Kong society, this humiliating language, did not disappear, but was further exaggerated through media communication.

Concluding remarks

Despite the inter-organisational/individual dynamics and the controversies embedded in the issue of democracy, the Umbrella Movement undoubtedly has etched itself into Hong Kong history. The scale of the movement and the forms of people's participation transcended previous pro-democracy movements. What's more, the Umbrella Movement unveiled a new era in the Sino–Hong Kong relationship, especially in terms of Hong Kongers' high-profile challenge to the Chinese central government's proposal and their quest for a self-determining fate.

Against the backdrop of China's rapidly developing economy and the Sino–Hong Kong economic partnership, Hong Kongers have shown a dramatic increasing trend in the assertion of Hong Kong identity and a decreasing identification with Chinese identity since 2008, according to a long-term survey conducted through the University of Hong Kong.[12] In the realm of social movements, a path showing activists' changing of movement discourse could also be identified. Back in the 1970s and 1980s, Hong Kong's movements were generally opposed to British colonialism and driven by Chinese nationalism, demanding a 'democratic handover' (Choy et al, 1998). After the 1997 handover, in 2003, a group of scholars, advocated a set of Hong Kong core values for the first time.[13] In subsequent years, a series of cultural preservation movements broke out in this city, during which a call was made by activists to re-examine and re-discover Hong Kongers' local history and local identity. Meanwhile, questions and criticisms have been raised about the closer Sino–Hong Kong relationship as well. Furthermore, as we previously mentioned, in 2012 hundreds of thousands Hong Kong people gathered at Civic Square and demanded withdrawal of the 'moral and national education' subject from the school curriculum. Chanting the slogan of 'anti-brainwashing by Chinese Communist Party', movement participants refused to call China their 'motherland' and advocated giving Hong Kong's next generation the freedom to choose which country they should love. Against such a backdrop of closer economic ties, but deeper Sino–Hong Kong cultural/political cleavage, the 2014 Umbrella Movement evolved beyond the expectations of either the OCLP or the HKFS. The slogan for the HKFS class boycott – 'self-determining our fate' – four characters in traditional Chinese calligraphy written on a stage board, has been etched in Hong Kongers' minds with the smell of tear gas and shouts of 'I want genuine universal suffrage'. Perhaps it will continue to be a banner of hope or fissure in future years.

Notes

[1] For the full document of the Basic Law, see: www.basiclaw.gov.hk/en/basiclawtext/chapter_4.html#section_1

[2] www.scmp.com/news/hong-kong/article/1617690/hong-kong-lawmaker-says-umbrellas-are-more-dangerous-tear-gas?page=all

[3] www.theguardian.com/world/2014/sep/29/umbrella-symbol-hong-kong-democracy-protests

[4] Facebook page: www.facebook.com/Protest.FemaleBodies.Future/?fref=ts

[5] Facebook page: www.facebook.com/AlexLester4everLove?fref=nf

[6] Facebook page: www.facebook.com/umbrellacensus?fref=ts

[7] See the news report by *Apple Daily*, 24 October 2014: http://hk.apple.nextmedia.com/news/art/20141024/18910801

[8] See the news report by *Apple Daily*, 29 October 2014: http://hk.apple.nextmedia.com/news/art/20141029/18916488

[9] See Facebook page: www.facebook.com/OccupyCentralMythKiller?fref=nf

10 See the case: https://goo.gl/ecF8pF
11 The case was reported by *Apple Daily*, 15 October 2014: http://hk.apple.nextmedia.com/enews/realtime/20141015/53021494
12 Find the chart showing the identity change here: www.hkupop.hku.hk/english/popexpress/ethnic/eidentity/poll/eid_poll_chart.html
13 For the full text of Hong Kong Core Values refer to: https://goo.gl/Tx1Pe1

References

Bennett, W. L. and Segerberg, A. (2013) *The Logic of Connective Action: Digital Media and the Personalization of Contentious Politics*. New York: Cambridge University Press.

Cartier, C. (2009) 'Regional formation and the post-colonial question: contemporary art in Hong Kong and the PRD', *Diaaalogue*, www.aaa.org.hk/Diaaalogue/Details/701.

Cartier, C. (2010) 'Power plays: alternative performance art and urban space in the political life of the city', in K. Louie (ed), *Hong Kong Culture: Word and Image*. Hong Kong: Hong Kong University Press, pp 25–40.

Castells, M. (2012) *Networks of Outrage and Hope: Social Movements in the Internet Age*. Cambridge, UK: Polity.

Choy, C., Wong, Y., Tsoi, Y. and Chong, Y. (1998) *From Identity to Indifference: Hong Kong Student Movement Since 1981*. Hong Kong: Hong Kong Humanities and Social Science Press.

Civic Party (n.d.) 'Timeline', www.civicparty.hk/?q=en/chronicle.

Coleman, J. (2014) 'Hong Kong protest: the symbols and songs explained', *BBC News*, 4 October, www.bbc.com/news/world-asia-china-29473974.

Crook, R. (2014) 'The history of the yellow ribbon', *BBC News*, 7 October, www.bbc.com/news/uk-29521449.

Eagleton, J. (2014) 'Umbrellas and yellow ribbons: the language of the 2014 Hong Kong protests' [Blog post], 4 November, http://blog.oup.com/2014/11/language-hong-kong-protests/.

Harrison, M. (2014) 'The Sunflower Movement in Taiwan', *The China Story Journal*, 18 April, www.thechinastory.org/2014/04/the-sunflower-movement-in-taiwan/.

Hong Kong Digital Photovision (2005) 'July 1 March: hope for full democracy' [Blog post], 3 July, www.hkdigit.net/2005/07/july-1-march-hope-for-full-democracy/.

Hume, T. and Park, M. (2014) 'Understanding the symbols of Hong Kong's "Umbrella Movement"', *CNN*, 30 September, www.cnn.com/2014/09/30/world/asia/objects-hong-kong-protest/.

Krischer, O. (2009) 'The art of covert intervention: Pak Sheung Chuen, *Art Asia Pacific*, 63, May/June, http://artasiapacific.com/Magazine/63/TheArtOfCovertInterventionPakSheungChuen.

Ku, A. S. (2007) 'Constructing and contesting the "order" imagery in media discourse: implications for civil society in Hong Kong, *Asian Journal of Communication*, 17(2), 186–200.

Swidler, A. (1995) 'Cultural power and social movements', in H. Johnston and B. Klandermans (eds), *Social Movements and Culture*. Minneapolis, MN: University of Minnesota Press, pp 25–40.

Part Two
Occupying and colonising

EIGHT

Introduction: occupying and colonising

Gavin Brown, Fabian Frenzel, Patrick McCurdy and Anna Feigenbaum

Introduction

All forms of protest have a geography and interact with the spatiality of the world in particular ways (Nicholls, 2009). This is particularly evident in the case of protest camps: they take form and materialise through an occupation of space, a piece of land, for an extended period of time. Many protest camps simultaneously occupy physical space *and* mediated space. In this sense, as well as occupying particular locations, by occupying mediated/media space they also have the potential to occupy people's imaginations, and occupy the media agenda for a while. The chapters in this section of the book primarily examine the contested politics of the physical occupation of land, its consequence and dynamics (Leidinger, 2015; Vasudevan, 2015a).

Ways of occupying

The act of occupying land or public space in the city can be motivated by many factors. Fundamentally, it constitutes a contestation of power within a given society and seeks to wrest actual and symbolic control over a given space or territory for a period of time. The tactical or strategic objective of a protest camp can significantly shape decisions about the place it occupies (as well as the form the occupation can, or is allowed, to take). While it is not our intention to set up a strong typology of camps, it is worth elaborating how camps with different objectives might use the land they occupy in different ways. First, there are protest camps that seek to protect a site, environment or community from unwanted developments. Of course, such camps are not purely defensive, as they proactively seek to stop something from happening. Examples of camps like this frequently arise out of environmental protest movements, seeking to stop the building of new roads (Doherty et al, 2007; Routledge, 1997), land occupations to block hydroelectric dams (Frenzel, 2014), or stop mining (Stahler-Sholk et al, 2014; Li, 2015). Second, there are camps, which assemble near a site which symbolises an injustice or wider social, political or environmental problem of some kind. Such camps may seek to disrupt the functioning of a power station (Frenzel, 2014), a business, or the embassy of a repressive regime (Brown and Yaffe, 2014). The tactical objective of this type of camp is to bear witness to the injustices at issue and mobilise further opposition to them. Third, there are those protest camps which function primarily as 'convergence spaces' (Routledge, 2003), bringing together activists working on a single cause (or a cluster of related concerns) to pool knowledge, share skills and develop new contentious repertoires and programmes of action. Symbolically, many activists and scholars locate the emergence of convergence space camps in the global *encuentros* organised by the Zapatistas in the jungles of Chiapas, Mexico in the early 1990s (Khasnabish, 2008). Other examples can be found in the HoriZone camp set up in parallel to the 2005 meeting of the G8 nations at Gleneagles (McCurdy, 2011). While most protest camps share this feature of bringing diverse people, practices and ideas together, this third type of camp is usually set up to accommodate people during an event, rather than the encampment being the protest act itself. A fourth type of protest camp is one that occupies a public space of national (or global) significance and symbolism to contest the legitimacy of the economic system or a national government (Robinson, 1994). These are the kinds of protest camps that came to international prominence and visibility in 2011 (Juris et al, 2012; Merrifield, 2013; Ramadan, 2013b). Of course, many examples here serve as a reminder that protests camps can (and, frequently do) serve more than one function simultaneously.

In this book we consciously expand our view of what a protest camp might be to consider the ways in which land occupations (Wolford, 2004) and squatting (Vasudevan, 2015a; 2015b) might also serve similar social, political and spatial functions. Similarly, the growing visibility of migration in Europe and other places around the globe (Gill et al, 2014; Papadopoulos and Tsianos, 2013) draws attention to how refugee camps (Ramadan, 2013a), and the encampments of migrants trapped on closed borders (Millner, 2011; Rygiel, 2011) simultaneously provide much needed shelter for people. These emergent encampments draw attention to the political, economic and environmental injustices and inequalities that migrants are fleeing, while at the same time creating a visible protest of the exclusionary immigration and border regimes.

As Sam Halvorsen points out in his chapter (Chapter Ten), drawing on ideas from Henri Lefebvre (1978) and John Holloway (2010), protest camps are spaces of 'territorial autogestion' in which groups of people develop forms of collective self-management autonomously from the state and corporate interests. These generative, prefigurative experiments in post-capitalist forms of social organisation have been repeatedly celebrated by activists and academics interested in the functioning of protest camps (Feigenbaum and Frenzel, forthcoming). We share that excitement for the possibilities offered by protest camps. Yet, we are also concerned by the different ways in which the occupation of land and public space by protest camps can have deeply problematic colonising tendencies. For example, when protesters occupy urban public spaces, they frequently invade spaces that homeless and other vulnerable groups have previously made their own. One key problematic here pertains to different views on visibility. While politically oriented squatters and campers often seek to increase the visibility of their encampments, destitute or homeless campers sometimes try to avoid the public gaze, because invisibility provides more security for their shelter.

In settler colonial contexts, it can be deeply problematic to celebrate 'occupying' others' land. This question was raised by a number of indigenous activists and their allies during the height of the Occupy movement in North America in 2011 (Decolonize Oakland, 2011; Kilibarda, 2012; POC National Statement, 2012). The contestation over the colonial implications of Occupy(ing) serves to highlight the connections between decolonisation and struggles for territorial control. As two chapters in this section highlight (see Thompson (Chapter Eleven), and Barker and Ross (Chapter Twelve)), indigenous groups across North America and elsewhere continue to use protest encampments and land occupations as a means of reclaiming sovereignty over stolen land, and maintaining control over land threatened with 'development' (Barker, 2012; Johnson, 1996).

The chapters in Part Two also question how certain 'publics' are brought into being by protest camps, while the existence of others might be elided or erased. These are fundamental questions about the complex (and contradictory) ways in which camps position themselves in relation to what is outside them. To occupy a space with a protest camp is to claim territory. But, over time, the defence of that territory and, in particular the physical demands bound up with the act of camping, can come to overshadow the original cause or demands of the camp. Chapters in this section also reflect on the constitutive power of the protest camps as a political and communicative space.

Here the spatial character of the protest camp as its own sphere of life and communication creates a disposition between the two, something that leads to various relationships from clear cut antagonism between 'the camp' and 'the outside' to more heterotopic overlaps, as well as more blurred boundaries in communication and action.

Overview of the chapters

This section consists of six chapters. Chapter Nine is written by a trio of British-based scholar-activists. In their chapter, Bertie Russell, Raphael Schlembach and Ben Lear examine the recent history of protest camps concerned with climate justice in the UK. The Camp for Climate Action was an environmental direct action movement active in 2006–11. Climate Camp adopted a repertoire of protest camps and direct action on the issue of climate change. Unlike previous protest camps in the UK that were set up to respond to a government proposal (such as road building, or the siting of US nuclear weapons) or summit camps that offered a convergence space for alter-globalisation protesters, the Climate Camp consciously choose the time and place for its emergence in an attempt to break from a previous cycle of 'summit hopping'. Climate camps emerged with the aim of combining high impact activism with low impact living and education on the root causes of climate change. The emphasis lay on demonstrating a radical politics in the present rather than an indeterminate future. Drawing on published statements and press releases, as well as extensive militant ethnographic research (Schlembach, 2011; Russell, 2014), the trio trace the development of this protest movement and analyse its attempts at embodying a prefigurative space. More than this, though, they question whether the act of camping, of continuing with the tactic of organising annual Camps for Climate Action ended up becoming as important for the campers as the environmental issues they were contesting and that this dynamic served to inhibit tactical innovation in response to a changing political climate. They argue that it was the refrain of the recurring camp-form that served as a straightjacket on the political imaginary. Responding to the issues raised in Part One, the chapter also asks whether the broad constituencies created in the climate camp diluted some of the more radical positions of climate activism, in particular in departing from the antagonistic positioning towards the political status quo. This is particular the case when climate camps focused on ostensibly neutral 'scientific evidence', which might be considered a de-politisation of the climate camp movement.In Chapter Ten Sam Halvorsen examines the case of the Occupy London camp(s) and argues that the protest camp is inevitably susceptible to fetishisation which he understands as the subordination of process to form. He begins by examining the work of Henri Lefebvre and John Holloway – two authors who discuss the challenges of creating counter power from below – in order to ground the discussion in theoretical debates surrounding fetishisation and institutionalisation. Based on militant research conducted with Occupy London the remainder of the chapter examines the losing of Occupy London's principal occupied space, the camp outside St Paul's Cathedral, and points toward a wider set of issues surrounding protests camps and territorial forms of struggle. In this regard, he returns to themes raised by Russell, Schlembach and Lear in their chapter about the refrain of the Camp for Climate Action. Halvorsen concludes his chapter by conceptualising the protest camp as an antagonistic form that necessarily exists against-and-beyond the social movements that constitute it.

The next two chapters both address the tense debates about the 'occupation' of public space by non-indigenous protest movements in the settler colonial context of North America. In Chapter Eleven, AK Thompson, critically evaluates the political claims advanced by anti-colonial critics of the Occupy movement in the United States since 2011 who proposed that the movement's allegiance to 'occupation' (the act of setting up protest camps, as Jessica Yee (2011) put it, in 'different places that symbolise greed and power') put it at odds with the politics of decolonisation. Drawing on theoretical contributions from Walter Benjamin, Frantz Fanon and Carl Schmitt, and through a review of two case studies (the 1968 student occupation of Columbia University and the 1969 occupation of Alcatraz by Indigenous activists) in which anti-colonial activists in the United States explicitly embraced occupation as a form of anti-colonial resistance, Thompson demonstrates that – far from being decolonisation's antithesis – occupation is in fact an inescapable feature of politics itself. In addition to providing pointed rejoinders to some of the Occupy movement's most vocal detractors, Thompson's case studies suggest that, although 'occupation' is undoubtedly part of the colonial repertoire, it can also be an effective aspect of anti-colonial resistance as well.

In the face of ongoing Canadian colonialism and displacement of Indigenous people, Adam J. Barker and Russell Ross argue in Chapter Twelve that blockading has become an important tactic through which Indigenous communities reassert their traditional forms of place-based culture and governance. Their chapter examines three important reclamation sites in Canada over the past 25 years, ranging from the spontaneous and relatively-short lived blockades of the Oka Crisis near the Kanesatake and Kahnawake Mohawk reserves in Quebec (1990), through the long-term Anishinaabe anti-clearcutting blockade at Grassy Narrows in northern Ontario (begun in 2002), to the growing and evolving anti-pipeline reclamation site in Unist'ot'en territory, in the British Columbia interior, which began in 2009. They argue that these three sites can reveal important lessons about Indigenous resurgence and the efficacy of protest camps as a tactic for reoccupying stolen land.

In Chapter Thirteen Uri Gordon draws from his own experience in protest camps to reflect on challenges of creating these home places in ways that contest and offer real alternatives to the state and representative democracy. The success and power of the politicising of the home place creates problems, in particular, when there is gap between the representation of this power in symbolic figures or spokespeople and the embodied power of the camp. Gordon points to the conflicted relationship between the engagement of social movement politics on a symbolic terrain and the actual lived reality of protest camps. In his auto-ethnographic account of the Israeli protest camps against housing shortages he indicates how the split between the mediatised 'founders' of the protest camp and the campers themselves eventually undermined the antagonistic power created in the camp (Fenster and Misgav, 2015; Schipper, 2015). Proposed reforms for a more horizontal structure of decision-making on a national basis were also deliberately undermined by a group of leaders and political advisers that usurped the political process. This finally led to the dissolution and defeat of one of the most powerful recent social movements in Israel. Gordon shows that protest camps draw their power from the lived experience in the camps, highlighting the centrality of the radical democracy experienced here.

Chapter Fourteen, by Maryna Shevtsova, compares two protest camps that occurred at Independence Square (Maidan Nezalezhnosti) – in Kiev, Ukraine – the first in 2004 and the second (Euromaidan) in 2013–14. This chapter examines how the two camps both resembled and differed from each other. The Euromaidan protest camp, Shevtsova argues, marks the development of Ukrainian civil society towards a more radically democratic and horizontal form of politics. The chapter covers issues as resistance practices used by the protesters, their resource mobilisation strategies, and the emerging approaches to governance and representation in the two camp's decision-making processes. Shevtsova highlights the growing Ukrainian nationalism present in the 2013 camp, and the participation of Nationalist and even fascist groups in the camp. Tensions thus emerged between two tendencies visible in Maidan-Sich 2014, namely the empowering moment of a more horizontal and self-organised protest camp and the emergence of a broader political constituency in the camp, which united less around a particular political outlook, but more broadly though a rejection of political elites and Ukrainian nationalism.

The last chapter of Part Two, Chapter Fifteen, written by Andrew Davies, examines Anna Hazare's August 2011 fast against corruption conducted in New Delhi, India. This fast galvanised one of the most high-profile political mobilisations in India for many years, and attracted widespread media coverage. Davies argues that viewing Hazare's fast and the accompanying infrastructures as a protest camp offers a more contextually grounded and nuanced understanding of the events surrounding the fast. Davies' contribution also broadens understandings of protest camps to include a wider range of occupations of public space. The chapter does this by examining the conceptual debate about civil society that structured many commentaries on Hazare's fast. These were often based on Partha Chatterjee's concept of 'political society', in which 'civil' society is seen as an elite zone which excludes marginal communities who instead occupy 'political' society. While conceptually useful, the chapter argues that a protest camps-based approach helps to interrogate the divide between civil/political society, and that such an approach to the Anna Hazare fast would create space for more ethnographic, grounded accounts of political practice.

Uniting all chapters is a sense of tension that emerges from the power of protest camps to bring together different people and their perspectives, often in opposition to the status quo and against governing elites, while creating their own constituent spaces of counter-power. The collective power of the many, while sometimes productive in contesting the status quo, also produces questions about the political orientation of camps themselves. The boundaries to the outside, often experienced physically in camps, may also serve the formation of new identitarian politics which might not necessarily be considered progressive, principally by excluding those who are not part of the camp. Indeed, the anti- or post-politics explicitly present in many of the camps discussed here, may find its reason precisely in the territorial and experiential form of organisation that represents political questions in space. Protest campers thus need to be reflexive about the dangers of territorial politics and find ways of addressing these contradictions head-on.

References

Barker, A.J. (2012) 'Already occupied: Indigenous peoples, settler colonialism and the occupy movements in North America', *Social Movement Studies*, 11(3-4), 327–34.

Barker, A. J. (2015) '"A direct act of resurgence, a direct act of sovereignty": reflections on idle no more, indigenous activism, and Canadian settler colonialism', *Globalizations*, 12(1), 43–65.

Brown, G. and Yaffe, H. (2014) 'Practices of solidarity: opposing apartheid in the centre of London', *Antipode,* 46(1): 34–52.

Decolonize Oakland (2011) 'Decolonize Oakland: creating a more radical movement', 4 December, http://occupyoakland.org/2011/12/decolonize-oakland/.

Doherty, B., Plows, A. and Wall, D., 2007, 'Environmental direct action in Manchester, Oxford and North Wales: a protest event analysis', *Environmental Politics*, 16(5), 804–824.

Feigenbaum, A. and Frenzel, F. (forthcoming, 2017), 'Austerity and the post-capitalist politics of protest camps: experiments in autonomy at Occupy London', in P. Bennett and J. McDougall (eds) *Popular Culture and the Austerity Myth: Hard Times Today*, London: Routledge. pp 123–38.

Fenster, T. and Misgav, C. (2015) 'The protest within protest: feminism and ethnicities in the 2011 Israeli protest movement', *Women's Studies International Forum*, 52, 20–29.

Frenzel, F. (2014) 'Exit the system? Anarchist organisation in the British climate camps', *Ephemera*, 14(4), 901–921.

Gill, N., Conlon, D., Tyler, I. and Oeppen, C. (2014) 'The tactics of asylum and irregular migrant support groups: disrupting bodily, technological, and neoliberal strategies of control', *Annals of the Association of American Geographers*, 104(2), 373–381.

Holloway, J. (2010) *Crack Capitalism*. London: Pluto Press.

Johnson, T. R. (1996) *The Occupation of Alcatraz Island*. Urbana and Chicago, IL: University of Illinois Press.

Juris, J. S., Ronayne, M., Shokook-Valle, F. and Wengronowitz, R. (2012) 'Negotiating power and difference within the 99%', *Social Movement Studies: Journal of Social, Cultural and Political Protest*, 11(3/4): 434–440.

Khasnabish, A. (2008) *Zapatismo Beyond Borders: New Imaginations of Political Possibility*. Toronto: University of Toronto Press.

Kilibarda, K. (2012) 'Lessons from #Occupy in Canada: contesting space, settler consciousness and erasures within the 99%', *Journal of Critical Globalisation Studies*, 5, 24–41.

Lefebvre, H. (1978) 'Space and the state', in N. Brenner and N. Elden (eds) (2009) *State, Space, World: Selected Essays. Henri Lefebvre*. London: University of Minnesota Press, pp 223–253.

Leidinger, C. (2015) *Zur Theorie Politischer Aktionen – Eine Einführung [A Theory of Political Activism: An Introduction]* Berlin: Edition Assemblage.

Li, F. (2015) *Unearthing Conflict: Corporate Mining, Activism and Expertise in Peru*. Durham, NC: Duke University Press.

McCurdy, P. (2011) 'The fragility of Dissent!: mediated resistance at the Gleneagles G8 Summit and the impact of the 7/7 London bombings', *Cultura, lenguaje y representación: revista de estudios culturales de la Universitat Jaume I*, 9, 99–116.

Merrifield, A. (2013) *The Politics of the Encounter: Urban Theory and Protest Under Planetary Urbanization*. Athens: University of Georgia Press.

Millner, N. (2011) 'From "refugee" to "migrant" in Calais solidarity activism: re-staging undocumented migration for a future politics of asylum', *Political Geography*, 30(6), 320–328.

Nicholls, W. (2009) 'Place, networks, space: theorising the geographies of social movements', *Transactions of the Institute of British Geographers*, 34(1), 78–93.

Papadopoulos, D. and Tsianos, V. S. (2013) 'After citizenship: autonomy of migration, organisational ontology and mobile commons', *Citizenship Studies*, 17(2), 178–196.

POC National Statement (2012) 'For people who have considered occupation but found it is not enuf', *DisOccupy*, 24 April, http://disoccupy.wordpress.com/.

Ramadan, A. (2013a) 'Spatialising the refugee camp', *Transactions of the Institute of British Geographers*, 38(1), 65–77.

Ramadan, A. (2013b) 'From Tahrir to the world: the camp as a political public space', *European Urban and Regional Studies*, 20(1), 145–149.

Robinson, S. (1994) 'The Aboriginal Embassy: an account of the protests of 1972', *Aboriginal History*, 49–63.

Routledge, P. (1997) 'The imagineering of resistance: Pollok Free State and the practice of postmodern politics', *Transactions of the Institute of British Geographers*, 28(3), 359–376.

Routledge, P. (2003) 'Convergence space: process geographies of grassroots globalization networks', *Transactions of the Institute of British Geographers*, 28(3), 333–349.

Russell, B. (2014) 'Beyond activism/academia: militant research and the radical climate and climate justice movement(s)' *Area*, 47(3), 222–29.

Rygiel, K. (2011) 'Bordering solidarities: migrant activism and the politics of movement and camps at Calais', *Citizenship studies*, 15(1), 1–19.

Schipper, S. (2015) 'Urban social movements and the struggle for affordable housing in the globalizing city of Tel Aviv-Jaffa', *Environment and Planning A*, 47(3), 521–536.

Schlembach, R., 2011, 'How do radical climate movements negotiate their environmental and their social agendas? A study of debates within the Camp for Climate Action (UK)', *Critical Social Policy*, 31(2), 194–215.

Stahler-Sholk, R., Vanden, H. E. and Becker, M. (eds) (2014) *Rethinking Latin American Social Movements: Radical Action from Below*. Lanham, MD: Rowman and Littlefield.

Vasudevan, A. (2015a) 'The autonomous city: towards a critical geography of occupation', *Progress in Human Geography*, 39(3), 316–37.

Vasudevan, A. (2015b) 'The makeshift city: towards a global geography of squatting', *Progress in Human Geography*, 39(3), 338–359.

Vasudevan, A. (2015c) *Metropolitan Preoccupations: The Spatial Politics of Squatting in Berlin*. Oxford: Wiley Blackwell.

Wolford, W. (2004) 'This land is ours now: spatial imaginaries and the struggle for land in Brazil', *Annals of the Association of American Geographers*, 94(2), 409–424.

Yee, J. (2011) 'Occupy Wall Street: the game of colonialism and further nationalism to be decolonized from the "Left"', *Racialicious*, 30 September, www.racialicious.com/2011/09/30/occupy-wall-street-the-game-of-colonialism-and-further-nationalism-to-be-decolonized-from-the-left/.

NINE

Carry on camping?
The British Camp for Climate Action as a political refrain

Bertie Russell, Raphael Schlembach and Ben Lear

Introduction

The security preparations for the London 2012 Olympic Games not only involved 'air security' in the form of surface-to-air missiles stationed on the roof of an East London tower block; organisers also had to reckon with the possibility of protests within the Olympic Park itself. After all, there had been recent waves of social unrest and peaceful occupations in the capital, from student demonstrations via the August 2011 riots to Occupy LSX which had encamped outside St Paul's Cathedral that previous winter. In a bizarre twist, for the purpose of delivering a 'safe and secure' Games, Home Secretary Theresa May thus had 'tents and camping equipment' banned from Olympic venues. The police were advised to deal swiftly 'with anyone who tried to flout the ban' (Home Office, 2012). That tents and camping equipment were explicitly highlighted as potential tools for civil disobedience tells us something about the nature of protest post-Occupy.

The symbolic value of the 'tent' as signifier of some form of 'radical protest desire' is *not* however universal, the act of camping fulfilling a different organisational role in different instances. This chapter reflects on the tent becoming not only a signifier – a potential weapon of opposition to government policies and national event management in Britain – but a *refrain*. Whereas the 'tent' may have been a symbol of protest in Occupy and post-Occupy Britain, the 'camp' had played a more vital function in the cycle of struggle that had come before it. Focusing on the Camp for Climate Action in Britain (climate camp hereafter) this chapter argues that 'camping' exceeded its role as either movement repertoire or protest symbol, becoming a central movement refrain that ultimately constrained the possibility of a development in political praxis.

The climate camp was a UK-based environmental direct action network which staged large-scale protest camps and actions between 2006 and 2011. Unlike previous protest camps in the UK which had been defensive or reactive in nature, the climate camp consciously set out to choose the time and location of its activity based on its own political agenda in an attempt to break from a previous cycle of 'summit hopping'. The climate camps set out to combine 'high-impact activism with low-impact living' alongside education on the root causes of climate change. With an emphasis on the use of horizontal consensus decision-making, these camps strove to embody a commitment to prefigurative politics; the emphasis lay on demonstrating a radical politics in the present rather than waiting for an indeterminate future. Over almost five years, it made headlines, allies and enemies as well as providing a space for developing the skills and politics of many activists who continue to work on climate-related issues or who are now involved in anti-austerity struggles.

Despite the apparent consistency of the organisation, in 2011 the climate camp disbanded itself at the end of a week-long strategy meeting. Contrary to any reading that would suggest this was due to a lack of 'good ideas' or personnel, or the passing into irrelevance of climate change as a political issue, this chapter argues that it was the *camp-form* itself that foreclosed any development in the organisation's praxis. Utilising Deleuze and Guattari's (2005) concept of *the refrain*, it is suggested that the camp-form went from operating as line of flight – a trajectory around which new forces could coalesce – to a straight-jacket of the political imaginary. Drawing on published statements and press releases, as well as extensive militant ethnographic research and our previous research (Pusey and Russell, 2010; Schlembach, 2011; Schlembach et al, 2012; Russell, 2014), we hope to illustrate that the camp-form cannot be reduced to either a symbolic gesture nor a protest tool, but must be understood as a complex compositional element that variously enabled and suffocated political opportunity.

While recognising the climate camp as a contested space (Saunders and Price, 2009) for the development of prefigurative politics, solidarities and affects within the broad environmental movement, we want to critically assess its political trajectory and attempts at instigating large-scale social change. We want to engage seriously with its central aims and analyse the relationship between these aims and the specific movement repertoire chosen – camping. As protest camps receive a new burst of theoretical attention in the wake of Occupy camps and those seen in Southern Europe (Frenzel et al, 2014), it is important that preceding movements which utilised the camp as a political form also receive analysis. The legacy of the climate camps is a mixed one, with some success in participant mobilisation, individual campaigns and 'public pedagogy' (McGregor, 2015) yet ultimately little effect on wider public discourse or systemic change (Bergman, 2015). While its mobilising power, in part based on the vibrant mix of prefigurative and mass direct action strategies (North, 2011), was relatively high in the period of low social struggle in which it operated we hope to highlight the risks a political movement faces of being 'locked' into specific movement repertoires that can take precedence over other considerations.

Situating the climate camps

In the initial phase of its lifespan, and in the discussions that led to its establishment, climate camp activists made frequent references to their political history and their involvement in the alter-globalisation movements and in environmental direct action (EDA) (Schlembach, 2011). The alter-globalisation movement had its British coming-out party in the summer of 1999 when several action networks came together in the City of London for the 'Carnival against Capitalism'. When the G8 returned to British shores in 2005, to Gleneagles in Scotland, it was met by large-scale protest. The *HoriZone*, an explicitly radical 'eco-village', was used as a base camp for the G8's more radical opponents.

While this tapped into an international process of anti-summit events, for many the specific national context was more important. Since the 1990s Britain had seen a wave of environmental direct actions, many of which were launched from protest camps. They had shown opposition to the road-building programme of the Thatcher government at Newbury bypass, delayed the construction of Manchester airport's second runway, and tore up fields of genetically-modified crops. Much of this had been under the umbrella label of the Earth First! network (Wall, 1999; Seel and Plows, 2000; Doherty et al, 2003; 2007; Plows et al, 2004). Thus, the *HoriZone* was an expression of the UK EDA movement as well as the G8 summit. It was here that the activists who would begin the climate camp met and began thinking through alternatives to summit hopping and forms of activity which would put climate change firmly on the agenda. From its conception, the camps were thus created at least in part as strategic attempts to break from the calendar of 'counter-summits' that had become a stultifying pattern of the alter-globalisation movement.

With its first manifestation at Drax power station in August 2006 – almost exactly one year after the 2005 anti-G8 protests in Gleneagles – the climate camp needs to be understood not as a separate entity to that which came before, but as a tactical move by some within the alter-globalisation movement to address this perceived shortcoming of the anti-capitalist left. Rather than a separate 'campaign' or 'organisation' emerging with a principle concern of addressing climate change, the climate camp was an outgrowth of the movement, an affirmative attempt to rupture the patterns of counter-summit mobilisations from which it came. While climate change was a concern in its own right, it was its potential to act as a conduit in the reformation of the anti-capitalist movement that led to it becoming a focus for a significant portion of the post-2005 radical left which formed the majority of the initial organising core.

By situating it within the context of ongoing campaigns and previous mobilisations, the important thing to note, then, is that the climate camp did not see itself as a social movement in itself. Rather it was to be regarded as an event or moment in a larger movement going back for decades which was international in outlook (Schlembach, 2011). Some even went so far back as to claim that climate camps were part of a movement of resistance against land enclosures. But in the specific context of the British anti-capitalist movement the climate campers also stood in a peculiar relation to the wider British left. In contrast to established coalitions or political parties, the camp organisers rejected the possibility of the network becoming a unified organisation and instead saw their camps as loose convergences of those prepared to use direct action and non-hierarchical decision-making to fight 'the root causes of climate change' (see Plows, 2008; Saunders, 2008; 2012; Mercea, 2013).

This political history is important if we want to understand the forms and practices that gave shape to the first climate camp and created its path dependency for later actions. To name just a few examples, the establishment of regional sub-groups in the camps, dubbed neighbourhoods or barrios, was an idea inspired by popular uprisings in Latin America and had become a popular organisational tool at other European convergences. The use of tripods to hold camping land, here made of scaffolding poles, had been successfully employed in tree defence camps in Australia and anti-roads protests in the UK. The consensus-models of group decision-making and the affinity group system for mass actions referred back to the criticisms of top-down control in political organisation brought by anarchist and feminist activists. In contrast to the Trotskyist organisations which dominated the British radical left, the climate camp was heavily influenced by anarchist perspectives (Frenzel, 2014).

The group's central events were large camps which took place annually from the summer of 2006 until 2010, attracting thousands of participants and significant media interest. Organised around the aims of 'low-impact living, education and high-impact direct action', they functioned as a base for mass direct action against chosen 'targets'. Schlembach et al (2012, 813) described the camps as such: 'An extensive programme of workshops and debates facilitated networking and strategizing, while an impressive logistical operation provided a working example of low-impact and non-hierarchical living.' They finally disbanded in 2011 to 'allow new tactics, organizing methods and processes to emerge in this time of whirlwind change' (Camp for Climate Action, 2011).

The first camp was established as a week-long protest not far from the coal-fired power station Drax, Yorkshire, in 2006. Several hundred people assembled to show dissent against an energy policy that was heavily in favour of non-renewable sources, foremost coal. Attempts to 'shut them down' were thwarted by a heavy police presence throughout the week of action, but the camp made international news headlines. Seemingly sanctioned by a scientific consensus that would dictate drastic social and lifestyle changes to limit the negative effects of anthropogenic global warming (Bowman, 2010), the group grew in size and notoriety when, in 2007, it pitched its tents on a squatted field in the vicinity of Heathrow airport, one of Europe's largest aviation hubs. The Heathrow camp saw the first large-scale political disagreement. Some believed that the focus on flying put the emphasis not so much on social change but on individuals' responsibilities to change their consumer behaviours and to 'fly less'. But buoyed by media attention and unprecedented opportunities to 'get our message out there', including on social media (Mercea, 2013), the 2008 camp returned to the issue of energy policy with a protest action at another coal-fired power station, Kingsnorth in Kent.

Throughout the course of their lifecycle, one noticeable effect of the climate camps was the resonance of camping as a form of action and its adoption into the wider radical protest repertoire. Climate camps were held in countries including France, Germany and Australia and these replicated the UK model (see for example Rosewarne et al, 2014). Receiving large media attention climate campers found it difficult to deviate from what appeared to be a successful tactic. As an example, in 2009 British activists mobilised against the G20 summit in London and, under the banner of 'G20 Meltdown', held a large protest outside the Bank of England. Alongside this the climate camp organised a day-long 'camp in the city' outside the nearby European Climate Exchange in order to focus explicitly on the negative effects of carbon trading. While anti-G20 protesters pushed against police lines to escape a containment cordon that was to keep demonstrators immobile, climate campers attempted to blockade Bishopsgate overnight using pop-up tents. In the event, both sets of protesters were confronted with aggressive public order policing, which tragically resulted in the death of uninvolved bystander Ian Tomlinson (Greer and McLaughlin, 2010; 2012; on the policing of the 2008 and 2009 climate camps, see Baker, 2011).

The final two climate camp events, one on Blackheath Common in South East London and the other on land belonging to the Royal Bank of Scotland's headquarters on the outskirts of Edinburgh, saw increasing attempts at 'soul-searching'. Activists put time aside to discuss the changing nature of the political landscape, after the banking crisis of 2008 had put the spotlight back onto global capitalism. The camp organisers actively invited criticism and fresh perspectives, as long as they were not considered personal gripes or partisan differences. What the camp wanted to discuss were fundamental questions over its direction and strategy, such as its relationship to the state or to workers' organisations. Such strategic questions also included the opportunities and limits offered by the camping refrain.

While the changing political context in which the climate camp was operating led to shifts in its choice of camping sites we can see a clear repetition of form. Each camp tried to achieve the agreed upon aims in roughly the same ways – through a programme of educational events, concrete examples of low impact living and forms of direct action – and there was a strong resemblance between all the camps. Indeed, much of the same equipment was used year after year, stored in organisers' homes or repeatedly borrowed from the 'activist tat collective' – a collective who provide activists with resources such as large marquees. The camp was clearly a reflection of a certain set of political positions and inherited movement repertoires which were (re)produced through the education processes at the camp. Part of the education offered at the camps was also practical in nature – it would not be unusual for someone to attend a camp and leave having participated in facilitating a meeting, helping with the cooking, cleaning or waste disposal.

Combined with a decision making structure which emphasises conservative and slow changes, the proliferation of these skills and perspectives helped to replicate the climate camps in the form in which they were begun. British environmental protest camps since then have tended to look very similar as well, for example those staged by 'Reclaim the Power'. The relative homogeneity of climate camps as a form of political activity stands in contrast to the relative difference between Occupy camps. Whereas Occupy's viral spread can be attributed to an easily imitable, yet also customisable, form of action and a political imaginary which captured the public mood in a period of political instability, the climate camp was reliant on slower processes of movement building.

Political tensions

Despite its easily recountable history, as expressed in a lineage of events, the camp wasn't a homogenous, monolithic structure. The rhythm of annual camps shouldn't be read as evidence of a cohesive and consensual politics. As Saunders and Price (2009) and others have pointed out, the climate camp was a contested political space in which differing perspectives and traditions encountered one another in an attempt to agree the common goals. Although the climate camp has its origins in radical politics, its public visibility as an organisation attempting to engage with climate change and its ethos of openness and participation meant it attracted a wide and diverse range of participants. As well as those who would identify with radical, anti–authoritarian politics various other groupings and political traditions were visibly engaged in the process. Some of these groups would less consciously identify with radical political traditions but were mobilised through a concern with climate change in and of itself. As one self-defined liberal camper wrote:

'Many people have come into climate camp not from anarchist, anti-capitalist or activist backgrounds, but because they see climate change as a huge threat and climate camp as one of the best ways of trying to stop it' (Camper, 2010).

These various perspectives existed in tension with one another, becoming clearly visible in certain discursive spaces (such as plenaries, workshops, social media and publications) as well as when trying to make decisions. The long-term strategy of the climate change movement and the 'solutions' it should be proposing were central sites of political disagreement. Despite the presentation (and common perception) of the climate camps as anarchist in ethos, based on principles of horizontal decision-making and direct action, they were a forum in which the role of the state was fiercely fought over (Schlembach, 2011). Many argued that given the cataclysmic nature of climate change and its time-bounded nature, the climate change movement did not have the time to tackle the wider injustices caused by the state and capitalism. For these participants, state-driven and/ or market-based solutions would have to be mobilised in the interests of minimising carbon emissions. The planet simply did not have time for radical politics and radicals would have to wait until after the climate crisis to talk about changing economic and political systems of power.Science was mobilised as a form of expert knowledge in an attempt to bypass these explicitly political disputes (see Bowman, 2010; Schlembach et al, 2012). Research around climatic tipping points helped amplify the power of the apocalyptic imaginary which was being mobilised (Skrimshire, 2008; Swyngedouw, 2010) and campers frequently resorted to the use of science to justify what were essentially political choices. Rather than placing the challenge of alternative visions of social organisation in the foreground, the Heathrow camp chose to march behind a banner claiming it was 'armed only with peer reviewed science'.

Perhaps the most visible clash between these perspectives took place between activist-organiser Ewa Jasiewicz and the journalist George Monbiot in the pages of the *Guardian* newspaper (Monbiot, 2008; Jasiewicz, 2008). Responding to Jasiewicz's argument against state and market-based solutions to the climate crisis Monbiot argued:

> She [Jasiewicz] claims to want to stop global warming, but she makes that task 100 times harder by rejecting all state and corporate solutions. It seems to me that what she really wants to do is to create an anarchist utopia, and use climate change as an excuse to engineer it. Stopping runaway climate change must take precedence over every other aim. (Monbiot, 2008)

This led to a backlash from those with a more radical perspective. At the 2008 camp, in response to several workshops and plenaries making these kind of arguments, a 'large group of anti-authoritarian participants' wrote a flyer (Autonomous Anarchist Campers, 2010) arguing that the climate camp 'risk[ed] losing contact with its anti-capitalist and anti-authoritarian roots'.

Hence despite the external appearance of coherence and homogeneity, there was an ever-present set of disagreements and concerns regarding the praxis of the organisation. These long-term political discussions were usually resolved unsatisfactorily with an 'agreement to disagree' or the simple recognition that we 'needed to continue talking about our politics'. This was not due to an organisational hostility to change; attempts were made to respond to these internal tensions, along with the shifting political context precipitated by the financial crisis. Camps outside the London carbon trading exchange (2009) or the RBS headquarters (2010) were conscious attempts to respond to these internal and external pressures. Individual campers also became involved in other struggles seeking to bridge the gap between ecological and more traditional workers' movement struggles.

Notwithstanding these individual attempts to experiment with the limits of 'confronting the root causes of climate change', the breadth of perspectives within the climate camp failed to materialise any substantial change in the praxis of the organisation. The consistency in the camp's praxis masked an organisation that had an ongoing plurality of forces looking to transform it, and a breadth of critiques which although often welcomed within the organisation's process, were not incorporated into a shift in strategy, function or form. This inertia in political praxis cannot therefore be understood as a result of an unwillingness to change, or a lack of a collective self-awareness of the need to develop different strategies.

Camping as a political refrain

In the 1988 film *Rainman*, Tom Cruise plays Charlie Babbit, a narcissistic yuppie with an auto-destructive streak fuelled by his own self-aggrandisement. Upon his estranged father's unexpected death, Charlie discovers that he has an older brother Raymond, played by Dustin Hoffman, an autistic-savant with a particular capacity for calculation and a near-instant photographic memory. Following Charlie's kidnap of Raymond from the Walbrook psychiatric institution, the plot develops around the two brothers' relationship as Charlie looks to exploit his older brother's capacity to card-count at Las Vegas casinos. While Cruise's character softens as he becomes used to Raymond's autistic idiosyncrasies, he is ultimately unable to prevent the older brother's return to the psychiatric institution.

Throughout the film, Raymond Babbit illustrates a number of repetitive tendencies, a common characteristic of autism. These are manifested in routines such as his insistence on purchasing his boxer shorts at a specific K-Mart, his repetition of an Abbot and Costello sketch 'Who's on First?', and watching his favourite television show *Wapner* – which he has scheduled to the minute. On the occasions where Raymond is unable to fulfil one of these routines, it leads to an uncontrollable fear and panic until the routine is restored.

Raymond's peculiar little routines exemplify quite dramatically what Felix Guattari called 'ritournelles' – *refrains*. These refrains are not

155

simply odd characteristics that 'belong' to a specific subject/assemblage, but are rather constitutive of the subject/assemblage itself:

> Every individual, every group, every nation is thus 'equipped' with a basic range of incantatory refrains… They [make] use of [them] to affirm their social identity, their territory, and their internal cohesion; because each member of the group 'belonged' to the same sound-shifter, the refrain thus took on the function of the collective and asignifying subject of the enunciation. (Guattari, 2007, 107)

These refrains, gathered and held in consistency with one another, are what constitute an assemblage – they are what define and produce the stable character and content of any given thing. If these refrains become disrupted, it threatens to pull the consistency of the assemblage apart, a return to chaos of the thing. If there is a threat or a disruption to Raymond's refrains there would be 'a mistake in speed, rhythm, or harmony' of Raymond himself – it 'would be catastrophic because it would bring back the forces of chaos, destroying both creator and creation' (Deleuze and Guattari, 2005, 343). The terror that Raymond experiences when faced with a mistake in the rhythm of his refrains is rooted in a direct attack on his existential self, an upsetting of the coordinates that define Raymond's capacity to exist in the world. Raymond *is* his refrains.

As Deleuze and Guattari outline, the refrain provides a point of order and a circle of control that contribute to the consistency of an assemblage, what makes an assemblage both functional and coherent. Yet at the same time the refrain is something which should allow an assemblage to 'go forth', to connect with other assemblages and to *become*, such that 'what just a minute ago was a constituted function in the territorial assemblage has become the constituting element of another assemblage, the element of passage to another assemblage' (Deleuze and Guattari, 2005, 357). Raymond provides an image of a malfunctioning assemblage, one in which the body has become completely beholden to the territorialising force of the refrain. Rather than the refrain facilitating the assemblage to go forth – which demands a radical openness to *difference* – it instead comes to suffocate and restrict the body. The refrain comes to function as a 'black hole', arresting other potentials and preventing the assemblage from entering into processes of becoming.

Rather than the climate camp *per se*, we can thus trace the 'camping' refrain through a very particular period, perceiving it as both a vector of transformation and asphyxiation of a broader movement. Emerging in the mobilisation against the G8 in Gleneagles, the 'self-sufficient autonomous camp' – itself a complex but generally static assemblage of compost toilets, tents, dietary requirements, sleep patterns or dress codes – assumed the total set of functions of the refrain. It at once provided a point through which to help ground a movement, a territory within which other assemblages could impress on one another, but also a force of deterritorialisation.

At this stage what cohered the assemblage of the alter-globalisation movement was not the camp – which fulfilled a logistical role – but rather the 'act' of the counter-summit. With the 'movement' having ceased to move, caught in a rhythm of counter-summits that limited potentialities, the 'camp' became a line of flight that ruptured the assemblage of the alter-globalisation movement. What fulfilled a function at Gleneagles became a territorialising force of the Camp for Climate Action.

This tension – between holding on to the initial thrust and knowing when it has become detritus – underpinned the climate camp's existence, and the inability to resolve it was ultimately functional in the organisation's collapse. The demand that we 'discuss our politics' became a mainstay of the monthly or bi-monthly gatherings. This desire was generally quite poorly articulated, and often spiralled into calls for the organisation to make statements regarding its anti-capitalist character. Yet what ran at the core of these calls was a questioning of the very function of the organisation itself – while the refrain of the camp had served as an 'element of passage to another assemblage', it was facing the danger of becoming instinctual routine.

The camp form increasingly went from being facilitator to inhibitor, from a space of possibility to a closure of potentials. Across two meetings towards the end of 2008, there was a concerted action by some to bring this question to the table – again couched within the need to 'discuss our politics'. Out of a weekend-long gathering of over 100 people (of which there were eight that year), this introspective review became sidelined to a ten-minute discussion so as to prioritise 'working group' time – the functional groups that ensure the camp was a regular manifestation. Suggestions that it could be possible for the climate camp to explore new avenues for action were rapidly closed down.

The following meeting attempted to extend the discussion, which ultimately became substituted by the need to 'spend less time discussing the issues' and spend more time 'planning actions'. During a further reflection at a national gathering regarding how the organisation should act – on what it could *do* – it was suggested by one participant that "it's not possible for the climate camp to *not* do a camp – it wouldn't be the climate camp! It's what we do" (personal notes). Whether this intervention was met with sympathy or derision is unclear, but what appeared as a particularly limited perspective on an organisation's capacity can retrospectively be read as an astute account of the assemblage's limits.

As with Raymond Babbit and his repetitive behaviour, there is no sense in looking for an exterior logic or rationale that explains the necessity of the act. The routine manifestation of a camp had become an end in itself, such that the possibility of *not* camping posed an existential threat to the entire assemblage.

Conclusion: metamorphosis?

Gathered in a wintery country-house in Dorset for a week-long residential gathering at the beginning of 2011, 80 participants in the Camp for Climate Action came to a near-unanimous decision to suspend their collective organising for the coming year. In what ultimately became its final utterance, the organisation released a statement entitled *Metamorphosis* which suggested that the cessation of activity was 'intended to allow new tactics, organising methods and processes to emerge in this time of whirlwind change'. In lieu of any proposal regarding how the organisation could move forward, it ended itself.

Our thesis has been that the *inability* of the climate camp to metamorphose – to become something other than what it was – was not due to some circumstantial lack of 'good ideas' or personnel, nor the passing into irrelevance of either climate change or the capitalist arrangement of social relations that drives it. To the contrary, it was the refrain of the camp-form that became the straight-jacket of the political imaginary. What had once provided a trajectory around which new forces could coalesce had become a suffocating centripetal force that *prevented* new political praxis from emerging.

Put simply, acting through anything other than the camp-form posed a threat to the consistency of the organisation. Political possibility itself – which is to say, what could be considered a site of contestation – had become constrained to the point where it was necessary to force a catastrophic mistake in the rhythm of the organisation. It was thus with regret that the wintery meeting in Dorset conducted a sort of participatory wavy-hands harakiri, ending the organisation in the name of the *principles* of the organisation itself – *the climate camp is dead, long live the climate camp!*

With the climate camp now unlikely to stage any phoenix-like return, what strategic lessons can be drawn from this analysis of 'the camp' as an object of political protest? First and foremost (and perhaps paradoxically), it is not the camp-form itself that deserves particular focus or merit, but rather the context in which it arises; it is the function that proves interesting, not the form. Sitting down on a bus is an occurrence that takes place millions of times a day on every day of the year, yet only one of these instances entered the collective memory of the Civil Rights movement. From a compositional perspective, there is nothing universal to be said about the camp-form, one can only appreciate what role it has played in the past, and dream of what may play that role in the future. As the Camp for Climate Action's final *Metamorphosis* statement indicates, as contexts change, so will the practices of movements.

As such, the analysis of the camp-form expounded in this chapter can be extended – at least in part – to similar phenomena, such as the role of occupations in the British student movement (Endnotes, 2013), the party-rave form of *Reclaim the Streets* (Wall, 1999), or indeed the cycle of summit protests that were central to the alter-globalisation movement. What is more important is that the analysis is useful not only in assessing movements of the past, but in challenging those who fetishise specific forms rather than interpreting radical social change as both socially contingent and historically specific.

While we have focused on the camp-form, we're not looking to imply that other elements were not at play in the rise and fall of the Camp for Climate Action. Rather, our intention has been to challenge the perception that the 'camp' was simply a tool, a tactic among many to be applied by an organisation in pursuit of its goals. To the contrary, as a refrain it had become fundamental to the composition of the assemblage, to the point that if you took away the tent, you took away the organisation. What the climate camp would look like without a tent was a question that ultimately the organisation itself couldn't answer.

References

Autonomous Anarchist Campers (2010) 'An open letter to neighbourhoods', in *Shift Magazine* and Dysophia (eds) *Criticism Without Critique: A Climate Camp Reader*, http://dysophia.files. wordpress.com/2010/01/cca_reader.pdf.

Baker, D. (2011) 'A case study of policing responses to Camps of Climate Action: variations, perplexities, and challenges for policing', *International Journal of Comparative and Applied Criminal Justice* 35(2)' 141–165.

Bergman, N. (2015) 'Climate camp and public discourse of climate change in the UK', *Carbon Management*, doi: 10.1080/17583004.2014.995407.

Bowman, A (2010) 'Are we armed only with peer-reviewed science? The scientization of politics in the radical environmental movement', in S. Skrimshire (ed) *Future Ethics: Climate Change and the Apocalyptic Imagination*, London: Continuum, pp 173–196.

Camp for Climate Action (2011) 'Metamorphosis: a statement from the Camp for Climate Action', http://london.indymedia.org/articles/7700.

Camper, A. (2010) 'Letter from a liberal', in *Shift Magazine* and Dysophia (eds) *Criticism Without Critique: A Climate Camp Reader*, http://dysophia.files.wordpress.com/2010/01/cca_reader.pdf.

Deleuze, G. (1988) *Foucault*, Minneapolis, MN: University of Minnesota Press.

Deleuze, G. and Guattari, F. (2005) *A Thousand Plateaus*, London: Continuum.

Doherty, B., Plows, A. and Wall, D. (2003) 'The preferred way of doing things: the UK direct action movement', *Parliamentary Affairs*, 56(4), 669–686.

Doherty, B., Plows, A. and Wall, D. (2007) 'Environmental direct action in Manchester, Oxford and North Wales: a protest event analysis', *Environmental Politics*, 16(5), 804–824.

Endnotes (2013) 'The holding pattern', in Endnotes (eds) *Gender, Race, Class and Other Misfortunes,* Glasgow: Bell and Baine, pp 12–56.

Frenzel, F. (2014) 'Exit the system? Anarchist organisation in the British climate camps', *Ephemera*, 14(4), 901–921.

Frenzel, F., Feigenbaum, A. and McCurdy, P. (2014) 'Protest camps: an emerging field of social movement research', *The Sociological Review*, 62(3), 457–474.

Greer, C. and McLaughlin, E. (2010) 'We predict a riot: public order policing, new media environments and the rise of the citizen journalist', *British Journal of Criminology*, 50(6), 1041–1059.

Greer, C. and McLaughlin, E. (2012) '"This is not justice": Ian Tomlinson, institutional failure and the press politics of outrage', *British Journal of Criminology*, 52(2), 274–293.

Guattari, F. (2007) *The Machinic Unconscious: Essays in Schizoanalaysis.* New York: Semiotext(e).

Home Office (2012) 'Tents banned from Olympic sites', *News Story*, www.gov.uk/government/news/tents-banned-from-olympic-sites.

Jasiewicz, E. (2008) 'Sunday in the camp with George', *Guardian*, www.guardian.co.uk/commentisfree/2008/sep/05/greenpolitics.climatechange.

McGregor, C. (2015) 'Direct climate action as public pedagogy: the cultural politics of the Camp for Climate Action', *Environmental Politics*, 24(3), 342–362.

Mercea, D. (2013) 'Probing the implications of Facebook use for the organizational form of social movement organizations', *Information, Communication & Society*, 16(8): 1306–27.

Monbiot, G. (2008) 'Climate change is not anarchy's football', *Guardian*, www.guardian.co.uk/commentisfree/2008/aug/22/climatechange.kingsnorthclimatecamp.

North, P. (2011) 'The politics of climate activism in the UK: a social movement analysis', *Environment and Planning*, 43(7), 1581–1598.

Plows, A. (2008) 'Towards an analysis of the "success" of UK green protests', *British Politics*, 3(1), 92–109.

Plows, A., Wall, D. and Doherty, B. (2004) 'Covert repertoires: ecotage in the UK', *Social Movement Studies*, 3(2), 199–219.

Pusey, A. and Russell, B. (2011) 'The climate crisis or the crisis of climate politics?', *Perspectives on* Anarchist, www.anarchiststudies.org/node/423.

Rosewarne, S., Goodman, J. and Pearse, R. (2014) *Climate Action Upsurge: The Ethnography of Climate Movement Politics*. Abingdon: Routledge.

Russell, B. (2014) 'Beyond activism/academia: militant research and the radical climate and climate justice movement(s)', *Area*, doi: 10.1111/area.12086.

Saunders, C. (2008) 'Double-edged swords? Collective identity and solidarity in the environmental movement', *The British Journal of Sociology*, 59(2), 227–253.

Saunders, C. (2012) 'Reformism and radicalism in the climate camp in Britain: benign coexistence, tensions and prospects for bridging', *Environmental Politics*, 21(5), 829–846.

Saunders, C. and Price, S. (2009) 'One person's eu-topia, another's hell: climate camp as a heterotopia', *Environmental Politics*, 18(1), 117–122.

Schlembach, R. (2011) 'How do radical climate movements negotiate their environmental and their social agendas? A study of debates within the Camp for Climate Action (UK)', *Critical Social Policy*, 31(2), 194–215.

Schlembach, R., Lear, B. and Bowman, A. (2012) 'Science and ethics in the post-political era: Strategies within the Camp for Climate Action', *Environmental Politics*, 21(5): 811–28.

Seeds for Change Collective (2007) 'How to make decisions by consensus', in Trapese Collective (eds) *Do it Yourself: A Handbook for Changing our World*, London: Pluto, pp 63–77.

Seel, B. and Plows, A. (2000) 'Coming live and direct: strategies of Earth First!', in B. Seel, M. Paterson and B. Doherty (eds) *Direct Action in British Environmentalism*. London: Routledge, pp 112–132.

Skrimshire, S. (2008) 'Approaching the tipping point: climate risks, faith and political action', *European Journal of Science and Theology*, 4(2), 9–22.

Swyngedouw, E. (2010) 'Apocalypse forever? Post-political populism and the spectre of climate change', *Theory, Culture and Society*, 27(2/3), 213–232.

Wall, D. (1999) *Earth First and the Anti-Roads Movement*. London: Routledge.

TEN

Losing space in Occupy London: fetishising the protest camp

Sam Halvorsen[1]

Introduction

This chapter argues that the protest camp is inevitably susceptible to fetishisation – the subordination of process to form – and as such proposes that it be reconceptualised as an *antagonistic* form of activism, torn between the need to institutionalise social movements and the drive to subvert any form of institutionalisation. I start by drawing on the work of Henri Lefebvre and John Holloway – two authors who discuss the challenges of creating counter-forms from below – in order to ground the discussion in theoretical debates surrounding fetishisation and institutionalisation. Although the problem of fetishising the protest camp was discussed within Occupy camps back in 2011 (for example, Kall, 2011) there has been little theoretical reflection. The remainder of the chapter examines the losing of Occupy London's principal occupied space, the camp outside St Paul's Cathedral, and points toward a wider set of issues surrounding protests camps and territorial forms of struggle. I conclude by conceptualising the protest camp as an antagonistic form that necessarily exists against-and-beyond the social movements that constitute them.

Occupy London came to life on 15 October 2011, inspired not only by events in New York but by the explosion of protest camps worldwide. The movement set up two protest camps in London's financial district, in the courtyard of St Paul's Cathedral and a small park called Finsbury Square, lasting for four and a half and eight months respectively, making them two of the longest-standing Occupy protest camps. As in camps elsewhere, Occupy London created numerous working groups, focusing on everything from food and welfare to its very own *Occupied Times* newspaper. At its peak there were around 3,000 participants, but for most of the time numbers were in the hundreds.[2]

The chapter focuses on Occupy London's most prominent protest camp, at St Paul's, and is based on research that combines a seven-month ethnography, 43 in-depth interviews and archive analysis. My involvement in Occupy London, first as an occupier and later as a researcher, led me to frame my investigation as militant research: an 'intensification and deepening of the political…[that] starts from the understandings, experiences, and relations generated through organizing as both a method of political action and as a form of knowledge' (Shukaitis and Graeber, 2007, 9). To this extent, my research has been oriented not solely around academic questions but also around activist debates and concerns. Integrating academic and activist debates, and bridging the divide between theory and praxis is a challenging and often problematic process. The arguments presented here necessarily represent my own political standpoints, even if I have attempted to capture the diversity of opinions contained within Occupy.

Form, fetishism and institutionalisation

Fetishism, in which the material appearance of things obscures underlying social relations and the *process* of development, has informed the Marxist theories of John Holloway and Henri Lefebvre. Although writing in different times, both authors provide damming critiques of 'the fetishised and fetishising forms of bourgeois "politics" and "economics"' (Holloway, 1991, 230) (for example, the commodity, the state, the political party, abstract space) and explore possibilities for creating counter-forms from below (for example, communes, assemblies, Soviets). The protest camp seems to provide one of the most popular examples of counter-forms in the early twenty-first century. Engaging with the writings of Holloway and Lefebvre in more detail exposes a core tension for social movements struggling to create new forms – on the perennial risk of fetishisation, separating form from content – and the dangers of (re)creating barriers to grassroots struggle.

Across his texts in the years surrounding 1968, Lefebvre developed the notion of *autogestion*, translated as 'self-management', to describe the basis for alternative forms of organisation. Lefebvre (1979, 135) presented *autogestion* as a group's 'refusal' to accept passively its conditions of existence', giving examples such as the Paris Commune, the Russian Soviets and the anti-colonial struggle in Algeria (Lefebvre, 1966). In contrast to the static, fetishised forms of bourgeois political economy *autogestion* 'introduces and reintroduces the only form of movement' (Lefebvre, 1966, 149) in which 'the members of a free

164

association take control over their own life, in such a way that it becomes their work [oeuvre]' (p 150). While Lefebvre was cautious not to over-prescribe how the form of *autogestion* should appear, he nevertheless hinted at two key characteristics.

First, *autogestion* needs to take on a territorial form, occupying spaces beyond the domination of the state. Lefebvre (1991, 292, 382, 416) highlighted the need for *autogestion* to occupy 'territorial entities' that are autonomous of state and capital, something he later referred to as 'territorial *autogestion*': 'exerting pressure against the summits of state power and leading a concrete struggle for concrete objectives' (Lefebvre, 1978, 250). Elsewhere Lefebvre stated, 'I believe that *autogestion* initiatives are rooted, embedded within the soil' (Lefebvre, 1976, 163), emphasising the need for the production of a material space in which *autogestion* could develop. The protest camp is a good example of this.

Second, although Lefebvre understood *autogestion* through its negation of the form of the state (at least in the long run), he was sceptical that this *negativity* would be sufficient to sustain the bottom-up power of *autogestion* (Lefebvre, 1969). For Lefebvre (1966, 147), the key challenge of *autogestion* was to move beyond negation and 'to constitute itself as a power which is not that of the state'. A key form that *autogestion* must take is therefore that of an institution (Lefebvre, 1969), an institution that moves both against and beyond the state. For Lefebvre the failure of *autogestion* to constitute itself in some form of institution risks it being reappropriated by the state and its multiple forms of bureaucracy. Lefebvre's insistence on the need to institutionalise *autogestion* stands in stark contrast to Holloway's approach.

Holloway's concept of 'cracks' initially appears to describe a similar form to Lefebvre's *autogestion*: they arise through a 'break with the logic of capitalist society' through which 'a different way of doing things' emerges (Holloway, 2010, 49). Like Lefebvre, Holloway is particularly concerned with breaking the dominance of the state form through a dialectical process of de-fetishisation, negating and pushing towards qualitatively different values to those of capitalist production. Holloway (2010, 27–28) also acknowledges the importance of having a territorial base for cracks, through which new social relations and values can develop, and points in particular to recent developments in Latin America (see Zibechi, 2012). Although Holloway (2010, 28) stresses that cracks are not only 'spatial ruptures' but may also exist as temporalities or activities, it is clear that territory provides one important basis for counter-forms.

In contrast to Lefebvre, however, Holloway is adamant that negativity must remain as the basis for counter-forms, and warns that attempts to institutionalise them would be disastrous. For Holloway (2010) cracks can only exist as negation, a 'doing' that negates 'labour', a 'power-to' in negation of 'power-over', and it is only from this negation that alternatives can emerge. Crucially, however, cracks only exist in movement, as a process of cracking, a 'constant moving against and beyond that which is' (Holloway, 2010, 209). For Holloway, lack of movement inevitably leads to cracks being reappropriated back into capitalist production, because lack of movement implies a pause in negation, a break in the flight from capital (see Chapter Nine by Russell et al). Moreover, the act of institutionalising a movement into a fixed form is a process of *identification* that makes it vulnerable to co-option by practices of capitalist production. Sharing the same concern as Lefebvre, on the risk of alternative forms being reappropriated by capital, Holloway arrives at a radically different conclusion.

Nevertheless, in a recent conversation with Michael Hardt, who shares Lefebvre's desire to institutionalise alternative forms in order to break with capital, Holloway acknowledges that institutions may be inevitable, as long as they are understood as a moment of subversion. As Holloway states, 'perhaps the movement creates new institutions, but only as the water in a stream rests for a moment in pools and then flows on' (October 2011, section 6). In other words, 'institutionalise-and-subvert…a repeated process of rupture, of breaking, of negating' (October 2011, section 5). This acknowledgment provides a bridge to Lefebvre's desire for institutionalising counter-forms.

I suggest that the compromise of 'institutionalise-and-subvert' provides a useful way of conceptualising the form of the protest camp: a fixed moment within a broader social *movement*. Holloway (2010, 20) suggests that cracks are 'questions, not answers', a movement of walking forward and asking questions in the constant experimentation with other worlds. The institutionalisation of these questions in the form of the protest camp is a necessary moment in order for the movement to take stock of itself, and consider whether they are asking the right questions, and not heading in the wrong direction. As this book demonstrates, the form of the protest camps serves numerous functions, and is a crucial space through which new social relations and values are produced. Examining the protest camp in more detail, however, demonstrates its tendency to become fetishised as an inherently positive moment of struggle, and this is a key lesson from Occupy London.

Occupy London and the tactic of the protest camp

Interviewing occupiers some six months following the eviction at St Paul's (which took place on 28 February 2012), many commented on how the protest camp was only ever a tactic. This was a sharp contrast with my ethnographic experiences at the camp in the Winter of 2011. Following my interviews, it became clear that almost everyone I spoke too did, at least by then (Summer/Autumn of 2012), now look back on the occupation as only a tactic; one moment within a broader movement. Charlotte, who was active at St Paul's and involved in the anti-eviction efforts, told me:[3]

> We need to be clear that occupying, and tent cities...they are not the end in itself, that is not the goal. The goal is to overthrow the capitalist system, or at least to fix the broken system so that it serves the interests of people and planet, to take back control of our lives and become the people who are making the governing decisions instead of letting someone else do it. (Interview, 7 January 2013)

While Charlotte is unclear as to the relationship between Occupy and 'the capitalist system', her goal appears similar to Lefebvre's *autogestion*, the creation of a system based on 'taking back' control of our own lives. What is important is that she sees the protest camp as only one way of doing this, and clearly not the only way. In other words, there is something else going on, of which the occupation at St Paul's (and in other spaces) was only a part. Paul, another camper at St Paul's, expressed this to me in similar terms:

> It [occupying] is a tactic, and also a practical necessity, we need to come together openly and occupy space but not because it's an end in itself, but because we're trying to build you know, we're trying to rebuild a new society from the ground up...so it's a tactical thing...but it's also essential. (Interview, 3 September 2012)

Paul is more explicit that while occupation is only a tactic it is a *necessary* tactic as new social relations must be developed through concrete material forms. Resonating with Lefebvre's notion of territorial *autogestion*, Paul sees occupying as an 'essential' tactic and implies that social relations must be constructed in a territorial form, 'from the ground up'.

The protest camp is a particular territorial form of struggle that serves numerous purposes, and has long been central to social movements such as Occupy. Several interviewees highlighted the importance of gaining media attention and challenging the privatisation of public space, among other functions. Speaking to Rosia, she highlighted the importance of having a physical space through the protest camp:

> The physical presence of the camp was important in keeping the movement together, in at least keeping us together physically and, allowing people to work together and I think in the absence of the camps we wouldn't have seen this. It is a lot harder to work together now. (Interview, 16 November 2012)

This materiality is a key characteristic of the protest camp, central to its territorial form (on the importance of materiality and camps, see Arenas, 2014; Feigenbaum et al, 2013; Vasudevan, 2015). Although Holloway's (2010) cracks may exist as temporal or activity-based ruptures, the importance of a material base should not be overlooked, and is an important argument for the need to produce protest camps. At the same time, it is the materiality of the protest camp, as a delimited territorial form, which facilitated its fetishisation.

Fetishising the protest camp

For some the protest camp not only had practical functions but it represented the intense commitment and sacrifices that occupiers were prepared to make. Jane, who camped at St Paul's, explained this significance to me:

> I think it [occupying] has been a tactic of its time, and I'm sure it will continue, you know as a big tactic, I mean obviously Occupy, the tactic of occupying means a lot of things, it's a confrontation which is one thing that maybe appealed to the public…it was a direct confrontation and a courageous one and won at some personal cost of people suffering. People who saw it from outside appreciate that this was serious, and sleeping in the cold and giving up their day jobs and missing their families, and letting down their friends and losing their homes in some cases, those personal costs were really quite important. (Interview, 13 December 2012)

Jane suggested that the commitment and sacrifice associated with the protest camp was central to the wider support gained by the Occupy movement. Indeed, the materiality of the concrete under the tents and the cold weather were seen as highly visible symbols for the movement's struggle. The logic of commitment and sacrifice is something that Adbusters – the 'culture jamming' magazine who put together the first callout to Occupy Wall Street – sought to utilise when considering how Occupy in North America could tackle the long, cold winter ahead of them in 2011. In a 'tactical briefing' they suggested the following strategy: 'Heroically we sleep in the snow…we impress the world with our determination and guts…and when the cops come, we put our bodies on the line and resist them nonviolently with everything we've got' (Adbusters, 2011, section 5).

Jane's argument was based on a similar logic, and led her to argue strongly in favour of camping at St Paul's for as long as physically possible, holding the space to show the world how determined occupiers were to change it. She expressed this sentiment both in conversations before the St Paul's eviction and several months later in a follow-up interview. Inevitably, however, long-term protest camp occupations can lead to activist burnout and be difficult to sustain over time (see Feigenbaum et al, 2013). By committing oneself to the particular form of the protest camp, however, occupiers were increasingly unable to distinguish between the form of the protest camp and the social movement. As Nick told me, many occupiers were *fetishising* the camp:

> I think [some people] often fetishise the tactic into what the movement was, and so they saw the occupation not as a tactic but as something in itself, like if you're not occupying something you are not Occupy, and I think that's a mistake, and I think it's shortsighted, and I think it's politically immature in a way I suppose, I mean you know not falling in love with your tactic. (Interview, 21 February 2013)

In falling in love with the form of the protest camp it became increasingly difficult to imagine Occupy beyond the encampment at St Paul's [see Russell et al, Chapter Nine]. Paul expressed this fetishisation of the protest camp to me in different words:

> Some people got lost, they couldn't see the woods from the trees, and all they could see was the camp, and didn't see any wider purpose…so that was one of the problems,

> you get a group of people for whom the camp is an end in itself. (Interview, 3 September 2012)

Indeed, speaking to occupiers back in the Winter of 2011, it seemed that many had subsumed the Occupy movement into the form of the protest camp. It was this fetishisation of the protest camp that made discussions over whether we should voluntarily leave, before being evicted by the state, even more difficult. While there were occupiers who believed that we should voluntarily give up the camp, their voices were being little heard back in the Winter of 2011.

Fetishism is a constant issue for activism, especially when it attempts to constitute itself as a specialist form of changing the world, somehow outside or detached form everyday life. Activism is necessarily an ongoing process that is bound up and part of the world it is changing, and fixing it into a particular form gives it the appearance of independent existence. This leads to 'the separation of constitution and existence' in which the process of constituting the protest camp becomes divorced from its existence in its territorial form (Holloway, 2012, 168). The danger of fetishising a movement to a particular form is that you lose sight of the processes that are producing it, and there is a subsequent 'subordination of *we do* to *what is*' (Holloway, 2002, 243).

Protest camps are a particularly effective form of activism, allowing for more intense moments of rupture to come together with everyday rhythms of social reproduction (Halvorsen, 2015). At best, they are dynamic and productive space-times of activism, allowing for new social relations and values to be generated in place. Nevertheless, in the struggle to maintain the form of the camp itself, against threats of dispersion and the fear of losing space, there remains the tendency for the protest camp to be confused with the social movement. In Occupy London it seemed that many activists forgot about the importance of what they were doing inside the camp. One outcome of this was that less attention was given to negotiating the oppressive power relations and hierarchies on camp, issues widely noted in Occupy worldwide, and stark reminders of the continuity with colonial practices of occupation[4] (see Jones, 2012; Juris et al, 2012; Khatib et al, 2012). Will, who was involved in the *Occupied Times* newspaper and was camping at St Paul's, explained this issue to me:

> I had felt for a while before eviction that the space was being fetishised and that it was no longer a plus, I felt that we should leave it, I felt that occupying was a tactic and not a lifestyle or an end in itself and basically I sort of thought

that occupying a space…had all these practical positives to it, but as things developed…I mean a lot of my friends had been alienated already by various things and I think a lot of people had gone away and the space was becoming something a bit different, and I felt that in America them losing their space had been a bit of a blessing in disguise to a degree…I think that actually Occupy London might be more than it is now had the space gone a bit earlier…but I was really conscious and careful not to use [the *Occupied Times*] as a platform for what I felt should happen, because I didn't want to impose, we didn't want to impose, anything on anyone. (Interview, 19 December 2012)

Will's quote is important not only for highlighting how fetishisation of form can lead to alienation, but also due to his acknowledgment that he was reluctant to share his critique of the protest camp prior to eviction, in particular through the medium of the camp newspaper. Will seemed to be torn between empathy with his alienated friends, and commitment to the form of the protest camp, but unable to find a channel for internal critique. In this way, a sense of inertia developed on camp, and with the absence of any pre-defined end date for the occupation it appeared that we were to stay indefinitely. In other words, Occupy London had become institutionalised in the form of the camp. Paul developed this point further to me:

One of the problems with Occupy is that it's good at starting but it's not very good at stopping [protest camps] when they are no longer effective and useful. It's got a start button, but it's impossible to get any consensus agreement to say that we're going to end, unless you decide beforehand that we're just going to occupy for a week or something…the problem for us, with Occupy in St Paul's, as good in many ways as it was, it was also turning into a black hole that you would just be sucked into, but you couldn't get out of it in order to be politically active. (Interview, 3 September 2012)

In the weeks following 15 October 2011, with no planned end date in sight, the Occupy *movement* was increasingly fixing itself to the *moment* of the protest camp, and in so doing antagonisms and critiques were seemingly pushed to one side in favour of constituting a positive form of struggle.

This problem was confounded as we were simultaneously dragged into the logic of the court case. Although many Occupy camps in 2011 were quickly evicted and with little warning, Occupy London was pulled into a long and drawn-out court case, instigated by the City of London Corporation, the owners of the land underlying the camp. As the end of 2011 approached, Occupy London was directing its attention towards events in court, and there was little room on camp for discussing the voluntary ending of the occupation. As I recalled in my research diary:

> The focus of our movement was increasingly on the court case, with large numbers going down the road each morning to the Royal Courts of Justice to support our defence. Meanwhile, back at St Paul's, plans were being made for eviction. The 'outreach' working group were putting together a list of supporters who could be contacted at short notice to help the resistance. A logistics team had been set up to start planning where to take all the tents and materials that had built up on camp. And media were trying to get as much publicity as possible around our cause.
>
> Recently, in my conversations with fellow Occupiers, I was broaching the topic of leaving St Paul's and ending the camp. 'Was it a good idea to hold the space indefinitely?', I asked, 'or should we decide to leave on our own terms before being forced out by the state, a prospect ever more likely as the court case proceeded?' Yet there was something of a taboo in having these discussions on camp. For many the idea that we would voluntarily give up the space seemed absurd, and even tragic. Late one evening I talked to an Occupier whom I knew to be wholly committed to keeping the camp for 'as long as it takes'. 'We have a duty to be here', he told me, 'to show them we really mean it, and we're not going to take it any more. This isn't some holiday, this is the real thing. Yes, it's not going to be easy, but that's not the point. If we just pack up and go now what would that say?' I noticed teardrops rolling down his face as he stared me in the eyes, 'This camp means the world to me, and so many others. I'm not gonna let anyone take it away.' (Field notes, 15 December 2011)

This passage demonstrates how the court case contributed to the fetishisation of the protest camp, with many Occupiers focusing their attention on the defence of the site and away from the practices taking place within it, and others developing a logic of sacrifice noted earlier, in which an endless protest camp was seen to exemplify commitment to struggle. Although many Occupiers demonstrated a reflexivity in interviews with me several months after eviction, acknowledging that the protest camp is a tactic, in the intensity of occupying this seemed much more difficult. To this extent the *affective* nature of protest camps noted by Feigenbaum et al (2013) may be one further cause of their fetishisation, in which an intense 'lived space' (Lefebvre, 1991) develops that captures the dreams and desires of occupiers.

On 23 December 2011 we heard that the court's decision would be postponed until the New Year, and while many breathed a sigh of relief, some of us were concerned that to let the camp continue for much longer would risk doing damage to a movement that was increasingly suffering from difficult internal tensions. Yet many occupiers had invested their time and hope into the possibility of the court case reforming the legal system. As Rachel told me:

> Although I think it was a pity that it wasn't possible to come to consensus over leaving St Paul's together with dignity, I don't think that we could have backed out of the court case, too many lawyers has really put their guts into it as well, and with luck there was always a possibility that the law could be stretched and changed and in that case I don't think that we could have walked away because it would have been ignoring the possibility of changing something.

Thus, while the form of the protest camp was being fetishised by occupiers from below, it was being simultaneously reified by a territorial logic of the state's legal apparatus from above. In both cases the protest camp was being understood as a fixed product, a fetishised thing, which ignored the *living* antagonisms (Holloway, 2002) that lay at its heart. A failure to pay attention to and negotiate these antagonisms meant that the camp became an increasingly unpleasant space, with many supporters being alienated by it. The bailiffs eventually turned up at St Paul's on of 28 February 2012, four and a half months after the camp started. While a core set of Occupiers made a valiant attempt at defending the camp against eviction, the turn out on our final day was nothing like it had been at the start of Occupy, and by the early hours of the morning the camp had been cleared.

Conclusion: the antagonistic form of the protest camp

The protest camp is a significant form of activism, as this book makes clear, allowing for new social relations and values to be built in place, bringing together exceptional moments of rupture with everyday practices of social reproduction. This chapter has demonstrated that the significance of the protest camp – both to activists and also to those who seek to evict it – made it highly susceptible to fetishisation. All forms of activism have a tendency to become fetishised, especially when they are understood as exceptional ruptures from the mundane sphere of everyday life (see Anonymous, 1999; Chatterton, 2006; Halvorsen, 2015). Yet the protest camp seems particularly liable to being approached as a 'temporary autonomous zone' (Bey, 1991) and Feigenbaum et al (2013) highlight *exceptionality* as a defining feature.

Among the literature on Occupy there has been recognition of the risk of 'fetishising space' (for example, Hammond, 2013; Marcuse, 2011). It has been argued that in confusing means with ends, Occupy risked undermining its broader goals for social change at the expense of defending and maintaining an occupied space. Yet it is not 'space' per se that is fetishised, rather it is the *form* of the protest camp (a particular moment in the production of space). Indeed, the radical potential of the protest camp lies in those *social relations* being developed in the production of space, social relations that form the basis of 'cracks' in capitalism (Holloway, 2010). The challenge for activists and academics engaging with protest camps is to avoid its fetishisation and to push our attention beyond the particularity of its form, towards the social movement underlying it.

Activists have been forced to re-imagine Occupy beyond the form of the protest camp following evictions. For example, Occupy Wall Street and the Spanish *indignados* successfully built new territorial forms for their struggles, such as Occupy Sandy in New York or the move into urban neighbourhoods in Spain (see Davis and Duerson, 2012; Moreno-Caballud and Sitrin, 2011). Occupy London has shown a level of reflexivity in its post-camp phase, suggesting that activists have acknowledged the risk of fetishising the protest camp, even if they did not confront this issue during occupation. First, there has been a shift to other place-based territorial forms, such as the occupation of Friern Barnet Library that allowed Occupiers to build new relations with a North London community. Second, there has been a shift to temporally bound occupations in which the losing of space is accepted from the outset, for example in the short-term occupations of Parliament square in the build up to UK elections in 2015.

From an academic perspective, and by way of conclusion, I propose that one means of avoiding the fetishisation of the protest camp is to conceptualise it as a necessarily *antagonistic* form that will always have to struggle against-and-beyond itself. In their study of protest camps Feigenbaum et al (2013, 178) claim that antagonism is a central feature, without which protest camps 'lose their raison d'être to some extent'. They suggest, however, that unlike key precedents such as Tahrir Square in Egypt, Occupy's protest camps were never based on a clear antagonism given that they rejected any unifying demands or axes of confrontation. Antagonism does not only exist in relation to some externality, but is also an internal feature of protest camps. I suggest the antagonistic nature of the protest camp is not only in response to the multiple internal tensions and divides that are brought to the surface through the practice of occupying (see Halvorsen, 2015), but also due to the fetishisation of the protest camp – as a fixed, territorial form – which will inevitably exist against-and-beyond itself.

On the one hand, social movements need to fix themselves to particular territorial forms such as the protest camp, forms that allows for Lefebvre's '*autogestion*' or Holloway's 'cracks' to develop. On the other hand, this fixing to form inevitably leads to the institutionalisation of activism, posing barriers to the continual *movement* of struggle. Holloway's notion of 'institutionalise-and-subvert' is useful here for pointing towards the antagonistic, or dialectical nature of struggle that constantly pushes against itself. New social relations and values need a material form to develop, but their reliance on a form tends towards their subordination to it. Any institutionalisation of a movement must be accompanied by a constant subversion of the form it takes. It is not enough to simply produce the counter-form of the protest camp: it must be constantly subverted. We could view social movements, like capital, as existing in a productive tension between fixity and motion (see Schrader and Wachsmuth, 2012), and there is thus a risk of celebrating Occupy for its fixity, without recognising the inherent limitations to its form.[5] Protest camps always have a duration to them, and if movements do not define it themselves it will inevitably be imposed from elsewhere. Often eviction can come too early, and without warning, and numerous external factors come into play (see Feigenbaum et al, 2013). Yet it is important to acknowledge that protest camps are inherently limited, and limiting, forms and a central challenge for struggles such as Occupy is to embrace the losing (and leaving) of space and the *movement* towards new forms. Protest camps provide social movements with an antagonistic form that have great potential but will always need to be overcome in the struggle to create better worlds.

Notes

[1] The author wishes to acknowledge financial support by the Economic and Social Research Council (grant number S/J500185/1).

[2] Activists continue to organise under the name Occupy London at the time of writing (Summer 2015). For information on their activities, past and present, see http://occupylondon.org.uk/

[3] Pseudonyms are used for interviewees.

[4] A discussion of the power relations between Occupy London activists and the homeless community outside St Paul's is beyond the scope of this chapter, but would well exemplify this.

[5] Others have argued that social movements could be understood through a *circulation of struggle* (Merrifield, 2013) or commons (Dyer-Witheford, 2006).

References

Adbusters (2011) 'Tactical briefing #18', *Adbusters*, 14 November, www.adbusters.org/blogs/adbusters-blog/adbusters-tactical-briefing-18.html.

Anonymous (1999) 'Give up activism', *Do or Die*, 9, 160–166.

Arenas, I. (2014) 'Assembling the multitude: material geographies of social movements from Oaxaca to Occupy', *Environment and Planning D: Society and Space*, 32(3), 433–449.

Bey, H. (1991) *T. A. Z: The Temporary Autonomous Zone, Ontological Anarchy, Poetic Terrorism*. Brooklyn, NY: Autonomedia.

Chatterton, P. (2006) '"Give up activism" and change the world in unknown ways: or learning to walk with others on uncommon ground', *Antipode*, 38(2), 259–282.

Davis, R. and Duerson, M. H. (2012) 'Occupy Sandy relief effort puts Occupy Wall Street activists in the spotlight again a year after Zuccotti Park', *Daily News*, 5 December, www.nydailynews.com/new-york/occupy-sandy-relief-puts-occupy-wall-street-back-spotlight-article-1.1213249.

Dyer-Witheford, N. (2006) 'The circulation of the common', paper presented at *Immaterial Labour, Multitudes and New Social Subjects: Class Composition in Cognitive Capitalism*, 29–30 April, Kings College London, www.fims.uwo.ca/people/faculty/dyerwitheford/Commons2006.pdf

Feigenbaum, A., Frenzel, F. and McCurdy, P. (2013) *Protest Camps*. London: Zed.

Halvorsen, S. (2015) 'Taking space: moments of rupture and everyday life in Occupy London', *Antipode*, 47(2), 401–417.

Hammond, J. L. (2013) 'The significance of space in Occupy Wall Street', *Interface: A Journal For and About Social Movements*, 5(2): 499–524.

Hardt, M. and Holloway, J. (2011) 'Creating common wealth and cracking capitalism: a cross-reading', *Shift Magazine*, www.herramienta.com.ar/revista-herramienta-n-49/creating-common-wealth-and-cracking-capitalism-cross-reading.

Holloway, J. (1991) 'The state and everyday struggle', in S. Clarke (ed) *The State Debate*. London: Macmillan.

Holloway, J. (2002) *Change the World Without Taking Power*. London: Pluto Press.

Holloway, J. (2010) *Crack Capitalism*. London: Pluto Press.

Jones, R. A. (2012) 'OWS and the class/race dynamic', *Socialism and Democracy*, 26(2): 30–32.

Juris, J. S., Ronayne, M., Shokook-Valle, F. and Wengronowitz, R. (2012) 'Negotiating power and difference within the 99%', *Social Movement Studies: Journal of Social, Cultural and Political Protest*, 11(3/4), 434–440.

Kall, R. (2011) 'Is Occupy Wall Street fetishizing public space?', *OpEdNew.com*, 6 November, www.opednews.com/articles/1/Is-Occupy-Wall-Street-Feti-by-Rob-Kall-111106-870.html.

Khatib, K., Killjoy, M., and McGuire, M. (2012) *We are Many: Reflections on Movement Strategy from Occupation to Liberation*. Oakland, CA: AK Press.

Lefebvre, H. (1966) 'Theoretical problems of *Autogestion*', in N. Brenner and N. Elden (eds) (2009) *State, Space, World: Selected Essays. Henri Lefebvre*. London: University of Minnesota Press, pp 138–152.

Lefebvre, H. (1969) *The Explosion: Marxism and the French Revolution*. London: Modern Reader.

Lefebvre, H. (1976) *The Survival of Capitalism: Reproduction of the Relations of Production*. London: Alison and Busby.

Lefebvre, H. (1978) 'Space and the state', in N. Brenner and N. Elden (eds) (2009) *State, Space, World: Selected Essays. Henri Lefebvre*. London: University of Minnesota Press, pp 223–253.

Lefebvre, H. (1979) Comments on a new state form, in N. Brenner and N. Elden (eds) (2009) *State, Space, World: Selected Essays. Henri Lefebvre*. London: University of Minnesota Pres, pp 124-137.

Lefebvre, H. (1991) *The Production of Space*. Oxford: Blackwell.

Marcuse, P. (2011) 'The purpose of the occupation movement and the danger of fetishizing space', http://pmarcuse.wordpress.com/2011/11/15/the-purpose-of-the-occupation-movement-and-the-danger-of-fetishizing-space/.

Merrifield, A. (2013) *The Politics of the Encounter: Urban Theory and Protest Under Planetary Urbanization*. Athens: University of Georgia Press.

Moreno-Caballud, L. and Sitrin, M. (2011) 'Occupy Wall Street, beyond encampments', *Yes Magazine*, 21 November, www.yesmagazine.org/people-power/occupy-wall-street-beyond-encampments.

Schrader, S. and Wachsmuth, D. (2012) 'Reflections on Occupy Wall Street, the state and space', *City* 16(1–2), 243–248.

Shukaitis, S. and Graeber, D. (2007) *Constituent Imagination: Militant Investigations/Collective Theorization*. Edinburgh: AK Press.

Vasudevan, A. (2015) 'The autonomous city: towards a critical geography of occupation', *Progress in Human Geography*, 39(3), 316–37.

Zibechi, R. (2012) *Territories in Resistance: A Cartography of Latin American Social Movements*. Oakland, CA: AK Press.

ELEVEN

Occupation, decolonisation and reciprocal violence, or history responds to Occupy's anti-colonial critics[1]

AK Thompson

The wish

A lot can change in two months. When intrepid activists descended on Zuccotti Park on 17 September 2011, few expected that they would spend the night. Within a month, their occupation had spread to dozens of other outposts across the land. A month later, most of the parks and squares had been cleared. Officially undaunted, the occupiers clamoured throughout 2012 to gain purchase in stormier, windswept fields. But it was no use: in a movement called 'Occupy', the struggle and the encampment were one.

Sooner or later, even great eulogies become historical footnotes. What, then, can be learned from Occupy now that its arc can be traced in a single meagre paragraph? According to Walter Benjamin, adopting a position downstream from an event's source could provide an analytic opportunity (1978b, 177). From such a position, he maintained, the critic might judge a current's force. Now that Zuccotti is a wasteland in a wasteland again (so sterile that even the office workers in adjoining towers won't eat lunch there), we can take stock of what we learned – and make lists of the questions that still demand answers.

Why, for instance, did the movement's renunciation of kleptocracy spread at such an epidemic rate, and how did a continent beset by tent cities in the autumn have little more to confront than a barricade's worth of hasty anthologies and slapdash monographs come spring? On the surface, the struggle to understand a movement's rise and fall seems to demand an analysis of the swirling vortices that guide the circulation of struggle. But while such an approach might help us to understand Occupy's degeneration from lighting rod to empty signifier, it's also true that it's likely to overlook the importance of foundational political *concepts*. However, once political concepts – and, indeed, the meaning of politics itself – are foregrounded, both the movement's contagious appeal and its rapid decomposition become instantly comprehensible.

Indeed, not since *The Port Huron Statement* has an American movement been so successful in revitalising our engagement with the conceptual bedrock of politics.[2] Among these concepts, perhaps the most cherished was 'democracy' itself. Ringing out with People's Mic choirs, the movement's General Assemblies could not help but remind us of the church-basement enthusiasm that, for Tocqueville, was the very heart of *Democracy in America*.

Even before there was 'democracy', however, there was 'occupation'. Perhaps more than any other term, noun or verb, it was occupation's destiny to spark debate – and these debates were as important as they were divisive. Reviewing them from our current downstream position, it becomes clear that movement fights about occupation's meaning allowed us to grapple, albeit indirectly, with a fundamental question whose answer continues to elude us: what does it mean to be political today?

The rapid diffusion of protest encampments during the fall of 2011 gives an indication of how conceptually generative 'occupation' had been. Nevertheless, the ferocity (to say nothing of the unresolved character) of movement debates suggests that this resonance owed largely to its indeterminacy. In many cases, 'occupation' became what Benjamin would have called a wish image – a vision capable of stimulating the longing for future happiness by recalling traces of the unrealised promise buried in the (mythic) past (1978a, 148).

Little wonder, then, that the late-capitalist disarticulation of social space (with its carcinogenic profusion of dead and transitory zones) stimulated recollections of an era when it was thought to be possible to foster a collective, exuberant 'we'. Eden, Winstanley's squatted wastelands, the Tennis Court Oath: each becomes a spark with the power to push the approximate present into the actualised future. Boomeranging through the past to stimulate its energetic élan, the wish image provides a vision of liberation that impels people to *act*. But how, and on what basis? The wish image doesn't say, and the concept has yet to find its object.

Although their sources are varied, wish images have consistently emerged from the Romantic current that has buoyed social movements since the end of the eighteenth century. In the immediate aftermath of Wall Street's catastrophic meltdown, movement Romanticism and the wish image 'occupation' revealed their profound affinity.

Figure 11.1: The Tennis Court Oath (Jaques-Louis David)

Figure 11.2: OWS General Assembly, 2012. (Photo by Wasim Ahmed)

Drawing on Mao (or maybe, sadly, Tyler Durden) and writing as The Imperative Committee, participants in the 2009 occupation of The New School issued a manifesto proposing that, as far as they were concerned, 'an occupation is not a dinner party, writing an essay, or holding a meeting'. Instead, it was 'a car bomb' (2009, 3). Conceived as the prelude to a messianic rupture in capitalism's base immediacy, it therefore followed that 'the coming occupations will have no end in sight' (2009, 12).[3] A little more than two years later, as Occupy Wall Street began showing signs of being possessed by what George Katsiaficas has called the 'Eros effect' (1987), activist Conor Tomás Reed proclaimed in the movement-based journal *Tidal* that, 'for many of us, "occupy" has become a verb to be sung'. This desire owed primarily to the fact that *the word itself*, when wielded by the right people, seemed to turn the world upside down.

> This rowdy crowd word, at once descriptive and prescriptive, aims to body-flip the logic of imperialism on its head. A radical people's occupation of public space doesn't erect checkpoints; it tears them down. Instead of usurping others' resources, we heartily pool our own for free distribution. (2011, 4)

From Mikhail Bakhtin's early-twentieth-century celebration of the medieval carnival (1984) to Naomi Klein's approving observation that the movement against globalisation responded 'to corporate concentration with a maze of fragmentation; to globalisation with its own kind of localisation; to power consolidation with radical power dispersal' (2000), the idea that struggle restores balance by reversing valuations has been as persistent as it has been seductive. In the western political tradition, such inversions can be traced back as far as Scripture, where – in Acts 17 – it is revealed that riots broke out in Thessalonica after Paul preached the Good News to unbelievers, who lamented: 'These that have turned the world upside down are come hither also… and these all do contrary to the decrees of Caesar, saying that there is another king, one Jesus.'

No sooner had the crop of new believers begun to savour their regicidal fantasies of deposing the One Percent's Caesars, however, than others began to take issue with occupation's new ubiquity. In their view, 'occupation' seemed irreparably tarnished by its association with the acts of conquest it was thought normally to denote. In their estimation, not only did the movement's preferred nomenclature alienate those who had endured histories of colonial violence at the hands of occupying forces, it also ensured that their efforts would fail. How, they asked, could a liberation struggle win if it rallied behind conquest's banner?

The anti-colonial critique

Barely a week into Zuccotti's Bakhtinian body flip, statements began appearing on the internet calling attention to the fact that the mobilisation had failed to address the *colonial* occupation that wrote America's story into the annals of humankind in letters of blood and fire. In a widely circulated *Racialicious* article, Indigenous writer and activist Jessica Yee suggested that – by encouraging 'organizers, protestors, and activists' to '"occupy" different places that symbolize greed and power' – the movement had signalled its insensitivity to the fact that 'The United States is already being occupied'. She went on to clarify: 'This is Indigenous land. And it's been occupied for quite some time now' (2011).

In response to the movement's careless framing, Yee enjoined protestors to consider how, instead of 'more occupation', what was needed was 'decolonization'. Moreover, since 'colonialism affects everyone', it was in everyone's interest to participate in its undoing. This was all the more true since, by her reckoning, 'colonialism also leads to capitalism, globalization, and industrialization'. 'How', she asked, 'can we truly end capitalism without ending colonialism?'

Although its defining attributes remained unspecified, 'decolonization' quickly became occupation's antithesis. And with the contest thus established, Yee's call gained traction in many cities. Over the course of a few short months, activists positioned within, alongside and in opposition to the growing Occupy movement initiated projects and set up websites with names like 'Decolonize Canada', 'Decolonize North America', 'Decolonize Oakland', 'Decolonize Occupy', 'DeColonize the 99%', and 'Decolonize The World'.

In the best interpretations, Yee's article was read less as an injunction to shut down movement operations than as a call to deepen them by exposing one of the primary contradictions underlying American experience. Thus it was that, on 4 December 2011, members of Occupy Oakland's People of Color caucus put forward a motion encouraging participants in that city's General Assembly to consider dropping 'Occupy' and adopting 'Decolonize' as their watchword. 'We want to open our movement to even greater participation', their proposal asserted. 'For many of us, including our local native communities, the terms "occupy" and "occupation" echo our experiences under colonial domination and normalizes the military occupations that the US is supporting in places such as Iraq, Palestine, and Afghanistan' (2011).

Speaking in favour of the motion, activists argued that the proposed name change would allow them to gain traction in communities affected by colonial occupation and conquest. In turn, such base building would help the movement to grow. Although the motion ultimately failed, the meeting's transcript reveals broad support for the 'name change' position.[4] According to one participant, 'the historical context of "occupy" doesn't fit with the goals of this movement'. According to another, 'the term occupy is racist' and, as a result, 'few people of color [were] involved' in movement activities. One participant reported how, 'as a Jewish person', they could not 'support Palestinian people in a movement named "Occupy"', while another expressed concern that, by 'using the language of our oppressors', the movement would be 'weakened' in a fundamental way.

Sentiments like these were not a west-coast anomaly. Speaking at a public forum two months after the 23 November 2011 eviction of Toronto's Occupy encampment, Indigenous Environmental Network organiser Clayton Thomas Mueller added his voice to those calling for the movement to change its name. 'No Native person ever called this movement "occupy"', Mueller said, 'and certainly no Palestinian ever did.'[5] On 24 April 2012, the authors of the POC Open Letter to the Occupy movement were even more direct when they declared that occupation was a 'failed political strategy'. And more: 'Liberation through occupation is impossible'.

Adopting a slightly more conciliatory tone in their retrospective analysis of movement gains, Baltimore-based authors Lester Spence and Mike McGuire conceded that, 'to the extent the fight against financial capital *is* a war', the term occupation helped to emphasise 'the fundamental nature of the struggle'. Nevertheless, since 'occupation' also 'denotes...white settler colonialism' and 'has a deeply regressive meaning' (Spence and McGuire, 2012, 56–57), they concluded by exhorting 'future iterations' of the movement to 'use symbols that reflect the realities of settler colonialism and refrain from using language that denotes 'occupation' (Spence and McGuire, 2012, 63).

When viewed as a strategic proposition, Spence and McGuire's recommendation seems to make sense. Nevertheless, across the continent, efforts to rename the movement were met with resistance. For many radicals, this resistance was enough to confirm their suspicion that the movement and its participants were irreparably racist. Such assessments should not be discounted; however, it's equally important to consider how the reluctance to dispense with 'occupation' might also have owed to the inadequacy of the proposed alternative. If the movement's use of 'occupation' was overly Romantic and insensitive to histories of conquest, it was equally true that the call to 'decolonize' (Yee) tended to lack the 'descriptive and prescriptive' (Reed) clarity of 'occupation' as a tactic of 'war' (Spence and McGuire, 2012) – and, hence (and following Clausewitz, 1989), of *politics* itself.

The call to 'decolonise' the Occupy movement was motivated by the sincere hope that America's history of violent conquest might finally, mercifully, be undone. But while there's no reason to suspect the motivations that compelled people to call for an end to the indiscriminate use of the term 'occupation', this should not lead us to conclude that the *analytic* basis of their exhortation should likewise be beyond scrutiny.

Returning to Yee's *Racialicious* article, the attentive reader is immediately struck by the important conceptual work accomplished by two distinct but interrelated rhetorical gestures. In the first, the movement's occupations are – by virtue of their common nomenclature – rendered as conceptual equivalents to the occupation that inaugurated colonialism in the Americas. Consequently, in the second, 'occupation' is posited as the logical antithesis to decolonisation, which is in turn held to be the only logical response to the founding violence of occupation.

These rhetorical moves reiterate conceptual habits that are pervasive among American radicals. Most evident in movement discussions about 'violence', such habits usually lead us to take note of what our enemy does and then to propose that – as a reflection of our opposition to their rule – we will do the exact opposite. In this way, resistance becomes a process of conceptual negation, of siding with the *representational* antithesis of the thing we oppose. 'They have power', said Melanie Kaye/Kantrowitz; 'we won't touch it with a ten-foot pole' (1992, 24).

So it is that we find ourselves launching assaults from the antithetical side of the conceptual divide. But what content might be attributed to such a negation? Yee never says. Although she briefly considers the tactical repertoire associated with 'occupation' (for example, occupying places that 'symbolise greed and power'), no such repertoire gets elaborated with respect to decolonisation. An oversight, maybe; or maybe an admission that the conceptual distinction cannot hold. Indeed, no less an authority than Frantz Fanon made clear that, when conceived as a *practical* and not merely a conceptual act, decolonisation is in fact much closer to occupation than Yee's comments would allow.

Like the OWS enthusiasts who cheered their movement's messianic reordering of the world, Fanon begins his decolonisation treatise on a Romantic note by proposing that, 'if we wish to describe it precisely', we would do well to recall 'the well-known words: "The last shall be first and the first last"' (1963, 37). But there's more: in a world cut in two, the will to decolonise first finds expression in the desire to *occupy the occupiers*. 'The look that the native turns on the settler's town is a look of lust, a look of envy', says Fanon. 'It expresses his dreams of possession – all manner of possession: to sit at the settler's table, to sleep in the settler's bed, with his wife if possible' (1963, 39). Comments like these may raise questions about Fanon's feminist credentials. Just as important, however, are those questions that might be raised concerning his implicit philology. It would not have surprised him (if he didn't know it already) that, throughout the sixteenth century – the very centerpiece of modern colonialism's 'age of discovery' – occupation was closely associated with sexual possession.[6]

Liberation owes nothing to negation; it is the fruit of reciprocity. Opposition to militarism calls on us to disavow 'class war' about as much as our conviction that picket lines mean 'don't cross' demands that we cede abortion clinics to the placard-wielding zealots who showed up first. Thus far, the history of American racism has made it harder to accept the same with respect to occupation; however, our collective failure to acknowledge occupation's inescapability as a necessary form of reciprocal violence has prevented us from advancing beyond the representational satisfactions associated with conceptual negation.

For the movement's Romantic enthusiasts, these satisfactions took the form of innocence as they carved out their micro-zones of autonomy while beseeching the State to safeguard their right to burlesque its sovereignty. For movement detractors, representational negation proved instead to be a reliable alibi. Responding to a force they didn't create but couldn't ignore, the most satisfying option was to declare it inadmissible.

History, meanwhile, records numerous instances in which radicals have explicitly embraced occupation as a term and tactic of explicitly *anti-colonial* resistance. Though it may not have been their intention, these movements help to reveal occupation's centrality to *all* forms of political action – whether carried out in the name of conquest *or* of liberation. Considered at their threshold, such acts make clear that politics without occupation is, in fact, inconceivable. Will it be *their* occupation or *ours* – and, if it is ours, what will we produce? These profane questions (only hinted at by the Occupy movement's regicidal wish images) are, in the final instance, the only ones that matter. A brief consideration of the 1968 occupation of Columbia University and the 1969 occupation of Alcatraz make clear the extent to which this is the case.

The occupation of Columbia University

In the spring of 1968, Columbia University was in tumult. The American student movement was at the height of its powers, and Students for a Democratic Society had not yet begun its downward spiral into sectarian rivalry. In fact, the group had begun forging meaningful alliances with other forces standing in opposition to the war in Vietnam and to the ongoing attacks against Blacks at home. It was in this context that, in 1968, the SDS chapter at Columbia University began to organise campaigns on two distinct but interrelated fronts.

Along the first, they attacked the University for its participation in the Military Industrial Complex and, in particular, for its involvement in the Institute for Defense Analysis. Along the second, they began to challenge Columbia's encroachment into Harlem and Morningside Heights. In particular, they mounted opposition to University plans to erect a gymnasium in Morningside Park.

Although the planned structure would occupy a large portion of the available green space, usage was to be restricted to Columbia affiliates. Serving the adjoining neighbourhoods of Harlem and Morningside Heights, the park was considered important territory by local residents who perceived the development as a form of territorial encroachment. In an article in the *New York Amsterdam News* of 27 April 1968 Victor Solomon of the Harlem chapter of CORE made these feelings clear when he declared: 'Harlem is a colony and is being treated like one' (cited in Bradley, 2009, p 57).

By the end of April, the SDS campaigns culminated in the occupation of several university buildings. For almost a week, protestors seized and held five separate structures and declared them to be 'free' space. At the centre of the occupation was Hamilton Hall. Not only had it been the first building to be seized, it was also held exclusively by black students and community-based militants. When the buildings were finally raided by police a week after they were first taken, Hamilton Hall was unique in that police took care not to be seen using force to remove the occupiers. At a rally held on the day of the arraignment hearing for students arrested during the occupation, one participant underscored his support for 'the students who have been carrying this struggle for the Harlem community against imperialistic, colonialistic attitudes of Columbia University that is trying to...turn Harlem into a colony' (Bradley, 2009, 99).

How did all of this transpire? To get a sense of the dynamics that marked those days, it's useful to turn to the pages of Columbia's student newspaper, *The Columbia Daily Spectator*. In addition to the breadth of the paper's occupation-related coverage, the publication's status as a daily produced by amateur journalists conspires to yield a relatively unedited account of the events. By following the story unfolding on the *Spectator's* pages, one can detect the eruption of anxieties concerning the meaning of politics even as they are coded in the careful tone of deliberations about race.

On 23 April, activists staged a demonstration in opposition to the construction of the gymnasium at Morningside Park. Charging that the new structure would intensify the university's encroachment into Harlem and Morningside Heights, the campaign coincided with the concurrent demand that the university become disentangled from the Institute for Defense Analysis. Writing about the demonstrations, *Spectator* journalist Michael Stern recounted how, after marching to the construction site in Morningside Park, 'protesters, led by members of Columbia's Students for a Democratic Society and Students Afro-American Society, tore down sections of the metal fence surrounding the site and fought with police for several minutes' (Stern, 1968, 1). Stern continues: 'After reiterating the charges that Columbia was discriminating against the community by building the gym on park land and refusing the community full use of the building's facilities, [SDS leader Mark] Rudd proposed that the crowd return to Columbia' (Stern, 1968, 2).

Upon returning to the university, the demonstrators began a spontaneous sit-in at Hamilton Hall, an academic building just off of the University's sprawling central green and adjacent to College Walk, the main artery bisecting the campus at 116th Street (which also bisects Morningside Park, immediately to the East of the University's walls). As the day wore on, the demonstrators made clear that their plan was to stay. According to the *Spectator*, 'At the midnight hour last night, several hundred of the demonstrators who had occupied Hamilton Hall since early yesterday afternoon, were readying themselves for an all-night camp-in in the corridors and the classrooms of the building.' According to the report's unnamed author, 'The unexpected and unprecedented siege of Hamilton Hall began...when more than 400 students and non-University demonstrators, exhilarated by the destruction of the fence surrounding the site of Columbia's new gymnasium, jammed into the building's tiny lobby and demanded to see 'the Man'' ('Protestors Crowd Into Hamilton Hall for All-Night Vigil', 1968, 1-2).

Although they had been central to the action at the construction site, the occupation of Hamilton Hall was not the work of SDS alone. For their part, political organisers from Harlem saw the occupation as an opportunity to help curb the university's encroachment into their territory. It therefore came as little surprise that – in the early hours of 24 April – 'black very militant community leaders' decided to 'blockade the building and close it down'. The decision to move from 'camp-in' to occupation thus arose not from white activists but rather from their 'very militant' counterparts. In response, 'the white students inside the building decided...to go along with the plans for barricading the building' (('Protestors Crowd Into Hamilton Hall for All-Night Vigil', 1968, 1-2). For some, this development was cause for apprehension.

According to *Spectator* reporter Robert Stulberg, 'the demonstration, which was initially sponsored by Students for a Democratic Society and the Student Afro-American Society, has apparently come under the control of black very militant community leaders'. In Stulberg's estimation, participants in the occupation included 'members of the Harlem chapters of the Student Nonviolent Coordinating Committee, the Congress of Racial Equality, and the militant Mau Mau Society' (Stulberg, 1968a, 1).

As the occupation developed, it yielded a nascent form of sovereign contestation. Owing to a recognition of the limits of demand-based politics and, at the same time, to the precariousness of their own claim to territorial control, the occupation produced intense negotiations about demands and the precise conditions under which they might be met. As Stulberg reported, 'the demonstrators...stated yesterday afternoon that they will not leave until all of their demands are met, and they will not send a group to negotiate their demands until the University agrees to give the demonstrators amnesty'. He continues: 'Among the list of six demands are requests that the University stop construction of the new gym in Morningside Park, sever its ties with the Institute of Defense Analysis and allow open hearings for all future judicial cases on campus' (pp 1–3).

Although they generally follow the repertoire laid down by modern social movements, these demands are interesting because they show how, in addition to underscoring the activists' opposition to the university's involvement in colonial violence both at home and abroad, they also set out to contest the configuration of sovereign power. This is achieved in an indirect manner, by trying to use existing laws to undermine the reach of the law itself. Thus it was that what began as a 'camp-in' staged to leverage demands developed into a civil war in miniature, in which control over territory became the means by which the struggle for sovereign determination of the law was sought.

The unease that this shift caused found expression in the pages of *The Daily Spectator*, where an op-ed entitled 'A Day of Warning' listed things about the anti-gym demonstration that needed to be condemned. Rounding out the piece, the author concluded by noting that 'control of the protest in Hamilton Hall has, to a great degree passed from Columbia students into the hands of people who are not members of the university community but are outside agitators whose interests and goals may bear little relationship to the ends desired by the demonstrators'. Despite the critical tone, however, the op-ed endorsed the call for an end to the gymnasium's construction – provided, of course, that it could be achieved through 'discussions with all interested community groups' ('A Day of Warning', 1968, 4). In the end, the threat of 'outside agitators' and black 'militants' concealed a more fundamental anxiety about the waning power of political-representational norms and the emergence of a new (but also more primitive and honest) political scene in which anti-colonial resistance took the form of occupation and struggle for territorial control.

According to the *Spectator*, 'the arrival of these militants raises another serious problem for the university: whether to call in city police to empty Hamilton Hall'. On the one hand, 'since they are taking part in an illegal demonstration inside a University building, the black leaders are trespassing on Columbia property'. Consequently, 'the University could attempt to have them removed by police on these grounds'. On the other hand, with the political polarisation intensified, 'any violence which might erupt from such a confrontation…could have repercussions far beyond the ivy-covered walls of the University' and, as such, needed to be seriously considered (Barry, 1968, 1-3). By outlining the problem in this way, the *Spectator* effectively demonstrated how, in the emergence of sovereign contestation between constituted power and a usurping one, it is constituted power that must work to maintain representational norms since doing otherwise concedes that an exceptional circumstance has, in fact, arisen.

The occupation of Hamilton Hall quickly led to both territorial and political polarisation, with the anti-colonial forces of occupation squaring off against their colonising counterparts. The headlines of the 25 April issue of the *Spectator* reveal how the sense of invasion had taken hold. 'Faculty Recommends Halt to Gym Construction: Campus Closed Down, SDS Holds [President] Kirk's Office', read the banner above the fold. Meanwhile, in another headline, the paper made the following ominous proclamation. 'Outsiders Influence SDS Action'.

Such warnings did little to prevent the action from spreading, however. Indeed, the front page confirmed that, since they last went to print, 'Protestors Occupy 2 New Buildings'. Penned once again by Robert Stulberg, the article explains: 'During the course of the day, which was marked by several near-violent outbreaks, members of Students for a Democratic Society barricaded themselves inside the office of President Grayson Kirk, while militant black students and community protesters remained in control of Hamilton Hall' (Stulberg, 1968b, 1). For their part, 'the administration decided to seal off the campus after receiving reports that militant black organizations in Central Harlem were planning to stage a mass protest at Columbia' (1968b, 1–2).

According to Victor Solomon, chairman of Harlem CORE, the Harlem community will demonstrate at Columbia today and everyday that black militant students and community members continue to hold Hamilton. Mr. Solomon said yesterday that a sound truck will travel through Harlem this morning to attract local people to Columbia. (1968b,1-2)

In their Editorial, the *Spectator* staff recounted how, 'faced with unsubstantiated rumors of community residents marching on Columbia to protest, the University all but sealed off the campus and locked many University buildings'. In this way, they lent 'credence to the charge that the administration considers the University to be a fortress surrounded by unfriendly natives'. But where the rumors unsubstantiated? On 27 April the paper's front-page headline read: 'Brown and Carmichael Appear at Hamilton'. According to Arthur Kokot,

> Black militant leaders H Rap Brown and Stokeley Carmichael forcibly entered the campus early yesterday afternoon, after which Mr Brown told a gathering of over 500 students assembled outside of Hamilton Hall, 'if the University doesn't deal with the brothers in there, they're going to have to deal with the brothers in the streets. (Kokot, 1968, 1)

Kokot's story continued:

> Mr Brown and Mr Carmichael entered the campus at 1:10 pm after breaking a police line defending the Amsterdam Ave. entrance to College Walk. They were immediately surrounded and escorted to Hamilton, by a group of forty black high school students and several other black persons… Mr. Brown emphasized the fact that black students are in control of Hamilton…The two black leaders had been aided in entering the campus by a group of approximately one hundred male and female young black students from several Manhattan high schools who had entered the campus around 11:20. (1968, 1, 4)

On the evening of 29 April, 1,000 cops are called onto campus to empty the occupied buildings. The lead story in the 30 April issue of the *Spectator* reads: 'In a brutal bloody show of strength from 2:30 until 5:30 this morning, New York City police, at the request of the

Columbia administration, cleared the five buildings held for the past week by student demonstrators.' The paper then goes on to give an in-depth account of how each building was evicted. Here, it's significant to note that no violence was used to clear Hamilton Hall: 'while police resorted to violence at other campus buildings to remove demonstrating students, a small detachment of the Tactical Police Force – without billy clubs – peacefully removed about a hundred black students from Hamilton Hall' ('University Calls in 1,000 Police to End Demonstration As Nearly 700 Are Arrested and 100 Injured', 1968, 1).

The occupation of Alcatraz

One year later, between 1969 and 1971, several hundred Indigenous activists occupied Alcatraz Island. According to movement participant Adam Fortunate Eagle, 'Alcatraz was a powerful symbol'. However, the action's significance did not arise primarily from the symbolic realm. For members of Indians of All Tribes, seizing the island was worthwhile in large part because it was thought to have 'enough facilities to give it some real potential'. In other words, the objective was not simply to *hold* the space but to *produce* something with and within it. As Fortunate Eagle recounts, activists hoped that the island's 'potential' could be used to 'galvanize the urban Indian community and reach out to the Indians on the reservation'.

> We developed our ideas of the practical, historical, and political reasons why Alcatraz should become Indian, and what exactly we would do with it. All of our thoughts were later incorporated into proclamations made at the takeover. (1992, 39)

Despite being a member of the 'local native communities' invoked by the Occupy Oakland People of Color Caucus in the preamble to their 4 December 2011 motion, Fortunate Eagle remained unfazed by the 'echo' of 'colonial domination' in the terms 'occupy' and 'occupation'. Indeed, as far as he was concerned, the homology between 'their' occupation and 'ours' was an important political discovery. And it's precisely for this reason that the activists that landed on Alcatraz are – in Fortunate Eagle's account – referred to as 'the occupying force', and that their arrival is described reverentially as 'the takeover' (1992, 54). The homology between 'their' occupation and 'ours' can be extended. Despite Reed's *Tidal* insistence that 'a radical people's occupation of public space doesn't erect checkpoints' (2011, 4), activist scholar Hannah Dobbs has noted that Indians of All Tribes secured Alcatraz by – among other things – painting 'giant 'no trespassing' signs, including one that read…"Warning Keep Off Indian Property'" (2012, 24).[7] Based on accounts such as these, it's clear that (regardless of the practice's apparent self-evidence today) positing resistance as the conceptual negation of the oppressor's terms was not yet hegemonic in 1969 – or even in 1992, when Fortunate Eagle published his reflections; or even among 'local native communities', despite the fact that this is where the allergy to 'occupation' is ostensibly strongest.

For Carl Schmitt, politics presupposes 'the distinction of friend and enemy'. Here, the political enemy is 'existentially something different and alien, so that in the extreme case conflicts with him are possible' (1996, 26–27). In this way, the goal of politics becomes: repulsing one's opponent 'in order to preserve one's own form of existence' (1996, 27). Although tainted by his association with fascism, Schmitt's formulation is nevertheless instructive when considering anti-colonial encounters. In Fortunate Eagle's account, deliberation enabled activists to 'agree on a name we could use to structure the occupying force and sign the proclamations – "Indians of All Tribes'" (1992, 43). Apart from the telling reference to his Indigenous compatriots as an 'occupying force', Fortunate Eagle's testimony highlights how the inauguration of politics is marked by the emergence of a 'we' – a 'form of existence', to use Schmitt's apt but misunderstood phrase.

Having landed on Alcatraz, Indians of All Tribes declared: 'We, the native Americans, re-claim the land known as Alcatraz Island in the name of all American Indians by right of discovery' (Fortunate Eagle, 1992, 44). Though the proclamation's gestural mimesis was no doubt meant to be – and indeed was – humorous, its political implications were impossible to ignore. For one, the 'we' that did the reclaiming amounted to a new people – a group that came together through reclamation and would not likely have emerged without it. Moreover, by making the claim on behalf of 'all American Indians', the occupiers effectively erased prior national divisions in an effort to conceptually extend the boundaries of their 'we'. Finally, by appealing to the 'right of discovery' (and thus drawing on a European colonial legal contrivance to legitimise their possession), Indians of All Tribes demonstrated that the realisation of their sovereign claim required that the legal claims of others be nullified.[8]

Having established the basis of their entitlement, the Indians of All Tribes proclamation enumerated the uses to which the island would be put. Significantly, all proposed uses concerned the development of the people's form of existence. These included: a centre for Native

American Studies, an American Indian spiritual centre, an Indian Center for Ecology, a Great Indian training school, and – finally – an American Indian museum.

Marked as it was by the weight of sovereign assertion, it's not surprising that the proclamation led Fortunate Eagle to consider the similarities between the actions of the occupiers and those that marked the conquest of the Americas. 'I thought of the Mayflower and its crew of Pilgrims who had landed on our shores 350 years earlier. The history books say they were seeking new freedom for themselves and their children, freedom denied them in their homeland.'

> It didn't matter that Plymouth Rock already belonged to somebody else; that was not their concern. What did concern them was their own fate and their own hopes. What a sad commentary on this country that we, the original inhabitants, were forced to make a landing 350 years later on another rock, the rock called Alcatraz, to focus national attention on our own struggle to regain the same basic freedom. (Fortunate Eagle, 1992, 56)

Alcatraz marked a watershed moment in Indigenous struggles in the United States. As historian Troy R Johnson reports, there were more than 65 major Indigenous occupations or actions in support of occupations in the period between 1969 and 1975. Many of these actions, which involved occupying abandoned military bases, explicitly mixed the struggle for legal recognition with the struggle to create new forms of Indigenous existence along post-national lines.

Citing the 1868 Sioux treaty right to occupy former Indian lands scheduled by the government to be declared 'surplus', United Indians of All Tribes occupied Fort Lawton on 8 March 1970. According to Johnson, 'Indians from Alcatraz Island made up the majority of the occupation force' (1996, 223). On the same date, 14 activists also occupied Fort Lewis, Washington (1996, 224). On 2 April 1970, another attempt was made to occupy Fort Lawton. According to occupation participant Bernie Whitebear, 'Alcatraz was very much a catalyst to our occupation here...If it had not been for their determined effort...there would have been no movement here' (Johnson, 1996, 225).

On 1 May 1970, Pomo Indians occupied Rattlesnake Island near Clear Lake California. Against the objections of the lumber company then claiming title to the land, they were 'allowed' to stay (Johnson, 1996, 225–226). On 9 May 1970, approximately 70 Mohawks from the

St Regis Indian Reservation occupied Stanley Island in the St Lawrence River, posted a 'no trespassing' sign, and reclaimed the island – along with its nine-hole golf course (Johnson, 1996, 226). According to Ward Churchill, 'Mohawks from St Regis and Canghawaga [Kahnawake]' partook in a similar action on 13 May 1974, when they 'occupied an area at Ganiekeh [Moss Lake], in the Adirondak Mountains'. After declaring the site to be 'sovereign Mohawk territory under the Fort Stanwix treaty', they 'set out to defend it (and themselves) by force of arms' (1996, 64).

Implications

Although they were important moments of anti-colonial struggle in America, the occupations of Columbia and Alcatraz were not anomalies. Moreover, they reveal that, rather than being decolonisation's antithesis, occupation has historically been a central tactic in the struggle to achieve it. The fight to determine what liberation might mean must first contest what – following Weber – we might call the state's monopoly on the legitimate use of occupation. Although it often remained insensitive to the colonial experiment from which it remained inseparable, the Occupy movement's wish images revealed that regicide was its guiding star. And, had they reached it, they would have opened clear lines along which decolonisation forces might have advanced.

Instead, the wish remained unclarified. And occupation (the concept without content) was set upon by decolonisation, its content-less antithesis. Had the conceptual problem been addressed, and had the strategic lines been more carefully drawn, our eulogy may have been a ballad instead. Having missed our opportunity, the least we can do is ensure that this footnote gets consulted.

Notes

[1]   An earlier version of this chapter appeared as '"Occupation" between conquest and liberation', *Situations: A Project of the Radical Imagination*, 6(1), 115–129.

[2]   Written in 1962 by Tom Hayden and other contributors at an SDS retreat in Port Huron, Michigan, *The Port Huron Statement* became a defining document of the American New Left. Throughout its pages, one notes a refusal both of America's stale bureaucratised democracy and of the horrors of Soviet-style authoritarian socialism. In their place, the SDS authors advanced a vision of participatory democracy that quickly became the movement's common sense.

[3]   Grad students will be grad students. Both the name 'the Imperative Committee' and the formulation 'the coming occupations' reveal the authors' debts to a particular strand of romantic insurrectionary thought associated with the work of Giorgio Agamben (author of, among other books, *The Coming Community*, 1993, Minneapolis: University of Minnesota Press) and elaborated by groups like the

anonymous Frenchmen who penned *The Coming Insurrection,* which was published under the name *The Invisible Committee* (2009, Los Angeles: Semiotext(e)).

4   Some commentators have observed that opposition to the resolution came primarily from white participants and, as such, should be read as further indication of the movement's insensitivity to questions of racism and colonialism; however, to the dismay of many activists, Boots Riley (frontman of revolutionary hip-hop act The Coup) also spoke in opposition to the proposal. This led to an interesting exchange, which can be read here: http://disoccupy.wordpress.com/page/2/.

5   This quote is taken from an unpublished statement made by Mueller at the event, recorded by the author.

6   On this point, see Sophie Lewis (2012).

7   As Feigenbaum, Frenzel, and McCurdy point out in *Protest Camps* (2013), protestors in Tahrir Square similarly erected barricades 'to protect the encampment' and preserve it as a 'space for democracy-building' (p 37).

8   Although Indians of All Tribes briefly cited nineteenth-century American treaty law to legitimate their claim, this action is best understood as an example of what, in his 'Critique of Violence', Walter Benjamin described as an act of violence that arises from the intent to exercise a right 'in order to overthrow the legal system that has conferred it' (1978c, 282).

References

'A Day of Warning' (1968) *Columbia Daily Spectator.* Vol. CXII, No. 101, 24 April, p. 4.

Bakhtin, M. (1984) *Rabelais and His World.* Bloomington, IN: Indiana University Press.

Barry, K. (1968) 'Challenge to Administration Strongest in School's History', *Columbia Daily Spectator.* Vol. CXII, No.101, 24 April, pp.1, 3.

Benjamin, W. (1978a) 'Paris, capital of the nineteenth century', *Reflections.* New York: Schocken Books.

Benjamin, W. (1978b) 'Surrealism', *Reflections.* New York: Schocken Books.

Benjamin, W. (1978c) 'Critique of violence', *Reflections.* New York: Schocken Books.

Bradley, S.M (2009) *Harlem Vs. Columbia University: Black Student Power in the Late 1960s.* Urbana, Chicago, and Springfield: University of Illinois Press.

Churchill, W. (1996) *From a Native Son: Selected Essays on Indigenism, 1985–1995.* Cambridge, MA: South End Press.

Clausewitz, Carl von (1989) *On War.* Princeton: Princeton University Press

Decolonize Oakland (2011) 'Decolonize: Oakland: creating a more radical movement', 4 December, http://occupyoakland.org/2011/12/decolonize-oakland/.

Dobbz, H. (2012) *Nine-Tenths of the Law: Property and Resistance in the United States.* Baltimore, MD and Oakland, CA: AK Press

Fanon, F. (1963) *The Wretched of the Earth.* New York: Grove Press.

Feigenbaum, A., Frenzel, F. and McCurdy, P. (2013) *Protest Camps: Imagining Alternative Worlds.* London: Zed.

Fortunate Eagle, A. (1992) *Alcatraz! Alcatraz!* Berkeley, CA: Heyday Books.

Imperative Committee, The (2009) *Preoccupied: The Logic of Occupation,* self-published activist pamphlet circulated during the New School occupation of 2009, http://reoccupied.files.wordpress.com/2009/04/preoccupied-printable-final.pdf.

Johnson, T. R. (1996) *The Occupation of Alcatraz Island.* Urbana and Chicago, IL: University of Illinois Press.

Katsiaficas, G. (1987) *The Imagination of the New Left: A Global Analysis of 1968.* Cambridge, MA: South End Press.

Kaye/Kantrowitz, M. (1992) *The Issue is Power: Essays on Women, Jews, Violence and Resistance.* San Francisco, CA: Aunt Lutte Press.

Klein, N. (2000) 'Does Protest Need a Vision?', www.newstatesman.com/200007030017.

Krokot, A. (1968) 'Two Black Leaders Support Strikers', *Columbia Daily Spectator.* Vol. CXII, No.104, 27 April, pp.1, 4.

Lewis, S. (2012) 'As odious as the word occupy', *Journal of Occupied Studies,* February, http://occupiedstudies.org/articles/as-odious-as-the-word-occupy.html.

Marx, K. (1954) *Capital, Volume 1.* Moscow: Progress Publishers.

POC National Statement (2012) 'For people who have considered occupation but found it is not enuf', *DisOccupy,* 24 April, http://disoccupy.wordpress.com/.

'Protestors Crowd Into Hamilton Hall for All-Night Vigil' (1968) *Columbia Daily Spectator.* Vol. CXII, No.101, 24 April, pp.1-2.

Reed, C. T. (2011) 'Step 1: occupy universities. Step 2: transform them', *Tidal: Occupy Theory, Occupy Strategy,* 1, 4, https://docs.google.com/file/d/0B8k8g5Bb3BxdcHI0bXZTbVpUbGVQSnRLSG4zTEx1QQ/edit?pli=1.

Schmitt, C. (1996) *The Concept of the Political.* Chicago, IL: University of Chicago Press.

Spence, L. and McGuire, M. (2012) "Occupy and the 99%." *We Are Many: Reflections on Movement Strategy from Occupation to Liberation.* Oakland: AK Press

Stern, M. (1968) '1 Arrested in Park in Violent Protest', *Columbia Daily Spectator,* Vol. CXII, No.101, 24 April, pp. 1-2.

Stulberg, R. (1968a) 'Protesters Say They Will Not Negotiate Until CU Grants Disciplinary Amnesty', *Columbia Daily Spectator*. Vol. CXII, No.101, 24 April, pp.1-3.

Stulberg, R. (1968b) 'Protestors Occupy 2 New Buildings', *Columbia Daily Spectator*. Vol. CXII, No.102, 25 April, pp.1-2.

'University Calls in 1,000 Police to End Demonstration As Nearly 700 Are Arrested and 100 Injured; Violent Solution Follows Failure of Negotiations' (1968) *Columbia Daily Spectator*. Vol. CXII, No.107, 30 April, p.1

Yee, J. (2011) 'Occupy Wall Street: the game of colonialism and further nationalism to be decolonized from the 'Left', *Racialicious*, 30 September, https://www.racialicious.com/2011/09/30/occupy-wall-street-the-game-of-colonialism-and-further-nationalism-to-be-decolonized-from-the-left/.

TWELVE

Reoccupation and resurgence: indigenous protest camps in Canada

Adam J Barker and Russell Myers Ross

Introduction: a history of blockades

> Disruption results in consequences
> remember Kanenhstaton Caledonia
> remember Gustafen Lake
> remember Ipperwash
> remember Oka
> rememeber Alcatraz and Eagle Bay
> remember Wounded Knee
> everyday is remembrance day
> everyday
> (excerpt from 'Forever' by Janet Rogers, 2015)

The history of the settler states of North America, Canada and the United States, can be told through stories of Indigenous peoples' struggles to maintain their lands in the face of relentless colonial displacement and dispossession (Dunbar-Ortiz, 2014; Daschuck, 2013; Harris, 2004). As settler states have relentlessly driven railways and roads through Indigenous homelands, while restricting Indigenous nations onto reserves, fractions of their former land-bases, direct actions to violate those colonial spaces can be a powerful act of resurgence for Indigenous peoples (Alfred, 2005; Simpson, 2011). In response, blockading has become an important tactic through which Indigenous communities reassert their traditional forms of place-based culture and governance. Blockades run the gamut from flashmob-style disruptions of urban intersections, highways and commercial spaces (Barker, 2015, 48–50) to what Dene political scientist Glen Coulthard calls the rarest form of blockade action: the 'more-or-less permanent reoccupation of a portion of Native land through the establishment of a reclamation site' (Coulthard, 2014, 166).

These reoccupations or reclamation sites may be comparatively rare forms of resistance, but they also represent some of the most important moments in Indigenous activism in North America. In the USA, the history of the American Indian movement and the resurgence of tribal sovereignty struggles in the 1960s and 1970s is inextricably wrapped around occupations: Alcatraz in 1969–71, the Bureau of Indian Affairs building in Washington, DC in 1972, and the town of Wounded Knee in 1973 (Deloria, 1985; Smith and Warrior, 1997). These occupations continue into the present, with the Winnimum Wintu, an 'unrecognised' tribe – meaning lacking official federal status – taking control of sacred river spaces in California (Fimrite, 2012), among many others.

Indigenous peoples in Canada are also a part of this history of anticolonial occupations. Canada is often falsely portrayed as a 'peaceful' nation, built on treaties rather than conquest (Regan, 2010), but the response of settler governments and communities to Indigenous activists tells a different story. In 1995, Ontario Provincial Police violently raided Ipperwash Provincial Park, which had been occupied by members of the Stoney Point Ojibway band as part of a decades-old long land claim. During the raid, police fatally shot protester Dudley George.[1] This standoff overlapped with an occupation near Gustafsen Lake in British Columbia, between August and September of 1995. Indigenous protesters occupied a private ranch on unceded Shushwap territory and the Canadian government responded by laying siege with federal police (Lambertus, 2004). And both of these protest camps followed on the heels of the most well-known standoff featuring blockades and occupations in Canadian history: the 'Oka Crisis' of 1990.

This chapter examines three important reclamation sites, ranging from the spontaneous and relatively-short lived blockades of the Oka Crisis near the Kanesatake and Kahnawake Mohawk reserves in Québec, through the long-term Anishinaabe anti-clearcutting blockade at Grassy Narrows in northern Ontario (begun in 2002), to the growing and evolving anti-pipeline reclamation site in Unist'ot'en territory, in the British Columbia interior, which began in 2009. These three reclamation sites differ greatly from each other, and occur over a 25-year period. We present them here as strategic exemplars (Stevensen, 2012, 602) of how Indigenous communities in Canada assert their embodied connections to the land through direct action protest camping. Every Indigenous protest camp is unique, but these three each demonstrate important lessons for resisting colonialism, capitalism and state violence, and also the necessity of respecting the individuality and diversity of Indigenous cultures, national identities and struggles for decolonisation.

Indigenous protest camps exist on a spectrum of direct action tactics related through the intent to selectively block access to Indigenous territories 'with the aim of impeding the exploitation of Indigenous people's land and resources' (Coulthard, 2014, 166). Indigenous protest camping must be seen through the framework of *re-occupation or reassertion of presence*: the reclamation of places claimed by colonial power and the reassertion of relationships to the land that underpin Indigenous societies and Indigenous identities which political scientists Taiaiake Alfred (Mohawk) and Jeff Corntassel (Cherokee) have argued are 'place-based' and 'oppositional' to contemporary colonialism (2005). Coulthard has written extensively on the importance of reoccupations and blockades for Indigenous political movements and anticolonial struggles in Canada, calling them expressions of a 'disruptive countersovereignty'. While there are many ways that Indigenous nations can and do exercise sovereignty, autonomy and self-determination (for example, Corntassel and Bryce, 2012; Hunt and Holmes, 2015), Coulthard contends: 'the material form that these expressions of Indigenous sovereignty took on the ground – the blockade, explicitly erected to impede the power of state and capital from entering and leaving Indigenous territories respectively – must have been particularly troubling to the settler-colonial establishment' (2014, 118).

Indigenous communities continue to find ways to assert this countersovereignty in the midst of the nexus of racist settler colonial narratives, state violence and capitalist exploitation of lands and peoples that underpins settler Canadian society. The successes of Indigenous reclamations under these conditions suggests that it is important for wider social movement scholars and grassroots activists to be aware of some of the unique histories and geographies of these actions.

Twenty-five years of reoccupations

This section examines the examples Oka, Grassy Narrows and Unist'ot'en, but it must begin with a caution that Indigenous reoccupations are for more frequent and numerous than most people realise. These include the Innu occupation of a military base in their homelands near Goose Bay, Newfoundland, the Haudenosaunee reclamation of lands being used for a suburban housing development near Caledonia, Ontario, and – depending on how a re-occupation or protest camp is defined – dozens of blockades designed to disrupt transportation and resource extraction, especially in British Columbia (Kilibarda, 2012, 27; Coulthard, 2014, 117). The three cases examined here are merely a glimpse of three reoccupations that have made a particularly large impact on the landscape of Indigenous anticolonial activism in Canada, but are far from the whole picture.

Oka

The Oka Crisis, the 'seventy-eight-day armed "standoff" beginning on 11 July 1990, between the Mohawk nation of Kanesatake, the Québec provincial police (Surete du Québec or SQ), and the Canadian armed forces near the town of Oka, Québec' (Coulthard, 2014, 116), changed the political landscape of Indigenous-settler Canadian relationships forever. Oka was the first contemporary conflict between Canada and Indigenous nations that involved state violence resulting in death, and as such, it continues to exert a major influence over how media portrays and most Canadians perceive other, ongoing Indigenous occupations (Wilkes and Ricard, 2007, 243). Sparked by a conflict over a Mohawk graveyard and surrounding forest known as The Pines – part of a century-long land claim by the community of Kanesatake, but targeted for development into a golf course by the local settler community – the Oka Crisis was initiated when Mohawk protestors blockaded a road to halt construction. The SQ responded with a massive show of force, and while one of their own – Corporal Marcel Lemay – was killed by stray fire, the Mohawk protesters remained. In the aftermath of the failed assault, the Mohawk Warrior Society, traditional Clan Mothers and Chiefs, and elected chief and council all took on various roles in expanding and defending the blockade, while the SQ and Québec provincial government convinced the Canadian federal government to loan Canadian military assistance. Limited incursions by the military met stiff resistance, but a low-level campaign of harassment – spot checking cars entering and leaving the community, refusing to allow food and medical supplies onto the reserve, and raiding community offices and gathering places on the pretence of searching for illegal weapons – served to deplete the strength of the protesters. Eventually the standoff ended in anticlimactic fashion: a negotiated stand-down by both sides, with little resolved. The Pines remained undeveloped, but the Mohawks' larger claims to land and sovereignty were unaddressed (for more, see Simpson and Ladner, 2010; Obomsawin, 1993; Mcleod, 1992; York and Pindera, 1991).

The Oka standoff can be seen as a case that pushes the boundaries of what we understand a protest camp to be or comprise. People did live within the boundaries of the protest action, in part because the main set of blockades were around the village of Kahnesatake – the Mohawk people's refusal to let their lands be developed or to accept the authority of the SQ or Canadian military on their lands resulted in their domestic spaces being placed at the heart of the wider reclamation action. Other pockets of Indigenous occupation popped up around this central space, such as camps blockading bridges, but the village remained the heart of all of these reoccupations. However, like many protest camps and occupations, the space that the Mohawk protesters reoccupied changed over the course of the conflict. The 'front lines' constantly shifted, both in response to state pressure and also through the improvisational counter-actions of the Mohawk protesters, including the solidarity actions of other Mohawk and Indigenous communities – such as erecting blockades and re-occupations in other locations, dividing the attention of the police and government – as the conflict progressed. At its height, Mohawk warriors from Kahnesatake controlled roads and forests all the way out to the major highway running near the reserve, and the neighbouring Mohawk people of Kahnawake kept and held the Mercier Bridge for several days. These spaces represent more than strategic junctures, however: they were spaces in which traditional knowledge and important contemporary skills and experience were brought to the fore and shared between warriors and community members, and across generational lines (Pertusati, 1996).

Grassy Narrows

'Grassy Narrows' is the colloquial way of referring to a long-running encampment and series of associated anti-logging blockades. Located 50 miles north of Kenora, Ontario, the Grassy Narrows blockade and protest camp takes its name from the Grassy Narrows First Nation – traditionally named and still often called Asubpeeschoseewagong Netum (Willow, 2010, 33) – an Anishnaabe community located in Kakipitatapitmok ('Slant Lake' in English). Due to clear-cutting and other resource extraction efforts, the community has experienced serious environmental degradation and increasing health risks (including mercury poisoning) over several decades. Like many Indigenous communities in North America, the economic conditions are depressed and the people politically marginalised. In 2002, in response to the increasing encroachment of logging activity, community members from Grassy Narrows established a semi-permanent encampment that was used as a focal point to organise other direct actions, notably a series of road blocks to prevent logging trucks and equipment from entering the area. The encampment has been occupied ever since, despite frequent changes in the number of people there and their affiliations, making it the longest ongoing Indigenous direct action protest in North America (for an extensive examination, see Willow, 2012; 2011; 2010). At various times, confrontations with both logging companies and police have become heated, with arrests and harassment of Anishinaabe and settler activists, and the blockades have been selectively expanded to other roads, access routes and construction or logging sites near the encampment in response. Activists of many different sorts, including those associated with environmental NGOs, the Christian Peace Keepers, and particular communities across Ontario and Canada, have irregularly participated with these blockades (Wallace, 2010), which has brought them into a variety of relationships with the encampment which, as will be discussed below, demonstrate the complexity of settler participation in Indigenous-led protest camps.

The reoccupation of Grassy Narrows is not situated where it is simply because of proximity to an extractive logging development. The place itself is described by the Anishinaabe as having inherent, pre-existing meaning for the traditional people of that territory. More than simply preventing the passage of agents of the state and logging corporations, the relationships that are practiced there are significant in and of themselves:

> The Grassy Narrows blockade is a site of overt resistance, but even more importantly, it is also a place where Anishinaabe people resist through the simple act of living. It is a place to articulate a contemporary Aboriginal sense of self in response to the constraints imposed by colonial social and political relations...
>
> The modest appearance of the Slant Lake blockade says a lot about its cultural significance. When activists at Grassy Narrows make plans to head to Kakipitatapitmok to fish, share a meal, enjoy a campfire, or spend a peaceful night, the physical barrier is not what they have in mind. No impermeable fortification ever stood here to stop the logging trucks...Here...people are the real blockade. (Willow, 2011, 267)

These place-based relationships are sufficiently important to the Anishinaabe of Asubpeeschoseewagong Netum to motivate many people to put themselves in the way of state harm by reoccupying the camp and defending the land from environmental destruction.[2]

Unist'ot'en

The Unist'ot'en Camp[3] was founded in 2009 and follows a similar trajectory to Grassy Narrows and Oka: it is an assertion of control over traditional territory, outside of 'official' reserve or First Nation boundaries, in response to the threat of environmental destruction from resource extraction. 'Unist'ot'en' refers to a clan of the Wet'suwet'en people, and the Unist'ot'en Camp is in the heart of their traditional territory and homeland. In their words, 'The Unis'tot'en Clan is part of the hereditary chief system which has governed Wet'suwet'en lands since time immemorial and is not subject to the Indian Act or other impositions of colonial occupation' (Unist'ot'en Camp, 2014). The Unist'ot'en Camp is not referred to as a 'blockade' by members, but rather a 'soft camp' or 'gateway'. The camp is constantly developing, but there are already a series of several buildings, including communal food storage and preparation areas, social and spiritual spaces, and the permanent home of camp leaders such as Freda Huson (Pablo, 2012). Although many in the camp identity as Wet'suwet'en, it is overall a mixed group of occupants, including both Indigenous and settler activists, some permanent, others who come from outside to help for limited periods of time. The camp is located around a bridge over Widzin Kwah (the Morris River), which is also an important river for salmon spawning and fishing, playing a key role in the traditional economy and culture of the area.

The location at the bridge over Widzin Kwah was chosen both because of its location in traditional territory and for tactical reasons: it is a natural bottleneck for at least three separate proposed oil and natural gas pipelines: the Pacific Trail Pipeline (PTP), Enbridge Northern Gateway (ENG), and Coastal Gaslink (CG). Countering the speculative geography of these pipelines, currently only lines on maps, the most prominent feature of the camp is the log cabin, occupied by Freda Huson and her family, constructed directly in the path of the pipeline corridor. The construction of the cabin began in 2010 and was completed in July 2012. Since 2011, the community that has coalesced around the site has engaged in a number of direct actions, including evicting surveyors working for Apache (PTP) and TransCanada (CG). They have also hosted a number of educational camps and encounters, in which outsiders from both Indigenous and settler communities come to the Unist'ot'en territory to help build structures, learn about the camp, and participate in drills and simulations such as a potential police raid or eviction. Camp members keep a close eye on who comes and goes in the territory, and where possible, confront and evict surveying crews and other employees of the pipeline companies (Prystupa and Uechi, 2014). The Unist'ot'en have also done a great deal of outreach, both confronting groups – including other Indigenous groups – whom they see as collaborating with the government or corporations threatening their territory, and organising days of action in distant locations like Vancouver, and involving other radical social movement organisations, including No One Is Illegal (NOII).

The Unist'ot'en Camp has been particularly active in blogging and has a strong profile on social media. As of this writing, photographer, filmmaker and writer Michael Toledano is visiting the camp and tweeting updates, information and observations amidst threats of a police raid (McSheffery, 2015a; 2015b). One recent tweet reads 'Normal day @ #Unistoten – salmon, sushi, healing centre construction, helicopter surveillance. Still under high alert' (Toledano, 2015). This tweet is accompanied by a series of four pictures, giving the much broader public a glimpse into the life at the otherwise remote camp. The camp has also been featured in investigative pieces by Al Jazeera and Vice Media (Al Jazeera Plus, 2014; Toledano, 2014), which have helped spread the message of the Unist'ot'en struggle to a much wider audience. Indigenous communities have previously used electronic media to good effect in organising mass actions, such as around the Idle No More protests in the winter of 2012–13 (Kino-nada-niimi, 2014; Barker, 2015, 51–52). Supporters of the Unist'ot'en Camp have been particularly effective in this regard and this is perhaps part of the reason why Unist'ot'en has received remarkably widespread support, from scholars and celebrities, to politicians and community organisations (McSheffrey, 2015b).

Resistance, resurgence, relationships: Indigenous reoccupations in action

Frenzel, Feigenbaum and McCurdy (2013, 15) have demonstrated that place has a massive impact on the spatialities of protest camps, arguing that 'while protest camps are symbolic spaces and often function as representational space, they draw their power from being in particular physical locations and from having particular infrastructural features'. This is nowhere more true than in the case of Indigenous protest camps. Here, we turn to some broad observations of Indigenous reoccupations that speak to both the power and unique qualities of these reclamation sites.

Settler colonialism and Indigenous resurgence

Indigenous reoccupations like those discussed here are part of the larger spectrum of blockade tactics, as discussed. These tactics are in the pursuit of the larger movements towards Indigenous resurgence (Alfred, 2005; Simpson, 2011). Indigenous peoples must survive while immersed in an environment of pervasive settler colonialism, which seeks to eliminate and erase Indigenous presence from the land (Battell Lowman and Barker, 2015; Veracini, 2015; 2010). As mentioned, Alfred and Corntasell have defined contemporary Indigenous identity as oppositional and place-based (Alfred and Corntassel, 2005). These two fundamentals of Indigenous identity are intertwined: it is through opposition to settler colonialism that Indigenous peoples are able to practice place-based traditions and cultures, and likewise the practice of these traditions and cultures amounts to a form of place-based resistance to settler colonialism. However, this conflict is often invisible to most settler people: settler colonial narratives strive towards a 'historylessness' that helps to replace histories of dispossession and displacement with stories of peaceful, gallant pioneers (Battell Lowman and Barker, 2015, 33–35). When Indigenous communities take up visible presence on the land – especially presence that disrupts the mobility of the capitalist economy of the settler state – this disruption forces issues of Indigenous discontent and struggles for freedom into the settler Canadian public discourse. In short, Indigenous reoccupations assert Indigenous identity across the boundaries of settler colonial space, which frustrates the drive for invisibility or transcendence of the settler colonial form.

Boundary crossing of this kind is not unique to Indigenous reoccupations. Rather, it is part of a common practice through which Indigenous nations exert their counter sovereignty contra settler colonialism. Kevin Bruyneel has discussed this 'thirdspace' of Indigenous sovereignty with respect to the way that Indigenous peoples have struggled against settler colonial racism that draws both spatial and temporal boundaries around indigeneity (2007). Indigenous nations exert their sovereignty by refusing to conform to settler colonial structures of displacement and systems of erasure, exerting influence on settler political and economic orders and reclaiming their collective authority with respect to the land. The reoccupation camps and blockades discussed here are particularly demonstrative of this because they cross multiple boundaries in an undeniably material way, from blocking bridges and roads to confounding pipeline construction and business development. Additionally, the use of social media and other forms of electronic communication to build linkages of solidarity and support further disrupts temporal boundaries that exile indigeneity to a pre-modern, pre-settlement time frame (Barker, 2015, 52–53).

Responses from state and corporate powers to these assertions of counter sovereignty are often violent. The military assaults on Oka and Grassy Narrows recall the deployment of the Northwest Mounted Police – the forerunners to the contemporary Royal Canadian Mounted Police – to break up Métis and Cree settlements that had declared sovereignty over the Red River territory of present day Manitoba (Nettleback and Smandych, 2010). Even the general settler Canadian public can be a threat, as demonstrated by the violent anti-Mohawk riots in nearby Chateaugay, Quebec, during the Oka Crisis, or the bombarding of a convoy of cars fleeing the Kahnestetake community with rocks (Obomsawin, 2000). While both the Unist'ot'en Camp and Grassy Narrows have seen police harassment and arrests, they have not yet experienced the sort of assault that occurred at Oka (and Gustafsen Lake, Ipperwash, Kanenhstaton/Caledonia, and others), though this may yet happen. In August 2015, the Union of British Columbia Indian Chiefs released a memorandum stating that they had knowledge that the RCMP were planning on raiding the Unist'ot'en Camp (McSheffrey, 2015a). The stakes for such a move were raised when, earlier that year, the Canadian government passed Bill C-51, an expanded suite of anti-terror legislation that some said was explicitly designed to criminalise Indigenous protest (Palmateer, 2015). Scott Morgensen (2011) has theorised that the biopolitics of settler colonialism construct any Indigenous presence in places claimed by the settler society as a threat, in need of elimination. The responses of both settler communities and governments to these reoccupations are clear demonstrations of this.

Identity and the land

As implied by the description of the practices of daily life in the Grassy Narrows camp, above, the social and cultural life of Indigenous reoccupation sites is an important feature of these spaces of Indigenous resurgence. To reiterate Willow's point, 'the people are the blockade'. Indigenous reoccupations are autonomous spaces where relationships are reworked at least partly shielded from the oppressive power of state and capital, and where Indigenous and not settler social and cultural discourses are considered the norm. In that context, the set of relationships being primarily pursued are those with the land itself.

Indigenous relationships to the land can be articulated as, in the words of Mohawk and Anishianaabe scholar Vanessa Watts (2013), 'place thought'. Watts describes this as a worldview that asserts that relationships between people and landbases and sacred places give meaning to human existence:

> Our truth, not only Anishnaabe and Haudenosaunee people but in a majority of Indigenous societies, conceives that we (humans) are made from the land; our flesh is literally an extension of soil. The land is understood to be female: First Woman designates the beginning of the animal world, the plant world and human beings. It is the femininity of earth itself that institutes all beings as literal embodiments of localized meanings. (Watts, 2013, 27)

These localised meanings are what Daniel Wildcat (Muscogee) and Vine Deloria Jr (Standing Rock Sioux) have described as the 'personality' of place: an emergent, autonomous identity that can be related to and communicated with (Deloria and Wildcat, 2001), partially through what Blackfoot scholar Leroy Little Bear has described as 'rituals of renewal' (Little Bear, 2004). Many social theorists, especially geographers, will likely note a similarity here to actor network theory (ANT), which Frenzel, Feigenbaum and McCurdy (2013, 12–13) assert is important for understanding protest camps. While there are some similarities, Watts argues that ANT cannot be said to function in the same manner as Indigenous place thought because it continues to rely on an ontological–epistemological divide that continues to embed 'the idea of human ownership over non-human things, beings' in social discourses (Watts, 2013, 30).

Consider the depth of the relationships between the Anishnaabe of Grassy Narrows and their lands as demonstrated by the ongoing efforts towards subsistence living and connections to cultural and social health (even at the possible expense of physical health):

> Acknowledging the continuing centrality of land-based subsistence in contemporary Anishinaabe life is prerequisite for understanding the political landscape of the Grassy Narrows blockade...For most families, wild foods – moose, beaver, venison, wild rice, berries, and fish – are anticipated seasonal supplements...Over time, I came to appreciate the cultural and symbolic values of land-based subsistence as even more significant than its material and interpersonal ones. When asked why, given her fears about toxic contamination, she didn't simply stop consuming

these items, Judy DaSilva was quick to reply: "It's not just something you quit," she said, "It's not just food for us; it's spiritual." (Willow, 2011, 269)

The community members position their spiritual responsibilities and commitments as necessary to maintaining vibrant and living relationships to the land, similar to the way that Songees educator and activist Cheryl Bryce articulates her invasive species pulls and public lessons as simultaneously insufficient but necessary to fulfil her responsibilities to the land and protect her peoples' cultural traditions (Corntassel and Bryce, 2012). Likewise, inside Indigenous reclamation sites the land itself is a vital, leading actor in the protest camp community rather than simply a site of contestation or material background for spatial struggles.

In addition to relationships between people and place, the reoccupations provide spaces for Indigenous communities to strengthen their internal solidarity and address inevitable community divisions. As Hayden King (Anishinaabe) pointed out during Idle No More, it is not only acceptable but actually a positive that there is space for disagreement within Indigenous protest movements (King, 2014). However, it is not often desirable to disagree in front of settlers generally, and especially not those who represent the interests of state and capital – even healthy disagreements are usually interpreted as signs of weakness, upholding an unfair standard of consensus that effectively silences Indigenous voices as 'too diverse'. By contrast, within the camps, there is a very different process of 'compensatory division' at play, strengthening the ties that bind the reoccupiers in enduring ways. Communications scholar John Jones describes compensatory division as the creation of rhetorical and/or technological 'divisions that are enacted in order to create the conditions under which new identifications can form' (Jones, 2014, 149). In the same way that protest camps create spatial divisions that differentiate the camp from society, protest campers engage in efforts to rupture identities in order that new, oppositional identities can be formed. These ruptures happen at different scales, with the Unist'ot'en Camp as a whole serving as a space from which to critique both Gitxsan (western neighbours of the Wet'suwet'en) deals with pipeline companies, and Carrier Sekani Tribal Council (a nearby band government) forums with PTP officials (Unist'ot'en Camp, 2012). Rather than a rift between Indigenous peoples, the divisions caused by the Unist'ot'en Camp's rhetoric and practice of land-based sovereignty resulted in community backlash against the secrecy of treaty and pipeline negotiations, resulting in an overall strengthening of solidarity with the Unist'ot'en Camp and blockading of the Gitxsan Treaty Office. On the more personal scale, social relationships are similarly worked out as community members work out complex relationships between band council governments, traditional or radical governance systems, warrior societies, community members who rely on resource extraction or development for employment, and so on. As described in the case of Grassy Narrows, the camp provided a space for Anishinaabe people to meet, talk, eat and work together, and work out how they could navigate the complex network of their political identities (Willow, 2011, 266–267).

Activists and solidarity

Indigenous reoccupations are far from internally homogenous – as described above, they are spaces that allow for productive disagreement. But more profoundly, reoccupations often serve as 'convergence spaces' for a variety of social movement actors and grassroots community members, Indigenous and settler. 'By participating in spaces of convergence,' argues geographer Paul Routledge, 'activists from participant movements embody their particular places of political, cultural, economic and ecological experience with common concerns, which lead to expanded spatiotemporal horizons of action' (2003, 345). This is evident in the way that Oka's influence continues to be felt on later reoccupations, including the prominence of the Unity Flag – better known as the Mohawk Warrior Flag (Doxtater, 2010) – which position Oka an important historical moment of counter sovereignty in action. The flag is significant as a symbol of resistance, but also because of its association with warrior societies, as many Indigenous communities were encouraged by the successes of the Mohawk Warrior Society – supported and guided by the Clan Mothers – to revive their own versions of these traditional roles and responsibilities (Alfred and Lowe, 2005).

Grassy Narrows and the Unist'ot'en Camp have been host to a variety of settler and other non-Indigenous activists, and this has at times been problematic. Routledge notes that convergence spaces are inherently spaces that facilitate interaction across differences, but also that uneven access to power and resources can create uneven forms of interaction and exchange (2003, p.345). This has certainly been the case in both Grassy Narrows and the Unist'ot'en Camp at times. Settler social movements, whether organised on liberal progressive (Grande, 2013), radical anarchist (Barker and Pickerill, 2012; Lagalisse, 2011), or environmentalist (Pickerill, 2009; McLean, 2013) ethics, have all had difficulties building respectful relationships with Indigenous peoples, often falling back into oppressive patterns of thought and behaviour. Social movements such as Occupy have at times shown an inability to accept Indigenous leadership (Kilibarda, 2012), and this can persist among activists participating in Indigenous reoccupations. Because of this, as community members and outside activists try to navigate the imbalances caused by the personal benefits of belonging to settler society (Battell Lowman and Barker, 2015, 84–89), trust is often built very slowly. Some activists at Grassy Narrows have been recalled as evidencing colonial behaviour – refusing to listen to the will of the community, pushing for aggressive action without consulting the community, occupying visible and vocal positions of leadership at the expense of Indigenous leaders – despite the common rhetoric of wanting to 'help' Indigenous communities (Wallace, 2010, 45).

The Indigenous leaders of the reoccupations have, however, developed ways of dealing with problematic outside activists. At Grassy Narrows, tensions around NGO actvists and community members arose over methods of organisation and leadership that differed between Indigenous and settler practices. The community responded by imposing their own frameworks of timing and protocol, sometimes encouraging outsiders to step up and take on more responsibilities, and at others excluding or ignoring the NGO activists who overstepped their roles (Wallace, 2010, 50–56). Meanwhile, those seeking to come to live and work at the Unist'ot'en Camp must submit answers to a questionnaire, with information on what skills and resources they will bring to the camp, how they will support themselves without burdening the community, and their relationships of accountability. Only those people whom the community invites may come to stay at the camp, although this should not be confused with segregation. Many people have and continue to come through the camp, and several social justice organisations have forged ongoing relationships with the Unist'ot'en Camp, including the largely-settler group Social Coast, who have participated in a number of Indigenous land reclamations around BC (Rose-Redwood, 2015). Perhaps what is more important is that the Unist'ot'en Camp has become strongly aligned with the migrant justice movement, NOII (Walia, 2013, 87–89) (see also Chapter Seventeen by Pascucci, Chapter Nineteen by Rollman and Frenzel and Chapter Three by Rubing which examine refugee protest and solidarity camps). NOII has worked to support the Unist'ot'en Camp because it opposes the same systems of colonialism, racism and capitalism that displace people around the word, forcing them to become 'economic migrants', travelling around the world pursuing 'stolen resources' because their own economies have been destroyed by neoliberal and neo-colonial interference (Walia, 2010, 81). Simultaneously, NOII's solidarity is predicated on the need to recognise that even racialised or undocumented populations can still be 'complicit' in processes of settler colonialism, and that state violence and control manifests differently for Indigenous peoples than for other people of colour, even if the source is the same. By not trying to collapse the struggles of racialised and displaced migrants into those of Indigenous peoples, NOII instead contributes to the 'expanding horizons' of the Unist'ot'en Camp, signalling the possibilities available for building new kinds of solidarity relationships in and through these spaces of Indigenous resurgence.

Conclusion: reflections on responsibility

As anarchist scholar Adam Lewis has argued, research can be a form of anticolonial struggle, but only when the researcher self-consciously engages his or her own power relations and academic privileges in constructing the research project and the intended impacts that it will have (Lewis, 2012). In that respect, by way of a conclusion we offer some personal observations on our relationship to these Indigenous reoccupations. We were young when Oka occurred, barely conscious of it as an event, and yet it has been ever-present in our education and activism because of the incredible impact that it made on settler Canadian and Indigenous peoples' alike. We have never been in a position to visit and directly support Grassy Narrows or the Unist'ot'en Camp, but we believe that their efforts are of profound importance, and that social movement scholars, activists and students who may read this piece need to be aware of these struggles. The way that Indigenous reoccupations 'trouble' (Coulthard's word) the settler colonial, capitalist systems of the Canadian political economy is instructive, but the diversity and individuality of these camps is important to understand as well. The particular shape of the camps – the way that communities are brought together or divided, the proximity to and interaction with river and forest spaces, the way that social and cultural dynamics in the camps are guided by Indigenous spiritual and political traditions – all help to reinforce and reaffirm particular sets of values that must be practiced in relationship to the land as well as in opposition to colonialism and capitalism.

Many Indigenous scholars, writers and historians have documented these and other important moments of Indigenous resurgence through reoccupations, many of which we have cited throughout as we rely on their understandings of how and why Indigenous reoccupation camps are organised. As Alex Khasnabish and Max Haiven have argued, research can make an especially useful contribution to social movements when it is conducted with an ethic of 'convocation' – that is, creating time and space for diverse voices to enter into sustained conversation (Haiven and Khasnabish, 2014) (see Chapter Twenty-one by Crane, which also examines this concept). It is our hope that readers interested in the possibilities offered by Indigenous resurgence as practices in place-based reoccupations will seek out the works and scholars whom we rely on. Works such as *This is an Honour Song* (Ladner and Simpson, 2010), *Red Skin, White Masks* (Coulthard, 2014), *Wasase* (Alfred, 2005), and *Dancing on our Turtle's Back* (Simpson, 2011) offer powerful visions of decolonisation that can be of use to many other social movements. The adoption of 'decolonisation' by many of those in NOII is important, and offers an intriguing possibility for growing relationships of solidarity and accountability across colonial divides (Walia, 2013, 247–276). A growing number of social movement scholars have identified Indigenous struggles as fundamental to addressing the inequality of capitalism and the violence of the state, as well as intersecting systems of patriarchy, racism and cis-heteronormativity (for example, Day, 2005; Barker and Pickerill, 2012). A wider understanding of and engagement with these camps should naturally accompany the question: how best to support these reoccupations, and how to build further relationships across space with other protest camps with similar ends?

Notes

[1] During a 2003–2006 inquiry into the Ipperwash clash, evidence was found that the Premier of Ontario, Mike Harris, pressured the Ontario Provincial Police to attack the occupiers. See Peter Edwards' *One Dead Indian* (2003).

[2] It should be noted that the level of threat from the state has recently increased. In 2015, a Canadian court ruled against the Grassy Narrows community, upholding the rights of logging companies over the territorial sovereignty of the Anishinaabe. While the decision may be appealed to the Supreme Court of Canada, in the interim the Grassy Narrows camp can now 'legally' be dismantled by the state.

[3] Spelled variously 'Unist'ot'en,' 'Unis'tot'en,' and 'Unistoten,' depending on the source. At present, little academic literature exists on the Unist'ot'en Camp, but the participants have extensively documented their efforts, and popular media and blogs have increasingly reported on the camp. Please see unistotencamp.com for more information.

References

Alfred, T. (2005) *Wasase: Indigenous Pathways of Action and Freedom.* Peterborough, ON: Broadview Press.

Alfred, T. and Corntassel, J. (2005) 'Being Indigenous: resurgences against contemporary colonialism', *Government and Opposition*, 40(4), 597–614.

Alfred, T. and Lowe, L. (2005) 'Warrior societies in contemporary Indigenous communities', background paper prepared for the Ipperwash Inquiry, www.numberswatchdog.com/numbers%20docs/WarriorSocietiesinIndigenousCommunities1.pdf.

Al Jazeera Plus (2014) *How to Stop an Oil and Gas Pipeline: The Unist'ot'en Camp Resistance* [documentary video], https://youtu.be/aiVxyLb1hJA.

Barker, A. J. (2015) '"A direct act of resurgence, a direct act of sovereignty": reflections on idle no more, Indigenous activism, and Canadian settler colonialism' *Globalizations*, 12(1), 43–65.

Barker, A. J. and Pickerill, J. (2012) 'Radicalizing relationships to and through shared geographies: why anarchists need to understand Indigenous connections to land and place', *Antipode*, 44(5), 1705–1725.

Battell Lowman, E. and Barker, A. J. (2015) *Settler: Identity and Colonialism in 21st Century Canada.* Halifax: Fernwood Press.

Bruyneel, K. (2007) *The Third Space of Sovereignty: The Postcolonial Politics of U.S.–Indigenous Relations.* Minneapolis, MN: University of Minnesota Press.

Corntassel, J. and Bryce, C. (2012) 'Practicing sustainable self-determination: Indigenous approaches to cultural restoration and revitalization', *The Brown Journal of World Affairs*, 18(2), 151–162.

Coulthard, G. (2014) *Red Skin, White Masks.* Minneapolis, MN: University of Minnesota Press.

Day, R. J. F. (2005) *Gramsci is Dead: Anarchist Currents in the Newest Social Movements.* Toronto: Between the Lines.

Deloria, V., Jr. (1985) *Behind the Trail of Broken Treaties: An Indian Declaration of Independence.* Austin, TX: University of Texas Press.

Deloria, V., Jr. and Wildcat, D. (2001) *Power and Place: Indian Education in America.* Golden, CO: Fulcrum Resources.

Daschuk, J. (2013) *Clearing the Plains: Disease, Politics of Starvation, and the Loss of Aboriginal Life.* Regina, SK: University of Regina Press.

Doxtater, K. (2010) 'From paintings to power: the meaning of the Warrior Flag twenty years after Oka', *Socialist Studies*, 8(1), 96–124.

Dunbar-Ortiz, R. (2014) *An Indigenous Peoples' History of the United States.* Boston, MA: Beacon Press.

Edwards, P. (2003) *One Dead Indian: The Premier, the Police, and the Ipperwash Crisis*, Toronto: Stoddart Publishing.

Fimrite, P. (2012) 'Winnemem Wintu tribe stages war dance as protest', *San Francisco Chronicle*, 26 May, www.sfgate.com/news/article/Winnemem-Wintu-tribe-stages-war-dance-as-protest-3588954.php.

Frenzel, F., Feigenbaum, A. and McCurdy, P. (2013) 'Protest camps: an emerging field of social movement research', *The Sociological Review*, 62(3), 457–474.

Grande, S. (2013) 'Accumulation of the primitive: the limits of liberalism and the politics of occupy Wall Street', *Settler Colonial Studies*, 3(3–4), 369–380.

Haiven, M. and Khasnabish, A. (2014) *The Radical Imagination.* Halifax: Fernwood Press.

Harris, C. (2004) 'How did colonialism dispossess? Comments from an edge of empire', *Annals of the Association of American Geographers*, 94(1), 165–182.

Hunt, S. and Holmes, C. (2015) 'Everyday decolonization: living a decolonizing queer politics', *Journal of Lesbian Studies*, 19(2), 154–172.

Jones, J. (2014) 'Compensatory division in the occupy movement', *Rhetoric Review*, 33(2), 148–164.

Kilibarda, K. (2012) 'Lessons from #Occupy in Canada: contesting space, settler consciousness and erasures within the 99%', *Journal of Critical Globalisation Studies*, 5, 24–41.

King, H. (2014) 'We natives are deeply divided: there's nothing wrong with that', in Kino-nda-niimi Collective (eds) *The Winter We Danced: Voices from the Past, the Future, and the Idle No More Movement.* Winnipeg: Arbeiter Ring Press.

Kino-nada-niimi Collective (2014) *The Winter We Danced: Voices from the Past, the Future, and the Idle No More Movement.* Winnipeg: ARP Books.

Lagalisse, E. M. (2011) 'Marginalizing Magdalena': intersections of gender and the secular in anarchoindigenist solidarity activism', *Signs: Journal of Women in Culture and Society*, 36(3), 653–678.

Lambertus, S. (2004) *Wartime Images, Peacetime Wounds: The Media and the Gustafsen Lake Standoff.* Toronto: University of Toronto Press.

Lewis, A. G. (2012) 'Ethics, Activism and the Anti-Colonial: Social Movement Research as Resistance', *Social Movement Studies*, 11(2), 227–240.

Little Bear, L. (2004) 'Land: the Blackfoot source of identity', in *Beyond Race and Citizenship: Indigeneity in the 21st Century* conference. Berkeley, CA: University of California.

Macleod, A. (1992) *Acts of Defiance* [documentary film]. Halifax: National Film Board of Canada.

McLean, S. (2013) 'The whiteness of green: racialization and environmental education', *The Canadian Geographer*, 57(3), 354–362.

McSheffrey, E. (2015a) '"It's definitely going down", says Grand Chief Stewart Phillip on Unist'ot'en Camp raid', *Vancouver Observer*, 28 August, www.vancouverobserver.com/news/its-definitely-going-down-says-grand-chief-stewart-phillip-unistoten-camp-raid.

McSheffrey, E. (2015b) 'Unist'ot'en Camp on "high alert" under rumours of police raid', *Vancouver Observer*, 27 August 2015, www.vancouverobserver.com/news/unistoten-camp-high-alert-under-rumours-police-raid.

Morgensen, S. L. (2011) 'The biopolitics of settler colonialism: right here, right now', *Settler Colonial Studies*, 1, 52–76.

Nettleback, A. and Smandych, R. (2010) 'Policing Indigenous peoples on two colonial frontiers: Australia's mounted police and Canada's North-West Mounted Police', *The Australian and New Zealand Journal of Criminology*, 43(2), 356–375.

Obomsawin, A. (1993) *Kanehsatake: 270 Years of Resistance* [documentary film]. Halifax: National Film Board of Canada, nfb.ca/film/kanehsatake_270_years_of_resistance.

Obomsawin, A. (2000) *Rocks at Whiskey Trench* [documentary film]. Halifax: National Film Board of Canada, www.nfb.ca/playlists/alanis-obomsawin-retrospective/viewing/rocks_at_whiskey_trench.

Pablo, C. (2012) 'Northern BC's First Nations people to stand firm against pipelines', *The Georgia Straight Online*, 26 September, www.straight.com/news/northern-bcs-first-nations-people-stand-firm-against-pipelines.

Palmateer, P. (2015) 'Testimony of Mi'kmaq activist Pam Palmater at committee studying Bill C-51', *Global Research* [website], 30 March, www.globalresearch.ca/canada-anti-terrorist-bill-c-51-to-criminalize-thoughts-of-indigenous-peoples/5439608.

Pertusati, L. (1996) 'The 1990 Mohawk–Oka conflict: the importance of culture in social movement mobilization', *Race, Gender and Class*, 3(3), 89–105.

Pickerill, J. (2009) 'Finding common ground? Spaces of dialogue and the negotiation of Indigenous interests in environmental campaigns in Australia', *Geoforum*, 40(1), 66–79.

Prystupa, M. and Uechi, J. (2014) 'TransCanada pipeline contractors "evicted" again in BC's north', *Vancouver Observer*, 25 July, www.vancouverobserver.com/news/transcanada-crew-evicted-unist-ot-en-camp.

Regan, P. (2010) *Unsettling the Settler Within*. Vancouver: UBC Press.

Rogers, J. (2015) *Peace in Duress*. Vancouver: Talon Books.

Rose-Redwood, R. (2015) '"Reclaim, rename, reoccupy": decolonizing place and the reclaiming of PKOLS', *ACME* 15(1), 187–206.

Routledge, P. (2003) 'Convergence space: process geographies of grassroots globalization networks', *Transactions of the Institute of British Geographers*, 28(3), 333–349.

Simpson, L. (2011) *Dancing on Our Turtle's Back: Stories of Nishnaabeg Re-Creation, Resurgence, and a New Emergence*. Winnipeg: Arbeiter Ring Press.

Simpson, L. and Ladner, K. (2010) *This Is an Honour Song: Twenty Years Since the Blockades*. Winnipeg: Arbeiter Ring Press.

Smith, P. C. and Warrior, R. (1997) *Like A Hurricane: The Indian Movement from Alcatraz to Wounded Knee*. New York: The New Press.

Stevenson, L. (2012) 'The psychic life of biopolitics: Survival, cooperation, and Inuit community', *American Ethnologist*, 39(3), 592–613.

Toledano, M. (2014) 'The view from Unist'ot'en: a camp that stands firmly in the path of Enbridge's Northern Gateway pipeline', *Vice*, 19 June, www.vice.com/en_ca/read/the-view-from-unistoten-a-camp-that-stands-firmly-in-the-path-of-enbridges-northern-gateway-pipeline.

Toledano, M. (2015) 'Normal day @ #Unistoten – salmon, sushi, healing centre construction, helicopter surveillance. Still under high alert [Tweet]', [@M_Tol] 30 August, https://twitter.com/M_Tol/status/637795593008484352.

Unist'ot'en Camp (2012) 'The uncertainty of pipelines in unceded lands', *Unist'ot'en Camp* [website], 7 November, http://unistotencamp.com/?p=65.

Unist'ot'en Camp (2014) 'Press release: Unist'ot'en clan refuse all pipeline projects', *Unist'ot'en Camp* [website], 18 June, http://unistotencamp.com/?p=950.

Veracini, L. (2010) *Settler Colonialism: A Theoretical Overview*. London: Palgrave Macmillan.

Veracini, L. (2015) *The Settler Colonial Present*. London: Palgrave Macmillan.

Walia, H. (2010) 'Transient servitude: migrant labour in Canada and the apartheid of citizenship', *Race and Class*, 52(1), 71–84.

Walia, H. (2013) *Undoing Border Imperialism*. Oakland, CA: AK Press.

Wallace, R. (2010) 'Grassy narrows blockade: reworking relationships between Anishinabe and non-Indigenous activists at the grassroots', *International Journal of Canadian Studies*, 41, 37–68.

Watts, V. (2013) 'Indigenous place-thought and agency amongst humans and non-humans (First Woman and Sky Woman go on a European world tour!)', *Decolonization: Indigeneity, Education and Society*, 2(1), 20–34.

Wilkes, R. and Ricard, D. (2007) 'How does newspaper coverage of collective action vary?: Protest by Indigenous people in Canada', *The Social Science Journal*, 44, 231–251.

Willow, A. J. (2010) 'Cultivating common ground: cultural revitalization in Anishinaabe and anthropological discourse', *American Indian Quarterly*, 34(1), 33–60.

Willow, A. J. (2011) 'Conceiving Kakipitatapitmok: the political landscape of Anishinaabe anticlearcutting activism', *American Anthropologist*, 113(2), 262–276.

Willow, A. J. (2012) *Strong Hearts, Native Lands: Anti-Clearcutting Activism at Grassy Narrows First Nation*. Winnipeg: University of Manitoba Press.

York, G. and Pindera, L. (1991) *People of the Pines: The Warriors and the Legacy of Oka*. Toronto: Little Brown.

THIRTEEN

Democratic deficit in the Israeli Tent Protests: chronicle of a failed intervention

Uri Gordon

Introduction

This chapter offers an insider's account and analysis of the failed efforts to democratise the Israeli Tent Protest movement and to impose accountability on its founders. Although one of the 2011 mobilisation's main banners was democratic revival and the power of collective decision-making, the attempt to implement these principles failed on the countrywide level. Behind the scenes of the lively camps, public assemblies and mass demonstrations, a fraught conflict was taking place between the movement's grassroots and its small group of founders, who had been crowned by the mainstream media as its leaders and with whom the political establishment had begun to engage. While declaring their commitment to transparency and direct democracy, the founders remained a closed group, rejecting or circumventing successive attempts to subject them to a countrywide delegate structure.

This story, despite having been arguably the most prominent topic of conversation among protest participants at the time, has received no sustained attention in scholarly discussions of the Tent Protests so far. What little literature does exist on these protests in Israel falls into three groups. The first contextualises the protests in Israel's political economy, explaining how neoliberal consolidation has created, as in other OECD countries, a precarious 'class-generational unit' (Rosenhek and Shalev, 2014, 43), young people of a middle-class background whose coming of age was marked by the fragmentation of old solidarities, and who now look forward to less economic security and lower standards of living than their parents'. The protests signify this cohort's break with its depoliticised, atomised and consumerist identities, while adding distinctly materialist agendas to the post-materialist ones associated with the New Social Movements (Herzog, 2013; Grinberg, 2013;

Levy, 2015). The second group of writings focuses on the movement's geographical dimensions, analysing the various spatial strategies used to 'activise' the protests (Marom, 2013); discourses of justice among movement-allied planners (Alfasi and Fenster, 2014); the importance of protest sites' lack of symbolic national resonance (Wallach, 2013); and the gendered and class dynamics animating the 'peripheral' camps in poor towns and neighbourhoods, which mobilised for a 'protest within a protest' (Misgav, 2013; Fenster and Misgav, 2015; Leibner, 2015). Lastly, the third group of texts criticises protesters' political timidity and their conscious choice to present an a-political front. Pointing to the protesters' reliance on the 'ambiguous yet profoundly Zionist notion of the sovereign people posed as a revolutionary subject' (Monterescu and Shaindlinger, 2013, 230), these contributions highlight the chilling effect of the anti-democratic, left-baiting discourses currently prominent in Israel, which caused protesters to avoid any mention of the occupation or settler colonialism in Israel/Palestine (Gordon, 2012; Shenhav, 2013; Rabinowitz, 2014).

In all of these sources, the present topic of democratic deficit has received only two brief mentions (Chalozin-Dovrat, 2012, 141–2; Ram and Filc, 2013, 36). This chapter attempts to close this gap. I open with an account of the movement's development and early tensions around leadership, and then recount the democratisation efforts from my own perspective. The analysis that follows critically relates the events described to the analysis and proposals forwarded by Jo Freeman in her well-known article *The Tyranny of Structurelessness* (Freeman, 1970). Concluding that its structural-functionalist framework is inadequate for explaining the dynamics involved, I suggest two related explanations as an alternative. The first derives from an emphasis on individual agency: the democratisation process failed because the founders were mostly junior media workers who brought their professional mentality into their leadership role, and were thus easily swept up by the frenetic press agenda, dismissing slower processes of deliberation as a luxury. Moreover, the founders had come to rely on three professional campaign advisors associated with the Israeli Communist Party, who were openly contemptuous towards horizontalism. The second explanation is a matter of political culture: lacking any background in radical politics, grassroots participants had no terms of reference beyond conventional notions of representation, transparency and accountability, and were unable to make the leap towards a fully anti-representational, horizontal and networked politics. This was coupled with a view of the mobilisation as a winnable short-term campaign, rather than one episode in a longer-term process of movement-building and consciousness-raising. Had the latter view prevailed, the struggle over representation could have been productively abandoned.

Two preliminary comments on method: first, while recent decades have seen participant observation gain legitimacy as a strategy for researching social movements from within (Lichterman, 1998; 2002; Gordon, 2012), the present account is somewhat irregular. It derives from an unplanned period of two weeks of intensive participation, wherein my engrossment in the movement's internal politics, cross-country travelling and round-the-clock communication took place without a scholarly project in mind. As a consequence, notes were taken in retrospect and what follows is the result of 'retroactive participant observation' (Sasson-Levy and Rapoport, 2003, 386) rather than a carefully planned research design. Second, my own role in the events was rather prominent, closely aligning with the concept of 'militant ethnography' (Juris, 2007; Uldam and McCurdy, 2013; Russell, 2015). As an approach to research, militant ethnography departs from pretences to disengaged and 'value-free' inquiry and instead takes full measure of the researcher-activist's insider's position and their role in shaping the movements and events they research. This includes 'weighing in during strategic and tactical debates entangled with complex relations of power' and 'the emotions associated with direct action organizing and activist networking' (pp 164–165). While a significant 'observer effect' is inevitable in such cases, this can still take place within a transparent and self-critical framework. It is in this spirit that I offer what follows.

Mobilisation and early tensions

While the first half of 2011 saw major pro-democracy mobilisations in the Arab world and anti-capitalist protests in Portugal, Spain and Greece, the parallel Israeli movements were limited to cost-of-living agendas and directed their demands towards the existing government. Rising fuel prices prompted a series of demonstrations and traffic slowdowns in the first half of the year (YNet News, 2011), organised largely through Facebook and Twitter by citizens who had not previously participated in any mobilisation. In June, a Facebook group calling for a boycott on overpriced cottage cheese (a popular product in Israel) attracted more than 100,000 members within days. The protest (Kraft, 2011) received significant media attention, and by the end of the month all three major dairy producers had announced price reductions. The first call for a protest camp in Tel Aviv was issued in early July. The instigator was Daphni Leef, a freelance video editor, who had to leave her rented flat due to renovations but soon discovered that a new rental would be beyond her means. She opened a Facebook event titled 'Emergency: pick up a tent and take a stand', where she announced that she would be pitching a tent on Rothschild Boulevard to protest against high housing prices. Leef was soon contacted by a number of her friends and acquaintances, who would organise the first tent camp. These included Regev Contes, a documentary and commercials film director; Stav Shafir and Yonatan Levi, both freelance journalists; Roee Neumann, a marketing student; Yonatan Miller, an actor; Julian Feder, a video editor, who unlike the others had a political background in the Trotskyist groupuscule 'Socialist Struggle' (CWI); and Yigal Rambam, an experienced activist from outside Leef's milieu who had been central to the fuel protests. The latter two would eventually break with the founders' group precisely over the tensions discussed here.

By the time the first tents were pitched on the boulevard, on 14 July 2011, the founders' publicity efforts in their own social networks had borne fruit: over 200 people joined the call and spent the night in the camp, most of them young residents of Tel Aviv, students or precarious workers in services or creative industries. A camp was set up in Jerusalem on the same day, and the movement soon received official endorsement from the National Union of Israeli Students (NUIS) and its chair, Itzik Shmuli. Within the first few weeks over 70 camps appeared in almost every Israeli town and city, with sitting areas and information stalls, meals and discussions, and local demonstrations and marches. In the smaller camps, most of the activity took place in the evenings, with the site being maintained during the daytime by a handful of organisers, often students with experience in youth movements and volunteering, as well as pensioners, unemployed people and teenagers on school holidays. The Rothschild camp, however, was of a different order of magnitude. Occupying the boulevard's kilometre-long central pedestrian stretch, the camp was a round-the-clock carnivalesque happening, with spontaneous speakers' corners and conversation circles, artistic performances and laptop hubs, and a constant stream of passers-by. Prefiguring later scenes at Zucotti Park, it also attracted a mélange of esoteric groups, from ultra-orthodox hippies and Scientology cultists to Project Venus enthusiasts and water fluoridation conspiracists.

The most obvious reason for the mobilisation's rapid spread was immediate, intensive and sympathetic media attention (Kimmel-Green et al, 2012). For six weeks the protests were headline news, as every major outlet seized upon an attractive story to break monotony of the summer's 'silly season'. In a manner unparalleled in the M15 or Occupy mobilisations, where journalists were treated with suspicion or even hostility, the Rothschild founders proactively coordinated with the corporate press from the start. The Rothschild camp founders quickly became media celebrities and figureheads through which the protests were reported. They were driven to maintain this role, keen to control messaging as the hard right began a campaign of rumours and disinformation (Genosar, 2011) intended to portray the protests as an 'astroturf' conspiracy initiated and funded by treasonous left-wing forces. It was the founders' embrace of the limelight, which set the scene for their ensuing conflict with the grassroots.

Yet several other factors contributed to the protests' spread. First, the tactic was familiar: small protest camps have been a feature of Israeli politics for decades, most often in the government quarter in Jerusalem but also in Tel Aviv and elsewhere. Over the years, well-publicised protest camps were set up by Ethiopian immigrants (Kaplan, 1988), disabled people (Rimmerman and Herr, 2004; Rimon-Greenspan, 2007), single mothers (Lavie, 2012; Herbst, 2013) and, since mid-2010, by the parents of captured Israeli soldier Gilad Shalit and their supporters (Sharim, 2013). Second, the conscript military background of many Israelis made for advanced organisational skills even in the absence of activist experience, with participants habituated to working quickly in small teams and using decentralised communication structures. Finally, camps in the major cities were soon joined by organisers, who had been involved in the Activism Festivals. This aspect deserves some attention because it helps explain the major generational and political change that occurred in Israeli grassroots activism through the 2000s. The first four Festivals were organised yearly from 2002 by Green Action, a radical group whose organisers had driven the direct action campaign against the Cross Israel Highway in 1998–99 and had a major role within the wider network of vegan anarch@-punks, radical NGO workers, artists, students and ravers who took up the Israeli iteration of the counter-globalist wave. Yet by 2005, following an internal crisis in Green Action, the festivals stopped being organised, as activists on the Israeli radical left almost entirely abandoned anti-capitalist causes in favour of solidarity work in the West Bank and the campaign against the Segregation Barrier (Gordon, 2010). The grassroots environmentalist vacuum was filled by a younger and relatively depoliticised network of students and itinerant workers, drawn to low-tech skills, alternative spiritualities, and the second-hand Deep Ecology of Daniel Quinn's novel *Ishmael* (Quinn, 1992). It was this network which took on reviving the Activism Festival in 2010, now adding a concert stage and orienting the event to the general public. While an explicit direct action agenda was no longer present, the event remained free, relying on 'magic hat' donations in the tradition of the Rainbow Gathering (Berger, 2006; Tavory and Goodman, 2009), and continued to employ a horizontal structure and consensus decision-making. Now, organisers of this new iteration of the Festival were playing an important part in creating camp infrastructures such as the field kitchen at Rothschild, which at its height fed some 500 participants daily.

Two weeks into the protests, polls indicated that they received 85 per cent public support (Perry, 2011). Yet precisely due to this popularity, and again in a manner unparalleled elsewhere, figures from the political establishment soon launched attempts to co-opt the protests. Tel Aviv mayor Ron Huldai came to the Rothschild camp on the first night, but was received with hostility and left. The same happened to right-wing parliamentarian Miri Regev the next day (see chronology in Oren et al, 2012, 23–33). On the fourth day of the protests, Prime Minister Benjamin Netanyahu publicly called upon the participants to support him in passing the National Housing Committees law – a move to further deregulate the construction industry which he had been planning since March, and was now presenting as a measure to deal with housing prices. In a blatant attempt to split the protests, Netanyahu also offered the NUIS several benefits such as a year of reduced bus tariffs for students – an offer which Shmuli and his aides wisely rejected.

As the founders organised to stave off co-optation efforts and hostile spins, they held on to their monopoly on media access. Acording to Rambam (in Shechter, 2012, 77),

> We became power-drunk very quickly. When additional camps began to emerge, Julian was the first to insist that we create a council of delegates from every camp. That we would loosen the reins, let go of the control. There was already a process going on of half-secret meetings and running off to [be interviewed on] morning and afternoon programmes…and suddenly the members of Dov Khenin's team in 'Ir Lekulanu' came in by the back door.

Ir Lekulanu ('City For Us All') was a left grouping created in 2008 for the Tel Aviv municipal elections, whose mayoral candidate was Khenin, a charismatic parliamentarian from the Arab–Jewish Israeli Communist Party. Rambam is referring to three individuals: Alon-Li Green, Khenin's parliamentary aide; Sharon Shachaf, a professional campaign manager who had run the Ir Lekulanu campaign; and her partner Noam Hofstadter, a Tel Aviv municipal councillor for Ir

Lekulanu. Three days into the protests they were invited by Yonatan Levi to become the founders' strategic advisors, and from then on they effectively called the shots. With their help, the first mass demonstration in Tel Aviv was organised for 23 July, with resources such as the stage and PA system paid for through donations collected from the public at the Rothschild camp and during the rally. The demonstration drew a surprising 20,000 participants and showed a remarkable level of militancy, ending with a blockade of a major junction and 15 arrests (Volinitz, 2011).

The first major concerns around representation now surfaced, prompted by the founders' control over who would speak at the rally. The ferment was especially felt in the Rothschild camp, which had taken on a life of its own while the founders moved to operate on a national level and conduct their meetings away from the boulevard, at an office space made available to Contes. The leadership vacuum was filled by Aya Shoshan, a radical who had just returned from Madrid where she had been active with the M15 mobilisation (Shoshan, 2012). Diving into activity at the camp, she was quick to teach the protesters the rudiments of popular assembly decision-making (compare Commission for Group Dynamics, 2011). A refreshing alternative to the usual Israeli mode of impatient and adversarial dialogue, these practices were nothing short of a revelation to the participants. Assisted by media attention to hand signals and other curiosities, the practices quickly spread to camps throughout the country. Yet a gulf had opened between the assembly's self-perception of sovereignty and the founders' autonomous decisions.

A day after the rally, Shoshan would later relate (Shechter, 2012, 2),

> There was almost violent rage in the camp, and suddenly I understood that I had a part in creating a very problematic situation…on the other hand, I really believed that this is how things should work. Initially I retreated a bit…but finally carried on, because why should a specific group of people decide how this whole thing is organised?

The founders attended a meeting at the camp, where they took a conciliatory tone. Daphni Leef reassured the participants that her

> team, which allegedly hides behind closed doors and makes decisions, doesn't decide anything, but only defends what is happening in the country from outside interests…When we need to send a response out quickly because we're subject

to a spin, we get together as six people to defend what is happening here. (Shakuf baOhel, 2011)

Stav Shafir, for her part, said that from the outset 'we dreamt about democratic consensus assemblies…Anyone who wants to speak or express their views, who wants to join the spokespersons' team, talk to the media – we will be glad. Contact us. I apologise that until now we have not done this in an orderly fashion' (Shakuf baOhel, 2011). In the background, the idea to convene a countrywide assembly was launched by Activism Festival veterans, among them Mor Huber, who took on the role of coordination between the camps. The first such meeting took place secretly in Hayarkon Park, with only specific people invited. It concluded with the decision to go back to the camps' assemblies, elect two representatives from each, and organise a new, publicly declared, countrywide assembly. That meeting, held a few days later in a lecture hall at Tel Aviv University, was by all accounts a disaster. The founders who attended hardly spoke at all, and along with the lack of an agreed methodology on how to run the meeting, little room was left for constructive dialogue. Participants had also come with very distinct ideas about what the meeting was about, and about the relationship between it and the Rothschild group. Many thought they had been invited by Leef to collaborate, not that the assembly was forced upon the founders. Further tensions were created by the fact that the founders had failed to consult anyone that morning, when they were invited to meet with President Shimon Peres at his residence in Jerusalem. Anxious not to be seen as disrespectful, they accepted. At the meeting, to which the press was also invited, Peres fawned over the protesters, calling them a 'generation of love' and calling for 'dialogue, not negotiations'. Coming out of the meeting, Shmuli was quick to declare that 'we are heeding the President's call and will arrive at any round table or framework in which we can have dialogue with the government' (Walla News, 2011). Many activists saw this as an intention to negotiate with the government without any mandate. What was worse, during the meeting it was revealed that the founders had sent Barak Segal – a student who had recently joined their closed group – to attend the 'Round Table' of organisations and youth movements, which was convening that same evening to discuss the 'demands' of the protests. The founders had kept this a secret throughout the entire meeting, but it was exposed by one of the attendees. The participants were infuriated, and the meeting broke up acrimoniously.

Diving in

It was at this point that my involvement with the movement began in earnest. I had already made first contact a week earlier, in Jerusalem. I had come up with my wife and toddler, from our remote home in the southern desert, to meet with Peace Cycle activists who had completed a 7,000-mile ride from the UK to Palestine. On the way, we passed by the Jerusalem tent camp that had been set up on a patch of lawn just outside the Old City walls. It was still a small affair, with perhaps 10 or 15 people present. As we dropped in, just to look around, I was collared by Micha, an anti-occupation activist with whom I had worked on successive Activism Festivals. The participants were in the middle of a meeting to decide whether to relocate to a new site, and were finding it very difficult to have a structured discussion. Micha asked if I could contribute from my experience in consensus facilitation. He also introduced me to a camp founder, Rona Orvano, an architecture student and president of the students' union at Bezalel art school. After going over the consensus process, I facilitated a successful discussion that resulted in a decision to relocate.

A week later, I was in Tel Aviv – again with my family, but this time on the way to the airport to visit my in-laws in the USA. We had only planned to stop by Rothschild on the way, but within minutes I was again collared into participation. This time it was Uri Porat, another Activism Festival veteran. Frustrated by the inexperience of many participants and the difficulty in making collective decisions, he quickly brought me up to speed on the recent days' events. I was already infected by the energetic atmosphere of the camp, and sensed that this was an opportunity for real positive influence. My other half, in a remarkable show of generosity for which I will be ever grateful, offered to fly without me while I stayed behind for a few days. She probably realised that if I passed on this opportunity, I would be unbearable for the entire trip. We went to the airport together, where I rescheduled my own flight ten days forward, and I returned to Rothschild.

Initially I had little enthusiasm for the protests, whose message was far from radical. As an anarchist I was unsympathetic toward appeals for the revival of the welfare state rather than an all-out critique of capitalism, and even more so towards the explicit side-stepping of the Israeli–Palestinian conflict, the occupation and the militaristic and racially stratified nature of Israeli society. But what motivated me was the understanding that the protests offered so many people their very first experience of collective action, a wide opportunity to engage in participatory decision-making and enjoy the resultant empowerment and transformation (compare Feigenbaum et al, 2013, 42). This was the one aspect I found inspiring, and which placed me in alliance with the grassroots forces seeking to redistribute power within the movement.I spent the next couple of days integrating myself into the movement, initially helping to set up a new and explicitly radical camp in Tel Aviv's Lewinsky Garden, a run-down area near the central bus station where homeless people and asylum seekers were already present alongside activists who had been supporting them against repression and racist attacks. I also began visiting other camps and making sense of the mix of established and new groups involved. A few nights after arriving, I helped to facilitate the Rothschild camp assembly. The leading activists were Aya and Noa Savir, a primary school teacher with crowd-control skills to match. By this time they had become more than neutral facilitators, and were actively promoting a two-point proposal: no to negotiations with the government, and a call to re-convene the national assembly as the only legitimate decision-making body for the protest movement. My non-tendentious facilitation was not what they were looking for, so I took a step back, and the decision was accepted by the camp's alternative to consensus – a 'clear visual majority'.

Later that night, I received a call from Rona Orvano. She had been co-opted into the founders' group and was at that moment sitting with them in Contes's office. Saying only that they were 'in a crisis', she recalled my facilitation in Jerusalem and suggested that I should intervene. I agreed and made my way there. As I entered the office, I couldn't help recalling the scene form *Pulp Fiction* in which The Wolf makes his appearance. Reeling from the failure of the countrywide assembly, rebuffed by the Rothschild decision that evening, and exhausted by weeks of pressure, the founders were in a state of anxiety and confusion. The media had begun to circulate unattributed reports about the protests 'losing momentum' and 'showing signs of division', and they were worried that the upcoming Saturday night's rally would be a failure. More than anything, my task was to help them calm down and collect themselves. I sat them in a circle, took on the facilitator's role, and had each one briefly express their view of the challenges. Once they had done that and the atmosphere had become much more relaxed, I suggested two points that they could adopt: a 'decision' that the rally on Saturday would be the largest yet (it ended up being just that, with up to 70,000 demonstrators), and a commitment to cooperate with the Rothschild assembly, hold off any further contact with the government, and attend the next countrywide assembly. The founders agreed.

The next morning I was contacted by Lin Chalozin-Dovrat, a Sorbonne doctoral student formerly active with the Women's Coalition for Peace, who invited me to meet with her along with Meretz activist Tal Grunspan and Mor Huber. Huber, as mentioned above, had become the movement's most effective networker, accumulating a contact list of activists in dozens of camps around the country. Seeing eye to eye on the issue of democratic deficit, we formed a networking team with the first task of organising another countrywide assembly. Over the next couple of days we busied ourselves spreading the word, finding an appropriate venue, and recruiting some professional group facilitators from Shatil (a trainers' group providing support and consultancy to NGOs) to accompany the process. Thanks to this preparatory work, the second countrywide assembly was much more constructive than the first, although tensions with the founders remained at the forefront. Leef and Shafir, who attended, endorsed the final decision to create a national steering committee with two delegates from each of five geographical districts, elected for a two-week tenure from among already-mandated camp representatives.

I spent the following week travelling far and wide, helping to arrange the selection processes in five district-wide meetings. Apart from anything else, these meetings were invaluable networking opportunities for geographically proximate activists (Routledge, 2003; Juris, 2005). Yet there remained a great deal of suspicion about the process, as well as misconceptions about numbers and representation. Tent delegates took it for granted that decisions in the new steering committee would be made by majority vote, and were thus concerned that their numerical representation would be inadequate. Indeed, the exact relationship between the local level of the camp, the mid-level of the district and the countrywide steering committee was never resolved, neither in terms of decision-making nor regarding issues of representation. Hence, it was also unclear how decisions would be taken on any of the three levels, although there was talk of a 'daily flow' of information and decision making between all three levels. Despite these difficulties, by the end of the week we had ten delegates to the national steering committee, and had also met individually with as many of the founders as we could, in order to ensure their willingness to cooperate with the process.

Given the amount of effort put into the process, the first meeting of the new steering committee was nothing short of shocking. I had simply not been aware of the extent of the three campaign advisors' influence on the founders, nor of their open contempt for the process I had just led. Instead of the spokescouncil I had perhaps naively envisioned, I found myself in the middle of a power-grab.

Shachaf, Green and Hofstadter took control of the space with an air of impatient entitlement, ejected the facilitator we had invited to guide the discussion, and announced the end of this 'toying with democracy' (Hofstadter's words). They told the delegates that they were there to help them get the camps in line with the strategy they had already settled on: a demand to reopen the national budget once Parliament was back in session. I sat there quietly, taking minutes, reluctant to step into power and challenge them. I could have spoken up and contested them. But after all, I was not elected by anyone. I hoped the delegates would be more assertive, but they were unable to step up. At that point I realised that the process was doomed. The democratic delegation process, aimed at lending the founders' ear to the grassroots, had run up against the will of the campaign advisors who already had it. I was comforted by the fact that the delegates did receive defined roles within the national campaign, and hoped that something would still come of it. My rescheduled flight took me away from the scene the next day.

The chain of events that followed is reconstructed from later conversations and accounts (TentOfHope, 2011). Apparently the founders continued working as a closed group, and avoided any further communication with the delegates beyond the first meeting. Assemblies continued to take place daily in individual camps, and weekly on the countrywide level, but even the watered-down structure the founders had seemed to accept was not implemented. This became apparent when, on 24 August, they convened a press conference along with leaders of the Labour–Zionist 'Dror Israel' movement, intended to present the document produced by the 'Round Table' meetings with demands towards the government – a document which no camp delegate had seen. This time there was far more vocal opposition from the grassroots, and activists from the peripheral camps broke up the event. Following the press conference, activists began to work towards another countrywide assembly. This was no longer a naive democratic process, but a conscious struggle for power, with preparatory work including 'secret' meetings and decisions in advance on who would be 'elected' as regional delegates, so that they could stand up to the founders.

The assembly convened in Ashdod, with 51 camp delegates and a number of the founders, and was very charged. In the heated exchange, the camp delegates asserted their loss of confidence in the founders. The final proposal that the meeting voted on was to establish yet another formal leadership group that would include the ten elected district delegates and three members of the founders' group. The decision passed by a small majority, leading to a difficult atmosphere.

Leef said that the decision was unacceptable and a slap in the face, and that it would lead to the founders leaving the struggle. Following another large demonstration on Saturday night, district delegates met with most of the founders on Sunday in an attempt to implement the decision. After several hours of discussions, the founders left the room for a consultation. When they returned they announced that the three who would join the district delegates would be Jonathan Levy (who did not attend the meeting), Alon-Li Green, and Oren Pasternak, a student leader. The district delegates rejected the proposal, seeing Leef and Shafir's decision to stay out of the team as an explicit attempt to undermine its relevance, keeping the power of media representation outside the new forum. Several hours of further talks spilled over to the street achieved no progress. For the grassroots, this was the final demonstration that the founders had no desire to work seriously with the grassroots, but only to draw out negotiations with them as they continued to operate as usual.

This was, as far as I can ascertain, how things ended. Within a week the movement began to peter out as the summer holidays ended, and with them the availability of free time and fair weather. Following the final Saturday night demonstration on 3 September – the largest in Israel's history, with up to 430,000 participants (Sherwood, 2011) – Shmuli declared the protests over as far as the NUIS was concerned, and media interest fell away as quickly as it had mounted. Camps were soon dismantled around the country, leaving only a handful of so-called 'no alternative' camps populated by the genuinely homeless. These too were forcibly evicted during the following months. The countrywide assembly continued to meet, however, and in line with a decision taken there many locales continued to hold weekly popular meetings and discussion circles for months to come. Two other important sub-networks outlived the camps: the 'Northern Front' coalition of activists from that part of the country, and the 'Periphery Forum' which brought together new and veteran activists from poorer towns and neighbourhoods, and which had had a very important role in mounting opposition to the founders and eventually in teaming up with the countrywide assembly to produce the result in Ashdod. All of these organised support for the 'no alternative' camps and discussed ideas for longer-term mobilisation. Other organisations which were created following the protests included the Social Guard – an activist presence in parliamentary committees – and a number of new cooperatives including the Bar Kayma social centre in Tel Aviv. In mid-September the Trajtenberg Committee, set up by the government in response to the protests, published its recommendations – most of them already parts of extant legislation that the government had failed to implement, and which have not been implemented since (Nagar, 2012). Shafir and Shmuli, for their part, began to prepare for political careers. Both ran in the November 2012 Labour Party primaries, were elected to top positions on the national list, and soon became members of parliament.

Analysis: the failure of formal structures

To seasoned activists, the events related above may immediately bring to mind a well-known analysis dating back 45 years – Jo Freeman's article *The Tyranny of Structurelessness* (Freeman, 1970; hereafter: 'TToS'). Addressing itself primarily to the feminist consciousness-raising circles of the time, it argues that these groups have made a dogmatic commitment to a lack of formal structures. This 'structurelessness', however, creates a void filled by informal hierarchies, constituted and perpetuated by in-groups of personal friends whose unaccountable interactions stand in for transparent decision-making. The lack of structures thus

> becomes a smokescreen for the strong or the lucky to establish unquestioned hegemony over others...the rules of how decisions are made are known only to a few and awareness of power is curtailed by those who know the rules, as long as the structure of the group is informal. Those who do not know the rules and are not chosen for initiation must remain in confusion, or suffer from paranoid delusions that something is happening of which they are not quite aware. (Freeman, 1970, 6)

The solution Freeman proposes is to acknowledge that inequalities are inescapable, but to formalise group structures so that the informal hierarchies re-constituted democratically. Since an elite is unlikely to renounce its power, even if challenged, 'the only other alternative is formally to structure the group in such a way that the original power is institutionalised...If the informal elites have been well structured and have exercised a fair amount of power in the past, such a task is feasible' (Freeman, 1970). As the informal elites become formal ones, rules for democratic control are introduced to broaden participation and create accountability. Positions which incur authority and decision-making power should be delegated by election, distributed among many participants, rotated often, and include a requirement to be responsible to the group. Information must be diffused widely and frequently, and everyone should have equal access to the group's money or equipment. As a result, 'the group of people in positions of authority will be diffuse, flexible, open and temporary' (Freeman, 1970, 8).

At first glance, the analysis and proposals of TToS appear highly relevant to the situation we were confronting: an unelected leadership created out of an informal friendship group, a grassroots movement excluded from its unaccountable decision-making, and an attempt, not to unseat the leadership, but to subject it to democratic accountability via formal structures. The founders would have remained the public face of the movement, given their access to national media, but what they said and did was to become more accountable and representative. Yet on a closer look, the events related above only highlight the analytical limitations of TToS, and the key flaw in its proposals.

To begin with, there were obvious differences in context. TToS addresses small, continuous face-to-face groups rather than a surging mass movement with a few weeks' life-cycle. Moreover, the 'in-group' here was not a clique that emerged due to the lack of formal structures, but rather a network of friends (or at least inhabitants of the same milieu) which had launched the movement itself. This discrepancy can be highlighted against Freeman's account of the 'Star system' (Freeman, 1970, 9):

> We live in a society which expects political groups to make decisions and to select people to articulate those decisions to the public at large...the public is conditioned to look for spokespeople. While it has consciously not chosen spokespeople, the movement has thrown up many women who have caught the public eye for varying reasons...women of public note are put in the role of spokespeople by default. This is one main source of the ire that is often felt toward the women who are labelled 'stars'.

Yet in the Tent Protests there were no sporadic stars 'thrown up' by events, but an organised group of people who consciously seized the opportunity to become stars with the savviness of media workers. The point is that the informal elite was not *created by* the lack of formal structures, as Freeman argues, but emerged in the deliberate interaction between the founders and the mainstream media.

What these discrepancies expose is the problematic at the centre of the TToS analysis: the complete bracketing of individual agency. It would not be an exaggeration to say that TToS is as blinkered a structural-functionalist account as can be found in 1970s American sociology. It approaches its object of study as a system, and it is only in terms of the system's formal and informal rules that the analysis proceeds, while the wills and designs of the people who inhabit the system have an anecdotal place at best. Thus friendship-elites 'are not conspiracies' but instead the result of inescapable structural factors – leading to the paradox whereby the elites are both hidden behind a 'smokescreen' and readily observable to 'anyone with a sharp eye and an acute ear' (Freeman, 1970, 10). Unless the latter organs are the sole provision of the social scientist, it is hard to see how an informal elite, based on friendship and enabled by structurelessness, could remain hidden or survive criticism for any extended period.

Such an extreme position in the structure–agency debate is overly deterministic in its view of the relationship between underlying structures and the behaviour of the human beings placed within them. It brackets the possibility of corrective agency on the part of the leaders themselves, who may realise their position is problematic and take steps to rectify the situation. Conversely, and crucially for our purposes, her functionalist premises lead Freeman to place far too much stock in the opportunities offered by formalisation of structures. If formal structures are the solution, then what happens when the informal elite group either rejects or circumvents them? What if the informal elite gains such independent and self-reinforcing level of public exposure that it no longer requires the loyalty of the grassroots in order to maintain its position?

This, I would argue, is what happened in the Tent Protests. Perhaps the internal structure would have been more democratic to begin with, had the founders been more experienced as activists and more genuinely committed to horizontalist values. Seeing the contradiction inherent in their prominence, they could have stepped back or even disappeared from the scene, leaving the movement truly unrepresented and uncontrollable. Yet most of them were junior media workers, who saw media reportage as the most important arena for struggle. This caused them to harmonise with the same frantic pace dictated by journalists, who needed immediate statements and responses to various spins and allegations. In this situation, a longer and more patient process of consultation with the grassroots naturally struck them as a luxury, if not an outright burden. To this was added the three campaign managers' condescending dismissal of horizontalism, or rather of a caricature thereof, as evinced by these quotes from Hofstadter and Shachaf (in Schechter, 2012, 129–130):

I think this approach, according to which any centre, any locus of decision making, is bad because the final goal is a different and democratic culture that we want to constitute, is mistaken. I don't believe in direct democracy. It's an amazing idea that can't work. In practice, it only deepened the rifts.

Direct democracy is one of things that are very nice in theory, but I've never seen anywhere where it worked. Most people have neither the time nor the patience to sit in front of their emails and sit all day in meetings and vote all the time. Most people have time to come to one demonstration a week.

Contes (quoted in Schechter, 2012, 130) expressed a similar sentiment: 'It was a campaign. That's all it was. These people, the psychotics in the camps, didn't understand that this stupid direct democracy thing isn't relevant here. Here there's no democracy. Here there's energy…there's no place for democracy when anyone off the street can participate.'

Set up against such hostility, the delegation process was doomed from the start – from the point of view of the advisors, it was nothing but a pacifying tactic towards the grassroots, which would allow them to maintain control. It was my own good faith that was unwarranted.

Analytically, the conclusion here is that critiques of power within social movements cannot sidestep the role of individual agency, and of individual's values and ideology, in shaping larger structures. This is especially true in extreme cases such as the Tent Protests, where power is concentrated in so few hands. In this context, the now-neglected sociological interest in small groups (Hare, 1994; Fine and Harrington, 2004) remains an attractive avenue for further research.

At the same time, it needs to be asked: how did the founders acquire such a degree of power that allowed them to ignore the pressures for accountability? The answer is that it takes two to tango: a great many participants in the grassroots acquiesced to the founders' leadership position, very few were prepared to challenge their power, and even fewer were prepared to rebel completely and to publicly reject their leadership. In a country like Spain such public rejection would have taken place immediately. The reason it did not happen in Israel was the hegemony of commonplace understandings of leadership and vertical organisation, and the relatively small presence of horizontalist approaches and practices. From the start, the idea of internal democracy within the movement was circumscribed within a representational model. In the camps, the most 'democratic' thing people imagined was to elect representatives.

Coupled with this was most participants' short-termist view of the movement's aims and possibilities. The camp activists wanted a national representative structure because they saw themselves as part of a finite campaign with winnable objectives. If the goal was to get the government to meet specific demands for policy and legislation, and if the founders would inevitably continue to represent the movement towards the government and the general public, then it was crucially important to them that their communication would be genuinely representative. This mindset was understandable, given the sense of urgency shared by protesters regarding the shortage of affordable housing, especially for those from the socio-economic periphery who took to the streets out of an acute economic distress. But had activists adopted a more cynical view, anticipating the government efforts to derail or ignore the protests, then the focus would have shifted to medium- and long-term goals: a change in public consciousness, political and economic self-education, and the seeding of stable groups and initiatives that would carry the lessons learnt from this mobilisation to the next episode. With such goals, the founders and their accountability would have appeared less important, and the conflict with them would have seeped much less energy that could have been better focused elsewhere.

As I write, Israelis are once again mobilising in mass – this time against the government's intention to hand over the country's recently-discovered offshore gas reserves to a private monopoly (Sachs and Boersma, 2015). Many of the limitations of the 2011 movement are still on display, especially the attempt to huddle behind an apolitical banner and avoid accusations of leftism; but perhaps the lack of media heroes this time around shows that other lessons from the Tent Protests have been learnt.

Acknowledgement

My thanks go to Aya Shoshan and Lin Chalozin-Dovrat for their corrections and comments, and for being such inspiring comrades.

References

Alfasi, N. and Fenster, T. (2014) 'Between socio-spatial and urban justice: Rawls' principles of justice in the 2011 Israeli Protest Movement', *Planning Theory*, 13(4), 407–427.

Berger, A. (2006) *The Rainbow Family: An Ethnography of Spiritual Postmodernism*, PhD thesis, St Andrews: University of St Andrews.

Chalozin-Dovrat, L. (2012) 'Representation', in Handel, A., U. Edelman, M. Givoni, N. Yuran and Y. Kenny (eds) *The Political Lexicon of the Social Protest*. Tel Aviv: Hakibbutz Hameuchad (in Hebrew).

Commission for Group Dynamics in Assemblies of the Puerta del Sol Protest Camp (Madrid) (2011) 'Quick guide on group dynamics in people's assemblies', *TakeTheSquare.net*, 31 July, http://bit.ly/20BCbgd.

Feigenbaum, A., Frenzel, F. and McCurdy, P. (2013) *Protest Camps: Imagining Alternative Worlds*. London: Zed.

Fenster, T. and Misgav, C. (2015) 'The protest within protest: feminism and ethnicities in the 2011 Israeli protest movement', *Women's Studies International Forum*, 52, 20–29.

Fine, G. A. and Harrington, B. (2004) 'Tiny publics: small groups and civil society', *Sociological Theory*, 22(3), 341–356.

Freeman, J. (1970) *The Tyranny of Structurelessness*, Combined web version, http://bit.ly/1drg1b2.

Genosar, S. (2011) Talk show, *Yediot Aharonot*, 9 September (in Hebrew), http://bit.ly/1iC63Zs.

Gordon, U. (2010) 'Against the wall: anarchist mobilization in the Israeli–Palestinian conflict', *Peace and Change*, 35(3), 412–433.

Gordon, U. (2012) 'Israel's "Tent Protests": the chilling effect of nationalism', *Social Movement Studies*, 11(3–4), 349–355.

Gordon, U. (2014) 'Participant observation', in R. Kinna (ed) *The Bloomsbury Companion to Anarchism*. New York: Bloomsbury.

Grinberg, L. L. (2013) 'The J14 resistance mo(ve)ment: the Israeli mix of Tahrir Square and Puerta del Sol', *Current Sociology*, 61(4), 491–509.

Handel, A., U. Edelman, M. Givoni, N. Yuran and Y. Kenny (2012) *The Political Lexicon of the Social Protest*. Tel Aviv: Hakibbutz Hameuchad (in Hebrew).

Hare, A. P. (1994) *Small Group Research: A Handbook*. New York: Ablex.

Herbst, A. (2013) 'Welfare mom as warrior mom: discourse in the 2003 single mothers' protest in Israel', *Journal of Social Policy*, 4(1), 129–145.

Herzog, H. (2013) 'A generational and gendered view of the tent protests', *Theory and Criticism*, 41, 69–96 (in Hebrew).

Juris, J. S. (2005) 'Social forums and their margins: networking logics and the cultural politics of autonomous space', *Ephemera: Theory and Politics in Organization*, 5(2), 253–272.

Juris, J. S. (2007) 'Practicing militant ethnography with the movement for global resistance in Barcelona', in S. Shukaitis and D. Graeber (eds) *Constituent Imagination*. Oakland, CA: AK Press.

Kaplan, S. (1988) 'The Beta Israel and the Rabbinate: law, ritual and politics', *Social Science Information*, 27(3), 357–370.

Kimmel-Green, H., O. Vlodavsky, D. Walter, E. Levi and E. Lila (2012) '"The protests resumed – (only) thousands came": coverage of the social protest in Israeli Media', *Keshev* analysis report (in Hebrew), http://bit.ly/1Qkx3JF.

Kraft, D. (2011) 'Cottage cheese becomes symbol of Israeli frustration with rising food prices', *Jewish Telegraphic Agency*, 20 June, http://bit.ly/1FkFZMv.

Lavie, S. (2012) 'The Knafo Chronicles: marching on Jerusalem with Israel's silent majority', *Affilia*, 27(3), 300–315.

Leibner, G. (2015) 'HaTikva Camp, 2011: the ambiguous agency of the marginalized', *Current Anthropology*, 56(11), 159–168.

Levy, G. (2015) 'From rights to representation: challenging citizenship from the margins post 2011', *Mathal*, 4(1), 1.

Lichterman, P. (1998) 'What do movements mean? The value of participant-observation', *Qualitative Sociology*, 21(4), 401–418.

Lichterman, P. (2002) 'Seeing structure happen: theory-driven participant observation', in B. Klandermans and S. Staggenborg (eds) *Methods of Social Movement Research*. Minneapolis, MN: University of Minnesota Press.

Marom, N. (2013) 'Activising space: The spatial politics of the 2011 protest movement in Israel', *Urban Studies*, 50(13), 2826–2841.

Misgav, C. (2013) 'Shedding light on Israel's backyard: the tents' protest in the context of urban periphery', *Theory and Criticism*, 41, 95–113 (in Hebrew).

Monterescu, D. and Shaindlinger, N. (2013) 'Situational radicalism: the Israeli "Arab Spring" and the (un)making of the rebel city', *Constellations*, 20(2), 229–253.

Nagar, N. (2012) 'The 2011 "Social Protest" in Israel and its aftermath', *Anuari del conflicte social* 2, 309–316, http://bit.ly/1j3f2lZ.

Oren, B. et al (2012) *The Field of Tents: Conclusions from the social Protests* (in Hebrew). Givat Ada: Self-published.

Perry, N. (2011) 'Poll: 85% support social protests', *Nana*,10, 2 August (in Hebrew), http://bit.ly/1gyNeEy.

Quinn, D. (1992) *Ishmael*. New York: Bantam/Turner.

Rabinowitz, D. (2014) 'Resistance and the city', *History and Anthropology*, 25(4), 472–487.

Ram, U. and Filc, D. (2013) 'The 14 July of Daphni Leef: the rise and fall of the social protest', *Theory and Criticism*, 41, 17–43 (in Hebrew).

Rimmerman, A. and Herr, S. S. (2004) 'The power of the powerless: a study of the Israeli Disability Strike of 1999. *Journal of Disability Policy Studies*, 15(1), 12–18.

Rimon-Greenspan, H. (2007) 'Disability politics in Israel: civil society, advocacy, and contentious politics', *Disability Studies Quarterly*, 27, 4.

Rosenhek, Z. and Shalev, M. (2014) 'The political economy of Israel's "social justice" protests: a class and generational analysis', *Contemporary Social Science*, 9(1), 31–48.

Routledge, P. (2003) 'Convergence space: process geographies of grassroots globalization networks', *Transactions of the Institute of British Geographers*, 28(3), 333–349.

Russell, B. (2015) 'Beyond activism/academia: militant research and the radical climate and climate justice movement(s)', *Area*, 4793, 222–229.

Sachs, N. and Boersma, T. (2015) 'The energy island: Israel deals with its natural gas discoveries', *Brookings Institute Policy Paper* 35, http://bit.ly/1j3p8TS.

Sasson-Levy, O. and Rapoport, T. (2003) 'Body, gender, and knowledge in protest movements: the Israeli case', *Gender and Society*, 17(3), 379–403.

Schechter, A. (2012) *Rothschild: The Story of a Protest Movement*. Tel Aviv: Hakibbutz Hameuchad (in Hebrew).

Shakuf baOhel ('Transparent Tent') (2011) Archived minutes of Rothschild camp assembly, 27 July, http://bit.ly/1NIqBwm.

Shanhav, Y. (2013) 'The carnival: Protest in a society with no oppositions', *Theory and Criticism*, 41, 121–45 (in Hebrew).

Sharim, Y. (2013) 'Israel's lost son: masculinity and race in the Gilad Shalit's affair', *Thinking Gender* paper, UCLA Center for the Study of Women, http://bit.ly/1QnDfyo.

Sherwood, H. (2011) 'Israeli protests: 430,000 take to streets to demand social justice', *Guardian*, 4 September, http://bit.ly/1STkN2s.

Shoshan, A. (2012) 'Interview: we want a change in the priorities, the system. We want democracy now!', *Palestine-Israel Journal*, 18, 2–3.

Tavory, I. and Goodman, Y. C. (2009) '"A collective of individuals": between self and solidarity in a Rainbow Gathering', *Sociology of Religion*, 70(1), 262–284.

TentOfHope (2011) 'Reports on new leadership efforts', Hatikva neighbourhood camp blog, http://bit.ly/1Qmz59N.

Uldam, J. and McCurdy, P. (2013) 'Studying social movements: challenges and opportunities for participant observation', *Sociology Compass*, 7(11), 941–951.

Volinitz, B. (2011) 'Housing struggle: thousands demonstrated at the protest rally in Tel Aviv', *Walla News*, 23 July (in Hebrew), http://bit.ly/1Q6QWAl.

Walla News (2011) 'President Peres to the protest leaders: "You've won the nation's heart"', *Walla News*, 1 August (in Hebrew), http://bit.ly/1QnDf1c

Wallach, Y. (2013) 'The politics of non-iconic space: Sushi, Shisha, and a civic promise in the 2011 summer protests in Israel', *European Urban and Regional Studies*, 20(1), 150–154.

YNet News (2011) 'Gas price hike leads to no-confidence vote', *YNet News*, 31 January, http://bit.ly/1W7NF97.

FOURTEEN

Euromaidan and the echoes of the Orange Revolution: comparing social infrastructures and resistance practices of protest camps in Kiev (Ukraine)

Maryna Shevtsova

What was striking to me when I first entered Maidan was the highest level of self-consciousness and self-organisation. There is…no police, but you feel so calm and comfortable as you have not felt for quite some time. And only later, when you leave this 'Island of Freedom' and see people wearing uniforms again, you just feel physical disagreement: 'why are they here?' (Roman,[1] personal communication, Dnepropetrovsk, 13 December 2013)

Introduction

This chapter explores the transformation of resistance, decision-making and spatial practices amongst participants of national-level anti-government protests in Ukraine in 2004 and 2013/14. Specifically, this comparative study looks at the way in which participants at two protest camps – both held at Maidan Nezalezhnosti in Kiev, but ten years apart – transformed the representational space of the square into a protest camp. An analysis of the differences between these two protest camps contributes to our understanding of the current social and political transformations taking place in Ukraine. To this end, by contrasting the (re)production of the space, spatial practices adjusted to the context of the protests and spatial representation, I argue that the particular characteristics of Maidan-Sich 2014 can be interpreted as reflecting the empowerment of the recently emerged civil society.

On 1 December 2013, several hundred people gathered in Kiev's main square – Maidan Nezalezhnosti (Maidan) – in response to the violent attacks that Ukrainian state security forces had inflicted on anti-government demonstrators in Maidan the night before. To show that their intentions were serious, demonstrators made it known that they would not leave the square until those responsible for the attacks were punished. Alongside this demand, a protest camp emerged that would remain at Maidan until 9 August 2014, more than eight months later, when Kiev city officials demanded that it be dismantled. During the protest camp's existence, it underwent a significant transition: it turned from a protest camp with mainly an occupation purpose to what participants themselves defined as '*sich*' – a place where people gathered and where collective decisions were taken and common tactics of resistance and defence developed. Both the general public and academics reacted to the resemblance between the 2013/14 Maidan protest camp and the protest camps organised in the same square in 2004 during the Ukrainian Orange Revolution (Salnykova, 2014; Wilson, 2014). However, such similarities are superficial; instead, I argue, it is more important to point out the often overlooked ways in which two protest camps differed. The differences highlighted in this study relate to new resistance practices used by the protesters, resource mobilisation strategies and new approaches to the camp's governance and representation in decision-making process. All these show the significance of the 2013/14 camp as a marker of the empowerment of Ukrainian civil society over the last decade.

In what follows I draw on accounts from the protests' participants and eyewitnesses, most of whom were present at Maidan in both 2004 and 2013/14. In total, I conducted more than 30 personal interviews in Dnepropetrovsk and Kiev between December 2013 and August 2014. I also draw on personal correspondence with the participants of the Kiev protest camp in 2004, along with secondary sources, such as news articles, the participants' online blogs, eyewitness accounts of the protests and television and radio interviews.[2] The chapter is structured as follows. First, I define the theoretical framework of this study. Next, I explore the similarities and differences between the two Maidan camps using the logic of Lefebvre's (1991) conceptual triad and focusing on the camps' spatiality, social infrastructure, resistance practices and decision-making processes. The conclusion briefly summarises my main findings and reflects on their implications for protest camp scholarship as well as for Ukraine's political landscape.

Appropriation of space, spatial practices and social transformations

This comparative study of protest camps is inspired by Lefebvre's (1991, 31) statement that every society, or each mode of production, produces its own space. Lefebvre's 'mode of production' refers to two sets of intersecting relations: *the social relations of reproduction* and the *social relations of production*. For the purposes of this chapter, I focus only on the relations of production (Lefebvre, 1991, 32). Lefebvre proposes the following conceptual triad, which can be employed as a framework for the comparative study of protest camps: *representation of space, representational spaces* and *spatial practice*. Representation of space, according to Lefebvre, refers to the 'order of the relations of production' (1991, 33): these are the 'frontal relations' of the space with the world outside that space. Their purpose is to manifest the meaning of the space to both insiders and outsiders. Representational space is 'space as directly lived through its associated images and symbols, and hence the space of "inhabitants" and "users"' (1991, 39).

Representational space embodies the symbolic value of the space as it is produced and understood, first and foremost, by the inhabitants of that space. By applying the concept of representational space to protest camps, one can explore the complex symbolism of the camp's inner life – as expressed through art, inner narratives or the social life that is hidden from external observers – and the ways in which it carries certain messages or values of a specific social formation. Given that protest camps are specific social formations, it makes sense to employ Lefebvre's concept of spatial practices that are related to 'production and reproduction, and the particular locations and special sets' (1991, 33). In the case of protest camps, these include daily life with its routines and realities, leisure and work, resistance and infrastructure building. Spatial practices refer to the ways in which space is used, or the modes of using the space, whereas representation of space and representational space both refer to the ways in which the space is perceived by different social actors. These elements of Lefebvre's triad should not be considered independently: it is their continuous interaction that produces the space of the protest camp. As Milgrom (2008, 270) observes, when the representation of space is produced initially, it already contains assumptions about the spatial practices of its users, their understanding of space, and the symbolism that displays the intentions of the people responsible for the production of that space. At the same time, the spatial practices of the space influence its production and its inhabitants' understanding of representational spaces (Milgrom, 2008, 270).

In order to compare the Maidan protest camps, I adjust Lefebvre's theory and employ the infrastructural research approach suggested by Feigenbaum et al (2013). As they argue, protest camps are a 'unique sociological phenomenon' functioning as representational space, where 'activists form individual and collective identities outside of institutionalized groups and organizations and the status quo' (Feigenbaum et al, 2013, 15). Focusing on the centrality of materiality, the authors suggest that we should look at protest camps through 'infrastructural lenses'. They go on to identify four key infrastructures – recreational, action, communication and governance – that can be used to examine structural differences and similarities in collective action within protest camps (Feigenbaum et al, 2013, 14).

I suggest using Lefebvre's conceptual triad as a perspective from which to compare and analyse the Maidan protest camps in Ukraine. In the Maidan events, we can see the development of new spatial practices together with the gradual transformation of representational space, which, in turn, reflects changes in the mobilisation and organisation of Ukrainian civil society. This connection, in particular, is important for understanding how newly emerged spatial or resistance practices in the camp led to changes in the governance of the two camps and their representation in decision-making processes. It also influenced the increase in internal tolerance of diversity. In the next section, I describe in detail the transformation of spatial practices and the representation of space in the Maidan protest camps over time.

Representation of space: why Maidan?

In the everyday speech of Ukrainians, the name 'Maidan' has long been used to refer to the territory of Maidan Nezalezhnosti (Independence Square) in the centre of Kiev. The square was given its current name after the fall of the USSR and with the independence of the state of Ukraine, and it has been used for political collective action ever since. Only 13 years after Ukraine gained its independence, in 2004 Maidan became a space of collective political agitation for a broad section of the Ukrainian population. In November 2004, as a response to electoral fraud during the presidential elections, campaigners for Viktor Yushchenko, the candidate who came second in the elections, called for his supporters to begin protests at Maidan. Beissinger quotes one of the observers as saying that 'what everybody expected was… much like the small demonstrations of 'Ukraine Without Kuchma' four years earlier'. What happened instead was a mass outpouring on the streets and swelling numbers, instead of diminishing ones' (Beissinger, 2011, 26). Estimates of the number of protesters on the streets of Kiev ranged from half a million to almost a million (Kuzio, 2006, 48). Demonstrators created a protest camp in central Kiev, with plans to stay until the government re-ran the presidential elections. Similar protest camps were soon established in many other large Ukrainian cities, such as Kharkov, Dnepropetrovsk and Lvov. Many of the camps remained even after the government ceded to public demands and held new elections. For the activists involved, the original 'Maidan' camp, which was one that continued after the new elections, acquired symbolic and political meaning. 'I would like to explain [to] you…why the camp was so important for us. This is all psychology, this is support. This is not to let anyone tell us that we stopped our fight at least for one day' (Oleg, personal communication, Kiev, 4 December 2004).

The new round of elections was held on 26 December 2004 and resulted in the victory of Viktor Yushchenko over Viktor Yanukovych. 'Nasha Ukrayina', a political coalition created by Yushchenko, presented his victory as a story of democratic revolution. However, once in power, the Yushchenko government disappointed the majority of the population and in the 2008 elections Yanukovych won the race for the presidency.[3] During Yushchenko's presidency, people continued to refer to the possibility of another 'Maidan' as a response to the negative political and economic developments in the country.[4] In the years that followed, there were some attempts to call for new protests: these included, in April 2010, a 'Maidan' against Kharkov's agreement,[5] and, in November 2010, a 'Fiscal Maidan'.[6] However, such attempts were insignificant in number and did not succeed.

The Orange Revolution made 'Maidan' a political and popular concept used by politicians and by protest movements in various contexts, sometimes as an argument and sometimes as a threat in political debates. It became common for the political actors of the opposition to use phrases such as 'We need another Maidan' and 'You will have to give the answers to Maidan'.[7] In this new context, 'Maidan' did not just mean a square in Kiev or a protest camp; rather, the expression embodied the popular will to hold the ruling elites to account.

Maidan 2013/14 started with a small group of student activists reacting to the news that President Yanukovych had withdrawn the Ukraine's application to the European Union's Association Agreement. Acting spontaneously, a group of no more than 100 people organised a protest camp in Maidan Square. In establishing the camp, the organisers consciously avoided using any party-specific political symbols; instead, they called themselves 'Euromaidan'. Egor Sobolev, one of the Euromaidan camp founders, described how things started.

> Someone got four small tables and chairs from one of the offices...and put on them labels 'FOOD', 'SECURITY', 'VOLUNTEERS'...and we were standing there like idiots, alone. Then someone brought a thermos, somebody put a box for donations – we still keep it! People were throwing some money there, we decided to buy tea, bread and cheese and give it to people who were coming. In the night it was still cold and raining, but in the morning more and more people came and so [the] camp's infrastructure was started.[8]

It was only after peaceful protesters were violently attacked by Ukrainian state security forces during the night of 30 November 2013 that participant numbers increased significantly. According to a poll conducted on 7 December 2013, 70 per cent of participants came to Maidan because they were outraged by the violence against protesters, while only 53.5 per cent expressed aspirations for Ukraine to join the EU.[9]

The choice of Maidan as the heart of the protests and the location of the biggest camps is related to its historical and symbolic meaning for Ukrainian people. It can be considered, therefore, a representation of space that carries an important message of democratic aspirations and expresses the willpower of the people of Ukraine. I turn now to an infrastructural analysis of Maidan's spatial practices in order to better capture the meaning and function of the camps as a representational space.

Analysing spatial practices: Orange Maidan versus Euromaidan

Most of the sources describing Maidan in 2013/14 commented that, in building its infrastructure, participants followed the successful experience of 2004 (Wilson, 2014; Åslund, 2015). However, such accounts overlook the difference in funding sources for the two camps. In 2004, major parts of the camp's infrastructure – tents, flags, banners and food, including oranges (orange was the colour of Yushchenko's party and fruit was distributed among the protesters as a symbol) – were delivered overnight together with the blankets, sleeping bags and heat generators essential in winter. At least a couple of members of Nasha

Ukrayina were usually present at Maidan and addressed protesters from the stage. Along with the many posters and flags displaying the slogan '*Yushchenko – TAK!*' ('Yes to Yushchenko'), this left observers in no doubt that not only was the protest against the anti-democratic actions of the government, but it also favoured one particular political force. Later, the initiative was widely supported by individual Ukrainians: people brought their own tents to Maidan and donated money, food and clothes to the protesters. However, the initial material contribution by Nasha Ukrayina indicates a significant level of centralised political campaigning and planning behind the camp. In his description of the development of the Orange Revolution, Wilson (2006) refers, for example, to the generous funding provided by Davyd Zhvaniia, a businessman and member of Nasha Ukrayina; this was used to buy the first tents, mattresses, bio-toilets and other supplies for the camp before donations from individuals started to arrive (2006, 126).

The funding of Euromaidan infrastructure was very different. In 2013/14, none of the opposition parties were prepared for a large-scale protest. The infrastructure of the camp was created by the protesters themselves rather haphazardly and remained insubstantial until 30 November 2013. After the general uprising in early December in response to the violence against the protesters, a large number of volunteers arrived. At this point, many small private companies and big businesses started to support Maidan, providing money or material resources, food, clothes and medical supplies.

What is important is that one cannot ignore the opportunities that the spread of the internet created for the mobilisation of resources. In 2004, social media networks did not exist as a powerful means of political communication and for disseminating ideas. Ten years later, smartphones and widely available internet enabled protestors to communicate and share ideas at very low cost. Most of my interviewees confirmed that they had learned about the uprising and the camp at Maidan through Facebook, Twitter or VKontakte (the Russian equivalent of Facebook). Social media networks were used to mobilise people and to provide the protest camp with material resources. Various on-line groups were created, such as 'Maidan SOS', where volunteers constantly updated lists of desired donations such as food items, clothes and medicines.[10]While the infrastructure of the two Maidan camps was organised in different ways, the 2013/14 camp developed a routine that was similar to the one that had existed in 2004. A large number of people came during the day for political discussions, while a smaller group of permanent inhabitants maintained the camp. Several protesters joined only for the evenings, after work. At night, the number of people in the camp was significantly smaller, but the participants ensured that there was always someone around for security reasons.

While infrastructure networks provided the protesters with their basic needs (heating generators, medicines, food, warm clothes and so on), a number of participants in the 2013/14 camp also engaged in the organisation of cultural events and public educational programmes. Rectors of several Ukrainian universities officially allowed their students to skip classes in order to stay in the protest camps, while some university professors came to Maidan and gave open lectures voluntarily. In December 2013, the so-called *Vidkrytyi Universytet Maidanu* (Open University of Maidan) was founded. For this initiative, a special stage was installed where university professors, activists, businessmen and artists could give lectures. At the beginning, the target audience was students, but the organisers soon found that there were many other people interested in the lectures – they even attended events held late in the evening and in freezing cold temperatures. As one of the organisers commented: 'We believe that the revolution is important not only on the streets, but also in the head...Having spent a lot of time at Maidan, we understood that what was missing here [was] intellectual content of a high quality.'[11]

Figure 14.1: People gathering around a piano at Euromaidan Protest Camp, 2013/2014 (Credit: Marco Ferraro)

Many participants interviewed who were active in both the 2004 and 2013/14 camps highlighted the significance of housekeeping, particularly in light of media representations; this has been an issue in many similar camps (Feigenbaum et al, 2013). The common concern of the camps' participants was not only to create a home place for the protesters but also to refute negative arguments made by the camps' opponents and to prevent disreputable portrayals in the media. 'Housekeeping' – that is, taking care of garbage in the camp and organising cleaning teams – was a crucial task for the protesters. There was also a strict 'no alcohol' rule in the 2013/14 camp. As the commandant of Maidan,[12] Andriy Parubiy, commented in his interview for *Argument* on 24 December 2014:

> We have the highest level of self-organisation...When we were attacked by 'Berkut'[13] they stole our portable kitchen, many things and left behind total chaos. I went to the stage and asked people to clean. And people...found somewhere the brooms and started cleaning...There should be no drunken people at Maidan...Of course, we cannot control everyone. But there is an order to take all drunken men outside the camp...We fully control the metro station under Maidan. Come there at 5 am and see [for] yourself that it has never been so clean before.[14]

One may argue, therefore, that there were obvious similarities in the representation of space in the two camps, especially during the initial stages of the 2013/14 Maidan; this would explain the constant references by outside observers of the events of 2013/14 to the events of the Orange Revolution. However, a close analysis of the ways in which the camps were established reveals the differences in spatial practices and in the perception of the two camps on the part of their inhabitants.

New decision-making and resistance practices

An important factor differentiating the two Maidan camps as representational spaces was the absence of any connection to a particular political party in the 2013/14 protest, as noted earlier. Wilson (2006) argues that, in 2004, Yushchenko's campaign team had not initially expected such a large public response to its call for action. However, the protest was planned and calibrated carefully: 25 orange tents (one for each of Ukraine's oblasts), complete with the party's symbol, were arranged around a stage in the middle of Maidan (Wilson, 2006, 123). This spatial arrangement confirmed and consolidated the protest camp as a place of action focused around a common goal and common leaders, with Yushchenko's party at its centre. When larger numbers of people headed to Kiev or started to establish protest camps in their own cities, they followed the spatial and aesthetic arrangement planned by the Yushchenko team. They installed not just tents, but orange tents, and raised orange flags with the party's symbols.

For participants of the 2013/14 Euromaidan protests, the presence of party political symbols was unacceptable. A survey conducted in December 2013 by Foundation Democrativ Iniciative after Ilko Kucheriv found that 92 per cent of protesters did not support any particular political party.[15] There was evidence of this when members of the *Bat'kivshchyna* party tried to display a portrait of their imprisoned leader and former Ukrainian prime minister Yulia Tymoshenko on the Christmas tree traditionally installed in December in the centre of Maidan Square. Maidan campers demanded the removal of the portrait, arguing that the camp did not support any political party but rather expressed the will of all the 'people of Ukraine'. As activists at the camp commented:

> It is not the Orange Revolution; there is no politics here. There [are] no rightists, no leftists. (Artem, personal communication, Kiev, 11 December 2013)

> Maidan is here not for NATO, not for the US or the EU. We are not for Tymoshenko, Klitschko, Poroshenko or Yatsenyuk…We are here because we are fed up with politicians using our taxes to buy villas and yachts instead of building the roads, schools and hospitals. (From the flyer distributed by the activists at Maidan, Kiev, December 2013)

An important difference between the two Maidan protests was the fact that the Orange Revolution passed peacefully, with no violence on the part of the government. In the case of Euromaidan, the escalation of the antagonism between the government and protesters eventually led to armed conflict. Maidan inhabitants' perception of the space changed significantly during the process, and observers witnessed the camp's transformation from 'Euromaidan' to '*sich*', the name adopted after the violent exchanges of February 2014.

The word *sich* refers to a fortified Cossack settlement: a form of self-governed semi–military community that existed in the territory of

Figure 14.2: Tires as barricades in Euromaidan, 2013/2014 (Credit: Marco Ferraro)

modern Ukraine and Russia between the sixteenth and the eighteenth century. The *sich* played an important role in the historical and cultural development of Ukraine and became a symbol of freedom and independence. When the state attempted to dissolve the camp at Maidan in February 2014 using special security forces, the residents responded by transforming it into an improvised fortress and calling it '*sich*'. As it was winter, people built barricades from stones extracted from the square's pavements, tyres and other available objects and covered them with freezing water. In a constant state of alert, residents created a governance structure inside the camp to oversee the camp's defence. Special groups called *sotnyas* were formed, inspired by the Cossacks' detachments. The move to using the term *sich* denoted the formation of a new organisational structure, which reflected new forms of mobilisation of both participants and resources, and reflected the need to develop new resistance practices in the camp. The act of staying in the protest camp in 2013/14 was not only an expression of disagreement with the government's politics but also a question of the survival of the autonomous camp.

The transformation to *sich* was also expressed in changes that occurred in decision-making practices. Many of my interviewees referred to the importance of being part of the decision-making process at the camp and were very excited talking about *Viche*; this is an old Slavic term referring to a general assembly of citizens in ancient and mediaeval Kievan Rus' who gathered to discuss common issues and take political decisions. *Viche* constituted one of the first forms of direct democracy in the Slavic states.[16]From 22 December 2013, thousands of protesters gathered every Sunday around the stage installed in the middle of the square in a modern version of the *Viche*. At the start of such gatherings, participants sang the Ukrainian national anthem: *Shche ne vmerla Ukraina*. If the motto of Maidan in 2004 was '*Razom Nas Bahato, Nas Ne Podolaty*' ('Together we are many, we cannot be defeated'), in 2013/14 every speaker greeted the people in the square with '*Slava Ukrayini!*' ('Glory to Ukraine'), to which people would respond '*Geroyam Slava!*' ('Glory to the heroes'), a phrase borrowed from the early twentieth-century Congress of Ukrainian Nationalists. The participants' turn towards nationalist practices, however, created space for right-wing groups to become more visible in the protest camp. Since the members of those groups were mostly fit, well-trained men, their role in the defence of the camp was central and widely appreciated. Yet their presence had some negative implications. It resulted in the emergence of a critique of the 'fascist nature' of the camp in the foreign press. Stories about Ukrainian fascists appeared not only in Russia, where the radical nationalist argument was one of the dominant features of such critiques of the events in Kiev,[17] but also in the Western media.[18]

Moreover, the presence of right-wing groups influenced the decision of activists belonging to minorities (in particular, feminist and LGBTI[19] groups) to be more discreet about their identity. The homophobic views of right-wing forces were well known, so, in order not to create conflicts and clashes in the camp, the LGBTI community made a conscious decision to protest at Maidan not as LGBTI activists but as Ukrainians fighting for European integration. Importantly, the views of right-wing groups were not the only reason for such discretion: the claim that the EU was imposing an obligation on Ukraine to legalise same-sex marriage was much used by anti-EU integration groups. The strategy chosen by the LGBTI community also served not to allow pro-Russian forces to speculate with their presence at Maidan.[20]It is worth noting that, while right-wing groups maintained a constant presence at Maidan, their role in the camp and their importance to the protest were definitely exaggerated by foreign media. Research conducted at Maidan with the financial support of the National Endowment for Democracy and International foundation 'Vidrodzhennya' shows that only 6 per cent of protest actions at Maidan were instigated by 'right-wing' groups, and, in general, members of right-wing groups took part in approximately 25 per cent of all protest events.[21] While this number is not small, and the activity of nationalist groups should not be ignored, it is also not large enough to corroborate claims about the 'fascist spirit' of the camp.

Many participants I interviewed mentioned what they felt was a highly democratic culture exhibited in the weekly gatherings at Maidan. Unlike in 2004, when the assemblies around the stage were usually followed by speeches by politicians from Yushchenko's party, everyone could speak at the *Viche* in 2013/14. For some of the participants, the *Viche* replaced the Ukrainian parliament in the sense that many felt that decisions taken there were the decisions of the people of Ukraine. A feeling prevailed of struggle for common goals and participants took on more responsibilities and became more politically aware and active than they had been in their 'before-Maidan' lives. As one of the interviewees commented:

> In 2004 I was a student and it was a lot of fun. We were driving in my friend's car around the city during the day, waving an orange flag, and spending nights in the tents. It felt like freedom. In 2013/14 there was no fun anymore; every evening I went to the camp after my day in the office and my wife and my daughter did not know if I would come back. But...I felt I was changing something; the destiny of my country depended on me...This time I was making decisions, and people next to me were making the decisions, and other people, who were not in Kiev, but supported us in any way they could from other places, trusted us and trusted the choices we were making, for them, too. (Bogdan, personal communication Kiev, August 2014)

Beissinger claims that 'participation in the Orange Revolution was more a short-term fluctuation in activism than a long-term general shift in societal values' (2011, 41). With regards to the 2013/14 camp, it is evident from my data that self-organisation and self-management increased, and that new modes of governance and decision making were introduced and put into practice. While one should remain critical of the intolerance expressed by right-wing groups in the camp, there were other signs described above that arguably point to a strengthening of Ukrainian civil society.

Conclusion

In this chapter, I have contrasted the two examples of protest camps in Kiev in 2004 and 2013/14. I have applied Lefebvre's conceptual triad for space production and an infrastructural analysis to examine these two protest camps. I have studied several characteristics that I consider of key importance for the camps' existence and maintenance – their representational spaces, resistance practices and decision-making processes – in an attempt to explain their similarities and point out their differences.

An important difference between the two camps relates to the self-organised nature of the camp in 2013/14 compared with the Orange Revolution, which was driven by one political party. My contestation is that the more autonomous and heterogeneous form of the second protest camp enabled the creation of a pluralistic environment and facilitated the interaction of various social groups that would not have united for common goals in different circumstances. This does not mean that Maidan 2013/14 was a totally inclusive space. I refer in this chapter, for example, to the constraints felt by LGBTI and feminist groups in the presence of right-wing forces in the camp. Obviously, over the life of the protest camp, which lasted for several months, there were tensions and conflicts between different groups of protesters. Despite this, the camp encouraged a productive cooperation between groups with quite different political and ideological views. At the same time, the protesters' armed confrontation with government forces in 2013/14 inspired the creation of new practices of resistance and decision-making. These practices drew to some extent on Ukrainian heritage; participants in the protest camp reproduced the resistance practices of Cossacks and their fortress or *sich* – practices that are strongly associated with Ukrainian history. On the one hand, the rise of a nationalist spirit created the conditions in which an alternative form of governance and decision-making could emerge; this was highly praised by the protesters themselves and akin to a more democratic and diverse organisational practice. On the other hand, however, it provided more space for the radical right-wing forces in the camp, which had some negative implications, as described in the chapter.

Changes in approaches to governance were reflected in new processes for appointing leaders, in the way in which leaders interacted with participants and managed the everyday routine of the camp, and at weekly gatherings known as *Viche*. Being part of the *Viche* gave many protesters a feeling of involvement and personal responsibility. This evolution of the Maidan protest camp into Maidan-Sich turned the space in the centre of Kiev into a self-governing organisational structure, which, according to many protesters, was considered a truly democratic environment where decisions were taken on behalf of the people of Ukraine. The events mentioned above therefore had a positive impact on the development of civil society in the country and on the birth of new leaders.

In summary, the developments that characterised the 2013/14 protest camp in Kiev and that are described in this chapter point to important shifts in political and social order in Ukraine, and the study of protest camps can provide insights into the political transformation that takes place around them. More research on the protest camp is needed in order to reveal more diverse aspects of this mobilisation and the camp's role in the transformation of Ukrainian society.

Notes

[1] For reasons of confidentiality, the names of the interviewees have been changed.

[2] All the interviews were conducted in Russian and the material gathered from online blogs and correspondence with the activists was in Russian and Ukrainian. The texts quoted in the chapter offer the translation made by the author.

[3] See Karatnycky, 2005.

[4] The opponents of Yushchenko and Maidan also employed this concept but in a negative context, for example by referring to people involved in the protest action as '*maydanutiye*' (literally, badly affected by Maidan).

[5] Protest attempts were initiated in April 2010 after President Yanukovych signed an extension agreement on the lease of Russia's naval base in Sevastopol for an additional 25 years.

[6] 'Fiscal Maidan' refers to protests in Kiev in November 2010 against the new tax code project.

[7] 'Maidan' rhetoric was used both by the politicians and by a wider audience. See, for example, Yushchenko's bloc will include the political forces following the ideals of Maidan, *Liga Novosti*, 5 November 2005, http://news.liga.net/news/politics/266452-v-blok-v-yushchenko-voydut-politicheskie-sily-kotorye-ispoveduyut-idealy-maydana.htm?no_mobile_version=yes.

[8] See Vspomnit vse: hroniki, lica i osobennosti Evromaydana (Remember everything: chronicles, faces and characteristics of Euromaidan), *Segodnya*, 23 December 2013, www.segodnya.ua/hot/maidan2013/vspomnit-vse-hroniki-lica-i-osobennosti-evromaydana-484621.html

[9] Demokratychna iniciatyva, 2013, Maidan 2013: Khto stoyit, chomu I za shcho? (Maidan 2013: who stands, why and for what?), Foundation Democrativ Iniciative after Ilko Kucheriv, www.dif.org.ua/ua/events/gvkrlgkaeths.htm.

[10] The websites of such groups were still active in 2015 but were being used to collect supplies for people in the conflict zone in Ukraine and to help refugees (see http://vk.com/maidan_sos, www.facebook.com/EvromaidanSOS/, https://twitter.com/sosmaydan).

11 See Evolyuciya pid Chas Revolucii: Vidkrytiy Universytet na Maidani (Evolution during revolution: Open University at Maidan), *Ukrains'ka Pravda*, 26 December 2013, http://life.pravda.com.ua/society/2013/12/26/147079/.

12 'Commandant' (комендант in Ukrainian) was a title given to the (non-political) leaders of the protest camp. Their duties covered quite a wide range, starting from construction of the camp, arranging regular food and medical supplies and cleaning to self-defence and military training for the security groups. The commandants were appointed by the non-formal leaders of the protest, who were elected spontaneously during the course of the protest action.

13 Special police of Ukrainian Ministry of Internal Affairs

14 See Komendant Maidana Andriy Parubiy: Maidan na prazdniki budet stoyat (The commandant of Maidan Andriy Parubiy: Maidan will stay for holidays), *Argument*, 24 December 2014, http://argumentua.com/stati/komendant-maidana-andrei-parubii-maidan-na-prazdniki-budet-stoyat.

15 Demokratychna iniciatyva, 2013, Maidan 2013: Khto stoyit, chomu I za shcho? (Maidan 2013: who stands, why and for what?), Foundation Democrativ Iniciative after Ilko Kucheriv, www.dif.org.ua/ua/events/gvkrlgkaeths.htm.

16 See Kachkovsky, L, 2000, Social organization of the Eastern Slavs, Day.Kiev.ua, 21 March, www.day.kiev.ua/en/article/culture/social-organization-eastern-slavs.

17 See Est li fashism na Maidane (Is there fascism at Maidan?), *MKRU*, 18 February 2014, www.mk.ru/specprojects/free-theme/article/2014/02/18/986509-est-li-fashizm-na-maydane.html.

18 See, for example, 'Prepared to die': the right wing's role in Ukrainian protests, *Spiegel*, 27 January 2014, www.spiegel.de/international/europe/ukraine-sliding-towards-civil-war-in-wake-of-tough-new-laws-a-945742.html; Euromaidan: the dark shadows of the far-right in Ukraine protests, *International Business Affairs*, 19 February 2014, www.ibtimes.com/euromaidan-dark-shadows-far-right-ukraine-protests-1556654.

19 Lesbian, gay, bisexual, transgender and intersex.

20 See Evrorevoluciya na Maidane. Rol i uchastie LGBT (Revolution at Maidan: role and participation of LGBT), Gay Alliance Ukraine, 19 December 2013, http://upogau.org/ru/ourview/ourview_590.html.

21 See Rol Pravogo sektoru na maydani bula v razi perebilshena-sociologi (The role of the right sector at Maidan was pretty much exaggerated – sociologists), TSN. ua, 10 July 2014, http://tsn.ua/politika/rol-pravogo-sektoru-na-maydani-bula-v-razi-perebilshena-sociologi-358441.html.

References

Åslund, A. (2015) *Ukraine: What Went Wrong and How to Fix It.* Washington, DC: Peterson Institute for International Economics.

Beissinger, M. R. (2011) 'Mechanisms of Maidan: the structure of contingency in the making of the Orange Revolution', *Mobilization: An International Journal*, 16(1), 25–43.

Feigenbaum, A., Frenzel, F. and McCurdy, P. (2013) *Protest Camps.* London and New York: Zed.

Karatnycky, A. (2005) 'Ukraine's Orange Revolution', *Foreign Affairs*, March 2005, www.foreignaffairs.com/articles/russia-fsu/2005-03-01/ukraines-orange-revolution.

Kuzio, T. (2006) 'Everyday Ukrainians and the Orange Revolution', in A. Åslund and M. McFaul (eds) *Revolution in Orange: The Origins of Ukraine's Democratic Breakthrough*. Washington, DC: Carnegie Endowment for International Peace, pp 45–68.

Lefebvre, H. (1991) *The Production of Space* (trans D. Nicholson-Smith). Oxford: Blackwell.

Milgrom, R. (2008) 'Lucien Kroll: design, difference, everyday life', in K. Goonewardena, S. Kipfer, R. Milgrom and C. Schmid (eds) *Space, Difference, Everyday Life: Reading Henri Lefebvre*. New York: Routledge, pp 264–83.

Salnykova, A. (2014) 'Barriers to inter-group deliberation in divided Ukraine', in J. Ugarriza and D. Caluwaerts (eds) *Democratic Deliberation in Deeply Divided Societies: From Conflict to Common Ground*. Basingstoke: Palgrave Macmillan, pp 89–111.

Wilson, A. (2006) *Ukraine's Orange Revolution*. New Haven, CT: Yale University Press.

Wilson, A. (2014) *Ukraine Crisis: What it Means for the West*. New Haven, CT and London: Yale University Press.

FIFTEEN

Civil/political society, protest and fasting: the case of Anna Hazare and the 2011 anti-corruption campaign in India

Andrew Davies

Introduction

On 19 August 2011, Khisan Baburao 'Anna' Hazare,[1] a 71-year-old (self-professed) 'Gandhian' activist led a march from Tihar Jail in South Delhi to Ramlila Maidan, a public space in the north of the city which had been the site of previous political agitations. Once there, Hazare had planned to 'fast until death' unless the United Progressive Alliance (UPA), the Congress Party-led ruling coalition government of India at that time, passed the Jan Lokpal Bill, which would create an independent, anti-corruption ombudsman. The UPA government had been the subject of numerous corruption related scandals, and was largely seen to be symptomatic of widespread corruption across Indian society. Hazare arrived in Ramlila Maidan and continued fasting,[2] taking his place on a permanent public pavilion which is located in the grounds. Other activists in the wider Jan Lokpal movement had prepared the Maidan for his arrival with assistance from state workers. Over the next days, thousands of people mobilised around the Maidan, and the protests attracted widespread mainstream and social media commentary. Hazare's fast lasted until 28 August, after the UPA pushed through the Jan Lokpal Bill as a direct result of events in the Maidan.

Hazare's fast became the most visible political activity in India during 2011, and in some cases, the fast and its associated protests were linked to the perceived global upsurge in protest activity in that year (Chatterji, 2013). Aditya Nigam (2012) specifically linked the Jan Lokpal protests to the wider events of 2011 such as the encampments of Tahrir Square and the Spanish Indignados as examples of a new wave of 'viral' protests. However, in this case, the process of 'encampment' was markedly different to the other protests of 2011 – in particular the tactic of an individual fasting was distinctive to other, often more collective forms of camp, which are discussed elsewhere in this volume (and also in Feigenbaum et al, 2013). However, the focus on the individual did create a sense of collective mobilisation, and the occupation and maintenance of the Ramlila Maidan as a space of protest is usefully illuminated through thinking about the space as a protest camp. Additionally, the August 2011 protests brought into sharp relief some of the tensions that exist across Indian society, together with concerns about the emergence of India's 'new' middle classes and their role in politics. Outside India, the Hazare movement has since received less attention. This is partially due to the political situation within India, as the Jan Lokpal movement fractured into different groups. Yet, the moment of the fast, I will argue throughout this chapter, can give us important insights into how a protest camps approach can give valuable insights into how conceptual categories like 'civil society' actually play out in practice.

As a result, while the chapter will discuss the context of the 2011 fast in Delhi, as well as discussing some of the material arrangements of the fasting site itself, the later parts of the chapter will think through how the fast became embroiled in debates about 'civil society' in India, especially in arguments that saw both civil society and the fast as markers for a political project by parts of the emergent Indian middle classes to attempt to restrict and challenge the Indian state. In order to do this, the chapter thinks through Partha Chatterjee's concept of 'political' society – which he has argued is a non-élite counterpoint to the more formally political 'civil society' – as an attempt to complicate readings of civil society. In particular, the chapter argues that, while useful, we need to complicate such bounded concepts, and that treating Anna Hazare's fast through the lens of the camp shows the porous boundaries between the conceptual categories like 'the state', 'political' and 'civil society'.

The Jan Lokpal campaign and Anna Hazare's August 2011 fast

The August 2011 Delhi fast was the culmination of a campaign which had been ongoing in many forms for some time, for example Hazare had been involved in community activism since the 1970s, and had begun specifically campaigning against corruption in the 1990s. However, the huge scale of the 2011 campaign for a Jan Lokpal Bill meant that Hazare became the figurehead for a political movement that drew unprecedented attention. The Jan Lokpal campaign had begun in February 2011 with a rally at Ramlila Maidan involving a number of anti-corruption activists including Arvind Kejriwal, Baba Ramdev and Hazare. Hazare had also fasted at Jantar Mantar, another site in Delhi, in April 2011. During this fast, Hazare's cause began to attract widespread support. Hazare also began to mobilise on a specifically 'anti-political' ticket, turning away politicians affiliated with formal political parties, which were seen as being closely involved in corruption. The protests in 2011 were all primarily mobilised as calls for stronger legislation than that being proposed by the UPA government. For instance, in April, Hazare's fast succeeded in improving the numbers of civil society actors who would sit on the committee, which drafted the Jan Lokpal Bill.

In light of the successful April fast, other activists involved in the wider anti-corruption movement began to plan similarly. Baba Ramdev, whose campaign in the anti-corruption movement was about 'black' money sitting in overseas accounts, occupied Ramlila Maidan on 4 June. Significantly, the preparations for this rally included the provision of extensive infrastructure in the Maidan, including toilets, a medical centre and media centres (Zee News, 2011). On 6 June, Delhi police raided the Maidan and detained Ramdev, leading to violent clashes between protestors and the authorities and tear gas being fired by the police. These clashes intensified the tensions between anti-corruption campaigners and the authorities. It was against this background that Anna Hazare announced in July that he was to fast in the Ramlila Maidan from 16 August onwards to get a stronger Lokpal Bill passed. There followed a protracted period of negotiation as the authorities attempted to refuse permission for the fast, while Hazare maintained his plans. On the morning of 16 August, Hazare was pre-emptively arrested to prevent him fasting, and was then remanded in custody after refusing to pay any bail. Protests against Hazare's detention soon occurred across India, and opposition political parties were swift to condemn the arrest. More negotiations followed, with Hazare beginning his fast in prison, and offers of permission to protest at different sites for different lengths of time being proposed. However, Hazare was allowed to leave Tihar Jail after three days on 19 August and proceeded through Delhi to Ramlila Maidan. There, Hazare fasted on a platform, often making speeches (together with other anti-corruption activists) that were broadcast live on the major Indian news channels, with activists making widespread use of social media to further disseminate these messages (Harindranath and Khorana, 2014). The Maidan attracted thousands of supporters daily, with marches and rallies on many days (over 100,000 people being present on 21 August), while the protests also attracted celebrities and politicians to the anti-corruption movement. There was also a committed infrastructure on the site, much of which was provided by the state against which Hazare was protesting, including food stalls, sanitation and medical aid, and even reports that post was being delivered to Hazare at the Maidan (DNA, 2011). These protest infrastructures mapped on to and extended existing facilities around the Maidan. For example, the platform which became Hazare's main stage is a permanent feature of the Maidan and was adapted for the fast, and the Maidan's role in previous political rallies meant that there was a significant body of knowledge available about how to best utilise the space. However, the scale of the August fast, both in terms of the length of time it would occupy the Maidan, and the numbers of people who it attracted to the site, was unprecedented and necessitated a degree of planning and coordination between a team of principle organisers from the movement (known in the press as 'Team Anna') and the authorities so that there was adequate food, water and sanitation on and around the site.

While Hazare's fast attracted support from across Indian society, it was also fraught with tensions, as politicians from opposition parties, including the Hindu-right Bharatiya Janata Party (BJP) and the Communist Party of India, attempted to make common cause with the protesters. Some commentators, such as Sitapati (2011) argued that the variety of intellectual trends present within the Anna protest was remarkable, both in providing a broad-based legitimacy to the movement, but also in its ability to hold together such disparate strands through its intervention at a particular moment when the UPA government was mired in corruption scandals. Notably, while the Jan Lokpal movement could hold together a number of positions, from pro-market liberalisation to neo-Gandhian, it largely excluded the Marxist-inspired Left, and it was from this quarter that most opposition to both Hazare and to the strategy of the movement came. Hazare himself is a controversial character – despite his avowed 'Gandhianism' many on the left in India see him as authoritarian in his conduct. Arundhati Roy (2011), writing in the Hindu newspaper, mounted an attack on Hazare's ability to manipulate the authorities and the media while in Delhi, stating:

> For three days, while crowds and television vans gathered outside, members of Team Anna whizzed in and out of the high security prison, carrying out his video messages, to be broadcast on national TV on all channels. (Which other person would be granted this luxury?) Meanwhile

> 250 employees of the Municipal Commission of Delhi, 15 trucks, and six earth movers worked around the clock to ready the slushy Ramlila grounds for the grand weekend spectacle. Now, waited upon hand and foot, watched over by chanting crowds and crane-mounted cameras, attended to by India's most expensive doctors, the third phase of Anna's fast to the death has begun.

Roy's scorn for Hazare was driven by her broader distrust of his tactics as authoritarian: He had previously made a number of controversial statements about Muslims, and had once stated how much he admired the BJP's then Chief Minister of the State of Gujarat (and now Prime Minister of India), Narendra Modi. Modi is particularly controversial, not least due to his unclear role during an anti-Muslim pogrom in the city of Ahmedabad in Gujarat during 2002, for which his critics see him as responsible. Combined with a high degree of middle-class participation (including a perception that many middle-class protesters were driven around the various marches by their chauffeurs), the fast succeeded in alienating much of the progressive left in India. However, the surprising coalescing of such disparate perspectives, from neo-Gandhianism to pro-economic liberalisation, mobilising on this scale was undoubtedly one of the key strengths of the movement. The end result of this mobilisation was that Hazare's fast was successful in the short term, forcing through a change in the law, with the UPA government having pushed through the Lokpal Bill during the night of 27 August.

Situating Anna Hazare's fast as political practice

Moving beyond the contextual information above, it is important to link ideas about protest, and more particularly camps, to the events of August 2011. Viewing Hazare's fast as a camp has the potential to open new understandings of both the fast as a protest and the varieties of social activities encompassed by protest camps. For example, while the fast did not involve 'camping' as it is popularly imagined, it was an occupation of space specifically for the purpose of contesting a major societal issue. The camp also bore a number of similarities to protest camp forms of political media strategies, as Hazare and other anti-corruption activists were able to use the media to put political pressure on the UPA, including live broadcasts of speeches and the crowds at the site, together with regular media briefings by members of 'Team Anna'. Indeed, the mediated nature of the fast formed a key aspect of the emergent politics of representation that developed in the site. This is discussed in more detail below, but the ability of the fast organisers to make Hazare's body (and the mass public body of the crowds in attendance) visible through integrating mainstream media facilities into the Ramlila Maidan site was a core component of the fast. It is useful here to follow Feigenbaum et al (2013) in thinking about the relationships of protest camps to media and communication as an ecology, rather than as a tool to achieve certain aims. By allowing a mainstream media presence on the Ramlila Maidan, as well as the variety of independent media and social media activities that were at work in less easily traceable ways around the fast, the Ramlila Maidan fast was unprecedented in the attention it drew to what was essentially a protest about a piece of political legislation. This was, I argue, key in the maintenance of the site as a space where disparate political and social identities could mobilise successfully, and certainly one lack in work on the Ramlila Maidan fast is detailed ethnographic work on how the political and social 'ecology' of the site was able to negotiate across difference between the various groups present on the site. However, unlike a strategic tool, the way this 'ecology' functioned was also productive of wider interpretations of the fast, most specifically those from the left who were excluded from the wider movement.

It is also important not to forget the importance of established political behaviours during the demonstration. Hazare's fast represents something deeply embedded within 'traditional' South Asian political norms, in particular in its use of fasting as a technique used by an individual or group to force political change. Fasting has been used as a technique of political protest for centuries, and has been an important tactic of resistance in India, from anti-colonial protests through to more recent protests about issues like the damming of the Narmada valley. Crucial here was the explicit attempt by Hazare to brand himself and the wider protests as 'Gandhian' (Sengupta, 2012). The political power of drawing on the philosophy and politics of Gandhi is clear, however, it has a number of important effects. First, it calls out to India's anti-colonial struggle. This positions the struggle against corruption as something that is equal to the historical struggle against colonialism, and is therefore of national importance. In doing this, it also solidifies boundaries between those who wish to struggle against corruption and those who don't. This antagonism helps to foster group cohesion by creating a negative category of 'the corrupt' to be resisted, and which in the case of Hazare was particularly applied to government officials and bureaucrats. However, this hardening of opposition is also problematic, creating limited space for political deliberation, as we shall see below.

The Maidan itself is a site with a long history of being used for political rallies – what is important for Hazare's claims to continuity with the Indian Independence Movement is that the site had previously been used to address crowds by the likes of Gandhi. This meant that the site was already known for being a 'political' space, and it also meant that received and embedded knowledges about using the space for political rallies had some influence. One of the striking things about the site during its occupation in August 2011 was its drawing upon a range of 'typical' performances and gestures that are often standardised throughout political rallies in South Asia. These included material gestures such as the use of Gandhi/Nehru hats (an important material marker of political identity in India), emblazoned with 'I am Anna' slogans in English and Hindi, through to more affective styles of political engagement, such as particular vocal styles by the speaker and his/her relation to the crowd, such as the call and response of stock phrases, through to more mundane, but still important, infrastructural decisions, such as building huge marquees to protect the crowd from the sun.

In addition to these well-practised repertoires being enacted in the Maidan, the focus was on the body of Hazare, whose platform at the eastern end of the maidan became a stage so that he, and others who occupied it, were clearly visible. This allowed 'the public', either through being there, or through the media to focus on his body as the subject of their gaze. This 'viewing' was not unproblematic, with mainstream media being provided with space for cameras, often in front of the public whose view of the stage was obscured (see the many videos online by activists for a sense of events at the Maidan – for example www.youtube.com/watch?v=K2I8UVORQp0). However, the almost uninterrupted access to images of Hazare's body, combined with the deployment of and easily identifiable target of the protest – 'corruption' – together with the ecology of well-established repertoires described above, meant that the mainstream media were able to disseminate the aims and objectives of the movement to an audience who were already well versed in many of the issues and their presentation. This also lies in marked contrast to mainstream media's confusion over the more nebulous goals of groups like Occupy or the Indignados, where broad-based discussions about the nature of democracy and capitalism were less easy to translate, and often led to confusion and/or misrepresentations of protesters by the media.

From another perspective, the Hazare fast is a 'new' form of political engagement, taking its shape from new media and protest activities. In this, Hazare's fast was different to many previous ones in that he made himself publicly visible throughout. Through the media ecology of the fast his supporters were able to project his struggle incredibly effectively. While people like Gandhi fasted in seclusion, the value of Hazare placing himself in a public place and allowing people to see him as he slowly inflicted violence upon his body is not to be underestimated. The body of Hazare became of wider importance to the movement, with the use of the 'I am Anna' hats mentioned above, mirroring techniques practised by activists in the Arab Spring (particularly Tunisia) and elsewhere in 2011. The mainstream media was central to this public projection – Rajagopal (2011) argues that the Anna campaign was the first instance where both English- and vernacular-language news media, which have traditionally been more and less conservative respectively in relation to protest agitations, came together to agree that a protest was a positive event which should be supported:

> The Anna Hazare campaign was remarkable in that, across the [English- and vernacular-] language media, the spectacle of popular mobilisation became a thing of unqualified virtue, discreetly signalled in the nomenclature 'civil society'. Civil society, unlike the state, was assumed to be free of corruption, as if one could distinguish between them so neatly. (Rajagopal, 2011, 20)

Rajagopal argues that this only increased the tendency to dichotomise into what he terms a 'with-us-or-against-us' approach to the protests. This combined with the highly mediated nature of the August 2011 fast in general meant that the terms of public debate quickly coalesced into oppositional debates, such as 'Corruption vs Non-corruption', or 'Civil Society vs The State'. This focus on 'civil society' is important to the perception of the 2011 fast – a large portion of discussion during and after the fast reflected concerns about the evolution of politics in Indian society, particularly in relation to the changes that have emerged since the liberalisation of the Indian economy that began in the early 1990s. As a result, it is necessary to turn here towards a more theoretical understanding of Indian society, particularly engagements with what Ajay Gudavarthy (2012) has termed 'post-civil society', or the workings of civil society in postcolonial India.

The camp and civil society

Recent debates about civil society in India have been dominated by Partha Chatterjee's concept of Political Society (Chatterjee, 2004;

2011a). Political society here is a postcolonial critique of the universalist project often promoted by advocates of 'global' civil society which emphasise civil society's potential for democratic change. Sceptical of these claims,[3] for Chatterjee, civil society, as a concept drawn from European enlightenment thinking, remains an elitist domain, and has never fully functioned in much of the global south, where large swathes of the population are excluded from civil society by being treated as 'populations to be governed' rather than 'citizens'. Seeing civil society as a domain belonging to the privileged, he argues that popular politics in much of the global south what he calls 'political society'. In political society, instead of being treated as individual, rights-bearing citizens, people are instead classified according to the Foucauldian language of governmentality according to the characteristics of the groups which they occupy (for example, as refugees, informal settlers, or according to communal identity). As a result, it is those groups who can make themselves visible, but who can also argue that they are the most worthy of aid, who are able to claim resources off the state. Thus, groups who are able to mobilise effectively and present their case in a way that a) the state can understand, and b) that the state sees as worthwhile (for example, fitting with the latest policy target or public demand) are more likely to receive the benefits of limited state resources. As a result, political society is where practices like clientalism, brokerage and other more-or-less formal activities take place as those excluded from civil society try to make themselves visible to the state. Political society then, is a space where, rather than the formal 'political' gestures of civil society, a series of mundane political activities are practised, such as visiting the office of a village official on a daily basis. It is also avowedly not a radical space of transformation, but a space where communities and individuals try to 'get by' by explicitly engaging with and utilising the state's facilities. Chatterjee's political society is not an alternative to civil society; it is instead a recognition that civil society is too limited a concept to grasp the messy, and often morally dubious, nature of politics as it is practised by those who sit outside the liberal political framework. When read in this way, the 2011 Ramlila Maidan protests are constructed as an action driven by predominantly civil society actors – middle-class, TV-watching, social media–using Indians who raged against their everyday encounters with 'political' society, such as:

> the daily experience of having to pay bribes to petty officials and functionaries to secure timely delivery of any service (for example, obtaining a ration card, installation

or restoration of a telephone line in cities, and water from canals, credit from banks and other inputs needed by farmers in villages), which is a basic right of every citizen. (Banerjee, 2011, 12)

To Chatterjee then, the Jan Lokpal movement remained fundamentally a concern of civil society – by creating a category of 'corruption' and seeing it as a problem largely created by government, which could only be solved by a large independent ombudsman, it remained a largely elitist project. Chatterjee explicitly ties this together with the increasing marketisation of Indian society – the most desired jobs in India now no longer lie in the civil service, but instead in the private sector. However, while the private sector is viewed as a place that rewards merit, government service is venal and corrupt.[4] This, as Harindranath and Khorana (2014) have argued, is an example of how the highly internet-mediated presence of the fast as a whole, together with the urban dominated emphasis of Indian civil society more generally, has skewed the ecology of anti-corruption so that its outcomes suited an internet-using, educated and relatively affluent middle class. To critics and academic commentators like Chatterjee (2011b), Appadurai (2011) and Menon and Nigam (2011), together with more publicly visible critics like Arundhati Roy, the Hazare protests were a *revanchist* attack on the state in order to secure the best solution for the middle classes who wanted to do away with government bureaucracy and replace it with private enterprise. By doing so, and removing some of the practices available to the poor as a part of political society which is 'corrupt', this is a reassertion of civil society as the predominant source of political negotiation within an idealised 'modern' India that is able to be a global capitalist power.

This view attracted much attention, but misses some of the complexity of how political relations between state, market and civil society actually play out in situations such as that of a protest camp. In a more balanced account Banerjee (2011) also argued that many of the critiques of Hazare mobilised by the left, especially accounts grounded in ideas of post-civil society like Chatterjee, did not provide any effective alternative or solution to corruption, especially when corruption remains endemic to so much of Indian society. In addition, by focusing on the problematic figure of Hazare, these critiques ignore, or at least hinder, any recognition of the variety of actors present within the broader Jan Lokpal movement. Not everyone who claimed 'I am Anna' by wearing a hat with that slogan was élite or 'middle class', nor were they all somehow 'duped' by the messages of 'Team

Anna' and the dominant mainstream media discourse. Indeed, since 2011, Hazare himself has become less visible as a political figurehead. Instead, Arvind Kejriwal and the Aam Aadmi Party ('Common Man's Party', or AAP) have become prominent. Kejriwal deliberately eschews any of the markers that are the traditional trappings of the political classes in India – for example he is famed for wearing the muffler of a working-class Indian during Delhi's cold winters rather than the formal attire that most (male) Indian politicians would wear. Kejriwal became a key figure as the Jan Lokpal movement splintered after Hazare's August 2011 fast. Unlike Hazare's distrust of formal political parties, the AAP's creation was an attempt to counter critics who said that the Jan Lokpal movement was undemocratic as it dictated terms to elected representatives. It was this difference of opinion between Hazare and Kejriwal supporters that formed one of the main fractures in the movement post–August 2011. Thus, what is interesting about the Ramlila Maidan fast is the way in which the fast as a 'camp' provided a space for keeping the movement together, yet also provided a moment for mobilising widespread discontent with democracy in ways which were, at least in part, productive of seemingly more progressive political outcomes, such as the AAP.

The critique of the fast from the progressive left ignores, or occludes that fact that the fast worked across a number of different spectrums, bringing in actors from left and right perspectives (and it is important to recognise the huge limitations of using 'left' and 'right' as terms to demarcate political differences here). Instead, thinking through the fast as a camp, offers productive ways through some of the problems of whether the fast was a site of more or less democratic accountability. As Rygiel (2012) has argued in terms of migrant and refugee camps, the camp both reproduces certain types of political behaviour, while limiting others. As a result, they can be sites where 'normal' politics is allowed to go on, or they can be sites of transgression – indeed, there was much about the August 2011 fast that was 'politics as normal' in an Indian context. This can, in turn, help or hinder whether those who take part in camps are actually accepted as citizens or not. Thus, instead of creating concepts to act as containers with strict boundaries, we should instead be examining the ways in which spaces like protest camps are run through with contradictions as old/normal/accepted political and social behaviours exist alongside new/marginal/radical practices. Seeing the 2011 fast this way helps to both ground it as a specific site, but also to think through how it fits into, but also cuts against, wider concepts. Perhaps then, instead of thinking about a division between civil and political society, it is possible to utilise what Sullivan et al

(2011) call '(un)civil' society. In this, and drawing upon Whitehead (1997), they argue that instead of dividing between civil and political society, Sullivan et al argue that organisations and movements that sit outside hegemonic forms (in their case, the Indymedia movement) are often represented as uncivil – sitting outside a (global) civil society that in fact continues to legitimise structural inequality. Sullivan et al rightly argue that the boundaries between 'civil' and 'uncivil' society are in fact porous and dynamic, and when we think through the Jan Lokpal fast in August 2011 with its connections to state, civil society and other actors, the fast provides a useful line of intervention into the somewhat binary nature of Chatterjee's thought.[5]

Thus, while the Hazare protest could be seen as an elitist civil society in action, the nature of the protest, and the way in which the fast was able to hold together a variety of political viewpoints shows us that the fast was both more variegated and more fractured than such unitary solutions would have us believe. The mainstream media ecology of the fast combined a number of recognisable protest repertoires and a wider discourse of corruption to be resisted/challenged and undoubtedly helped to stabilise relations around the fast during its event. However, Ramlila Maidan, rather than being an unproblematic space where limited deliberation took place, was in fact much more dynamic, as the subsequent split between Hazare and Kejriwal shows. While the fast's anti-authoritarianism was construed as creating a site which limited the space for democratic deliberation, this obscures the process of negotiation and bartering behind closed and open doors that must have taken place in order to get the Ramlila Maidan to function as a site during the fast. These included high level negotiations between the various different political parties and movements who came together on the site, including such varied groups as the police, municipal sanitation officers and mainstream media producers, but also incorporated a variety of more mundane, everyday acts of social reproduction, such as the appearance of food vendors and street hawkers selling 'I am Anna' hats and other merchandise around the Maidan. These actors are clearly visible throughout the protests, and could represent the actions of individual hawkers taking advantage of the crowds to boost their income, through to more structured forms of labour organising that take place throughout India's informal sector. It is too simplistic to see these smaller-scale actors as being a part of a non-élite 'political' society, as it is unclear how they intersected with the wider protest movement, whether they were included as a part of the organisation of 'Team Anna' or were simply tolerated as part of wider street theatre surrounding the protest. Thus, thinking about the

2011 fast as a space of ongoing social relations, rather than as a space of conceptual rigidity, helps to blur the lines between categories of the state, civil and political society.

Conclusions

It is important to think about Anna Hazare's 2011 fast as a protest camp as this approach helps to problematise some of the narratives which formed about the fast in the years since it took place. The first of these is the construction of the protest camp as an elitist space, one which is conflated as being utilised by civil society actors and/or India's new middle classes. Treating the site as a camp allows for a more situated account which sees the Ramlila Maidan as a more dynamic space, where, if not '(un)civil society' was practised, at least the negotiations between state, media, political parties, other civil society organisations and everyday protestors were worked through. That the Maidan did not collapse into chaos during the fast is evidence of a certain type of social reproduction taking place, which involved actors from a variety of social backgrounds mobilising to maintain the site as a habitable and workable space, and this more grounded level of analysis of the Maidan has been generally lacking.

This is not to say that there was not present an overarching narrative driven in often class-based terms. The heavily mediated site, with its banks of TV cameras, together with the mainstream media's access to high level members of 'Team Anna' allowed a certain discourse to emerge from the site, and this was one which largely excluded (and indeed antagonised) voices from the progressive left with its perceived 'middle-classness'. This is also important as it means that analysis of protest camps should be attuned to these class-based politics which often sit in the background of the more material, situated and affective discussions of the construction and maintenance of protest camps. However, this cuts both ways, as the most vigorous academic engagements with the fast have tended to privilege the conceptual, particularly in relation to the nature of civil society, at the expense of the more grounded. In this case, there are probably further discussions to be had about how these 'middle-class' discourses were debated and negotiated in and around the site of the fast itself – in general there has been a lack of ethnographic engagement with the spaces of the fast – and how these debates then filtered into the wider media ecology of the protest as a whole, especially as 'Team Anna's' relationship with the mainstream media has often been assumed as dominant in shaping the fast's narrative. What this chapter makes clear is the potential for a protest camp's approach to challenge existing accounts (from both 'the progressive left' and 'the middle classes' and elsewhere) of the fast, and by extension other related forms of protest, and therefore to provide space for alternative readings that can ground and contextualise more theoretical discussions of concepts such as civil/political society.

Notes

[1]   'Anna' is a word common to many South Asian languages meaning 'Elder Brother'.
[2]   He had begun fasting while in Tihar jail, where he had been since 16 August 2011.
[3]   Important here is Chatterjee's intellectual history as a member of the Subaltern Studies Collective in the 1970s and 1980s.
[4]   This, of course, conveniently forgets the role of the private sector in the various corruption scandals that afflicted the UPA government.
[5]   This is something recognised by Chatterjee himself (see Chatterjee, 2012).

References

Appadurai, A. (2011) 'Our corruption, our selves', *Kafila*, 30 August, http://kafila.org/2011/08/30/our-corruption-our-selves-arjun-appadurai/.

Banerjee, S. (2011) 'Anna Hazare, civil society and the state', *Economic and Political Weekly*, 46(36), 12–14.

Chatterjee, P. (2004) *The Politics of the Governed*. New York: Columbia University Press.

Chatterjee, P. (2011a) *Lineages of Political Society*. New York: Columbia University Press.

Chatterjee, P. (2011b) 'Against corruption = against politics', *Kafila*, 28 August, http://kafila.org/2011/08/28/against-corruption-against-politics-partha-chatterjee/.

Chatterjee, P. (2012) 'The debate over political society', in A. Gudavarthy (ed.) *Reframing Democracy and Agency in India: Interrogating Political Society*. London: Anthem Press, pp 305–322.

Chatterji, M. (2013) 'The globalization of politics: from Egypt to India', *Social Movement Studies*, 12(1), 96–102.

DNA (Daily News & Analysis) (2011) 'Ramlila Maidan is Anna Hazare's new postal address', www.dnaindia.com/india/report-ramlila-maidan-is-anna-hazares-new-postal-address-1580281.

Feigenbaum, A., Frenzel, F. and McCurdy, P. (2013) *Protest Camps*. London: Zed.

Gudavarthy, A. (2012) *Reframing Democracy and Agency in India: Interrogating Political Society*. London: Anthem Press.

Harindranath, R. and Khorana, S. (2014) 'Civil society movements and the 'Twittering Classes' in the postcolony: an Indian case study', *South Asia: Journal of South Asian Studies*, 37(1), 60–71.

Menon, N. and Nigam, A. (2011) 'If only there were no people, democracy would be fine...', _Kafila,_ 22 August, http://kafila. org/2011/08/22/if-only-there-were-no-people-democracy-would-be-fine/.

Nigam, A. (2012) 'The Arab Upsurge and the "viral" revolutions of our times', _Interface: A Journal For and About Social Movements_, 4(1), 165–177, www.interfacejournal.net/wordpress/wp-content/uploads/2012/05/Interface-4-1-Nigam.pdf.

Rajagopal, A. (2011) 'Visibility as a trap in the Anna Hazare Campaign', _Economic and Political Weekly_, 46(47), 19–21.

Roy, A. (2011) 'I'd rather not be Anna', _The Hindu_, 21 August, www.thehindu.com/opinion/lead/id-rather-not-be-anna/article2379704.ece.

Rygiel, K. (2012) 'Politicizing camps: forging transgressive citizenships in and through transit', _Citizenship Studies_, 16(5–6), 807–825.

Sengupta, M. (2012) 'Anna Hazare and the idea of Gandhi', _Journal of Asian Studies_, 71(3), 593–601.

Sengupta, M. (2014) 'Anna Hazare's anti-corruption movement and the limits of mass mobilization in India', _Social Movement Studies_, 13(3), 406–413.

Sitapati, V. (2011) 'What Anna Hazare's movement and India's new middle classes say about each other', _Economic and Political Weekly_, 46(30), 39–44.

Sullivan, S., Spicer, A. and Böhm, S (2011) 'Becoming global (un)civil society: counter-hegemonic struggle and the Indymedia network', 8(5), 703–717.

Whitehead, L. (1997) 'Bowling in the Bronx: the uncivil interstices between civil and political society', _Democratization,_ 4(1), 94–114.

Zee News (2011) 'Ramlila ground gets ready for Ramdev's fast', http://zeenews.india.com/news/nation/ramlila-ground-gets-ready-for-ramdevs-fast_710292.html.

Part Three
Reproducing and re-creating

SIXTEEN

Introduction: reproducing and re-creating

*Fabian Frenzel, Anna Feigenbaum, Patrick McCurdy
and Gavin Brown*

Introduction

Protest camps occupy a unique position within collective action as they are not only the site of protest but they simultaneously double as home places (hooks, 1990; Roseneil, 2000); places where participants are fed, cared for and sheltered. Previous parts of this book have examined how protest camps manifest their protest in relation to space, and the ways in which they enable and nourish the assembly of diverse participants, creating coalitions of protestors that may form significant challenges to the status quo. In this part the focus turns inward, looking at practices of social reproduction and the re-creation of everyday life in protest camps and the politics which underwrites this.

A politics of social reproduction

It is important to first clarify that the constructions of many protest camps as home places is not simply an accidental side effect or by-product of this form of protest. Rather, it is often deliberately pursued and actively promoted as a social movement politics. In the case of many camps such politics takes inspiration from at least two significant political debates on the radical left.

First, re-creating the protest camp as home takes on the 'question of organisation', and in particular the notion of prefiguration (Breines, 1989; Pickerill and Chatterton, 2006; Day, 2005; Frenzel, 2014; Nunes, 2014). A debate of means and ends, or tactic and strategy, the question of organisation in left-wing movements goes back to nineteenth-century conflicts between anarchists and socialists. While socialists broadly aimed for the working-class organisation to capture state power and use this power to implement a socialist and communist order, many anarchists instead argued for a dismantling of the state in the process of revolutionary transformation (Gordon, 2008; Ward, 1973). In the political analysis of anarchists, political power had to be built from the bottom up, overcoming the authoritarian structures manifest in states with new forms of radically democratic organisation. The poles of vertical versus horizontal organisation were rarely this clear cut, and historically many socialists were engaged in attempts at creating new forms of alternative living from the bottom up, for example the alternative and utopian communities that formed in the nineteenth century by socialists such as Richard Owen (Miliband, 1954).

Conversely, many anarchist movements, like the Catalan anarchists in the 1930s, did not hesitate to take and use state power when the opportunity arose (Bookchin, 1994). Despite these obvious overlaps the two poles of left-wing answers to the questions of organisation, remained significant dividing lines. They came to the fore again in the 1960s as many leftists felt the need to distance themselves from the political project of states in which socialist and communist parties had taken power (Breines, 1989; Ward, 1973). As these states engaged in increasingly fierce repression of opposition voices and pursued top-down control, the anarchist pole became more attractive to many on the left, represented in the political formation of the 'new left'. A key tenet of the movements that emerged in this context was the idea of prefiguration, now increasingly explicit in programmatic and political action (Bookchin, 2015; Breines, 1989; Cornell, 2011). Accordingly, political organisation in the movements had to pre-figure the political organisation of the desired political order. Tactics, including the running of day-to-day organisational affairs had to be aligned with the strategic aims. No longer were means to be justified by the ends of political action (Bookchin, 2015; Cornell, 2011).

Second, in looking at protest camps as home places, one needs to consider the politicisation of social reproduction, particularly following feminist critiques of political organisation that became increasingly influential since the 1960s (Dalla Costa and James, 1972; Federici, 2012). According to the feminist critique at the time, political organisations on the left often mirrored the patriarchal order of the status quo, relegating the question of social reproduction to a secondary importance, both theoretically and practically. Theoretically this concerned the devaluation of social reproduction in the dominant Marxist reading of the political economy where it was considered as 'non-productive labour' and thus not as an important domain of labour struggle (Federici, 2004). In more practical terms this concerned the secondary role of women in the labour movements' organisational structures and the limited recognition of feminised labour in the movements themselves. This critique demanded, along the lines of the anarchist critique, that social movement organisation must became more conscious of the necessary labour of social reproduction and equally prefigure such consciousness in feminist organisational principles. Feminists in the US, Britain and Germany were also at the forefront of pioneering protest camps as a new social movement tactic in these countries (Costello and Stanley, 1985; Leidinger, 2011; Roseneil, 2000)

Both debates thus provided the background to a new composition of struggle in which protest camps occurred. They are forms of social movement organisation that have been both powerful in contesting the status quo and prefiguring organisational structures that allowed movements to experiment with and implement the desired new forms of organisation, conscious of demands for radical democracy, as well as the politicising of social reproduction. Of course protest camps were not the only organisational forms in which these issues were experimented with. The development of political organisations based on neighbourhoods as in Argentina after the uprising of 2001 (Sitrin, 2006), basis groups as in the environmental movements of the 1970s (Rucht, 1990), theme specific collectives like networked local No Border groups or affinity groups that form at protests (Brown, 2007; Trapese Collective, 2007), the rise of communes and squatting as specific tactics of urban social movements (Hancox, 2014; Kuhn, 2014; Vasudevan, 2015), and more spontaneous and voluntary forms of participation in social movements all reflected this shift (Beck, 1997; Offe, 1987).

In Part Three we will therefore reflect not only on the experience of protest camps but also look at a number of examples where social movements' tactics involve a focus, both theoretically and practically, on the politicising of social reproduction, for example in building occupations and autonomous homeless tent cities. The chapters show the complexities involved in comparing protest camps to such forms of protest that more immediately address participants' needs for housing and care.

When social reproduction is politicised, a number of issues appear on the political agenda that need more careful reflection, for example, questions concerning the balance between social reproduction and more confrontational forms of political contestations (as well as the highly contested expectations about who should participate in each of these functions). Because protest camps can become a temporary home for many people, questions of physical, psychological and symbolic safety (especially for women and minority groups) have frequently been the cause of tension within camps. How do campers struggle to realise some of their political hopes within the space of the camp – not just their 'big' hopes for a more just, equal and sustainable society; but their hopes for a transformation of everyday social relations between people?

Because protest camps prefiguratively embody alternative ways of being, they can serve as powerful inspirations long after specific camps cease to exist. The new focus of social reproduction thus brings challenges, but also exerts an immense political power, often played out in a politics of the everyday that has a unique ability to form collective pluralities in antagonistic struggles.

Chapters in Part Three

This becomes tangible in Chapter Seventeen, Elisa Pascucci's contribution on the protest camp of Sudanese refugees in Cairo in 2005. This little-known protest camp started off as a protest against increasing deportations of Sudanese refugees from Egypt following the Darfur peace accord. The protests targeted the UNHCR bureau in Cairo and eventually transformed into one of the most significant social movement mobilisations prior to the 2011 uprisings at Tahrir Square in Egypt. While not planning the protest to be a camp, the refugees responded to the immediate need for housing and shelter for many refugees and started to camp out. While continuing their protests the Sudanese refugees increasingly built semi-autonomous structures of a precarious new home place. This in turn increased the attraction for other Sudanese refugees, and the camp as well as the protest grew, eventually also mobilising Egyptian supporters, both from more religious and political backgrounds. As Pascucci argued the camp thus succeeded in influencing not just those who actively took part in it but also Egyptian civil society. In this sense the refugee camp arguably served as an inspiration to Egyptian social movements prior to Tahrir. This is indicative of the immense power of politicising social reproduction.

This is equally the case in Marcella Arruda's discussion of the Marconi occupation in São Paolo, in Chapter Eighteen. The occupation of an inner-city high-rise office building does not constitute a protest camp. However, in politicising the housing question by collectively and publicly occupying empty real estate, the Marconi occupation follows a similar politics. The contribution also points to shared challenges between occupied building sites and protest camps. Arruda highlights the development of infrastructures that fulfilled the aspirations of the squatters, in transforming the office building into housing. They also sought to maintain practices of prefiguration that spoke to the broader public. But as the centrally organised structure of this squat was established and the occupation became relatively secure, several of the squatters retreated to a more private understanding of their new home place and stopped pursuing collective structures. In the end, the occupation began to collect rent from participants, and replaced the self-run kitchen and collective daycare with paid workers. The occupation thus transformed into what could be described as autonomous housing. Along the way it lost some its political edge, no longer pushing an antagonistic stance to the status quo.

The occupation of an empty plot of land in Kreuzberg, Berlin, is the topic of a further contribution by Niko Rollmann and Fabian Frenzel in Chapter Nineteen. The authors observe how the related issues of gentrification and urban poverty played out as activists took over the plot to prevent the development of high-end real estate. The emerging protest camp started to attract increasing numbers of destitute and homeless participants and increasingly re-orientated its focus towards an attempt to provide autonomous housing. As in the previous chapter, this engendered a number of problems, albeit differently addressed in this camp. Quickly a split occurred between those protest campers who prioritised the political struggle against gentrification and those more involuntary occupiers (Schein, 2012) who sought a place of shelter in the main. While several attempts were made to combine the causes, the challenges proved significant. The occupiers' own daily lives took up much energy and little power was left to collectively organise their lives and address the increasingly pressing issues of safety, hygiene and a long-term strategy. This example shows the challenges faced by protest camps to fully provide care and social reproduction, when participants bring limited resources into the camp.

Safety and security are also the focus of Claire English's discussion, in Chapter Twenty, of migrant solidarity and the 'No Border' camps of Calais, France. English highlights the challenges of building a home place and negotiating safety in the particular case of a solidarity protest camp set up within an informal refugee camp. The mutual conduct by campers, including the respect for private spaces needs to be permanently negotiated in all protest camps. In the case of Calais No Borders, such negotiations sometimes ended up reproducing existing power relations between different participants. This includes the perspective of many male participants that they are not overly concerned with safety, as well as the assertions of some female refugee supporters that they felt their safety was compromised predominantly because of the behaviour of particular refugee men. Thus some women decided to organise to patrol the 'Afghan area', an approach that uncannily mirrors the construction of stereotypes and ghettoisation by the state. As in Calais, several protest camps have worked to agree safer spaces policies aimed at regulating shared space (across multiple axes of social difference), but as English's analysis confirms, this is often done as a formal act without much discussion. Moreover, the question of who should and how to implement and sanction such rules on behaviour is always fraught.

Nicholas Jon Crane highlights yet another problem deriving from the politicising of social reproduction in the camp, by asking what is actually reproduced. He contends that protest camps may become institutions that serve to maintain the status quo, rather than challenge it, when their immediate political contestation declines. In his study of the educational function of Mexican protest camps, his reading of social reproduction concerns the formation of political identities. Protest camps have been shown to be central in the formation of activist identities, but are also often credited with the politicisatiom of formerly 'non-activist' participants (Feigenbaum, 2010; Frenzel, 2011; Leidinger, 2011). In Crane's study, in Chapter Twenty-one, the opposite effect is observed as protest camps now form a routine part of the political subjectivation of Mexican student protestors. While radical positioning is fostered in the camp, it is equally linked to a specific youthful moment in the life of the participants. The state thus manages to contain the antagonistic gestures in the camps as those of a 'naturally oppositional youth'. Crane suggests the necessity of better understanding the conditions in which protest camps provide a rupture that may not be easily integrated and appeased.

Overall the chapters thus provide many perspectives on the ways in which protest camps and related forms of protest politicise social reproduction. They thus also relate to debates about care and its ethics (Bellacasa, 2011; Mol, 2008; Stengers, 2010). Arguably many protest camps discussed here respond to the broader retrenchment of the state from the provision of care prompted by neoliberal politics. In doing so they face the dual challenge to contest the retreat of the state while prefiguring autonomous alternatives of care provision. As the chapters in Part Three show, this dual strategy is at times riddled with contradictions. At the same time, the reflective accounts presented here also provide some ideas towards how the challenges can be tackled and thus allow recurring debates to advance.

References

Beck, U. (1997) 'Subpolitics: ecology and the disintegration of institutional power', *Organization and Environment*, 10(1), 52–65.

Bellacasa, M. P. de la (2011) 'Matters of care in technoscience: assembling neglected things', *Social Studies of Science*, 41(1), 85–106.

Bookchin, M. (1994) *To Remember Spain: The Anarchist and Syndicalist Revolution of 1936*. San Francisco, CA: AK Press.

Bookchin, M. (2015) *The Next Revolution*. London: Verso

Breines, W. (1989) *Community and Organization in the New Left, 1962–1968: The Great Refusal*. New Brunswick, NJ: Rutgers University Press.

Brown, G. (2007) 'Mutinous eruptions: autonomous spaces of radical queer activism', *Environment and Planning A*, 39 (11), 2685–2698.

Cornell, A. (2011) *Oppose and Propose: Lessons from Movement for a New Society*. Oakland, CA: AK Press.

Costello, C. and Stanley, A. D. (1985) 'Report from Seneca', *Frontiers: A Journal of Women Studies*, 8(2), 32–39.

Dalla Costa, M. and James, S. (1972) *Women and the Subversion of the Community*. Bristol: Falling Wall Press.

Day, R. J. F. (2005) *Gramsci is Dead: Anarchist Currents in the Newest Social Movements*. London: Pluto Press.

Federici, S. (2004) *Caliban and the Witch*. New York: Autonomedia.

Federici, S. (2012) *Revolution at Point Zero: Housework, Reproduction, and Feminist Struggle*. Oakland, CA: PM Press.

Feigenbaum, A. (2010) '"Now I'm a happy dyke!": creating collective identity and queer community in Greenham women's songs', *Journal of Popular Music Studies*, 22(4), 367–388,

Frenzel, F. (2011) 'Entlegende Ort in der Mitte der Gesellschaft Die Geschichte der britischen Klimacamps', [Fringe places in the middle of society A history of the British climate camps] in A. Brunnengräber (ed) *Zivilisierung des Klimaregimes: NGOs und soziale Bewegungen in der nationalen, europäischen und internationalen Klimapolitik [Civilising the climate regime: the role of NGOs and social movements in national, European and international climate change politics]*. Wiesbaden: VS Verlag für Sozialwissenschaften, pp 163–186.

Frenzel, F. (2014) 'Exit the system? Anarchist organisation in the British climate camps', *Ephemera*, 14(4), 901–921.

Gordon, U. (2008), *Anarchy Alive! Anti-Authoritarian Politics from Practice to Theory*. London: Pluto Press.

Hancox, D. (2014) *The Village Against the World*. London and New York: Verso.

hooks, bell (1990) *Yearning: Race, Gender, and Cultural Politics*. Boston, MA: South End Press.

Kuhn, A. (2014) *Vom Häuserkampf zur neoliberalen Stadt: Besetzungsbewegungen in Berlin und Barcelona* [*From housing struggle to the neoliberal city: Squatter Movements in Berlin and Barcelona*]. Münster: Westfälisches Dampfboot.

Leidinger, C. (2011) 'Kontroverse Koalitionen im politischen Laboratorium Camp: antimilitaristisch–feministische Bündnisse und Bündisarbeit als kontingente, soziale Prozesse', ['Contested coalitions in the political laboratory protest camp – anti-military feminist groups and their group work as contingent social practice'] *Oesterereichische Zeitschrift fuer Politikwissenschaft*, 40(3), 283–300.

Miliband, R. (1954) 'The politics of Robert Owen', *Journal of the History of Ideas*, 15(2), 233–245.

Mol, A. (2008) *The Logic of Care: Health and the Problem of Patient Choice*. Abingdon: Routledge.

Nunes, R. (2014) *The Organisation of the Organisationless: Collective Action After Networks*. London and Berlin: Meta Mute & Anagarm Books

Offe, C. (1987) 'Challenging the boundaries of institutional politics: social movements since the 1960s', in C. Maier (ed) *Changing Boundaries of the Political: Essays on the Evolving Balance Between the State and Society, Public and Private in Europe*. Cambridge and New York: Cambridge University Press, pp 63–105.

Pickerill, J. and Chatterton, P. (2006) 'Notes towards autonomous geographies: creation, resistance and self-management as survival tactics', *Progress in Human Geography*, 30(6), 730–746.

Roseneil, S. (2000), *Common Women, Uncommon Practices: The Queer Feminisms of Greenham*. London: Cassell.

Rucht, D. (1990) 'Campaigns, skirmishes and battles: anti-nuclear movements in the USA, France and West Germany', *Organization and Environment*, 4(3), 193–222.

Schein, R. (2012). 'Whose occupation? Homelessness and the politics of park encampments', *Social Movement Studies*, 11, 335–341.

Sitrin, M. (2006) *Horizontalism: Voices of Popular Power in Argentina*. Oakland, CA: AK Press.

Stengers, I. (2010) *Cosmopolitics I*. Minneapolis, MN: University of Minnesota Press.

Trapese Collective (2007) *Do It Yourself: A Handbook for Changing Our World*. London: Pluto Press.

Vasudevan, A. (2015) *Metropolitan Preoccupations: The Spatial Politics of Squatting in Berlin.* Oxford: Wiley Blackwell.

Ward, C. (1973) *Anarchy in Action.* London: G. Allen and Unwin.

SEVENTEEN

From 'refugee population' to political community: the Mustapha Mahmoud refugee protest camp

Elisa Pascucci

Introduction

Over the last decade, migrant and refugee protests have emerged as one of the most significant phenomena through which citizenship and belonging are contested and redefined 'from the margins', both in Europe and along its externalised borderland (Balibar, 2004; Tyler and Marciniak, 2013). The sit-ins held by undocumented migrant workers in Murcia, Southern Spain in 2001 (Bañón Hernández and Romero, 2013), and the African refugees' protests in Tel Aviv's Levinsky Park, as well as the camps set up by rejected asylum seekers in central Vienna and in Berlin's Oranienplatz in 2012–13 and the collective known as 'Lampedusa in Hamburg' are all examples that highlight how political mobilisation against migration governance is increasingly taking the form of protest camps.

In Europe as well as in the broader Mediterranean region, migrant and refugee protests have often intersected with, emulated, and in some case anticipated recent struggles against austerity, authoritarianism and neoliberal capitalism (see Tyler, 2013). In Egypt, the focus of this chapter, public collective mobilisation and street politics have characterised the social landscape for decades (Kandil, 2011). Slum dwellers, factory workers, Islamists, ethno-religious minorities and other marginalities (Ayeb and Bush, 2013) have all been important actors in the long-term political and social struggles which led to the events of 2011–12 (Elyachar and Winegar, 2011). Cairo being home to a large population of urban refugees (Goździak and Walter, 2012). The role of migrants and refugees in Egyptian popular politics has also often been significant. Nonetheless, it remains less explored in academic literature concerned with the country's recent history.

This chapter traces the origins and dynamics of one of the biggest public protests in the history of postcolonial Egypt: the encampment set up by Sudanese refugees in Cairo in front of the United Nations High Commissioner for Refugees (UNHCR) office, in September 2005. The refugee protests, which lasted for over three months, came to be known as 'the Mustapha Mahmoud camp', from the name of the park, and of the adjacent mosque, in which they took place, in the neighbourhood of Mohandeseen, in Giza. Initially triggered by UNHCR's decision to suspend refugee status determination procedures for Sudanese applicants following the 2005 Sudan Comprehensive Peace Agreement, the protests revolved around the more comprehensive lack of effective 'durable solutions' to the refugee condition in Egypt. During the three months of protests, around 3,000 Sudanese migrants of different ethnic, religious and social backgrounds moved to the Mustapha Mahmoud Park, and the camp existed as a nearly self-sustaining city, counting on networks of solidarity and that were both local and transnational. Protesters also advanced formal, written requests to UNHCR, demanding enhanced legal protection and financial assistance. However, attempts at negotiations with UN office failed, and on 30 December 2005, the camp was forcefully evicted by Egyptian security forces, causing around 27 deaths.[1]

The analysis presented in this chapter is based on interviews with the Mustapha Mahmoud protesters conducted by local researchers affiliated to the Forced Migration and Refugee Studies (FMRS) Centre of the American University in Cairo and on reports released by UNHCR, non-governmental organisations (NGOs), and local press during the three months of protests. In addition to that, the chapter uses interviews, conducted in Cairo in 2012 and 2015 in the context of a broader research project on refugee politics and humanitarianism in Egypt, with Sudanese community activists who had visited the camp, or had been in contact with refugees who had taken part in the protests, as well as with Egyptian activists who organised a yearly commemoration of the camp in an independent cultural centre in central Cairo.[2] Not only does this approach allow for different perspectives on the protests to emerge, but it also highlights the camp's enduring effects on Cairo's refugee communities, political activists and civil society more generally. While protest camps are generally defined by 'temporariness' and 'exception' (Ramadan, 2013), methodologies that include the analysis of their 'legacy' can provide important alternative insights on the politics of their temporalities.

Anticipating the now substantial body of work on migrant and refugee protests (Edkins and Pin-Fat, 2005; McGregor, 2011; 2012; Mountz,

2011; Rygiel, 2011; Tyler, 2013; Tyler and Marciniak, 2013), in their important contribution Caroline Moulin and Peter Nyers (2007) described the refugee protests that took place in Cairo in 2005 as an act through which the governmentality of international aid was 'politicised' by the refugees. Theorising the protests as an expression of 'global political society' (Moulin and Nyers, 2007; see Chatterjee, 2004), they thus argued that they worked through attributing 'to the empirical form of a population group' target of international humanitarian operations 'the moral character of a community' (Chatterjee, 2004, 57, cited in Moulin and Nyers, 2007, 362). Moulin and Nyers's (2007) discussion, however, focused almost exclusively on the discursive appropriation by the refugees of the language and legal categories of international humanitarianism. This chapter suggests instead that it was also through the social and material infrastructures that sustained everyday life in the protest camp that the Mustapha Mahmoud refugees constituted themselves as a collective political subject.

The focus on the camp's infrastructures helps to illuminate two interrelated dimensions of the Mustapha Mahmoud camp. First, in line with a growing body of critical scholarship in development and humanitarian studies, it foregrounds the material and spatial dimensions of humanitarianism and migration governance and of their contestation (Duffield, 2011; Ramadan, 2013; Smirl, 2008, 2015; Squire, 2015). Second, it highlights the complex entanglement of social reproduction and political autonomy that characterise protest camps. Recent research has shown how camps define themselves as autonomous spaces not only through antagonistic stances and organisational differences that distinguish them from the external world, but also, and crucially, through 'biopolitical experiments' that involve the mundane, embodied and affective aspects of living together, particularly in relation to care and reproductive labour (Frenzel et al, 2013). As 'platforms that allow the reproduction of life' (Simone, 2004, 408) within protest camps, infrastructures such as living spaces and communication technologies and are thus essential in defining protest camps as experiments in political autonomy. This chapter examines the role of camp infrastructures in refugee protests, showing how, through them, populations normally framed as passive recipients of aid are able to experience care and mutual help autonomously from humanitarian agencies. In doing so, the analysis highlights the complex, contradictory and ambivalent character of the autonomous political subjectivities forged through the camps.

The chapter proceeds as follows. First, it outlines the background of the camp in relation to the history of the Sudanese refugee question in Egypt. Second, it analyses the camp's infrastructures focusing on the following elements: its location and connections to the external world; the experiences of mutual care that characterised everyday life in it, and the violent eviction by Egyptian security forces. The conclusions then offer some reflections on the camp's legacy, as well as on the similarities between refugee protests and the encampments that characterised the Egyptian uprising of 2011–12.

The Sudanese diaspora and the refugee question in Egypt

Sudanese are one of the largest migrant groups in Egypt. Geographical and cultural-linguistic proximity have facilitated exchanges and mobility between Egypt and Sudan throughout the postcolonial era. In 1976, the Wadi El-Nil (Nile Valley) Treaty ratified the terms of the reciprocal treatment for citizens of the two countries. Sudanese nationals were permitted to enter Egypt without a visa and were, at least on paper, allowed legal access to employment, welfare and ownership of property (Kagan, 2012). Although Egypt was already a signatory of both the 1951 Refugee Convention and of its 1967 Protocol, this regime applied equally to all categories of migrants. Largely integrated, many Sudanese in Egypt engaged in transnational political activities, and a number of Sudanese associations were active in Egypt's major cities (Al Sharmani and Grabska, 2009). The existence of a solid network of diasporic community associations, encompassing highly politicised groups with transnational links to Sudanese political movements, both in the homeland and in other states, played an important role in the Mustapha Mahmoud protests.

In the 1990s, the condition of Sudanese communities in Egypt changed dramatically. Growing geopolitical instability led to a remarkable increase in the number of displaced people in the Nile region (Grabska, 2005) and, in 1995, the Wadi El Nil Treaty was abrogated, and entry visas introduced.[3] A system of migration management was thus created in which UNHCR – according to the Memorandum of Understanding with the Egyptian State signed in 1954, and till then almost entirely unapplied – became the agency in charge of refugee status determination and refugee assistance (Kagan, 2012). As in other countries in North Africa and the Middle East, UNHCR thus became a 'surrogate state' (Slaughter and Crisp, 2008) within the Egyptian state. The establishment of the agency as a quasi-sovereign actor is effectively captured by the slogan 'We live in a country of UNHCR', used by the Mustapha Mahmoud protestors (Moulin and Nyers, 2007; Kagan, 2012).

As a result of these changes, for Sudanese associations and community groups in Cairo, refugee advocacy became a central issue around which to organise their activities. Many of them – like the two Darfuran organisations whose members were interviewed for this chapter – were established or developed in the early 2000s thanks to the official recognition as CBOs (community-based organisations) by UNHCR, and the access to UN funding which it granted. This led Sudanese organisations in Cairo to incorporate the language of humanitarianism and refugee advocacy into their pre-existing experiences of political mobilisation, often developed in contact with militant groups in Sudan. This process is of particular importance in the genesis of the Mustapha Mahmoud camp, as one of these organisations, *Refugee Voice*, founded in Cairo in January 2005, played a fundamental role in setting up the initial sit-in (FMRS, 2006).

While its language and categories were appropriated by refugee organisations, the system of humanitarian governance put in place by the UN's 'surrogate state' was undergoing changes that would lead to growing frustration and hostility among refugee communities. In the second half of the 1990s, shifts in development and humanitarian policies that were global in scale had led UNHCR to revise its interventions, particularly in the field of socio-economic assistance (Hyndman, 2001; Hunter, 2009). Starting from the early 2000s, cuts were implemented which affected direct assistance in the form, for example, of reimbursement of medical expenses or grants for children's primary education. For Sudanese people in Cairo, one of the most immediately visible consequences of the defunding of assistance was a reported increase in the number of evictions due to difficulties in paying rent (Sperl, 2001; FMRS, 2006). It is highly significant that many of the refugees who joined the Mustapha Mahmoud protests, often moving with their families and all their belongings to the park, affirmed to be experiencing housing problems (FMRS, 2006).

UNHCR's inconsistent attitude in managing programmes of resettlement to third countries also contributed to the widespread perception of a complete lack of 'durable solutions' for Sudanese people in Egypt. Although the total number of resettled refugees had progressively increased from less than 300 in 1994 to 4,110 in 2004 (Kagan, 2011), that same year major changes in recognition policies dramatically affected Sudanese refugees' prospects for resettlement. In June, after the ratification of the Comprehensive Peace Agreement between the Sudanese government and the Sudan's People Liberation Army, UNHCR Cairo decided to suspend individual refugee status determination (RSD) procedures for Sudanese applicants. Instead, all

Sudanese asylum seekers were provided with UN *yellow cards*, granting temporary humanitarian protection against repatriation. According to the FMRS's analysis (FMRS, 2006), the change was intended to enhance – rather than decrease – the space for protection of Sudanese people in Egypt: given the new perspectives for enduring peace in Sudan, individual claims for asylum would have been legally debased. However, many among Cairo's Sudanese communities felt that the new procedures were leaving them in a legal impasse. As a measure of temporary humanitarian protection granted on a collective basis and subject to reassessment every six months, *yellow cards* precluded access to resettlement programmes, leaving people in a prolonged condition of uncertainty.

The first collective protests in front of the UNHCR Cairo premises took place a year before the main protest camp was put in place. In August 2004, a few dozen asylum seekers and refugees gathered in front of the agency's offices in Mohandeseen. Protesters presented a document criticising the cuts to assistance programmes, and requested a formal meeting with UN representatives. As in the 2005 protests however, the office maintained a rather ambiguous attitude towards the protesting asylum seekers. While formally maintaining its intention to listen to their claims, UNHCR expressed doubts on the legitimacy of the protesters' representatives. As attempts at negotiations eventually failed, scuffles erupted among the protesters over divergences on issues of representation, in which the UNHCR premises were slightly damaged. The police were called to intervene and disperse the demonstration, resulting in ten people getting injured, and over 22 refugees being detained. At the end of the protests, as the FMRS (2006) researchers note, the issues raised by the migrants remained unaddressed.

The sit-in in the park in Mustapha Mahmoud square began on 29 September 2005. According to *Refugee Voice*, the organisation that called for the initial rally, around 70 people attended the initial demonstration. However, in the space of a couple of weeks, numbers grew to over 500 people. In a press report released in October 2005, UNHCR repeatedly claimed most of the migrants involved were rejected asylum seekers – 'closed files', in the agency's jargon – and, as such, did not have any legitimacy to advance claims for protection and resettlements (FMRS, 2006). However, reports by local researchers, testimonies by migrants and activists and other statements released by UNHCR itself later in 2005 who visited the camp confirm that recognised refugees and asylum seekers were also present.

The protest camp location: contesting humanitarian space, forging solidarities

As refugees and asylum seekers, many of the migrants who joined the protests had regular contacts with UNHCR, and had experienced access difficulties in the form of long waiting times, and scarce or unclear information. Since the early 2000s, the work of UNHCR Cairo, in line with a tendency towards the securitisation of aid work that is global in scale (Smirl, 2008; 2015; Duffield, 2010; Grant and Thompson, 2013), has been marked by increasingly rigid security protocols, and by architectural and logistic arrangements that determined a sharp separation between the aid workers and their beneficiaries. These spatial practices played a significant role in determining the set-up and development of the Mustapha Mahmoud protest camp. After the protests that took place in 2004 described above, in order to prevent further rallies near its premises, UNHCR decided that first contacts with applicants would be moved to the Mustapha Mahmoud Park, located around a block away from their premises (FMRS, 2006). For the whole year that preceded the beginning of the protest camp in September 2005, all initial interviews were held in the park by case workers supported by interpreters. As FMRS researchers note, the 'holding of asylum seekers and refugees "at arm's length"' can be seen as 'a physical representation of the increasing distance between UNHCR and the population it purported to protect' (FMRS, 2006, 11).

The decision added another cause of frustration to what was already an extremely tense situation. Refugees were showing increasing dissatisfaction with the ways interviews were carried out, and complained about the behaviour of UNHCR security personnel controlling the park. The location of the Mustapha Mahmoud camp thus exposed the built environment in which humanitarian aid is delivered as a contested site of international politics (Smirl, 2008).

The location of the protest camp, however, also had another important function. Large enough to accommodate a high number of people, and relatively close and well connected to central Cairo, the Mustapha Mahmoud park proved strategic in ensuring visibility to the protests, and allowed them to develop important connections with the urban environment. This is shown also by the fact that the square where the park is located is a popular site for political demonstrations in Cairo. On several occasions between 2011 and 2013 it was chosen by Egyptian protesters of various political orientations, including the Muslim Brotherhood, as the gathering point for marches against the military rule that followed the ousting of Hosni Mubarak. Its location was thus one of the several infrastructural and material elements that Mustapha Mahmoud shared with the Egyptian public protests that preceded the 2011 uprising – a point that will be further elaborated upon below.

Public visibility worked to attract media attention to the requests advanced to UNCHR by the refugees and, perhaps what is more important, provided protesters with the opportunity to build networks of material support. As the protests grew larger, the initial encampment rapidly developed into an increasingly self-sustaining city, with living spaces made up of tents, as well as communal kitchens, schools and clinics. It became evident how, for many refugees and asylum seekers who were joining the protests, including families with children, the camp was turning into a main point of reference for housing and social services provision, particularly medical care. Local NGOs and human rights groups thus started to offer assistance in the form of collected blankets, food and financial donations (Azzam, 2006).

Help, however, did not only come through the 'humanitarian calls for actions' of local civil society. In the weeks that followed the initial sit-in, the relations of religious and national solidarity into which refugees were immersed both locally and transnationally materialised in many unexpected ways. Protesters could count on the possibility of accessing water, food, temporary shelter and bathrooms, from Sudanese friends living in Mohandeseen. Similarly, the material support offered by the adjacent Mustapha Mahmoud mosque turned out to be essential for their daily subsistence. Protesters had access to the mosque's courtyard and prayer rooms, which they could use to take regular rests. Moreover, as the start of the protests coincided with the beginning of Ramadan 2005, the Mosque's Mufti, Ali Gomaa, 'issued a *fatwa* approving *Sadaqah* for all Sudanese refugees during *Eid Al-Adha*' (Azzam, 2006), thus allowing the protesters to become the beneficiaries of the Ramadan charity by the many Egyptian Muslims attending the Friday prayer. As already mentioned, the protesters could also rely on the solidarity of Sudanese associations and individuals both in the homeland and in western countries, not only in the form of donations and material support, but also in securing media visibility to their cause through websites such as Sudanese Online.

Infrastructures of care beyond humanitarianism

Thanks to its multifaceted connections with the surrounding environment, and to the local display of solidarity, the camp's infrastructure developed significantly already during the first month of demonstrations. According to the FMRS researchers, by mid-November 2005,

> The ground was covered with a layer of mats and blankets. Luggage and other items formed partitions with narrow walkways between living spaces. Separate sections were built for men and for women and children...at first, sheets were hung as shelter from the sun. As the weather turned colder, the sheets were replaced with tarps. Meals were prepared in a communal kitchen area on gas stoves, with food bought with money pooled from those in the park and shared...Makeshift shops inside the park offered snacks. (FMRS, 2006, 26)

As already mentioned, these infrastructures became an immediate and concrete alternative to the precarious housing arrangements and livelihood strategies of many Sudanese people in Cairo, in particular providing shelter to homeless refugees. This is clearly expressed in the following quote, from an interview with a migrant conducted in Cairo in 2011:

> A lot of people went there with their suitcases, the children, money, everything, I remember...a lot of people had no house, or a very bad house...No jobs obviously, nothing to do. So if you haven't got a house or are paying a lot of money for it...why wouldn't you leave it, why wouldn't you join other refugees who are offering food, if you can stay there in the tents? (Male, 38 years old, Sudan. Interview, Cairo, 10 December 2011)

Existing literature has shown how migrant and refugee makeshift encampments often act as a substitute for insufficient and dysfunctional asylum and social services (Sigona, 2003; 2015). However, in this case a camp originally set up as a protest sit-in took up this function, maintaining both its explicitly politicised character and its acquired 'practical' purpose, which constitutes a far less documented phenomenon. Nevertheless, considering practical purpose is important in order to understand the political subjectivities at work in camps. Analyses of recent anti-austerity camps in Europe and in the US are particularly useful in this regard. Commenting on the issue of homeless people who joined the Occupy Wall Street encampment in Manhattan in 2011, Barbara Ehrenreich (2011) has argued that urban protest camps work through both exposing and offering alternatives to the highly precarious life of the disenfranchised in neoliberal cities. The material infrastructure built by campers thus acquires political significance in itself, reinforcing and often exceeding the demands which they articulate discursively.

Also in the case of Mustapha Mahmoud, refugees' experiences of extreme precariousness were both publicly shown through the camp and reflected in the lists of requests advanced to the UNHCR. While most of the latter revolved around the refusal of repatriation and the search for durable legal solutions to the Sudanese question in Egypt, the protesters were also asking that UNHCR assistance mandate be carried out more effectively. This involved not only protecting refugees from abuse and arbitrary detention by Egyptian security forces, but also 'taking care' of vulnerable households and individuals. Point number 11 of the list circulated on 26 October 2005, for instance, explicitly asked UNHCR 'to care about vulnerable categories as elders, minors without family members, and women at risk' (Moulin and Nyers, 2007, 365).

Moulin and Nyers (2007) have seen in these claims the assumption and re-appropriation by the refugees of the languages and socio-legal categories of humanitarianism. For them, refugees' requests amounted to a 're-taking of the governmentality of care, inserting refugee voices into the bureaucratic processes of categorization, population-making, and care that govern their life' (Moulin and Nyers, 2007, 366). The analysis of the material and spatial modalities through which the camp was set up and sustained itself confirms and complements these insights. While asking for enhanced protection and more substantial aid interventions, the refugees were in fact also transforming the regime of self-reliance de facto imposed through cuts to UNHCR assistance budgets into the autonomous infrastructure of an emerging political community. The daily work of taking care of children, elderly people, and those who were ill or disabled, or simply needed to be provided with food and shelter, became a fulfilling experience. Care was autonomously shared in the space that was set up to contest the failings of care provision by the international humanitarian agencies. While asserting their autonomy, the protesters were also reflecting back to the agency its own inconsistencies and inadequacies. Mustapha Mahmoud articulated a dual and somewhat contradictory stance towards UNHCR as a governance actor, thus constituting an example of what McNevin (2013) has singled out as the main element characterising the political claims of irregular migrants, namely their ambivalence.

Most of the testimonies collected during the Mustapha Mahmoud events highlight the protesters' feelings of pride at their ability of 'taking matters into their own hands', in spite of the harsh living conditions in the camp. In the short reports written by researchers and activists who visited the camp between October and December 2005, the living spaces are described as surprisingly clean and tidy, considering that an estimated 3,000 people were taking part in various activities, or just hanging out, in the park during the day time. These accounts underscore how people felt increasingly driven to take care not only of each other but also of the 'things' they were sharing and of the living spaces they had all contributed to construct. Nearly every day, speeches were delivered in which the people present at the sit-in were invited to 'respect the place' because it was 'their community' (FMRS, 2006, 27), practices that one of the interviewees described as fostering feelings of safety and security.

> 'And the rest of Egypt, for a lot of Sudanese people, has never been safe. The camp was safe. And you move in there and you found people in the same situation as you, because a lot of people are…they do not know each other'. (Interview, Cairo, 12 June 2012. Male, age unknown, South Sudan, unemployed)

To be sure, this rhetoric should not be idealised. A small number of interviews also report physically abusive behaviours by community leaders within the camp, and some of the visitors described a sharply gendered division of labour. Feelings of safety and protection were coupled with perceptions of the potential violent threat coming both from internal divergences and external attacks. To deal with these, the camp developed its own security system. Visitors were asked for identification documents before being allowed access to the park, and checked for whether they were carrying weapons or alcohol. The food and beverages donated were also often checked to make sure they were not attempts at sabotage through poisoning (FMRS, 2006). Like in the Tahrir encampments of 2011–12, self-managed security measures became essential not only in order to keep the physical space of the camp safe and orderly, but also for the protesters' to assert their capacity for political organisation. Although emerging also from the initial intention to expose and contest UNHCR's growing securitisation, Mustapha Mahmoud thus de facto ended up mimicking the UN office's security practices. This element further highlights the complex and contradictory character of migrant and refugee protest camps as autonomous spaces.

Egyptian police had also been present around the camp, the square and the surrounding streets since the beginning of the demonstrations. Many protesters reported having good relations with police officers – police liaisons being often a necessary element of the infrastructure of protest camps in different contexts (Feigenbaum et al, 2013). For many of the Sudanese refugees involved, the protest camp had been the first occasion to experiment a somewhat 'peaceful' relation with Egyptian state authorities, as opposed to the threat of police harassment, arbitrary detention and even deportation which they experienced in everyday life.[4] This liaison, however, was only possible through the mediation of UNHCR. As the position of the office, which had been ambivalent since the beginning of the protests (Moulin and Nyers, 2007), shifted towards a more overtly oppositional stance, the condition of the camp gradually became more problematic. By the beginning of December 2005, all attempts at negotiations between the refugees' representatives and the UNHCR had failed. On 22 December a formal letter was sent by UNHCR to the Egyptian Ministry of Defence which communicated that their efforts to reach a negotiated solution had failed – an act that local activists and researchers regarded as having 'pav(ed) the way for the forced removal' (FMRS, 2006, 33; Moulin and Nyers, 2007).

The camp's violent eviction and the legacy of the Mustapha Mahmoud protests

The events that took place in the night between 29 and 30 December are worth reporting in detail, as they powerfully speak to the inherent 'fragility' of the political community grounded in – and limited to – the material and spatial practices of protest camps. At around 1 am on 30 December 2005, police started to fire water cannons at the camp every 15 minutes. These were alternated with rounds of talks in which authorities repeatedly offered to transfer the refugees to a 'safe' camp site outside of the city, a proposal that the protestors refused because of lack of information about the location and characteristics of the site. A couple of hours later, according to eye witnesses, 'riot police began "warming up" by chanting slogans, running in place, and jumping up and down' (FMRS, 2006.). The accounts collected among protesters reveal how, in just a few hours, the feelings of safety, belonging, and even excitement and pride that had characterised the protests in the previous days were replaced by pervasive fear and uncertainty.

Water cannons were turned on for the last time at dawn, when, blocking escape routes, security forces entered the park and started to forcefully remove people. Although Egyptian authorities have systematically denied excessive use of force during the operations, protesters and eye witnesses among local residents reported use of tear gas, electrified batons, violent beating up of children and women, and even gun shots. Testimonies by the people who survived the attack convey a sense of loss of control, and a heightened perception of being powerless and vulnerable.

> I was not aware of anything until they were hitting me. I think there were five policemen for every refugee. When we started to defend ourselves, there were many more coming. They came and attacked. I saw one person I knew. They were beating him and when he fell down, they broke his neck. One of the police broke his neck with his baton. One pregnant woman also died in the same place. (Interview with demonstrator, collected by FMRS researchers, Cairo, 13 January 2006, FMRS, 2006, 36)

In many cases, the beating continued when protesters were already on the vans that would have transferred them to local prisons. The crackdown left at least 27 people dead, while over 650, including individuals holding official refugee status, were detained for months and in most cases released only after the direct intervention of UNHCR (FMRS, 2006).

The extremely violent epilogue highlights how, as political communities formed by people who mobilise collectively 'out of place' (Moulin and Nyers, 2007) migrant and refugee protest camps are also inherently vulnerable to state violence. The central role played by infrastructures in the constitution of camps enhances their vulnerability. Since the development of these political communities is so strictly dependent on the physical spaces and material practices that allow the protests to take place, forcible removal by state authorities has the power to put a sudden and definite end to the camp as a political experiment. Arguably, through the physical annihilation of the communal space they created and held for a limited period of time, the Mustapha Mahmoud refugees were put back into the voiceless position occupied by migrants and refugees with uncertain legal status.

Their infrastructural precariousness highlights the importance of temporariness as an element that contributes to the complex and contradictory character of migrant and refugee protest camps. Yet, as Moulin and Nyers (2007) reminds us, acknowledging the 'fragility' of their protests should not lead to reproducing narratives that univocally victimise refugees, and 'establish(es) them *only* as abject populations to be governed and controlled' (Nyers, 2007, 371). In the Mustapha Mahmoud case, the Egyptian state's attempt to violently suppress the refugees' political mobilisation expressed through the camp – facilitated by UNHCR's failure in recognising the legitimacy of the protests – can be regarded as only partially successful. Nearly two years of ethnographic research among Cairo's Sudanese refugee communities and, to a lesser extent, local NGOs, highlighted in fact how Mustapha Mahmoud had what can be defined as its own 'legacy'. Methodologies for the study of protest camps, I suggest, should pay attention not only to how camp practices circulate locally or transnationally, but also how they are transmitted and their memory preserved through time.

The tragic epilogue of the protests had consequences which were still sharply felt when research for this chapter was conducted, six years after the removal. The following comments by a Sudanese community worker express views that were shared by many of the Sudanese and Darfuran refugees interviewed in 2011–12 and 2015.

> You know, all that [the protest camp] had two main consequences: first of all, for years, nobody went to UNHCR anymore. Obviously, who could trust them anymore? There was also this sense that there was nothing left to do in Egypt, like there is nothing left, no hope to change things. It was like...and then, the second consequence is that people started going to Israel. If there is nothing left to do in Egypt, for a lot of people this is the only thing they can do, even if it is deadly dangerous... (Interview, Cairo, 20 June 2012. Male, 38 years old, Sudan, community worker)[5]

The consequences of the protests, however, were surely not limited to widespread feelings of distrust towards the UN agency.

> I think we all still remember, even Egyptians do. People don't talk about that as much because here it is never easy to talk about politics. But even the people who arrived after that, even if they are not Sudanese, like the Oromo, even among them there is respect for the Mustapha Mahmoud people. (Interview, Cairo, 20 June 2012. Male, 38 years old, Sudan, community worker)

The quotes above highlight the impact of the protest camp both on the Cairo activist scene and on other refugee communities, beyond the Sudanese one. In December 2011, when research for this chapter was conducted, a candlelight vigil was held in central Cairo to commemorate the Mustapha Mahmoud's deaths. A yearly event, the memorial was organised by a group of activists and artists associated with the Townhouse Gallery, a local cultural and exhibition centre and NGO, and with the popular festival known as *Al Fann Midan* (Art is a square).[6] Most of the activists who participated had been involved in the Tahrir protests of 2011 and 2012. Commenting on that experience, some of them drew parallels between the forced evacuation of the camp and the repression suffered by protesters in Tahrir Square.

The case of the Ethiopian–Oromo community, also mentioned in the quote above, reminds us instead how the infrastructural 'know-how' of the protest camp was appropriated by refugee mobilisations in the years that followed Mustapha Mahmoud. In 2011–12, sit-ins were still taking place regularly in front of the UNHCR premises in Cairo. Motivated largely by the same claims advanced by the Mustapha Mahmoud protesters, they were still organised mostly by Sudanese people – who remain, at the time of writing, one of the largest refugee groups in Egypt. However, smaller protests were also emerging that involved the Cairo Oromo community, which had grown significantly in numbers since 2011. In 2013, in correspondence with 'the Nile crisis' between Egypt and Ethiopia, these experiences resulted in a major protest camp, which lasted around a month, and gained significant international visibility.[7] In conversations with Oromo refugees and community organisers which I had in 2015, Mustapha Mahmoud was often mentioned as a point of reference. The Oromo protesters had learned how to formulate slogans, become visible, and organise communal kitchens from the accounts of the Mustapha Mahmoud protests that circulated among the refugee communities gravitating around the UNCHR Cairo office. This is arguably the most significant legacy of the camp: having materialised an alternative experience of community, and made publicly visible – and available for re-appropriation – the concrete practices that made it possible.

Conclusions

Mustapha Mahmoud was one of the biggest refugee protest camps ever documented in the global south. Examining protesters' testimonies collected between 2005 and 2015, the chapter's methodological approach has highlighted three elements in particular. First, the chapter has focused on the infrastructures that allowed the Sudanese refugees to live together for over three months in the encampment in central Cairo. The camp provided the protesters with a very concrete material alternative – in terms of food, shelter and even medical care – to increasingly inadequate programmes of humanitarian assistance. While exposing both the inaccessibility and the operational inefficiencies of UNHCR, Mustapha Mahmoud constituted a space where refugees could experience safety, protection and mutual assistance and do so autonomously from aid agencies. The chapter has thus shown how attention to the materialities and spatialities that allow for social reproduction within camps is essential for understanding the relation between refugee protests and humanitarian governance.

Second, while the analysis of the forced eviction has highlighted the inherent fragility and temporality of protest camps' infrastructures, ethnographic research conducted in Cairo over five years after the protests has shown their enduring legacy among refugee communities and Egyptian activists alike. These findings suggest that temporariness is not the only dimension characterising the temporalities of protest camps, and that research should pay attention to how camps' languages and practices are transmitted across time.

Finally, the chapter has shown how, as an experience of autonomous political and community life, the camp was also, 'a site of contradictions' (Moulin and Nyers, 2007, 371). Sealed-off by an efficient, self-managed security apparatus, 'governed' by representatives and community leaders, offering rather organised medical and school services to people in need and not immune – in its own internal dynamics – from prevarication and violence, the camp constituted a rather ambivalent collective political subjectivity. In it, communication with governance actors – often expressed appropriating their language – coexisted with radical autonomy and self-sufficiency, and the contestation of the inadequacies of humanitarian agencies with the emulation of some of their most dysfunctional practices.

These ambivalences should not come as a surprise. At a global level, camps – refugee camps, but also, among other things, temporary detention facilities – constitute in fact the fundamental spatial paradigm of migration governance. Refugee protests can thus be regarded as a 'struggle(s) over the very meaning of these spaces' (Rygiel, 2011, 4). Between contradictions, setbacks and extreme vulnerability, they nonetheless constitute attempts to re-appropriate and rebuild the camp 'from below' (Papadopoulos et al, 2008, cited in Rygiel, 2011, 4). As the crisis of refugee and migration governance in North Africa and the Mediterranean region deepens because of the instability that followed the Arab uprisings, such attempts at re-appropriating its spaces, practices and languages become an ever more significant political phenomenon.

Notes

1 Twenty-seven is the number of deaths recorded in official governmental accounts of the eviction. The figure has been often contested by Sudanese community associations and NGOs in Cairo, according to whom the real number is higher.
2 Names of informants have been withheld to protect confidentiality. Interviews were conducted both in English and Egyptian Arabic. Translations by the author.
3 The treaty was partially re-instated in 2004 through the Egyptian–Sudanese Four Freedoms Agreement, but with no substantial changes as to the condition of Sudanese refugees in Egypt (Kagan, 2012).
4 For an analysis of refugee detention and deportation in Egypt, see www. globaldetentionproject.org/countries/africa/egypt/introduction.html.
5 The reference here is to the border crossing between Egypt and Israel through the Sinai peninsula, see www.hrw.org/reports/2008/11/12/sinai-perils.
6 At the time of writing, the *Al Fann Midan* festival, established in the month that followed the 2011 uprising, was suspended due to restrictions to public gathering imposed by the Abdelfattah Elsisi government.
7 See www.aljazeera.com/indepth/inpictures/2013/06/201361711365644208.html.

References

Al-Sharmani, M. and Grabska, K. (2005) 'Living on the margins: the analysis of the livelihood strategies of Sudanese refugees with closed files in Egypt', *Working Paper* 6, Cairo: Center for Migration and Refugee Studies, American University in Cairo.

Al-Sharmani, M. and Grabska, K. (2009) 'African refugees and Diasporic struggles in Cairo', in D. Singerman (ed) *Cairo Contested: Governance, Urban Space and Global Modernity*. Cairo: American University in Cairo Press, pp 455–473.

Ayeb, H. and Bush, R. (2012) *Marginalities and Exclusion in Egypt*. London: Zed Books.

Azzam, F. (2006) 'No way forward, no way back', *Al Ahram Online*, http://weekly.ahram.org.eg/2006/780/sc15.htm.

Balibar, É. (2004) *We, the People of Europe? Reflections on Transnational Citizenship*. Princeton, NJ: Princeton University Press.

Bañón Hernández, A.M. and Romero, S. R. (2013) 'Ánimo. Estamos con vosotros. Messages of solidarity written in a visitors' book during a sit-in conducted by a group of immigrants in Spain', *Discourse and Society*, 24(1), 3–26, doi: 10.1177/0957926512463633.

Chatterjee, P. (2004) *The Politics of the Governed: Reflections on Popular Politics in Most of the World*. New York: Columbia University Press.

Duffield, M. (2010) 'Risk-management and the Fortified Aid Compound: everyday life in post-interventionary society', *Journal of Intervention and State Building*, 4(4), 453–474, doi: 10.1080/17502971003700993.

Edkins, J. and Pin-Fat, V. (2005) 'Through the wire: relations of power and relations of violence', *Millenium: Journal of International Studies*, 34(1), 1–24, doi: 10.1177/03058298050340010101.

Ehrenreich, B. (2011) 'Throw them out with the trash: why homelessness is becoming an Occupy Wall Street issue', *TomDispatch. com*, www.tomdispatch.com/post/175457/tomgram%3A_barbara_ehrenreich%2C_homeless_in_america/.

Elyachar, J. and Winegar, J. (2012) 'Revolution and counter-revolution in Egypt a year after January 25th: fieldsights – hot spots', *Cultural Anthropology Online*, 2 February, www.culanth.org/fieldsights/208-revolution-and-counter-revolution-in-egypt-a-year-after-january-25th.

Feigenbaum, A. (2014) 'Resistant matters: tents, tear gas and the 'other media' of occupy', *Communication and Critical Cultural Studies*, 11(1), 15–24, doi:10.1080/14791420.2013.828383.

Feigenbaum, A., Frenzel, F. and McCurdy, P. (2013) *Protest Camps*. London: Zed.

FMRS (Forced Migration and Refugee Studies) (2006) *A Tragedy of Failures and False Expectations: Report on the Events Surrounding the Three Month Sit-in and Forced Removal of Sudanese Refugees in Cairo.* FMRS programme, September–December 2005, Cairo: American University in Cairo.

Frenzel, F., Fegeinbaum, A. and McCurdy, P. (2013) 'Protest camps: an emerging field of social movement research', *The Sociological Review*, 62: 457–474, doi: 10.1111/1467-954X.12111.

Goździak, E. and Walter, A. (2012) *Urban Refugees in Cairo.* Washington, DC: Georgetown University Institute for the Study of International Forced Migration, http://issuu.com/georgetownsfs/docs/urban_refugees_in_cairo.

Grant, R. and Thompson, D. (2013) 'The development complex, rural economy and urban–spatial and economic development in Juba, South Sudan', *Local Economy*, 28(2), 218–230, doi: 10.1177/0269094212468400.

Hunter, M. (2009) 'The failure of self-reliance in refugee settings', *Polis*, 2, 8–46, www.polis.leeds.ac.uk/assets/files/students/student-journal/ma-winter-09/meredith-hunter-winter-09.pdf.

Hyndman, J. (2001) *Managing Displacement: Refugees and the Politics of Humanitarianism.* Minneapolis, MN: University of Minnesota Press.

Kagan, M. (2011) 'Shared responsibility in a new Egypt: a strategy for refugee protection', *Scholarly Works* paper 677, http://scholars.law.unlv.edu/facpub/677.

Kagan, M. (2012) 'The UN "surrogate state" and the foundation of refugee policy in the Middle East, *Scholarly Works* paper 781, http://scholars.law.unlv.edu/facpub/781.

Kandil, H. (2011) 'Revolt in Egypt' *New Left Review*, 68, 17–55, https://newleftreview.org/II/68/hazem-kandil-revolt-in-egypt.

McGregor, J. (2011) Contestations and consequences of deportability: hunger strikes and the political agency of non-citizens. *Citizenship Studies*, 15(5), 597–611, doi: 10.1080/13621025.2011.583791.

McGregor, J. (2012) 'Rethinking detention and deportability: Removal centres as spaces of religious revival', *Political Geography*, 31, 236–246, doi: 10.1016/j.polgeo.2012.03.003.

McNevin, A. (2013) 'Ambivalence and citizenship: theorising the political claims of irregular migrants', *Millennium*, 41(2),182–200, doi: 10.1177/0305829812463473.

Moulin, C. and Nyers, P. (2007) '"We live in a country of UNHCR": refugee protests and global political society', *International Political Sociology*, 1, 356–372, doi: 10.1111/j.1749-5687.2007.00026.x.

Mountz, A. (2011) 'Where asylum seekers wait: feminist counter-topographies of sites between states', *Gender, Place and Culture: A Journal of Feminist Geography*, 18(3), 381–399, doi:10.1080/096636 9X.2011.566370.

Ramadan, A. (2013) 'From Tahrir to the world: the camp as a political public space', *European Urban and Regional Studies*, 20(1), 145–149, doi: 10.1177/0969776412459863.

Rygiel, K. (2011) 'Bordering solidarities: migrant activism and the politics of movement and camps at Calais', *Citizenship Studies*, 15(1), 1–19, doi:10.1080/13621025.2011.534911.

Sigona, N. (2003) 'How can a Nomad be a "refugee"', *Sociology*, 37(1), 69–79, doi: 10.1177/0038038503037001445.

Sigona, N. (2015) 'Campzenship: reimagining the camp as a social and political space', *Citizenship Studies*, 19(1), 1–15, doi: 10.1080/13621025.2014.937643.

Simone, A. (2004) 'People as infrastructure: intersecting fragments in Johannesburg', *Public Culture*, 16(3), 407–429, doi: 10.1215/08992363-16-3-407.

Slaughter, A. and Crisp, J. (2008) 'A surrogate state? The role of UNHCR in protracted refugee situations', in G. Loescher, J. Milner, E. Newman and G. Troeller (eds) *Protracted Refugee Situations*. Tokyo: United Nations University Press, pp 123–140.

Smirl, L. (2008) 'Building the Other, constructing ourselves: spatial dimensions of international humanitarian response', *International Political Sociology*, 2, 236–253, doi: 10.1111/j.1749-5687.2008.00047.x.

Smirl, L. (2015) *Spaces of Aid: How Cars, Compounds and Hotels Shape Humanitarianism*. London: Zed Books.

Sperl, S. (2001) *Evaluation of Urban Refugee Policies in Egypt*. Geneva: UNHCR Evaluation and Policy Analysis Unit (EPAU)

Squire, V. (2015) 'Acts of desertion: abandonment and renouncement at the Sonoran Borderzone', *Antipode*, 47(2), 500–516, doi: 10.1111/anti.12118.

Trombetta, L. (2015) 'More than just a battleground: Cairo's urban space during the 2011 protests', *European Urban and Regional Studies*, 20(1), 139–144, doi: 10.1177/0969776412463373.

Tyler, I. (2013) *Revolting Subjects: Social Abjection and Resistance in Neoliberal Britain*. London: Zed Books.

Tyler, I. and Marciniak, K. (2013) 'Immigrant protest: an introduction', *Citizenship Studies*, 17(2),143–156, doi:10.1080/13621025.2013.78 0728.

The Marconi occupation in São Paulo, Brazil: a social laboratory of common life

Marcella Arruda

Social change arises...through the dialectical unfolding of relations between a) technological and organizational forms of production, exchange and consumption, b) relations to nature, c) social relations between people, d) mental conceptions of the world, e) labour processes and production of specific goods, geographies, services or affects, f) institutional, legal and governmental arrangements, g) the conduct of daily life and activities of social reproduction. (David Harvey, 2010)

The city is man's most consistent and on the whole, his most successful attempt to remake the world he lives in more after his heart's desire. But, if the city is the world which man created, it is the world in which he is henceforth condemned to live. Thus, indirectly, and without any clear sense of the nature of his task, in making the city man has remade himself. (Robert Park, 1929)

Introduction

The Marconi occupation is a squat in downtown São Paulo, Brazil, organised by the Movimento Moradia Para Todos (Movement for Housing for All) (MMPT). In an abandoned office building, occupied in 2012, protesters struggled to materialise their political hopes inside the camp: everyday social relations between people were transformed, with the aim of achieving a glimpse of a more just, sustainable and equal society. By 'creating other ways of being in the world' (Osterweil, 2004, 503), Marconi became an example of a social movement protest strategy, providing housing but also challenging the capitalistic status quo and encouraging a search for individual and group identities. Those alternative relations and structures were ephemeral constructions: the elements that constituted the protest camp vanished over time, stressing the existing tension between 'making protest' and 'making home'. Issues were intertwined and collided in the everyday existence of the inhabitants of this social laboratory. Despite the short life of the initiative, it still reverberates and the experience is still embodied in those people who were involved.

This chapter analyses what happens when the camp exists in order to offer a practical solution to housing and social reproduction. It is divided into three sections: the first contextualises this case study against the backdrop of the Brazilian protest landscape, while the second analyses the Marconi occupation through a key set of protest camp infrastructures and practices. The chapter ends with a reflection on common life and social reproduction, considering how such practices contribute to the creation of new and alternative forms of democracy through the transformation of everyday relations – the challenge of 'making home' and 'making protest'.

Right to the city: squatter and occupy movements in Brazil

Protest has always been present in Brazilian culture and society. In the context of a globalised city, where the price of urban land is rising every day and where there is no concern with welfare – there is a considerable shortage of affordable housing in general and a public policy of locating social housing on the city's periphery, with no infrastructure – movements have fought in São Paulo since the 1970s for the right to a more inclusive and just city. These movements were fundamental to ending the period of dictatorship and to democratising the country in the subsequent decade – a democracy that continues to manage the country today.

The pressure exerted by social movements pushes the state to ensure access to the commons by creating public policies, but their tactics also build a path towards the realisation of such policies: a real democracy is practised in the movements' squats. The occupations not only aim to provide housing, but are also social laboratories for experimentation with other realities, creating new, alternative and self-managed ways of relating to the city and society. Not unlike protest camps, they combine social reproduction with certain political demands, operating on both a pre-figurative and a symbolic plane of political action. That challenge, however, requires that social movements adopt a two-sided approach:

opening up cracks in the public arena but also empowering citizens to appropriate that space.

> Cracks are unstable, cracks are constantly on the move, always opening up again, joining up with other cracks. Not only is this the only viable way in which we can make sense of radical social transformation, but, in addition, it corresponds to what is actually happening at the moment. Thus, we can think of a crack as being a space of negation and creation, refusal and creation, when we say 'No', we won't accept the logic of capitalist relations here in this space and this moment; we are going to do things according to a different logic. (Holloway and Susen, 2013, 24)

One really important movement on Brazil's political scene – and one that goes against the hegemonic power of dominant discourses and practices – is the Movimento dos Trabalhadores Rurais Sem Terra (Movement of Landless Workers) (MST). MST is a social movement that was founded in the 1980s in the interior of Brazil, in response to the modernisation of the country and of agriculture during the dictatorship. The movement started to organise itself in opposition to extensive plantations, the mechanisation and use of toxic chemicals in agriculture, and its main tactic – which it still uses today – was to set up camps in large estates that were unused by their owners. The aim was to provide people with land, but also with a greater voice in public decisions and power in political disputes.

Although there are differences with the structures of many protest landscapes, squats such as Marconi can be understood as an urban variation of the land occupation movement in the countryside of Brazil, a specific form of protest camp with a visible presence in the Brazilian context. Both confront the state and the institution of private property; they do so partly through political action demanding urban and more general land reform, but mainly by realising place-based protest – the movements respond to the issue by adopting a practical solution and occupying empty and abandoned places (Figure 18.1).

Marconi is a squat established by MMPT, an organisation that emerged in 2000 and fights for Article 6 of the Federal Constitution of Brazil to become a reality: this article assures social rights in areas such as education, health, work, dignified housing, leisure and safety, and is a key promise of the Brazilian constitution. The movement defends low-income populations and their right to pay an amount for housing that is proportional to their revenue, not an amount

Figure 18.1: Façade of the building occupied by MMPT (Credit: Julia Malafaia)

that depends on property bubbles and price volatility; this is why they fight for social housing as a way of guaranteeing people's right to the city. Most of the time, whether someone can live in the city centre or in a good neighbourhood is determined by whether they have the money to afford the expensive rent. However, in downtown São Paulo, for example, there are more than 150 empty buildings that could be transformed into social housing. The activists aim to secure the social function of property by occupying these abandoned empty buildings in areas where the necessary infrastructure exists, and through the subsequent expropriation of the buildings by the Housing Secretariat, the housing authority of the city, which transforms them into social housing. However, in the context of the urban dynamics of the contemporary city, this approach is still the exception. As Engels (1872, 23) illustrates in *The Housing Question*:

> The growth of the big modern cities gives the land in certain areas, particularly in those areas which are centrally situated, an artificially and colossally increasing value; the buildings erected on these areas depress this value instead of increasing it, because they no longer belong to the changed circumstances. They are pulled down and replaced by others. This takes place above all with workers' houses which are situated centrally and whose rents, even with the greatest overcrowding, can never, or only very slowly,

increase above a certain maximum. They are pulled down and in their stead shops, warehouses and public building are erected.

The awareness of the necessity for an accessible and inclusive city is, however, growing: in March 2013, MMPT had 4,013 families associated with it, who support the movement by participating in its protests. MMPT is part of a network of organisations called Central de Movimentos Populares (Union of Popular Movements) (CMP) which has around 35,000 activists in the country. The CMP network helps reinforce the political power of MMPT in its negotiations with the public sector, through the support of other movements. One example of its collective political achievements is the compromise it reached with the mayor in expropriating 24 properties that had been squatted by various movements in downtown São Paulo.

This political pressure was also effective because of the squats, which amplified the issue of social housing: by transposing the frame of the housing debate from the mayor's office to the streets, the spaces of contestation helped raise awareness of the failure of public services for the whole of society, in turn lending more political power to the movements. The appropriation of such sites and their insertion into this landscape represent a symbolic statement against its context, and a heterotopic space is built:

> There are also, probably in every culture, in every civilization, real places – places that do exist and that are formed in the very founding of society – which are something like counter-sites, a kind of effectively enacted utopia in which the real sites, all the other real sites that can be found within the culture, are simultaneously represented, contested, and inverted. Places of this kind are outside of all places, even though it may be possible to indicate their location in reality. Because these places are absolutely different from all the sites that they reflect and speak about, I shall call them, by way of contrast to utopias, heterotopias. (Foucault, 1967)

The process of representing, contesting and inverting society's values and sites is evident in the dynamics that happen inside the Marconi occupation. For a short period of time, the squat constituted a 'homeplace' – 'a site of resistance and nurturance' (bell hooks, 1990, 41–49) – where there was a strong sense of solidarity, community and care between the activists, which contrasted with values relating to property, consumption and individualism in the rest of society (Figure 18.2). bell hooks' concept of 'homeplace' refers to a safe space for growth and development, where we can 'nurture our spirits'. This 'safe space' was experienced by the people who cooked lunch for everyone, who played with their neighbours' children in the corridor, who decided which phrase to write and the colours in which to paint the flag 'While you don't wake up, we fight for you', who protested with their saucepans in the streets after they received notice of a court order that establishes the owner's right (and often leads to evictions). Their communal or common life was built through day-to-day relations, and the inhabitants created values as they performed activities together.

Figure 18.2: The sign reading 'I love my occupation' in a common room which each inhabitant should clean once a week (Credit: Julia Malafaia)

MMPT was the initiative of an activist called Edinalva Franco, who had participated in social housing movements since adolescence. At a certain moment, she decided to create her own. In 2012, MMPT activists took part in their first squat: they occupied an abandoned mansion in downtown São Paulo. Only then did the movement start to expand – although it was always closely linked to the figure of Edinalva Franco. They put a sign on the door, and people started to come to their meetings, to understand the history and objectives of MMPT, and to get involved in the fight for dignified housing. Marconi was the second occupation undertaken, with around 100 people. The collaboration was born out of necessity, as an immediate response to the housing crisis which affects many people in São Paolo. Once the squat had begun, adaptations needed to be made to the building to fulfil the needs of the residents, such as organising work schedules for collective activities and reforming the space – infrastructure was therefore established to respond to the requirements of 'making protest' and 'making home'.

Marconi occupation as an urban protest camp

In 2013 I and two other members of an initiative called Muda (Portuguese for 'change' and 'seed') undertook a four-month residency in Marconi. Our aim was to take an empathetic approach to the issues involved in the right to the city and the homeplace, and to study and contribute to building this 'space where there is a desire to constitute non-capitalist, collective forms of politics, identity and citizenship' (Pickerill and Chatterton, 2006, 730).

> The idea of the right to the city…primarily rises up from the streets, out from the neighbourhoods, as a cry for help and sustenance by oppressed people in desperate times. How, then, do academics and intellectuals (both organic and traditional, as Gramsci would put it) respond to that cry and that demand? (Harvey, 2012)

Bearing David Harvey's question in mind, the residency combined an academic perspective with a more practical and embodied approach, and constituted an experience that shaped the analysis discussed in this chapter. It is: '[a]n approach to research that combines creative and academic research practices, and supports the development of knowledge and innovation through artistic expression, scholarly investigation, and experimentation. The creation process is situated within the research activity and produces critically informed work in a variety of media (art forms)' (Research Creation, nd).

From this research, it was possible to understand which structures, resources and strategies had been inherited from other protest camps and which were a result of this specific context and circumstances (physical, social and environmental). Therefore, Marconi can be defined as an ongoing assemblage of many different practices that change according to the people involved and the limitations and resources that arise in the space. This section aims to draw out patterns in the ways in which planning strategies and resources became entangled in this specific protest landscape, building a 'small, self-managed city, a "heterotopic space" of exchange and innovation' (Juris, 2008, 129) with a particular configuration. To articulate this analysis, the infrastructures of the space were divided into four key organisational dimensions, which, of course, interact dynamically with each other: communication, action, governance, and recreation or domestic (compare Frenzel et al, 2014).

Communication infrastructure

Communication is a strategy that crosscuts all the other modes of operation; it complements them and allows them to work through its potential and on a variety of scales (between inhabitants, with collaborators and with the whole of society). The actions organised by the movement are physical but have repercussions that go beyond the events themselves; just like the Climate Camp Movement in the UK, the Marconi occupation exists in two forms simultaneously – as a protest camp and as:

> an organisational framework that links campers and supporters with more regular gathering and exchanges including national organising meetings and large social media networks. The actual camps here arguably become a particular form of mobilization of a movement that exists beyond the camp with the benefit of enabling a longer lasting strategy. (Frenzel et al, 2014, 7)

Social media and independent platforms have an important role in internal communication, while activist journalists help ensure that the relevant issue appears on the agenda of mass media and internationally. However, the main strategy of most of the movements still depends on face-to-face communication, bringing people together to share, plan and build.

> Direct action takes the alienated, lonely body of technocratic culture and transforms it into a connected, communicative body embedded in society. Taking part in direct action is a radical poetic gesture by which we can achieve meaningful change, both personal and social. Direct action is the central strategy of creative resistance, a strategy that, unlike the rationality and objectivity of most politics, revokes

the emphasis on words and reason and demands the acknowledgement of intuition and imagination. (Jordan, 1998, 134–135)

The actions realised inside the Marconi occupation and in its surroundings, which are performed by its inhabitants and by a network of collaborators, function mainly as protest (political pressure), protection (the physical and symbolic nurturing of the activists) and integration (with collaborators, other movements and civil society). However, the Occupation itself plays an important role in multiple ways; it, too, exists as a protest, a protection and an integrative action simultaneously, in that it is a direct intervention in the space being contested, it builds a community that supports people in need, and it creates a laboratory for a democratic society.

Action infrastructure

As far as protest action is concerned, the moment when the protesters break into an abandoned building (the act of squatting) is one of its most important tactics. Other common strategies in the repertoire of protest camps include camping in front of institutional venues, building barricades, and organising manifestations and riots. In these cases, the practical and theoretical preparation of the activists before the protest action is fundamental. This preparation can cover learning how to use an iron bar to break into a building, learning how to face police repression, and understanding the activists' position in society and their right to protest.

This is the moment when protection becomes relevant: actions that back up the protesters and help them overcome the challenges, practically and psychologically. Informal spaces where social relations take place, such as encounters with coordinators or neighbours, or the provision of legal support by municipal lawyers who defend the protesters in court, are the site of actions that help provide a nurturing environment. Also, workshops, lectures and debates give the protesters argumentative tools and empower the inhabitants to be able to justify their actions.

The protesters put their knowledge into practice when they are in contact with other social movements and civil society: inside the Marconi occupation, participants used to host debates on relevant issues about social change, bringing in academics, civil society and high-school students. Integrative actions such as these create a 'convergence space' that gathers together mobilised citizens and activists and becomes a place of sharing, planning and articulation:

> common ground between various social movements, grassroots initiatives, non-governmental organisations and other formations, wherein certain interests, goals, tactics and strategies converge. It is a space of facilitation, solidarity, communication, coordination, and information sharing. It is both virtual – enacted through the internet – and material, enacted through conferences and various kinds of direct action such as demonstrations and strikes. (Routledge, 2000, 35).

Acting on the initiative of Muda, we promoted events in the area surrounding the space with the aim of connecting more directly with the public, integrating the activists into the wider society, and raising awareness of the fight among people who were not already aware of it or who had to overcome layers of prejudice to get involved. In addition, events were organised in the streets because there was an understanding that the city was the living room of the building – a place where people could host the rituals of daily life and display affection. A connection between people (activists or not) arises from contact and relationships, from looking beyond what the people represent. Empathy is triggered when scenes of domesticity are created: one example was the breakfast organised on the street in front of the building.

Events happened with the collaboration of both residents and owners from markets in the neighbourhood. The process of organising the breakfast, as well as the meal itself, created a space of engagement and allowed a change in perspective, and it transformed the street politics of the surrounding area. The restaurant owner who lent the chairs, for example, did not want to collaborate in the beginning; he thought that, since the start of the squat, the number of robberies in the neighbourhood had increased. However, after a process of building trust, he decided to help, and on the morning of the breakfast he met his neighbours and revised the previous image he had had of them.

On that morning, one could see children going up the stairs of the building and calling out to everyone, the younger ones going down the stairs with tables, and the older ones heating water for the coffee. In the streets, residents wore MMPT T-shirts, the waitress from the bakery on the corner provided orange juice, families invited to the event through Facebook brought croissants, curious homeless people were encouraged to have a cup of coffee, intrigued passers-by asked what was happening, and a policeman stopped to say that it was an illegal appropriation of public space. The dynamics of this public space, usually a place for crossing, with no permanent activity and not much interaction, were inverted, opening up a crack for the creation of bonds and for more democratic relationships. This temporary site of affect opened the space to 'transformative practices of listening and becoming' (Mezirow and Taylor, 2011), proving how sensations and bodily experience contribute to shift people's perspectives towards the unknown, to the other:

> The events were particularly successful in getting people to meet, overcome the stultifications of shyness, begin to listen to one another, and build and transmit excitement… Without any expectation that a group with a common goal should form, these events provided a space for a range of people from many different backgrounds to experience 'being-in-common'. (Gibson-Graham, 2006, 24)

Instead of trying to achieve an ideal concept of community economy, what was understood was the importance of recognising moments of 'being-in-common' in all economic subjects and forms that exist in relations of interdependence that can be negotiated and explored. During the events mentioned above, those relations happened organically, and this experience could be shared between the activists and other inhabitants of the city. The crack that the Marconi occupation creates in this urban reality, therefore, was broadened into a specific space and time, thereby creating a temporary autonomous zone (Hakim Bey, 1986). This can be seen as one of the main challenges for the Occupation and MMPT: to legitimise the existence of this gap and to deal with society's prejudice towards it. This prejudice was the result of many years of stigmatisation and a lack of appreciation of the protesters' fight and is also due to the weight Brazilian citizens give to the violation of private property.

Other urban interventions organised by Muda that broadened the crack and activated the dynamics and politics of Rua Marconi included: Urban Objects, a food cart and mobile playground built with the residents and architecture students; and the Real Estate Bubble, an inflatable architectural space built of recycled plastic bags in collaboration with the Spanish collective, Basurama, and the Cooperative of Garbage Pickers of Glicério. The interventions had 'vibrant materiality', as Jane Bennet puts it: spaces defined by an assemblage of objects, bodies and interactions (Bennet, 2009). In the case of the Real Estate Bubble, it also problematised the issue of the right to the city, exposing how the phenomenon of gentrification creates an exclusive city, configured only for those who can afford it.

Governance infrastructure

These actions were proposed during the assemblies that happened once a week; a consensus would be reached on whether the action was pertinent or not and how the residents would be involved in its organisation. Usually, the people involved in the events were the participants of the leisure working group, or people who had links to and relationships with us. As part of the governance system (Figure 18.3), each resident had to choose a group with which to work: leisure, communication, education, cooking, cleaning, guarding, and so on. The groups were autonomous but also needed to work together with the coordinators of the building in specific cases. It is possible that this structure was more formalised than those in other protest camps, partly because of the formalisation of the Marconi occupation itself: a building made of concrete, with clear limits to how it could be transformed. All the residents were expected to participate in the Saturday assemblies. The governance processes were based always on a vote, sometimes using a blackboard to facilitate this. A coordination meeting was also held once a week. The difference between these meetings tended to

Figure 18.3: Entry door of the building with the coexistence rules of the occupation (Credit: Julia Malafaia)

relate to the issue under discussion and the format of the meeting: necessities and problems regarding the building and social rules were themes of the assemblies (with all the residents present), while new MMPT strategies and bureaucracy were discussed by the coordinators in meetings of those people who helped the movement externally (most were not residents of the occupations). However, the assemblies were usually the last resort in resolving conflicts: first, the decision-making processes happened in informal relations and everyday spaces, such as the hallway, the staircase or the queue to get lunch. The staircase and the corridors were the heart of the building: places for meeting, playing, talking and exchanging. Just as Rem Koolhaas points out in 'Strategy of the void': 'imagine a building consisting of regular and irregular spaces, where the most important parts of the building consist of an absence of building' (Koolhaas, 1995, 603).

Domestic infrastructure

In the Marconi occupation, the relation between the subject and the object of architecture is redefined, and the place's value lies in the relationships that happen inside the building, the crack that is characterised by a charged nothingness. Living there, we could see that energy flowing; the sense of belonging, trust and collective identity of the inhabitants used to grow every day, mainly because of the activities developed between them. A climate of solidarity and a feeling of community helped strengthen the bonds and provide a little stability to the extreme vulnerability to which these people are susceptible. The domestic infrastructures were based in an ethic of care, which reinforced the idea of the occupation as a heterotopic space in which there is a disruption of hegemonic practices and aesthetics: 'this marks how the protest camp becomes "a place out of place", where the rituals of daily life – from cooking and bathing to parenting and displaying affection – become offered as an "alternative aesthetics" to those of the normative, surrounding geography' (Cresswell, 1996, 124).

The domestic infrastructure of the squat contrasts with the capitalist status quo and the dominant discourse – of possessing huge apartments, with lots of private and individual rooms, a lift, and no spaces that promote interaction between neighbours. The Marconi occupation's character is that of a collective and fragmented house: the apartments (old offices) are only 12 square metres in size, there is one bathroom per floor, and there is one collective kitchen for the whole building as well as washing machines shared by the residents.

A day-care nursery (Figure 18.4), a library, a cinema and a space for meetings were created, strengthening the ties between neighbours and with the squat itself, and highlighting the lack of truly accessible infrastructure in the city. In addition, residents tried to be self-sufficient in their everyday practices: the municipal market donated food, but the residents produced compost and collected rainwater for their own garden. However, logistics and management were also necessary in order to allow the domestic infrastructure to work together with the political infrastructure: 'The place where more work must be done concerns how we align questions of individual wellness, community well being, and antagonism toward the state. There is no single formula. There are only better experiments…Here we start to see an articulation of an emancipatory bio-politics' (Feigenbaum et al, 2013, 221).

Figure 18.4: Kindergarten and day care centre self-managed by the occupiers (Credit: Julia Malafaia)

Conclusion

Common life and social reproduction

At one specific moment, the Marconi occupation could be considered a protest camp: it had a symbolic role that 'mobilized protest campers, validated their cause and enlarged the scope of the issue at hand' (Gamson and Wolfsfeld, 1993), reflecting the unjust conditions of part of the population back to the state and to wider society. The site embodied this issue and provided it with visibility, since the building is located in the heart of one of the richest cities in the world, close to institutional centres and in a location that millions of people pass through every day. It conformed to the concepts of a contested space, symbolically looking at the question of people's right to the city; a convergence centre, in the sense that it built a network of activists (and academics) who passed through the space; a representational space, which stood for the cause of social housing and the right to the city; and a homeplace, similar to intentional communities, causing obvious disruptions in people's normative daily lives and domestic infrastructures.

In the everyday practices of the Marconi occupation, there was a clear tension between an emancipatory politics and bio-politics; the former represented the empowerment of the activists while the latter was a resistant response to the hegemonic power and control practised upon their lives. For a while, the residents, who positioned themselves in relation to others and to the space in their search for individual and collective identities, experienced autonomy: 'the personal is political'. Through experiences of labour and leisure, affect was produced; transformative encounters created bonds between the activists themselves and with the space, and therefore accumulated value.

> The process of disclosing new worlds involves complex movements between identification with new subject positions, exploratory acts of self-transformation, and the fixing of new 'dispositional patterns of desire' that become part of what we experience as subjection (Connolly, 1995, 57). At any point in the history-making process, an individual is caught in two places, experiencing the dissatisfactions and disappointments of what they know and habitually desire and the satisfactions and surprises of what is new, but hard to fully recognise and want. The individual needs external nourishment and encouragement to sustain acts of self-cultivation, to see changing themselves as contributing to changing worlds.' (Gibson-Graham, 2006, 162)

In the Marconi occupation, structures of social care were recreated to nurture this community of resistance (Federici, 2012), encouraging new forms of political participation and individuation. This recreation also involved the ways in which resources were commonalised and surpluses redistributed. One example was the community kitchen: it was managed by some of the residents, but all of the inhabitants could access and benefit from it – the surplus was distributed to everyone. Another example was the food cart, an open platform and common resource for the activists to gain additional income through selling their food in the streets, and to generate and distribute value in an autonomous and self-managed way.

A crisis of social reproduction

This also, however, became the issue that led to the domestic structures of the protest camp changing: residents started to argue about whether non-producers of social surplus could have a say in how that surplus was appropriated and distributed, and for which social ends. This discussion mirrored the debate of the whole democratic system, and was what recreated the infrastructures and practices of the camp.

One hypothesis is that when the activists were not aligned in their potentialities, desires and intentions, conflicts and tensions started to arise. Once those frictions increased further, some of the residents left – and they tended to be those who had played more active roles. The activists understood the importance of value and affect: they needed to feel that they belonged to this place, that they were free to be themselves and to be part of a community. Perhaps because the residents acted sometimes out of obligation or fear of punishment, and were there in order to achieve individualistic dreams (to own their own house in the future, for instance), the 'nowtopia' was not strong enough for people to engage permanently in the construction of this new world. Circumstances changed and put an end to the experience of the Marconi occupation as a protest camp.

Today, people do not contribute to the collective anymore; there are no groups of common or shared activities. And those who work in the building are paid by MMPT. There was a crisis in social reproduction inside the squat regarding both labour power and life, which occurred once the reproduction of the residents became completely dependent on waged labour and the infrastructures of care, based on cooperative relationships, collapsed. In a way, it is interesting to see how people value their work more highly when they receive a more tangible reward for the time and effort they invest in labour. However, in this case, the residents do not have the consciousness of being part of something, of forming a collective identity.

By studying the Marconi occupation through the framework of the protest camp, we can include a discussion of social reproduction and care, questioning how surpluses are produced (through labour power and life) and redistributed. By analysing the change in the occupation's dynamics, we can understand the importance of potential, value and care. 'Of course, social reproduction retains its dual nature in the production of labor-power as a commodity and the production of human social relations and cooperation.

By considering how the Marconi occupation was a heterotopic space for a specific moment in time, we can see how the activists experimented with other forms of being and other practices of labour and value, moving beyond capital. Processes of production and social reproduction are necessarily entangled, so would it not be a solution to integrate them, to produce commons, against capitalist domination and exploitation? This occurred in the cooperative activities of the squat, which arose from necessity but provided a structure of care and solidarity. For a moment, there was a commonalisation of resources: people had access to the means of subsistence (that they themselves produced) without having their labour power exploited. What if those extra-economic activities of social reproduction were enough to create another way of 'being-in-common', producing and redistributing surplus value for all? What if those activities are what it takes for the commons to be produced and nurtured to keep the individual alive and the community preserved, but without creating pressure on the generation of a surplus?

References

Bennett, J. (2009) *Vibrant Matter: A Political Ecology of Things.* Durham, NC: Duke University Press.

Bey, H. (1986) 'The end of the world', *Chaos*, 6, 18.

Brown, G., Dowling, E., Harvie, D. and Milburn, K. (2013) 'Careless talk: social reproduction and fault lines of the crisis in the United Kingdom', *Social Justice*, 39(1), 78–98.

Connolly, W. (1995) *The Ethos of Pluralization.* Minneapolis: University of Minnesota Press.

Cresswell, T. (1996) *In Place – Out of Place: Geography, Ideology, and Transgression.* Minneapolis, MN: University of Minnesota Press.

Engels, F. (1872) [1975] *The Housing Question.* London: Co-operative Publishing Society of Foreign Workers.

Federici, S. (2012) *Revolution at Point Zero: Housework, Reproduction, and Feminist Struggle.* Oakland, CA: PM Press.

Feigenbaum, A., Frenzel, F. and McCurdy, P. (2013) *Protest Camps.* London: Zed.

Foucault, M. (1967) 'Of other spaces: utopias and heterotopias', *Architecture/Mouvement/Continuite*. October, 1984 ['Des Espace Autres', March 1967. Translated from the French by Jay Miskowiec].

Frenzel, F., Feigenbaum, A., and McCurdy, P. (2014) 'Protest camps: an emerging field of social movement research', *Sociological Review*, 62(3), 457–474.

Gamson, W. A. and Wolfsfeld, G. (1993) 'Movements and media as interacting systems', *The Annals of the American Academy of Political and Social Science*, 114–125.

Gibson-Graham, J. K. (2006) *A Postcapitalist Politics*. Minneapolis, MN: University of Minnesota Press, p 162.

Harvey, D. (2010) 'Organizing for the anti-capitalist transition', *Interface*, 2(1), 243–261.

Harvey, D. (2012) *Rebel Cities: From the Right to the City to the Urban Revolution*. London: Verso.

Holloway, J. and Susen, S. (2013) 'Change the world by cracking capitalism? A critical encounter between John Holloway and Simon Susen', *Sociological Analysis*, 7(1), 23–42.

hooks, bell (1990) *Yearning: Race, Gender, and Cultural Politics*. Boston, MA: South End Press.

Jordan, J. (1998) 'The art of necessity: the subversive imagination of anti-road protest and Reclaim the Streets', in G. McKay (ed), *DiY Culture: Party and Protest in Nineties Britain*, London: Verso, pp 129–151.

Juris, J. S. (2008) *Networking Futures: The Movements Against Corporate Globalization*. Durham, NC: Duke University Press.

Koolhaas, R. (1995) *S, M, L, XL*, New York: Monacelli Press.

Mezirow, J. and Taylor, E. W. (2011) *Transformative Learning in Practice: Insights from Community, Workplace, and Higher Education*. Oxford: John Wiley and Sons.

Osterweil, M. (2004) 'A cultural political approach to reinventing the political', *International Social Science Journal*, 56(182), 495–506.

Park, R. E. (1929) 'The city as a social laboratory', in T. V. Smith and S. D. White (eds) Chicago: An Experiment in Social Science Research. Chicago, IL: University of Chicago Press, pp 1–19.

Pickerill, J. and Chatterton, P. (2006) 'Notes towards autonomous geographies: creation, resistance and self-management as survival tactics', *Progress in Human Geography*, 30(6), 730–746.

Research Creation (nd) *Research Creation*, www.mun.ca/arts/research/creation.php, St John's: Faculty of Humanities and Social Sciences, Memorial University of Newfoundland.

Routledge, P. (2000) '"Our resistance will be as transnational as capital": Convergence space and strategy in globalising resistance', *GeoJournal*, 52(1), 25–33.

NINETEEN

From protest camp to tent city: the 'Free Cuvry' camp in Berlin-Kreuzberg

Niko Rollmann and Fabian Frenzel

Introduction

Focused on issues of gentrification, the 'Free Cuvry' camp existed from March 2012 until September 2014 and was one of Berlin's most visible post-Occupy protest camps. The camp attracted a lot of attention, with reactions ranging from outright condemnation to uncritical idolisation. Many people – whether protest campers, local residents or visitors – also experienced Free Cuvry as extremely complex, contradictory and unpredictable. While, at times, it was a protest camp against gentrification, it was also a refuge, an anarchist utopia, a 'no rules' zone, a crime scene, a health hazard, an expression of Berlin's housing shortage and an indicator of Berlin's increasing social polarisation. Based in Berlin's district of Kreuzberg, adjacent to the river Spree, it was located on prime privately owned real estate. During its existence, it was inhabited by up to 120 people from a variety of backgrounds, including a number of recent migrants to the city, temporary visitors and tourists.

The Free Cuvry protest camp combined the expressive and activist features of a protest camp against gentrification and the features of a tent city (Heben, 2012), a semi-autonomous shelter and refuge for some of Berlin poorest inhabitants. In their self-organisation the campers made several attempts at reconciling the camp's dual characteristics as both a protest camp and a tent city: providing autonomous organised housing and care, while blocking the development of high-end speculative real estate. The challenges encountered in the process are paralleled in the ways that many urban protest camps consist of political organising and the providing of autonomous care and social reproduction (Feigenbaum et al, 2013).

This chapter draws on reflections on protest camps (Feigenbaum et al, 2013; Frenzel et al, 2014) and tent cities (Heben, 2012) to situate Free Cuvry. We focus in particular on the tensions between the protest camp's political character and its attempts at providing autonomous care and social reproduction. Our purpose is to better understand how these tensions materialise, for example around expending resources to provide care, the varied ability of more destitute participants to find time to take part in political debates, and the question of how to successfully build coalitions between different campers. Such concerns have been touched upon in discussions of previous camp experiences, for example in the context of Occupy camps (Halvorsen, 2015; Schein, 2012; Ehrenreich, 2011). Building on these debates, we also consider the specific conditions in which Free Cuvry emerged in its location in Berlin-Kreuzberg: a city district with a long history of social struggles and anti-gentrification activism. In the 1980s Berlin-Kreuzberg was home to a strong squatting scene that continues to influence the urban fabric to date. While most former squats in Kreuzberg today have been formalised, the housing struggles of the 1980s have resulted in a highly supportive urban environment for housing activism.

In this context we analyse how Free Cuvry self-organised. This includes a focus on the infrastructures of social reproduction and the ways in which campers organised their daily life in the camp. We will also analyse the camp's political organisation, looking at the workings of plenaries and other organisational structures. The analysis also highlights the role of outside supporters of the camp (non-resident political activists and neighbours of the Free Cuvry) and the motivations (or lack of) for their involvement with the camp. This analyses aims at better understanding the processes in which political coalitions can be built between protest camps and their environments, particularly in cases where there is a strong focus on autonomous social reproduction and care.

The chapter concludes by discussing some of the consequences emerging from the Free Cuvry encampment, in particular with regards to the specificity with which local contexts influence the emergence and characteristics of camps and tent cities. More generally, we suggest that the need to combine autonomous care and political protest brings to the fore the class basis of different activist politics. Activist politics in such contexts will likely be based on coalitions of different groups rather than being carried by uniform collectives. We suggest that protest camps can be considered as places where such coalitions can be formed, when activists are willing to overcome dogmatic views on political organisation and operate pragmatically towards emerging political opportunities.

Figure 19.1: View over the Free Cuvry protest camp from the river Spree (Credit: Niko Rollmann)

Methods

Telling the story of the Free Cuvry occupation, based on primary research with camp participants and people involved with the camp, as neighbours and supporters, poses a number of methodological and ethical questions. This chapter is based to a large degree on the observations and experiences made during the authors' visits to the camp, between June 2013 and its eviction in September 2014. Pursuing participant observation in the tradition of militant ethnography (Juris, 2007; Uldam and McCurdy, 2013) the authors took a consciously embedded and partisan perspective on the camp. In addition, a broad range of data was collected from semi-structured interviews and open conversations. The interviewees and research participants included eight of the former camp residents, as well as 21 people involved with the camp including supporters, political activists, volunteers of charitable organisations, politicians, social services employees, government workers, local shopkeepers, neighbourhood residents and others. The interviews lasted from 30 minutes to two hours. The interviews were held without recording devices in most cases, because many research participants were reluctant to be recorded. Notes were taken of the interviews, often after the interviews took place.

The chapter additionally draws on research carried out by the urban geographer Jan van Duppen (2010) and a group of ethnology students from Berlin's Free University. These two research projects have provided some important insights on which this research built. The former covers a period prior to the protest camp occupation and the latter has not been published, but was shared with the authors. Secondary data was also acquired from a small number of newspaper and magazine articles, including three interviews of camp residents by a charitable organisation and later published by the organisation for fundraising purposes. There was also email correspondence with ten people connected to the camp, in such cases where face-to-face interviews were impossible.

The work of assembling data on Free Cuvry was at times challenging. The camp's inhabitants were primarily focused on action and were not so much concerned with documenting their own life. They also had to organise their everyday survival and – as far as the activists among them were concerned – work out political strategies and gather support. Written records and other forms of documentation were hard to come by in these circumstances, with some activists also putting an emphasis on secrecy. Furthermore, outsiders such as journalists or other people asking questions were often seen as intruders who could not be trusted (correctly so since most of the press coverage was vitriolic and superficial). Many of the camp's residents also wanted to remain 'invisible' and were consequently reluctant to talk to strangers or broadcast their situation.

The analysis of the data was pursued, for the purpose of this chapter, in order to compile a potentially broad perspective on the protest camp, while privileging the voices of those directly affected and involved. This partisan perspective however does not mean that we take liberty with establishing the facts. While many perspectives expressed here are subjective, we also aim to provide an account of the Free Cuvry that enables a broader consideration of the strategies for protest camps and other movements. Our work also aims to feed back into organisational processes around the Free Cuvry in Berlin, where we remain in close contact with many research participants.

Protest camps between political action and social reproduction

In the study of social movements there has been an increasing focus on better understanding the social and cultural environments in which movements operate (Melucci, 1996). This 'cultural turn' was prompted partly by the realisation that social movements do not simply pursue political aims, but that they also create social spaces and political communities (Offe, 1987; Crossley, 2002). In cultural and social spaces, political ideas are developed. At times, such spaces also enable the implementation of some of the ideas formulated within them. This ability has been likened to the generating of alternative worlds, which can be traced historically, as well as forming a significant part of contemporary social movement politics (Feigenbaum et al, 2013). Such 'worlding politics' (Stengers, 2005) have been pursued significantly in anarchist inspired movements, who for some time prioritised the formation of alternatives in the here and now (Day, 2005; Gordon, 2007). Particularly with the arrival of what has been called New Social Movements, or the New Left, from the last 1960s onwards in Western Europe and the United States, the tendency towards the production of autonomous spaces has come to the forefront (Cornell, 2011). This is well expressed in the notion of prefigurative politics, emphasising the desire to align the form of politics and its organisation with the content and aims of the movement (Breines, 1989). The shift is reflective of the increasing wariness with which activists viewed the self-declared socialist and communist states formed on the basis of authoritarian political organisation (Frenzel, 2014).

One important outcome of this new orientation is the increasing use of protest camps as a social movement form. Feigenbaum et al (2013) have highlighted that protest camps became attractive to New Left politics because they seemed to enable the formation of collective power outside of large-scale organisations such as trade unions or parties. As many protest camps organise spatially, they allow for key organisational elements such as membership and rules to be place-specific and emergent rather than transcendental (Frenzel, 2014). Protest camps also seemed to enable organisation based on more horizontal forms of leadership and historically they often tried to realise this (Leidinger, 2011; Frenzel, 2014). As protest camps historically developed, they combined a number of different purposes through the creation of specific infrastructures towards these purposes. Some of these travelled between camps as materialised knowledge, creating immanent and form-based convergence (Feigenbaum et al,

2013). Frenzel (2014) has pointed out that protest camps made 'partial organisation' possible and cater for a politics oriented towards the spontaneous, non-committal and affective.

What is important is that protest camps, in contrast to more institutional forms of political organisation such as trade unions or political parties or more event-based protests like demonstrations, also often form home places for their participants (bell hooks, 1990; Feigenbaum et al, 2013). The creation of a home, a place where one can find shelter, food and relaxation at the site of protest, remodels classical notions of the separation of private and public space. In many protest camps we find the politicisation of what is normally considered a private domain such as, for example, aspects of social reproduction like the provision of food and care. Sometimes there is also the privatisation of what is normally considered 'political'. This includes the emergence of informal leaders or elders, whose decisions on organisational matters may, for example, trump democratic decision-making processes involving all participants.

Overlaps between the private and the political thus may cause challenges and tensions. Most protest camps require a set of infrastructures dealing with governance and organisation, enabling the setting of rules and the negotiation of practices. Camps can at times suspend the necessity of fixed rules. Frenzel (2014) has shown that the more antagonistic a camp is positioned in relation to its outside, the less relevant internal rules and procedure seem to be. Over time however the tensions that arise from combining protest with the creation of alternative communities in which people live tend to come to the fore. This is particularly the case when the provision of a caring alternative home place requires significant resources of collective organising. This involves the work of providing food and shelter, or securing social reproduction and also addressing the psychological needs of participants.

Halvorsen (2015) has highlighted that the necessities to maintain social reproduction at the site of the camp, in his study of the Occupy camps in London, can clash with the more overtly political, 'activist', orientations of some participants, who prioritise more explicitly political work, such as the formulation of demands or the pursuit of direct action such as blockades. Capacity to do both may be limited and participants have their own priorities that influence how they decide where to invest their energies. In some cases, this may lead to a situation where camps reproduce gender divisions: for example, when women end up doing the work of social reproduction, the caring for the home place, while men are more engaged with the work of representation politics, strategic discussions and political action (Halvorsen, 2015). For many participants such a reproduction of gender-based role divisions is deeply problematic. We would like to emphasise here that protest camps do not necessarily manage to overcome the limits of the status quo from which they aim to differ, in particular in the attempts to provide alternative worlds. However, protest camps often vividly display such failings or problems in ways that allow for a broader reflection among participants and observers about these challenges that arise in the attempt to simultaneously protest and build alternative worlds. This is also the case in the domain of social inequality, particularly with regards to homeless and destitute participants in protest camps.

This chapter thus investigates the Free Cuvry as a protest camp in the context of these broader struggles, aiming to add to what we consider an emerging field of social activism. While not exclusively pursued in protest camps, attempts to create autonomously provided shelter often take the form of the camp, as in the case of Cuvry. In addition, the political focus of the Free Cuvry, beyond providing shelter, was to protest against and prevent gentrification, therefore also addressing the housing question. A better understanding of the Free Cuvry, being both a protest against gentrification and a home place for some of the poorest residents of the city, may contribute to some of the questions that have emerged at the cross-sections of protest camps and tent cities. We argue that while the case is in many ways highly specific, there are some important insights to be taken from it. Before addressing those common questions, this paper will first introduce the specific setting in which the Free Cuvry emerged.

Life and politics in Kreuzberg

The Free Cuvry camp was located in Berlin-Kreuzberg, a neighbourhood that, for decades, has been emblematic of housing activism, with an active squatting scene, and support for alternative lifestyles defining the local habitus (Kuhn, 2014; Vasudevan, 2015). A derelict and peripheral neighbourhood in the years of Berlin's separation, Kreuzberg experienced an influx of low income groups and, in particular, of Turkish labour migrants, as well as forming a broadly alternative, leftist and alternative scene.

Kreuzberg's eastern part, where the Free Cuvry was located, was particularly isolated during the separation with the Berlin Wall to its west, north and east. For many West Berliners, it was a district of almost ghetto-like reputation, leading to the district sometimes being perceived of as an enclave within the enclave that was West Berlin. In return, many in the Kreuzberger alternative scene felt a unique sense of local autonomy, represented also in the strong representation of the Autonomen movement in the local left (Geronimo, 2012). In this sense Kreuzberg was also understood as place where one was able 'to do his/her own thing'. The ruins and wastelands left behind by the war and post-war de-industrialisation provided space for all kinds of unconventional activities (Colomb, 2012).

During the 1980s, Kreuzberg also remained a district with widespread relative poverty. In this context any tendencies towards gentrification, for example the opening of more expensive shops or restaurants, were radically contested, sometimes with radical action, such as the vandalising of expensive cars. Today, the squatting scene is largely attributed with preserving the historical housing stock of Kreuzberg (Kuhn, 2014; Colomb, 2012). The broader alternative scene at the heart of the district advanced many social and political ideas that are today broadly considered mainstream, including gender equality, gay and queer rights, anti-nuclear and alternative energy policies, bike-friendly urban cultures, and many more (Holm and Kuhn, 2011; Kuhn, 2014; Novy, 2013; Colomb, 2012; Vasudevan, 2015). At the same time the isolation of Kreuzberg also resulted in a local alternative culture sometimes reminiscent of provincialism and highly resistant to any change. This includes to this day an ambivalent and often hostile attitude to newcomers, reflected, for example, in common anti-tourism attitudes in the district (Colomb and Novy, 2016).

Since the opening of the Berlin Wall, and in particular over the last decade, Kreuzberg has been at the forefront of unprecedented gentrification pressures, as the neighbourhood moved geographically to the centre of the reunited city. The alternatives realised in the neighbourhood also created a unique charm that has significantly increased its appeal and its cool. As a result, rental markets have exploded, and property prices increased across the neighbourhood. A strong political awareness of gentrification continues and so do the struggles against it. This includes a number of campaigns against displacement, mobilisations against new real estate developments and in solidarity with the poorest residents. Some activist groups also continue attempts to 'de-valorise' the neighbourhood with targeted attacks on expensive cars and high-end housing developments, echoing the struggles of the 1980s (Colomb, 2012; Holm and Kuhn, 2011). Kreuzberg's unruly past and these momentary conditions are directly connected to the history of the Free Cuvry camp (Novy, 2013; Colomb, 2012; Vasudevan, 2015).

Free Cuvry's emergence

The camp emerged on an empty plot of land adjacent to the river Spree, located on the corners of Cuvrystrasse and Schlesische Strasse. The last building on the plot, a storage facility dating back to the 1950s, was demolished in 1999. Over the years, several attempts to develop the site failed: investors ran into financial trouble, there were conflicts between the site's owners and the local authorities or neighbourhood residents. The site achieved certain fame when the renowned street artist 'Blu' painted two huge murals on the walls of adjoining buildings in 2007 (Henke, 2014).

Figure 19.2: View over the Free Cuvry with Blu grafitti on the right (Credit: Niko Rollmann)

In the 1990s, the site seemed to be a typical Berlin wasteland; typical as Berlin's architectural fabric had been punctuated by war damage as well as by factory closure and stagnating economic development in the post-war years. The plot was open and many residents used it autonomously, making good use of its location right next to the river Spree and the relatively wide vistas it provided in the dense inner city. Urban geographer Jan van Duppen carried out a research project there from July 2009 until June 2010, including an intensive on-site study. He observed a wide variety of activities: people came to rest at the riverside, have a drink, consume drugs, eat, walk their dogs, fish, spray graffiti, admire Blu's murals, engage in 'guerrilla gardening', hold meetings, produce video clips and use the site as a toilet (Van Duppen, 2010).

A first occupation of some the site occurred in September 2011. The squatters had no direct political intentions, according to one of the initiators of the occupation interviewed for this research. Rather, the aim was to create a form of free and unconventional living on the site. The occupation did not take up much space and did little to disturb other uses and thus remained uncontroversial. However, controversy arrived at the site the following winter. In early 2012 the site's potential for conflict came to the fore: funded by the car maker BMW, the so-called 'Guggenheim Lab' proposed to take over the site temporarily to create a debating forum on issues of urbanity (Colomb, 2012). Some politicians supported the idea, but local political activists saw this initiative as a potentially significant driver of the gentrification of the neighbourhood. They also resented the involvement of BMW. In addition, many local residents felt that they had not been consulted over the project. In March 2012 the Guggenheim lab decided to move to a different site in Berlin, stating that threats had been made against them (Spiegel Online, 2012).

At the same time the self-declared 'non-political' squatters who had occupied the site in the previous autumn, returned. This time they built tepees to provide themselves with more comfort, creating more substantial infrastructures. Mobilised by the recent political upheaval over the site, their second occupation was more visible and also attracted a number of more politically oriented squatters. Local anti-gentrification campaigners from the so-called 'Reäuberläb' that had formed in opposition to the Guggenheim Lab (their name played on that of the Guggenheim Lab, and is loosely translated as 'Robbers Lab'), used the site to stage a neighbourhood festival in June 2012. The Reäuberläb campaigned openly for an experimental use of the site, for example by setting up a bar to stage regular cultural events. These more expressively political activities did not escape the attention of the site's owners, the 'Nieto GmbH & Co Verwaltungs-KG'. They notified the squatters that the site would be cleared by the end of July 2012. The threatened eviction mobilised more anti-gentrification campaigners, with the site becoming the topic of political discussions across Berlin. While Reäuberläb activists always stated that they wanted to work with the squatters already living there, different perspectives emerged within the camp. There was a fear by some of the squatters that the events, including the loud music played, would draw unwanted attention to the site.

Leading up to the threatened eviction, the Reäuberläb organised a series of events, culminating in a music festival during the days of the expected eviction. On the morning of 24 July, two trucks with material for building fences turned up at the site, ostensibly to shut down access to the site on the behest of the owners. But the owners had not secured an eviction order. Faced with dozens of protesters, but no police support, the builders had to abandon their plan.

That was the end of the first attempt to evict the squatters. Despite this success for the squatters, the friction between people with different perspectives on the purpose of the camp increased. Some of the original squatters felt uncomfortable with the politicisation and the growth of the site. According to one of the early campers, up to a hundred people lived on site by July 2012. He also mentioned a growing number of thefts on site, which led him and some of the other original squatters to leave. Taking the tepees with them, they set up a new camp, that they called 'Teepee Land' at another nearby empty plot on the river Spree.

The Free Cuvry, however, had survived the first eviction attempt by the owners and was for now a fully political camp. Once the dust had settled, the Reäuberläb activists saw it as their next task to ensure the camp's survival over the coming winter. This included the building of more substantial infrastructures. Tents were replaced by more solid constructions; firewood, warm clothes and blankets were gathered. Meanwhile, a lot of the 'summer guests' left as it got colder, with only a small number of residents, perhaps a dozen, remaining. A weekly plenary consisting of camp residents, Reäuberläb members and activists from local political groups was set up as a governance infrastructure. The camp survived the winter, but as spring 2013 came, it had lost some of its political character. While the activists from outside continued with their support, most of the camp's residents no longer participated in the meetings of the plenary. Many resident squatters shared the sentiment against the owners, but no sustained political actions and no alternative concepts for the site were developed in this period.

The site owners, however, had developed new plans. Convinced by local politicians to seek consultation, they presented a new development plan at a public meeting in June 2013. The scheme included 250 flats, a kindergarten and shops. The plans did not go down well with those present at the meeting. After a number of disruptions during the presentation, the owners were finally completely shouted down and left the meeting. Most of those present at the meeting seemed to be against any development of the site. Many also objected to the fact that only 10 per cent of the flats would be built as 'affordable housing'.

In response, there was some political activity, including an anti-eviction demonstration on 26 June 2013, but it was of a sporadic nature and often seemed to be driven by non-residents of the camp.

Making ends meet

An increasing focus of camp residents' activities concerned their own social reproduction, highlighted in the changing, and somewhat improving material infrastructure of the camp. In summer of 2013, small wooden huts had largely replaced the tents and teepees, that had dominated the site since the summer of 2012. The population of permanent hut-dwellers had grown. Increasingly the camp's population consisted of several distinct groups: politically oriented squatters, local Berlin 'street kids' (often in a punk outfit), homeless Eastern Europeans and a small number of African refugees. As in the previous winter, the winter 2013–14 saw the camp's population decline down to between 20 and 40 people but it rose again in spring 2014 to over 100. After that, there was a continuous rise in the population, driven largely by Roma from Bulgaria and Romania who arrived at the site from spring 2014.

Political organisation was increasingly difficult because of language barriers and the varying aims of the residents. By the end of the summer of 2013, the different groups had claimed separate 'neighbourhoods' within the site, within which the cultural homogeneity was larger. In this way the site and its large space 'worked' for the residents. There were some basic agreements, for example concerning thoroughfares. Open access to the river was also maintained. Newcomers would negotiate their place needs within the smaller neighbourhoods in a largely informal fashion. While much of this informal negotiating worked, conflicts sometimes occurred over space. Several of the residents interviewed indicated that such conflicts were sometimes solved by resorting to (threats of) violence, rather than political negotiations.

Social reproduction and the organisation of life in the camp were challenging tasks. From the start, there were no proper toilets, no water pipes and no electricity. These conditions affected camp residents very differently. Among the residents significant differences existed in regards of their social status and access to resources. A few of the camp's inhabitants were officially registered as Berlin residents (which involved having a fixed address) and thus able to claim social benefits. A small number of people were also able to draw on resources and savings. Some people had flats at their disposal, and did not need to stay at the site. But at the site there were also an increasing number of people who joined the camp largely out of necessity. The openness of the site during the occupation offered refuge and protection and enabled precarious survival in the city.

Residents' activities give a clear indication of their priorities. On a normal day many residents would be involved in collecting returnable bottles, firewood and other useful objects, begging, busking, juggling, producing self-made jewellery, drawing postcards and pictures or taking on odd jobs. Some were active as fire artists or sold street papers comparable to Britain's *Big Issue*. A few also worked in cafés or bakeries. Others had more unusual jobs, like guiding tourists across the camp or selling old tyres. Fishing in the river Spree and urban gardening provided additional resources. The rubbish containers behind local supermarkets were also relevant since the goods they held, items past their sell-by date, were often still fit for consumption. A few of the camp's residents were involved in petty crime, mainly small-scale theft. Whatever their individual 'trade' may have been, the squatters usually showed a high degree of solidarity, helping others when necessary. They often perceived the camp's population as a large family.

The reproduction of life in the camp also depended on external structures. Several state and volunteer institutions, such as the 'Bürgerhilfe' support centre, the 'Fixpunkt' medical service, the 'Sankt Marien Liebfrauen' church and other organisations supported the camp dwellers, as did local shops and bakeries – and a number of individuals. Apart from providing advice, assistance, food, water, clothes and other goods, they sometimes also allowed the camp's residents to use their toilets.

The squatters were often on the move during the day. They had to make a living, maintain their huts and go to support organisations for help. Much time was also spent looking for people one needed to speak to, with only a small number of the squatters having mobile phones or regular access to the internet. Travelling was often time-consuming because many of the camp's inhabitants had no bicycle and no money for public transport.

Many people also suffered from health problems. The most common problems were tooth decay, skin diseases, lice and other parasites, drug- or alcohol-related conditions, poor nutrition and lack of exercise. In addition, there was a high stress level related to the constant struggle to 'keep going'. And there were, of course, tensions between some of the squatters that occasionally erupted into violence. As one of the camp's residents graphically expressed it: 'You can run as fast as you want – but the shit always catches up with you!'

While most of the camp's residents shared the conditions and routines described above, there was a fundamental difference between the ones who wanted to live there and those who had to. This reflected the differentiation made by Schein (2012): some squatters came from middle-class backgrounds which meant that the camp was a voluntary, lifestyle and perhaps political choice for them. But, for most of the campers, it was a different story: the camp was a crucial element of their survival in the city. This caused severe problems for the ability of the camp to organise politically. Few residents were able or willing to spend time in plenary meetings, when more essential concerns had to be addressed. But political organisation was also rejected on more romantic grounds. Also outsiders sometimes tended to romanticise the camp, referring to the spontaneous music 'jams' at the camp fires and the squatters' apparent freedom.

The Monday plenary

In spring of 2014, a number of changes in the camp led to the re-establishment of a governance infrastructure in the form of the 'Monday plenary'. One reason was the arrival of the last group of settlers, the Roma, which led to some complaints from other camp residents. They experienced this influx as an invasion and worried about a surge in thefts and the 'territorial' behaviour of some of the Roma. At the same time, residents from the surrounding streets and café and restaurant owners started to complain to the authorities. They stated that the Roma were involved in 'aggressive begging' and theft. Complaints by neighbours of the camp however did not only focus on the Roma. In an interview one said that she thought the site was no longer accessible. Free Cuvry had turned into a dirty and 'unpleasant' location where many did not feel safe any more. The sheer size of the camp also led to concerns over rubbish, rats and hygiene more generally. On the site itself, several violent confrontations between the Roma and other groups – especially the Eastern Europeans – occurred, often over questions of territory. The rejection of the Roma in particular (both in the camp and by its neighbours) was at times driven by open racism against the Roma. Several camp residents interviewed articulated racist resentments. The decisive reason for a renewed attempt at political organisation, however, was external pressure. In June 2014 rumours of an imminent eviction started to spread, while several articles appeared in newspapers that quoted neighbours and local politicians calling for a solution to the situation, often at least implicitly making the case for an eviction.

Figure 19.3: Activities on the Free Cuvry in summer 2014 (Credit: Fabian Frenzel)

In the light of these external pressures, the solidarity of some neighbours with Free Cuvry was reignited. They complained about the negative reporting and often racist undertones that fuelled it. They pointed out that the problematic conditions of the site were mere expressions of certain social realities and a lack of political will to address the needs of the camp's inhabitants. In this situation, new momentum arose to support the camp, re-establishing it as a symbol of resistance against gentrification. The public awareness of the settlement had also risen considerably, which meant an increasing potential for political support. For a moment in the summer of 2014, the Free Cuvry was almost trendy.

On 26 July, a large theatre event was staged there. More important, though, was the 'Day of Open Cuvry' on 2 August. It included a public discussion, involving neighbours, supporters and residents. In this public meeting participants formulated the camp's problems and drew up a list of priorities: improving the sanitary conditions at the site; helping the Roma in accessing social services; fighting violence, sexism and homophobia; upgrading the camp's organisational structure; resisting a possible eviction; mobilising the support of leftist groups; and, working out concepts for the future of the site. A new plenary, the 'Monday Plenum', emerged from that discussion. The new plenary saw as its main tasks to improve the conditions on the site and prevent an eviction of the squatters. This involved gaining support from local politicians to install toilet facilities on site, among other things.

Just as the political organisation of the site seemed to take shape, however, the political pressure on the site also rose. With the arrival of the Roma, several children had begun to live on site. In mid-September the city authorities threatened to take the Roma children into care homes because, the officials claimed, they were not being taken care of properly. The Monday plenary attempted to respond to this threat by seeking negotiations involving Berlin-based Roma cultural associations and city officials. However, many Roma from the Free Cuvry site also decided to leave the camp temporarily to avoid having their children taken away from them.

The eviction

On the evening of 18 September 2014, a fire broke out in the south-western part of the camp and quickly engulfed several huts. The blaze's fast spread and the unusually high flames seemed to indicate a firebomb attack. Soon, the fire brigade and the police arrived and the camp's residents were asked to leave the site for their safety and to enable investigations into the causes of the fire. In the course of the night and morning, the police decided to use the situation to permanently evict the Free Cuvry camp. The residents were initially told that they could return to their huts after the fire had been extinguished and a forensic investigation had been conducted. In the morning, with additional police in place, the residents, as well as the public, were finally told that an eviction of Free Cuvry was being implemented. The whole site was fenced off and residents were only allowed back, one or two at a time, with police escort, to retrieve their possessions.

The police officially stated that the squatters left the camp voluntarily because of the fire – a claim in stark contradiction to all the statements made to the authors by the camp's residents. The officers also arrested four Eastern European residents on suspicion of arson. They allegedly set fire to the shed of an African resident after a fight. However, all those arrested were soon released without charge. The cause of the fire was never established. Several residents we spoke to accused the police, or the owner of the site deliberately starting the fire to create a pretext for the eviction, and all agreed that the fire provided the police with a convenient opportunity to clear out the camp. A few days after the eviction, the camp was literally razed to the ground by bulldozers, leaving hardly any trace of the community that had existed here.

The eviction left some 120 people homeless. While some residents could rely on alternative accommodation, most were out on the streets and in smaller green spaces in the neighbourhood. The police repressed and dissolved any attempt made by the former residents to stay together as a group over the next few days. Several protest actions took place on the day of the eviction and in the following weeks and months. Perhaps the most publically visible protest was the decision by graffiti

Figures 19.4 and 19.5: After the eviction the buildings were bulldozed to the ground (Credit: Niko Rollmann)

artist 'Blu' to remove his famous, large-scale murals from the site to prevent them becoming selling points for future real estate plans on the site (Henke, 2014). Several other protests continued over the site, which, at the time of writing, remains an empty plot.

Conclusion

In the introduction to this chapter we highlighted how many protest camps attempt to combine expressive protest with the creation of alternative spaces of social reproduction that sustain daily life. We discussed the ways that camps sometimes struggle to reconcile those two elements, and how combining them can pose challenges. These challenges are often related to the merging of private and public spaces inside the camp. Certain forms of political protest require a logic of action and strategy that may clash with the logics and requirements of sustaining home spaces. The aspiration to provide home spaces in combination with protest action is also related to resources. The provision and maintenance of the infrastructures of protest and social reproduction requires a lot of energy. In many urban protest camps the provision of care and social reproduction is met by a larger demand of those who find themselves in destitute or precarious conditions, for example those who are homeless. We highlighted the larger, perhaps global, context in which protest camps today increasingly also concern the housing question and homelessness. Urban protest camps are attractive for some destitute and homeless city dwellers because they provide relative safety and access to more resources. In light of the attempts of housing movements and poor urbanites to provide autonomous housing solutions, protest camps also potentially form spaces where coalitions can be built to support such struggles. In their provision of home places, protest camps reveal their potential to prefigure autonomous solutions to the housing question. But when camps attempt to provide alternative comprehensive care and social reproduction for people in need, its broader politics and strategy will be dominated by this conjuncture. Furthermore, the collaboration between 'voluntary' and 'involuntary' campers is difficult, often fraught, because of a lack of reflection about some campers' relative privilege, complications from cultural barriers and mutual misunderstandings between the groups.

In the experience of Free Cuvry, it is possible to identify a clear split between what Schein (2012) has referred to as voluntary and involuntary occupiers. To some extent this separation was also reflected in the dual character of Free Cuvry, as a camp that protested against gentrification and aimed to prevent the building of high end real estate, and as a camp in which some of Berlin's poorest inhabitants aimed to create autonomous shelter. The Free Cuvry occupation came into being as a protest, but it quickly became what would later be described as a community, a village, or by some more derogatory commentators, a favela or a slum. The project showed the potential of combining practices of protest and care, as the anti-gentrification protest worked like a shield under which a number of involuntary occupiers could seek cover from the usual repression. From within this shield, these involuntary occupiers could, at least in theory, build collective organisation that addressed their social exclusion. This shield function evidently worked for those who joined Free Cuvry and used it as a base for a more autonomous self-organisation of their life. But these necessities prevented, in many cases, a more political engagement with the site, leading to a tendency of individualisation of living in the camp.

This was problematic for two reasons: first, it meant that there was an increasing lack in the overall quality of the care provided in the camp, with problems such as rubbish and sanitation that required collective structures not being addressed. Second, there was hardly any work done towards developing a strategy to harness the symbolic power of the anti-gentrification camp for the development of a long-term alternative proposal for the site. In the absence of political organisation, conditions deteriorated on site, and formerly sympathetic neighbours turned against the Free Cuvry. Only the threat of eviction, a result to some extent of the declining solidarity among neighbours, brought supporters back to the site with the explicit aim to re-politicise the camp. The Monday plenary made some slow progress towards this aim, but the new drive was undermined by the eventual eviction in September 2014.

Much of the Free Cuvry experience is very specific to the context in which the occupation occurred. It emerged in an environment characterised by a relatively high tolerance towards squats and protest camps. A camp-like occupation of high value private land over more than two years was partly enabled by the very specific place the camp was in. Even in a place like Kreuzberg where much knowledge exists over the potential of alternative lifestyles to enrich urban commons, the same form of long-term integration would have had to be envisioned and pursued to enable the camp's survival. The Monday plenary also started working on such a vision, imaging a communalisation of the land in a community land trust and to develop Free Cuvry into an autonomous but stable and legalised tent city. The example of the tent city movement in the US shows that such projects are not necessarily pipe dreams any longer (Heben, 2012). The pursuit of such a long-term strategy, however, would have required a political coalition beyond the camp and its supporters in the Berlin radical left, to local councillors at least.

In circumstances where Free Cuvry attracted a group of highly diverse residents, many of whom had to focus on immediate concerns of survival and social reproduction, the scope for such strategic considerations was small. Moreover, a strategy of communication and coalitions with local politicians is highly controversial among protest movements in the city. After a number of 'consultation processes' and 'listening exercises', many activists see no viable strategy in working with existing institutions. In the absence of a strategy and long-term goals, the default politics of the site was increasingly dominated by a 'free for all' spirit. In the long run, both the camp's autonomous ethos and its diverse population made co-operation (beyond a reaction to threats of eviction) very difficult.

It thus seems that some stronger focus on building a political strategy for the camp and concerted attempts at political organisation would have been necessary to enable the building of a more permanent institutionalised form. It is also important to note what the camp did achieve, over more than two years of existence, in the absence of much strategy: it managed to hold an investor at bay, as its ragged appearance mocked expensive and prestigious gentrification projects across the city. It also challenged the shiny 'New Berlin' image the city's authorities were so keen to promote. And even with the camp gone, the site still showed considerable strength as a political symbol – provoking regular actions and attempts at re-occupation.

For a broader consideration of the role protest camps play in the global housing struggle, the Free Cuvry experience offers evidence of new urban movements that address the housing question, resisting the impositions of global rent regimes and real estate speculation in anti-gentrification activism. By building communities, tent cities, and camps where shelter and care is autonomously provided, these newly forming movements show the potential to actively pursue alternatives. They can combine insights from decades of squatting experiences in affluent societies of the global north, with strategies for the self-organisation of autonomous housing solutions pursued in the global south. However, future camps and occupations will have to come to terms with the significance of the unfolding social crisis and be realistic about available resources This will require acknowledging the limits of what autonomous shelter and care provision can do, and it may require a willingness, at times, to work pragmatically with progressive urban authorities.

References

Apin, N. (2014) *Bier, Sonnenuntergang, Pfandflaschenkrieg*, HAU theatre program for its 'Treffpunkte: Das Private im öffentlichen Raum' [Beer, Sunset, Bottlewar, HAU theatre programm for its 'Meetingpoints: The Private in Public Space'] season 1–26 October, 28–29.

Breines, W. (1989) *Community and Organization in the New Left, 1962–1968: The Great Refusal*. New Brunswick, NJ: Rutgers University Press.

Colomb, C. (2012) *Staging the New Berlin: Place Marketing and the Politics of Urban Reinvention Post-1989*. London and New York: Routledge.

Colomb, C. and Novy, J. (2016) *Protest and Resistance in the Tourist City*. London and New York: Routledge.

Cornell, A. (2011) *Oppose and Propose: Lessons from Movement for a New Society*. Oakland, CA: AK Press.

Crossley, N. (2002) 'Global anti-corporate struggle: a preliminary analysis', *British Journal of Sociology*, 53(4), 667–691.

Davis, M. (2006) *Planet of Slums*. London and New York: Verso.

Day, R.J.F. (2005) *Gramsci is Dead: Anarchist Currents in the Newest Social Movements*. London; Ann Arbor, MI: Toronto: Pluto Press.

Ehrenreich, B. (2011) 'Throw them out with the trash: why homelessness is becoming an Occupy Wall Street issue', *TomDispatch. Com*, www.tomdispatch.com/archive/175457/barbara_ehrenreich_homeless_in_america.

Featherstone, D. (1997) 'Regaining the inhuman city: the "pure genius" land occupation', *Soundings*, 7(Autumn), 45–60.

Feigenbaum, A., Frenzel, F. and McCurdy, P. (2013) *Protest Camps*. London: Zed.

Frenzel, F. (2014) 'Exit the system? Anarchist organisation in the British climate camps', *Ephemera*, 14(4), 901–921.

Frenzel, F., Feigenbaum, A. and McCurdy, P. (2014) 'Protest camps: an emerging field of social movement research', *The Sociological Review*, 62(3), 457–74.

Frenzel, F. (2016) *Slumming it: the tourist valorisation of urban poverty*. London: Zed.

Geronimo (2012) *Fire and Flames: A History of the German Autonomist Movement*. Oakland, CA: PM Press.

Gordon, U. (2007) *Anarchy Alive!: Anti-Authoritarian Politics From Practice to Theory*. London; Ann Arbor, MI: Pluto Press.

Halvorsen, S. (2015) 'Taking space: moments of rupture and everyday life in Occupy London', *Antipode*, 47(2), 401–417.

Heben, A. (2012) *Tent City Urbanism*. San Bernardino, CA: CreateSpace Independent Publishing Platform.

Henke, L. (2014) 'Why we painted over Berlin's most famous graffiti', *Guardian*, www.theguardian.com/commentisfree/2014/dec/19/why-we-painted-over-berlin-graffiti-kreuzberg-murals.

Hernádi, S, (2015) 'Eine Favela in Berlin?' [A Favela in Berlin?], *MieterEcho*, 372(February), 10.

Holm, A. and Kuhn, A. (2011) 'Squatting and urban renewal: the interaction of squatter movements and strategies of urban restructuring in Berlin', *International Journal of Urban and Regional Research*, 35(3), 644–658.

hooks, bell. (1990) *Yearning: race, gender, and cultural politics*. Boston MA: South End Press.

Jeffrey, A., McFarlane, C. and Vasudevan, A. (2012) 'Rethinking enclosure: space, subjectivity and the commons', *Antipode*, 44(4), 1247–1267.

Juris, J. S. (2007) 'Practicing militant ethnography with the movement for global resistance in Barcelona', in S. Shukaitis and D. Graeber (eds) *Constituent Imagination*. Oakland, CA: AK Press.

Keseling, U. (2014) 'Die Berliner und der Kampf um Freiraum' [The Berliner and the struggle for free spaces'], *Berliner Illustrirte Zeitung* (weekend supplement of the *Berliner Morgenpost*), 22 June, 4–5.

Kuhn, A. (2014) *Vom Häuserkampf zur neoliberalen Stadt: Besetzungsbewegungen in Berlin und Barcelona* [*From housing struggle to the neoliberal city: Squatter Movements in Berlin and Barcelona*]. Münster: Westfälisches Dampfboot.

Leidinger, C. (2011) 'Kontroverse Koalitionen im politischen Laboratorium Camp – antimilitaristisch-feministische Bündnisse und Bündisarbeit als kontingente, soziale Prozesse' ['Contested coalitions in the political laboratory protest camp – anti-military feminist groups and their group work as contingent social practice'], *Oesterereichische Zeitschrift Fuer Politikwissenschaft*, 40(3), 283–300.

Melucci, A. (1996) *Challenging Codes: Collective Action in the Information Age*. Cambridge and New York: Cambridge University Press.

Müller, S. (2014) 'Deutschlands erste Favela' ['Berlin's first Favela'], *Stern*, 33, 88–96.

Novy, J. (2013) '"Berlin does not love you": notes on Berlin's "tourism controversy" and its discontents', in M. Bernt, B. Grell and A. Holm (eds), *The Berlin Reader: A Compendium on Urban Change and Activism* Bielefeld: Transcript, pp. 223–237.

Offe, C. (1987) 'Challenging the boundaries of institutional politics: social movements since the 1960s', in C. Maier (ed) *Changing Boundaries of the Political: Essays on the Evolving Balance Between the State and Society, Public and Private in Europe*. Cambridge and New York: Cambridge University Press, pp 63–105.

Schein, R. (2012) 'Whose occupation? Homelessness and the politics of park encampments', *Social Movement Studies*, 11(3–4), 335–341, doi.org/10.1080/14742837.2012.708834.

Spiegel Online (2012) 'Back to the lab: Guggenheim cancels "high risk" Berlin project', *Spiegel Online*, www.spiegel.de/international/zeitgeist/guggenheim-lab-cancels-berlin-project-a-822853.html.

Stengers, I. (2005) 'The Cosmopolitical proposal', in B. Latour and P. Weibel (eds), *Making Things Public: Atmospheres of Democracy*. Cambridge, MA: MIT Press, and Karlsruhe: ZKM/Center for Art and Media, pp 994–1003.

Uldam, J. and McCurdy, P. (2013) 'Studying social movements: challenges and opportunities for participant observation', *Sociology Compass*, 7(11), 941–951.

Van Duppen, J. (2010) 'The Cuvrybrache as free place: the diverse meanings of a wasteland in Berlin', MSc dissertation in Urban Geography, July, Utrecht: Utrecht University.

Vasudevan, A. (2015) *Metropolitan Preoccupations: The Spatial Politics of Squatting in Berlin*. Oxford: Wiley Blackwell.

Wacquant, L. (2008) *Urban Outcasts: A Comparative Sociology of Advanced Marginality*. Cambridge: Polity.

TWENTY

Security is no accident: considering safe(r) spaces in the transnational Migrant Solidarity camps of Calais[1]

Claire English

Introduction

The issue of migrants coming together in large numbers in Calais gained political significance in two waves. During the 1990s, after the fall of the 'communist' regimes of Eastern Europe, people arrived in Calais fleeing the former Yugoslavia, including an influx of Kosovan families and children (Rumford, 2012, 2). A second wave occurred following the 11 September attacks and the raft of new 'anti-terror' legislation linking immigration, especially of Afghanis and Iraqis, with 'national security' issues (Rumford, 2012, 10) sparking the attention of the mainstream press. The continued ill-treatment of migrants, despite its illegality under international law prompted a solidarity camp of international activists, local French people and the migrant communities in Calais forming a collective organisation and space to organise from, this group has come to be known as Calais Migrant Solidarity.

This chapter assesses the work of Calais Migrant Solidarity over the past six years as a project and experiment in ways that activists collectively reproduce themselves as a multitude or community of many in the camps of Calais. This is undertaken through bringing a much-needed feminist analysis to the organisational practices in this collective, while paying attention the highly emotionally fraught environment tempered by the wide-ranging subjectivities and experiences of those involved. One suggested method for mediating disputes and disagreements is the mobilisation of safer spaces policies to regulate individual behaviour in the camps, and this chapter will analyse this method. Specifically, this chapter examines notions of safety, Otherness and 'intersectional inclusion' (Roestone Collective, 2014) and looks at the ways that activists negotiate individual experiences of 'negative' affect (especially 'bad' feelings like being unsafe or vulnerable or at risk). It is hoped that it might be possible to find ways to collectivise experiences of vulnerability, enacting an individually and collectively differentiated construction of solidarity through the spaces created together.

Methodology

My examination of the practices and conceptual underpinnings of safety in migrant solidarity organising emerges from my participation, particularly over three years (2011–2014) in both London and Calais with London No Borders and Calais Migrant Solidarity, No one is Illegal and similar groups. I also conducted 15 personal interviews with solidarity activists sourced directly through my personal activist networks. Additionally, I draw on activist resources such as grievance policies, materials associated with solidarity camp training days, activist trauma support literature and other social movement documents, particularly regarding safe(r) space policies and trauma or activist support. My research is largely conducted as an 'insider' activist and relates to the common problems raised by activists about the ways that we organise with others. I have chosen to focus on the communities with whom I am directly involved rather than attempting to summarise the experiences of migrants travelling through in Calais, who are clearly the recipients of much more specific and concrete attempts by the border authorities to compromise their physical and emotional safety in systematic ways.

Within the collectives in which I participate there has been a shift in recent years towards embracing concepts such as safer spaces, community accountability and grassroots justice. This has happened in an attempt to transform current models of conflict resolution that could otherwise depend on the systemically racialised models of punishment such as incarceration or institutionalisation, or models that rely on social isolation such as expulsions. Drawing on the wisdom and practices of organisations such as INCITE! Women of Color Against Violence, Reclaim Justice Network (http://downsizingcriminaljustice. wordpress.com), Critical Resistance (http://criticalresistance.org) and the Creative Interventions Toolkit (www.creative-interventions.org), my interviews with solidarity activists revealed that individuals and collectives are attempting to consolidate a more effective and anti-oppressive ethic of care in dispute resolution processes – although there is as yet no consensus on either the best outcomes or practices associated with this.

Safer spaces policies

Safer spaces policies, in particular since the Occupy camps during 2011, have relied upon the supposed power of creating a written document that announces a space as safe, and the hope that people will either self-regulate or be prepared to be 'called out' in case any oppressive behaviour occurs (Coalition for Safer Spaces, 2010). For activist networks such as Occupy and Calais Migrant Solidarity, part of establishing an anti–authoritarian ethic is in the mobilisation of 'safer spaces' policies[2] to deal with those activities or attitudes perceived as oppressive or violent that occur *within* the core locations of the camps or organisations concerned. Chronologically, these policies emerged alongside particular activist projects focusing on models of transformative/restorative/community 'justice', that radical individuals use to deal with issues of sexism, racism, homophobia, transphobia or even assault that occur in these communities and spaces (CARA, 2007; INCITE!, 2013). Such approaches are used as an alternative to calling in the police or other state agencies to settle these matters. The 'safer spaces' policy and recent activist projects concerning community justice come partly from an acknowledgement that the legal systems in mainstream society cannot regulate sexual (Serisier, 2013) or other sets of personal relations in a way that is either fair or adequate. There are various critiques of safer spaces that have emerged in recent years. These will be discussed in the final section of this chapter and are related to the key questions of this chapter: is it desirable for people in social movements to always feel safe? Who tends to be 'Othered', or carry the 'bad feelings' in situations of conflict?

By seeking to identify safety as an affect constructed around an unspoken agreement on 'correct' behaviour and 'incorrect' behaviour this can lead to a politics of regulation and normalisation, based on the idea that there is a majority who understand the ethical/moral/desirable conduct, and they are responsible for admonishing those who do not adhere. This not only relies upon the idea that there is or can be a shared understanding of this behaviour across all experiences, but also may exclude and further isolate those with no relationship to these 'norms', or subject positions that escape normative classification. Overall this chapter intends to reflect on the way notions of safety were established and negotiated at the Calais No Border Camp 2009 and in Calais Migrant Solidarity as an organisation in the aftermath of the camp.

Calais Migrant Solidarity and No Border camps

Calais Migrant Solidarity is an activist collective established at the end of the Calais No Border protest camp in the summer of 2009. No Border camps are one of the No Border network's main projects, organised on local as well as international scales and attracting from a couple of hundred to thousands of participants. These camps are set up as spaces in which to exchange experiences, to engage in political education and debate, and take direct action against the regime of border controls (Alberti, 2010, 140). Normally the presence of activists in the location of the camp is short lived. CMS and its on-going presence in Calais is an exception made possible by consistent fundraising and streams of activists volunteering their time. In keeping with the protest camp ethic, historically the group has provided a place for visiting activists to sleep. These places have included 'the office', 'the hangar', and different squatted spaces including more recently an encampment next to the Tioxide factory.[3] In addition to being sleeping spaces for visiting activists these places often serve as a place of encounter for different groups of migrants who don't often necessarily interact with each other. These places have brought together Afghans, Syrians, Iraqi-Kurds, Egyptians, Sudanese, Eritreans, among others, and allowed space for discussion. The No Border Network and its camps tend to focus on direct action politics, aiming at political interventions rather than the provision of direct assistance for migrants and there are on-going arguments about how to negotiate our activism alongside our critiques of attempts at the recuperation of voluntary social work through ideas such as 'the big society' (Ishkanian, 2014) and its prescriptive ideas of citizenship.

Reflections on safety and space at the Calais No Border Camp

At my arrival in Calais for the No Border Camp in 2009, there was three days left of preparation before the official start date. There were a number of activities that needed to be carried out; digging toilets and building showers, setting up the 'welcome tent', and writing a safer space policy. I noted in my fieldwork for my master's thesis that it was much easier to find volunteers to dig toilets than write guidelines about safety and protest camps (English, 2010, 6). Finally, the task was taken on by a working group of mostly young men who were keen to take oppressive behaviours seriously, but weren't especially sure where to begin (English, 2010, 6). The original version in English was delayed until only an hour before the opening meeting and the translations of the document (most meetings were translated into six languages) weren't finished until the camp was nearly over. Many participants considered this a failure in collective responsibility.

On the fourth day of the camp, a group complaint was brought to the evening general meeting. There were reports of 'Afghan men' unzipping women's tents and attempting to enter them without invitation, resulting in accounts such as this, '

A lot of women...felt unsafe at the camp with incidents of men hanging round tents asking women if they could come in and sexual harassment. However, in true DIY[4] form women organised to improve this situation, taking turns patrolling the area' (www.lasthours.org.uk/articles/no-border-in-calais/).

The nature of the complaint was one that brought the as yet uncatered for questions of safety and security at the camp to the fore. At the Calais No Border camp we had neither a collectively agreed safer spaces policy nor an alternative to expelling or penalising those who acted outside of (un-agreed) norms. When no consensus was reached at the general meeting as to how to move forward, a group of women called their own meeting to discuss what to do. In the meeting a number of strategies were put forward. Those who felt upset were to speak in confidence with members of the trauma support team. This team included Sofia, whom I interviewed. She confirmed that there was a level of distress at the camp that was difficult to deal with, as not only were tents being unzipped, but there were number of complaints about aggressive British men who had been drinking too much among numerous other safety concerns.

As there is always a pressure to 'put aside' issues that appear to pose gender against race when organising in Calais (interview with Rita[5]) a response was formulated with little debate. In effect a group of women set up a 'security group' to patrol the sleeping areas.[6] Perhaps not unlike the development of Neighbourhood Watch groups, the intention of which are to be community minded but can inadvertently lead to the racialisation of 'suspicious behaviour', the security group was cause for concern for many at the camp.

Problematising the 'Feminist Security Group' and white women as bearers of morality

The Feminist Security Group comprised of a group of volunteers (mostly women, many from the queer bloc) regularly monitoring the encampment at night in shifts of two to four hours. This would involve walking through the tents with torches asking if everyone was 'feeling okay' and encouraging those who seemed 'too intoxicated', to go to bed. For many, these 'patrols' created an incredibly awkward presence at the camp. It was only in place for the final two nights of the camp before everyone returned to their homes. Seemingly there was not enough time to reflect or discuss the call-outs that emerged to form this group, including 'Who is available to monitor the Afghan area?' (cited in English, 2010, 8).

Postcolonial theory can help to understand that such a situation in some ways mirrors a colonial discourse in which white women are mobilised as bearers of morality, piety and sexual purity against the 'uncivilised Other' (Perry, 1997, 501). Perry writes that 'as individual wives, architects of female society, or even as available objects of male desire, white women were constructed as natural agents of social control' (1997, 502). This is not to accuse those involved in the group as guilty of 'civilisational thinking'. It is however important to notice that the intersectional thinking was missing from the analysis here, bringing forth a drive to posit those from a certain 'race' against those of a certain 'gender' with little attention to social and historical factors shaping this analysis.

The Feminist Security Group, and its critics, mobilised understandings of power in particular ways. An example of this is below,

> My skin colour means I am less likely to suffer violence at the hands of the police, and many other less obvious unearned privileges…(but) My gender, or people's perception of my gender, means that I am often seen as a second-class citizen, especially by those who come from *heavily patriarchal societies*. In Calais I have met many people who have become my friends, but I have also had moments where the inferiority with which people regard me has become…obvious, talking about me in a derogatory way… following me to my tent during the camp, and refusing to engage with me…because of my gender. The jungle has been described as an 'open prison', made of predominantly men, and because of this I can understand some of the reasons for these behaviours, but it does not make it acceptable.[7] (Calais9, 2009, emphasis added)

A generalisable environment of safety for all those participating in the camp is the goal of a safer space policy, but enabling an equalised 'level' space is neither desirable nor possible according to some of my interview participants. Fifteen Interviews were conducted with No

Borders Activists and feminist activists in 2013. Those mentioned in this chapter are anonymised and referred to as Kavita, Mia, Anna, Rita Sofia, Jack, and Jeremy. Some argue that the way to end sexism in solidarity movements is to 'stick around through the drama and earn your stripes with the oppressed group in question'. But this is neither possible nor desirable for most people. Is it possible to reach an idea of safety collectively? Can we find an agreement that respects the needs of marginalised communities and the vulnerabilities that we each bring to the solidarity camp? Could a policy regulating safety in the camp have averted this situation? In the remainder of this chapter I attempt to locate four considerations that my interviewees believed necessary in order to negotiate 'safer practice' within transnational migrant solidarity organising.

Four considerations for safer spaces and migrant solidarity projects

Safety and substances and limits

One of the critiques of collectives that use existing, codified safer space policies agreed upon before an event was that in many ways they'd become what was referred to as a 'box-ticking' activity.

> I mean sometimes there's a piece of paper that people write stuff on, so they're 'doing' safe spaces but…you get to meetings and actually they're not creating a safe space… People talk about safe spaces, consensus decision-making, vegan food, and it just becomes something that comes with it rather than anything meaningful. (Interview with Anna)

This is reminiscent of the themes in Sara Ahmed's examination of how the Race Relations Amendment Act (2000) has shaped a new politics of documentation. She argues that the distinction between 'meeting the requirements', 'fulfilling the requirements' and 'compliance' is crucial (Ahmed, 2007, 595). This can be extrapolated to safer spaces policies. Putting up a policy on the wall (meeting the requirements), asking people to read the policy upon entering the space or even signing a document saying that they will act accordingly (fulfilling the requirements), and creating an organising space that is safe(r) than the outside world (compliance) all differ dramatically.

Kavita noted that the process of creating safer space is achieved collectively and is more important than the document itself,

Kavita: The point originally wasn't the document *but the process of getting there* and now it's like, well, if we've lost the document we can print one off the internet…And it will probably be from North America so it will use expressions that most of us don't use here like 'Folk of Color'. Like, who? (Interview with Kavita).

The purpose of a safer spaces policy is to ensure that people wishing to share an organising space will agree to behave appropriately for the culture of that space, even if it is not an agreement they participated in composing. Kavita pointed out that there is likely to eventually be a situation where people do not agree with the ideas prescribed by that policy and asked, what then? '

It's all very social contract as well isn't it? Sign something, agree to something. What if you don't agree? Cos the point of the Safe Space policy is surely that when it's controversial you're undone. Unless something's done to enforce it…So unless there's some come-uppance to it.'This led on to a discussion linked to the earlier ideas of community accountability and transformative justice referenced in the introduction[8] but with the caveat that there is an added level of complexity when someone involved in your project is unable to comply with safer space policies due to their methods of managing their vulnerability, that is, through the use or overuse of substances. This is relevant as the environment in Calais is one of a high stress a lot of the time, mostly caused by impeding immigration raids or police harassment. I witnessed this tension during my fieldwork, March 2013 and throughout my involvement with CMS since its establishment. Some people are suffering with post-traumatic stress symptoms or other mental health problems resulting from their time in warzones or due to difficult personal circumstances. There is very little support in Calais for either migrants or activists.[9] In some cases this can lead to self-medicating, often in the form of alcohol consumption. The presence of alcohol can indicate a less-than-safe environment for some people, ex-addicts, and abuse survivors, among others. Whether this immediately makes the space unsafe is not clear though. My experience of the office in Calais is that it is often fairly contained during the day, but can become quite drunken and rowdy in the evenings with those who are not attempting to cross the border that night attempting to unwind with activists and local people. I wrote the following fieldnotes during my most recent trip to Calais,

We (Virginia and I) were the only women in the office of about 30 men and were getting attention, but no one hassled us – they were seemingly just pleased to have different company. One guy followed us around, but I think it was more because he was confused than aggressive, and he was visibly drunk. He kept asking 'You take me in car, England, yes?' and then going away for a minute before returning again. He repeated this to us about 50 times, it was more tiresome than intimidating, but he was a big guy and I didn't really know what he thought we could do for him – he'd be much too big to hide in a car. In the end he followed us to the car that was taking us to the train station. He was still repeating the same question and wouldn't let us shut the car door – that felt something between scary and painful – I could feel his frustration. I felt really sad about that guy. He was too drunk to be nimble enough to cross to the UK that night, I wondered how long he'd been trapped in the office drinking cans of beer asking women not to take the train, and realised it could have been a long time. It didn't feel to me that the guy was dangerous, just stuck. In lots of ways, stuck. (Fieldnotes, March 2013)

Alcohol consumption, be it recommendations of limited intake or total sobriety have featured in discussions about how to run communal spaces in other activist spaces such as Occupy Wall Street and Occupy Sandy.[10] When demands for 'safe' behaviours from all individuals were made, some people were being isolated from the group, including the homeless people who usually slept on the sites of the demonstrations who were told off for being noisy and drunk, 'badly behaved', and disturbing the activists who were trying to sleep.[11] Thus an attempt was made to develop guidelines to prevent exclusionary demands for 'safety'.

This is also a theme that comes through in some literature on safer spaces. The Roestone Collective describe safer spaces as a 'relational work' (2014, 1347). By examining safe spaces through the relational work of creating and maintaining them, they find that this reconfigures the experience of space as safe or unsafe (2014, 1348). In other words, it is through a critical cultivation of these kinds of spaces (be they aiming for 'safety' or simply attempting to open the possibility for engagement from as many people as possible) that these policies begin to matter. While safety is a question of collectivising agreement where possible, it is also a question of material needs, including infrastructure and our ability to find funding for crisis situations, for example to re-accommodate someone assaulted at an encampment.

Safety in/as separation

Within activist communities some hold the belief that by organising 'autonomously' individuals can be free of or buffered from oppressive social relations. By 'autonomous' this means the formation of independent groups of people who face specific forms of exploitation and oppression – including but not limited to people of colour, women, queers, trans or gender nonconforming people and others.[12] In my fieldwork in Calais there were various reported experiments with 'women only' sleeping spaces for both activists and migrant communities. I learned during my fieldwork that this format was eventually abandoned as many of the women had travelled with male comrades or lovers and wanted to be able to sleep in the same space as them. Connected to this there was a rule outlined in the office that activists (though this was only mentioned in relation to women's safety) would be strongly advised not to sleep overnight in the migrant camps without another activist with them. This rule relied upon the assumption that women are more likely to be safe alone with other activist (mostly white) men in the office than with the migrant men in the jungles. Not everyone agreed. Janeska, to whom I spoke during my fieldwork in August 2013, recounted the following series of events,

> When I was in Calais another activist approached me and said, "I know the rules are that women shouldn't hang out in migrant circles by ourselves overnight…But right now the activist house is full of men I don't know and actually the migrant house is full of men I do know who I've been socialising with for three months and…I just don't care I'm gonna sleep up there with them" and at the end of the day what argument can you make about that? If that's where she feels safe then that's fine. I mean actually what happened was there was a raid really late at night and she got scared and it didn't work out that there was a safe space for her in the activist house or in the migrant house…there was nowhere. (Janeska, personal communication, 2013)

Trying to mediate the complexities of solidarity work in Calais through encouraging coalescence around identity may obscure the intersectional and personal experiences of both what feels oppressive and what feels safe, leading to assumptions about what particular groups need in order to be involved in the project. Following black feminist scholars, the Roestone collective argue that what is needed to challenge patriarchy is experimentations with intersectional inclusion. To foster this, one interviewee's suggestion was that groups spend more time in collective reflection (interviews with Rita and Sofia, 2013), but there are surely many other ways to do this.

Safety in reflexivity

Most of the people I interviewed who had spent time in Calais were amenable to, and some desperately keen for, a discussion of collective safety. However, there was a resistance to it as well. There was both a feeling that as activists 'they didn't need it personally' (interviews with Jeremy and Jack), that it was something likely to be needed by others, and that this somehow meant that the discussion should be initiated only by those others. Jack said that he had seen Trauma Support Spaces and Safer Spaces (which he thought of as the same or very similar) at camps before but,

> To be honest I've never really interacted with them, I've probably got a distorted view...I've really only heard people in the trauma support group come along to meetings...and I've thought, 'Hmmm, this all sounds a bit wishy washy.' Now maybe if I was actually in trauma and in need of some support I would find it really helpful...but I've not actually engaged with it...(Interview with Jack)

The interview with Jack was interesting, his personal experience of discomfort or lack of safety in activist movements was tied more to fear of physical assault from outsiders (fascists, for example) than it was to mediating experiences or interactions between activists. He was able to reflect upon the fact that women, queers and migrants might need extra support, but he was 'waiting for their lead' (interview with Jack). The interview with Jeremy was similar in tone when reflecting on his experience of organising in migrant solidarity groups,

> At times the gender composition has been unbalanced... most of the time when organising, going on actions... gender has never been brought up at all, which is not necessarily a good thing...The problem is that I don't really know how to discuss these things with a lot of the people

in the migrant community. I don't think I yet have the tools to do that. (Interview with Jeremy)

I asked Jeremy how he thought that the tools could be gained to talk about forms of gendered and racialised oppression present within the collective, and whether he thought people would set aside the time for that. He answered that he thought that more recently people had become interested in intersectional politics and that the climate to talk about it was upon us 'if time could be allocated' but he was doing his own work on the issue as an individual activist.

> The intersectional politics that I've encountered has always come from outside of solidarity networks as it's difficult to set aside time and...I think that's bad...I feel like No Borders is constructed by intersectional politics and it's included in it but it's never talked about explicitly..., but then I'm trying in my own way to construct and understand these differences through the actions that I commit. (Interview with Jeremy)

It is important to learn from these contributions. Stengel and Weems (2010) and bell hooks (1990) argue that in the quest for safety we must remember that discomfort does not impede learning. The Roestone Collective argue that individuals in collective environments should feel 'safe enough' – but not necessarily comfortable – to voice their opinions and constructively respond to their peers. This is the kind of atmosphere of reflexivity that may be necessary to change the culture of silence around safety and Otherness in shared organising spaces. It is not easy to talk about how each person experiences safety within these shared spaces, but creating an atmosphere where we attempt to reflect on these differences is perhaps a place to start.

Safety in complexity

In this final section I would like to look at the way an atmosphere of safety may be constructed through universalising particular actions or traits as 'normal' and 'to be expected' from particular groups but not others, exacerbating Orientalist and gendered tendencies in collective thinking. The Roestone Collective observe that strategies to create safety often fail to critically engage with the paradigms that underlie harassment and discrimination (2014, 8), that is, structural and institutional forms of oppression such as racism and sexism may not be addressed in trying to create safer spaces, if they are designed to moderate individual behaviour rather than looking at systems of power. This can result in the following

> I think in Calais you're often in the situation where your race defines you more than your gender, so the westerners that come over to do No Borders migrant solidarity actions are often seen as a homogenous group, some of them are obviously targeted or treated differently because of their gender but I think that race is more of a division in that space than gender. (Interview with Jeremy, Feb 2013)

There is a certain expectation from some activists in Calais that anyone who comes to do solidarity work will agree to be in the space 'primarily' to show solidarity to migrants (fieldwork, March 2013). This has at different times resulted in complaints that women are not being taken seriously, as their concerns are not as important as those arising from the 'division put in place by race' (interview with Jeremy). The attempt to 'rank' forms of oppression is one of the many reasons that an intersectional analysis has had an impact on the politics of solidarity, at least in intention if not in practice. This, along with a desire to universalise categories of 'all women' and 'all men' to avoid racial or cultural essentialism, can in fact lead to the marginalisation of women and non-binary people and an entrenching of sexism and (Orientalist) racism. The following section is from an interview with Sofia about her time at the No Border Camp in Calais as a volunteer at the trauma support group, and as a woman sleeping in a tent alone for the duration of the camp. She described the aftermath of some women reporting being harassed by men,

> *Sofia*: some migrants did try to go into people's tents. One of them tried to come into my tent, maybe about one or two o'clock in the morning and he came again a couple of times…And I didn't feel safe there. But the frustration about this wasn't that he was a migrant…And I knew because of working at the trauma support that drunk European men were making huge trouble too…at the camp, so it wasn't about people coming from Afghanistan.

The way that Sofia recounted this event shows the pressures that have been consistently present in discussions of gender and race in Calais Migrant Solidarity since before its inception. There was a pressure to both hold migrant men and activists to account in the same way so as to not be making excuses based on someone's race on the one hand. On the other hand, there was pressure to ignore certain elements of sexism in the camp because of the difficulties associated with embodying a migrant subjectivity. Seemingly this left the migrants in a position where they could not be expected to understand someone pointing 'get out of my tent' – on account of vagaries attributed to cultural background. Both of these conclusions are reductive, and while a communication directly about these sorts of issues is difficult, especially when you cannot find a translator in the middle of the night, the camp reached a crisis point because a series of problematic assumptions were made on the basis of gender, race and or cultural background. The importance of working through intersectional politics in migrant solidarity projects seems particularly necessary when reflecting upon this and other negotiations of collective safety. Engaging in the work of thinking-through how to make our spaces better is vital to the continuation of effective spaces for solidarity and in order to foster shared spaces to reproduce ourselves as the people we would like to be.

Conclusion

This chapter has sought to explore the different conceptions of safety in migrant solidarity collectives to further identify ways that activists may inadvertently reproduce processes of Othering in the work that is undertaken in our spaces. Othering is perpetrated in a number of ways including the mobilisation of Orientalist conceptions of masculinity, and the desire to universalise individual subjectivities that may in fact have been shaped differently through colonial legacies and other structural forms of inequality. The chapter has instead suggested looking to practices of 'intersectional inclusion' as proposed by scholars including the Roestone Collective as a way to avoid establishing a hierarchy of oppression and subsequently silencing some marginal voices. In the production of safer spaces, one of the lessons is that people should feel 'safe enough' but not necessarily comfortable, as the best spaces for learning are not always spaces that feel completely easy, especially for those from more privileged positions in society. I've proposed some considerations for those that wish to pursue safer space policies as a method of engaging with questions of safety in light of the insights from my fieldwork and interviews.First, an atmosphere of (relative) safety is processual. It is the act of collective writing and discussion that give safer spaces policies their usefulness, not the performance of a small working group producing a piece of writing to stick on a wall. The inclusive collective writing process may avoid alienating some people who would otherwise reject the idea of shared rules or guidelines. In the process of writing it is worth considering who fails to be cared for when creating a safer space – if you are creating a set of rules that might be broken, what happens to those individuals? Every set of guidelines produces dissidents (those who disagree with your rules), assailants (those who forcefully break those rules), and those who might break them as part of their personal issues – such as those with mental health problems, substance users and addicts. There are also infrastructural considerations that need to be taken in to account when dealing with conflicts. Activist organisations need to care for people's safety in exchange for their willingness to do emotional labour. This may include the provision of separate spaces for those involved in the conflict to sleep at night and sometimes even for translators or those supplying counselling services. Our ability to provide relative safety is therefore reliant upon volunteers, funding streams and the maintenance of structures that allow for conflicts to be resolved as fairly as possible. Last, reflexivity is an integral part of any collective that aims at the ongoing participation of marginalised groups. It is paramount to solidarity work – activists should aim to never be 'too busy fighting' to reflect.

Notes

[1] Fifteen interviews were conducted with No Borders Activists and feminist activists in 2013. Those mentioned in this chapter are anonymised and referred to as Kavita, Mia, Anna, Rita Sofia, Jack, and Jeremy.

[2] A safer space is a supportive, non-threatening environment that encourages open-mindedness, respect, a willingness to learn from others, as well as physical and mental safety. It is a space that is critical of the power structures that affect our everyday lives… Everyone who enters a safer space has a responsibility to uphold the values of the space (Coalition for Safer Spaces NYC, 2010).

[3] Some more information on the Tioxide encampment can be found here: https://calaismigrantsolidarity.wordpress.com/page/2/.

[4] DIY in this instance refers to a 'Do it Yourself' style of politics, where activist communities aim to resolve their problems within the community rather than relying upon 'professionals' or the state. This can be installing plumbing and electrics etc, and so on, in squats and social centres, through to finding community solutions to problems of theft, assault, aggression etc.among others (for examples, see McKay,: 1998,; Feigenbaum et al, Frenzel, McCurdy: 2013).

[5] The names of my participants have been anonymised to protect their identities.

[6] Each year there is a donation of tents to Calais Migrant Solidarity following the music festivals in the UK such as Glastonbury. The tentsse donations are invariably made up of the cheapest tents available from the biggest commercial retailers. As a result, there were around 200 tents that looked very similar at the camp in Calais, many were set up next to the activist tents, which were also mostly the cheapest

tents available. One could argue in this situation that if men were unzipping the wrong tents, so possibly, was everyone else -- because so many of the tents looked exactly the same. This is not to discredit those who were being harassed. I am noting this point about the tents because it was a fact strangely absent from reflections at the time.

[7] The harassment of women at the camp and in ongoing ways for the CMS network is something that remains urgent and largely unspoken about. For further discussion on this see English (2014).

[8] These forms of justice attempt to find clarity around how best to seek emotional or physical compensation from those who have made others feel unsafe, including, what is punishment without banishment? What helps survivors believe their attacker has changed and is ready to reengage with the community they have damaged? These questions are not ones this paper will attempt to solve, but the work in this area is inextricably linked with discourses of safety and space.

[9] Some information on Trauma Support for activists in Calais has been produced, but it barely touches on issues of structural oppression and relates more to activist burnout than post- traumatic stress, https://www.activist-trauma.net/assets/files/ATnobor_A5_4pp_leaflet.pdf.

[10] A guide was developed called 'Mindful Occupation', http://mindfuloccupation.org/files/booklet/mindful_occupation_singles_latest.pdf which has a series of suggestions about how people suffering the eaffects of trauma or 'stuck replaying a memory' can 'stay embodied', i.e.that is, in the present, by avoiding alcohol.

[11] 'Sentiments within Occupy that criminalizeise and scapegoat '"the crazies"' often primarily target participants who are homeless and/or people of color. These racist and classist assumptions distract from the ever-present threat of police brutality and depict Occupy as divided and unstable to '"the outside".' (Occupy Mental Health Project, 2012: 9).

[12] More information about this here: https://libcom.org/library/non-negotiable-necessity-autonomous-organizing.

References

Ahmed, S. (2007) 'You end up doing the document rather than doing the doing: Diversity, race equality and the politics of documentation'. *Ethnic and Racial Studies*, 30(4) 590–609. ISSN 01419870

Alberti, G. (2010) 'Open Space Across the Borders of Lesvos: The Gendering of Migrants' Detention in the Aegean' *Feminist Review* (94)1, 134-147

Calais9 (2009) 'Calais Migrant Solidarity', https://calais9.wordpress.com/calais9-zine-text-only

CARA (2007) 'Taking Risks: Implementing Grassroots Accountability Strategies' in *The Revolution Starts at Home*, https://lgbt.wisc.edu/documents/Revolution-starts-at-home.pdf, pp 64-80

Coalition for Safer Spaces (2010) 'What are and Why Support 'Safer' Spaces? Available at: https://saferspacesnyc.wordpress.com/

English, C. (2010) 'Securing solidarity: feminism, migration and agency in the "Jungle" of Calais', MSc dissertation (unpublished), London: London School of Economics and Political Science.

English, C. (2014) 'Bordering on reproducing the state: migrant solidarity collectives and constructions of the other in safer space', in S. Price and R. Sanz-Sabido (eds) *Contemporary Protest and the Legacy of Dissent*. London: Rowman and Littlefield.

Feigenbaum, A., Frenzel, F. and McCurdy, P. (2013) *Protest Camps*. London: Zed.

hooks, bell (1990) *Yearning: Race, Gender and Cultural Politics*. Boston, MA: South End Press.

INCITE! (2013) 'Organising for Community Accountability: How Do We Address Violence within Our Communities? http://mail.incite-national.org/sites/default/files/incite_files/resource_docs/6685_toolkitrev-cmtyacc.pdf

Ishkanian, A. (2014) 'Neoliberalism and violence: the Big Society and the changing politics of domestic violence in England', *Critical Social Policy*, doi: 10.1177/0261018313515973.

Lasthours.org (2009) 'No border in Calais', www.archive.lasthours.org.uk/articles/no-border-in-calais/.

McKay, G. (1998) *DIY Culture: Party and Protest in Nineties Britain*. London: Verso.

Occupy Mental Health Project (Editors) 2012. 'Mindful Occupation: Rising Up Without Burning Out' Icarus Project, AK Press: Oakland

Pendleton, M. and Serisier, T. (2009) 'Beyond the desire for law: sex and crisis in Australian feminist and queer politics', *The Australian Feminist Law Journal*, 31, 77–98.

Perry, A (1997) 'Fair Ones of a Purer Caste: White Women and Colonialism in Nineteenth-Century British Columbia,' *Feminist Studies*, 23, 501–24.

Roestone Collective, T. (2014) 'Safe space: towards a reconceptualization', *Antipode*, 46(5), 1346–1365.

Rumford, C. (2002) Borderworker: 'Looking at how people construct, shift and dismantle borders' available at: https://borderwork.wordpress.com/case-study-calais-france/

Serisier, T. (2013) 'Queer spaces, sexual violence and the desire for safety', V. Bell (ed) *Queer Sexualities: Diversifying Queer, Queering Diversity*. Oxford: Oxford Interdisciplinary Press.

Smith, A. (2013) 'Unsettling the privilege of self-reflexivity', in F. Twine and B. Gardener (eds) *Geographies of Privilege*. Abingdon: Routledge.

Smith, A. (2014) 'Beyond the pros and cons of trigger warnings: collectivising healing', http://andrea366.wordpress.com/2014/07/13/beyond-the-pros-and-cons-of-trigger-warnings-collectivizing-healing.

Stengel, B. and Weems, L. (2010) 'Questioning safe space: an introduction, *Studies in Philosophy and Education*, 29(6), 505–507.

TWENTY-ONE

Political education in protest camps: spatialising dissensus and reconfiguring places of youth activist ritual in Mexico City

Nicholas Jon Crane

Introduction

Protest camps require and facilitate political education. But political education can also undermine the potential of protest campers to elicit radical change. This chapter examines several protest camps in post-1968 Mexico City to reveal how young protest campers cooperate in political education to the effect of reconfiguring places of activism and cultivating spaces of politics. It shows that protest camps can productively stage encounters between different senses of the world, and that political education can intensify spatial expressions of political antagonism. At the same time, the chapter also shows how political education can sometimes obstruct the reconfiguration of places of activism. Here, political education is a mode of social reproduction that carries with it the tendency toward stability. On the one hand, then, I examine practices of political education through which protest campers prefiguratively embody alternative ways of being that challenge established vocabularies and identities of the place in which they are situated. On the other hand, I show that, as a 'protest camp pathology' (Feigenbaum et al, 2013, 229), political education maintains parts of the social–spatial order against which protest campers have ostensibly converged.

These arguments are informed by fieldwork in Mexico City where protest camps have become a highly visible form of youthful agitation. From 2010 to 2014, I worked in central Mexico twice per year, primarily alongside young activists. Many of these young activists identified as student activists, even if they were not enrolled in school. These activists had reason to claim a student activist identity. Alongside the official left (for example, political parties like the 'centre-left' PRD), extra-institutional left groups including independent unions, social movements, mutual aid organisations and art collectives, have historically lionised the 1968 student movement as a force of progressive change. Shared reverence for the movement can be traced back to 2 October 1968, when – ten days before Mexico City began hosting the Olympics – forces loyal to the Institutional Revolutionary Party (PRI) shot and killed hundreds of activists who had converged in Tlatelolco. Many young activists today look to this massacre – often simply referred to as 'Tlatelolco' – as an event that inaugurated an enduring genre of conflict; they use it to identify the repressive essence of the state and the heroic self-sacrifice of the student left arrayed against it. In doing so, they arguably reduce political geographies in the five decades since to an uncomplicated binary of oppositional conflict between the state and what, after McAdam et al (2005), I call a 'movement family'.

This chapter is organised into four sections and a conclusion. My first section clarifies three key concepts: place (of ritualised activism); subjectification; and space (of politics). The second section examines the role of political education in maintaining protest camps, and highlights the role of storytelling in both the pursuit of alternative ways of being and also the delimitation of young people's politics. The next section suggests that political education in protest camps can reveal capacities otherwise denied from extant scripts of young people's lifecourse and thereby cultivate spaces of politics. Finally, the fourth section shows how young protest campers may disrupt a depoliticised lifecourse by forging solidarities unaccounted-for in places of ritualised activism. I break these four sections according to thematic emphasis in order to explore them in analytical detail. Where they overlap, it is because the themes they address are interrelated. I conclude by briefly reviewing the chapter's contributions and situating the argument within protest camps scholarship.

Placing activism, cultivating spaces of politics

In July 2012, activists for a revivified *Movimiento de Liberación Nacional* (MLN) established and maintained a camp in Mexico City's central plaza (the *Zócalo*) as part of a wave of protest against the *imposición* (fraudulent election) of President Enrique Peña Nieto (now in office, 2012–18). For these activists, Peña Nieto embodied the return of the PRI to Mexico's executive branch 12 years after its defeat by the right-wing National Action Party (PAN) in 2000. Critics of the PRI had long argued that a façade of democracy during the regime's seven decades of post-revolutionary political dominance (1929–2000) allowed Mexican elites to obscure the fraud, corruption and repression on which they relied to maintain control. But after two terms under the PAN, and after suffering an upsurge in drug war violence under President Felipe Calderón (2006–12), 38 per cent of a once cynical electorate was evidently either nostalgic for or bought off by the old political machine. Analysis of the MLN protest camp in the wake of this election allows us to clarify key concepts for the arguments that follow: place, subjectification and space.

The location of the July 2012 MLN camp was itself significant. These protest campers were doing as thousands of activists had done in that site for decades. After Lise Nelson (2003), one can examine the *Zócalo* for how social movement discourses have come to be 'sedimented' in it and how protest campers might not only enact predictable rituals of activism but may also reject their assignation of a role, experiment with unaccounted-for ways of being, and thereby spatialise dissensus. This refusal of one's particular place in social–spatial order is usefully understood as *subjectification*, which is to say, the process by which one becomes a 'subject of action' (May, 2009, 115).

The subjectification heralded by a protest camp is contingent upon the meanings and materiality sedimented in the place it might reconfigure. *Place*, here, is understood in relational terms. For Doreen Massey (1994, 154), places are 'articulated moments in networks of social relations and understandings'. Places may be fleetingly stabilised around specific meanings or material arrangements, and may accordingly reflect a policed allocation of ways of being in that place (compare Rancière, 1999, 29). But, against any appearance of timeless stability, Massey (2005, 11–12) argues that places are rife with 'loose ends'. The examples in this chapter suggest that protest campers can successfully exploit these loose ends to create spaces of politics. Places of protest camping are neither pre-given nor stable. Rather, the sedimentation of meanings and material infrastructure in a given place is both a constraint upon and condition for political interventions by which protest campers might spatialise dissensus.

The *Zócalo* is a site popularly understood to represent the Mexican nation and political power. Examples abound. Veronica Crossa (2009) reveals the symbolic importance of the *Zócalo* in a study of neoliberal policy through which a growth coalition excluded and displaced street vendors who had, for decades, used the Historic Centre as an informal marketplace. For Crossa, the coalition's appreciation of the normative power of the *Zócalo* is implicit in their 'Rescue Programme' to cultivate an image for the city that appeals to investors. In the *Zócalo* and elsewhere in Mexico City, the would-be displaced inhabitants of the place refused the allocation of particular ways of being to particular places – they refused a policed order of the status quo. And, as part of that refusal, they drew on the symbolic and material importance of the place to expose the wrong immanent to this reordering of place for moneyed tourists (Crossa, 2013).

Another acknowledgement of the *Zócalo's* symbolic importance – one that refers explicitly to rituals of activism – is evident in the 1997 performance by Mexico City artist Francis Alÿs, *Cuentos Patrióticos*. The performance was captured by video and is typically exhibited as a series of photographs (for example, in a permanent exhibit for 1968 in the UNAM Cultural Centre in Tlatelolco). *Cuentos Patrióticos* consists of a 'multiplication of sheep' that follow Alÿs around the flagpole in the centre of the plaza (Debroise and Medina, 2014, 440–441). For a contemporary public, it is a story of the insistent return of state repression and attendant demand for heroism with reference to which many activists make sense of post-1968 politics. Across disparate examples, then, the *Zócalo* is acknowledged as a place in which to perform either Mexican identity or dissent vis-à-vis what is acceptable as such. The MLN campers protesting against the *imposición* of Peña Nieto in 2012 can therefore be seen to have appropriated this site both to make their protest visible and to facilitate the tactical use of identities and vocabularies that had settled in the *Zócalo* in previous waves of protest.

My analysis of how student activism in post-1968 Mexico City is constrained suggests that young people enact a sedimented repertoire of contestation and thereby stabilise a social–spatial order. This chapter suggests that political education in protest camps can intervene in this repeated inscription of a predictable repertoire. But again, the process of subject formation heralded by a protest camp is contingent upon symbolic and material resources in the place. Pedagogical interventions in protest camps exceed and also paradoxically need the certainties of the status quo in order to take shape. That is to say, protest campers become subjects of action from out of the policed allocation of ways of being in that place, and their refusal of assigned roles through political education gives form to the camp as a contingent space of politics.

In the *Zócalo*, protest waves, neoliberal urban planning, rituals of national pride, and so on, together articulate the place from out of which protest campers might spatialise dissensus. Protest campers also play a role in this articulation. For example, the place of the MLN's post-electoral protest camp in July 2012 was produced in part by supporters who pitched the tent, hauled water jugs, paid for photocopies, donated chairs, painted banners, or volunteered time at an information table. These quotidian practices creatively drew upon resources already sedimented in and apparently proper to the place. Protest campers arranged these materials in a way that had, through previous waves of protest, come to be acceptable in the place.

MLN campers retained 'organizational remnants' from previous campaigns (Taylor, 1989): a tangible infrastructure that included weather-resistant posters hung from sturdy rope along which visitors could learn about the context of the post-electoral activism.

Figure 21.1: Material infrastructure for political education in the July 2012 protest camp of the *Movimiento de Liberación Nacional* (photo by the author)

These posters functioned as a pedagogical intervention. They situated the activism of 2012 in a more enduring struggle against repressive state power. In that sense, they established contemporary activists within a lineage or movement family. But the posters not only enabled protest campers to enact predictable rituals of place-based activism; they also opened the camp to unaccounted-for political engagement from visitors and passersby. The posters facilitated refusal of a social–spatial order – with resistance here and its adversary there – that the camp may otherwise have maintained. Amid the pervasive 'student-led' post-electoral agitation under the sign of #YoSoy132 (Gómez, 2012), the protest campers in the *Zócalo* tactically adopted sedimented social movement discourses to address a receptive public (the post-1968 student left) and also to call forth a new subject of action – a 'we' that the name 'post-1968 student left' could not contain. As I elaborate in the following three sections, this practice of political education arguably called forth a collective subject that exceeded the figure of the heroic student, and disrupted the depoliticised lifecourse along which young people are presumed to become political in post-1968 Mexico City. In that sense, the posters in the MLN camp reflected a pervasive tension within political education between innovation and reification. I continue mapping this tension in the pages that follow.

Protest camps as sites of learning

Examples from post-1968 Mexico City suggest that 'learning' in protest camps (Feigenbaum et al, 2013, 219) can both facilitate the social reproduction that is essential to camps' endurance and also sometimes promote rituals of activism that undermine political antagonism. One such example – in this case, of student activists appropriating university infrastructure for political education – reveals the simultaneity of these countervailing processes and suggests a fluid relationship between formal and informal education (compare Mills, 2016). Here, lessons learned through political education include the target of a given struggle (neoliberalism in higher education), the logic of that struggle (mutual aid in the face of competition-inducing reforms), and skills (the facilitation of meetings, independent media production, and so on). More generally, this example shows that political education can create space for realising capacities to act politically outside the constraints of an assigned role, and without permission from external authority.

The pedagogical work of recreational or community-based camping movements has historically been conservative, and has asserted the values of a compartmentalised people against influence from outside (Feigenbaum et al, 2013, 6–9). Examples of contemporary protest camps suggest that political education in these sites can also reify identities and vocabularies sedimented in a given place. But examples also reveal that protest campers use political education to challenge an unjust social–spatial order, and they paradoxically do this by drawing upon material and symbolic resources afforded by that order (compare Feigenbaum et al, 2013, 39). Examples show that political education makes perceptible the creative capacity of protest campers, and can accordingly facilitate recognition of how, 'in many areas of our lives, we are already co-authors of the world' (Chatterton, 2005, 547).

In July 2011, the *Comité de Lucha UAM-X* (Struggle Committee at Universidad Autónoma Metropolitana in Xochimilco, Mexico City) opened a free school seminar to friends and followers of their profile on the social media platform Facebook. In a private group, the organisers distributed academic and activist articles for a discussion of their political conjuncture. Amid a process of neoliberalisation secured by repressive state power, the Comité selected texts on Mexican politics in 1968 and 1999 – years immediately recognisable to seminar participants as the dates of celebrated student movement mobilisations.

The seminar would happen in an *aula provisional* (makeshift classroom) that the Comité had appropriated. When I arrived at UAM-X for the meeting, I quickly found the organisers because they strategically occupied a highly visible site adjacent to the cafeteria. Subsequent trips to UAM-X revealed that the Comité had made a durable claim on this site. That morning, a young man wearing a shirt for the electrical workers' union SME managed a table for the distribution of photocopied zines and pamphlets, t-shirts, videos and fliers that situated the Comité within an array of civil society organisations, autonomous movements, and the as yet barely legible agitation that would soon take as #Occupy and then #YoSoy132 in 2011–12.

In still other ways, the Comité organisers deliberately sought to exploit the political potential that inhered in their place. For example, they managed connections to people not yet integrated with the Comité by situating their table at a highly trafficked site where student clubs and others post fliers for upcoming events. This decision invited political engagement from visitors and passersby, and particularly from other UAM-X students who might look to the walls for announcements of student-centred events. But even as the Comité opened itself to outsiders, it purposefully managed these potential links on its own terms (compare Chatterton, 2005, 554). When I approached the table that day, one young man greeted my audibly non-native Spanish with a clear desire to make sense of my place vis-à-vis the group's political identity. He briefly vetted me through conversation about the then-recent paramilitary repression of the Triqui community in San Juan Copala, Oaxaca. Only then, apparently regarding me as at least unthreatening, did he suggest I return in 20 minutes so that we could walk to the classroom together.

The *aula provisional* resembled a shipping container and was tucked away in a less trafficked part of campus. The Comité used the space to organise actions, create propaganda and host meetings. The tables around which we sat to wait for the other seminar participants were covered with piles of material (fliers, stickers, pamphlets) to be organised for the table, the Comité's public face. Among the materials were fliers for a march (a *kaminata*) discussed later in the chapter, and stickers for *No más sangre* (No More Blood), the name under which activists were then promoting a wave of nationwide demonstrations against the drug war of President Felipe Calderón (2006–12). With the arrival of a seventh attendee, one of the Comité members (a UAM-X sociology student) initiated our discussion by identifying key themes: the neoliberalisation of higher education in Mexico and abroad, and the past and contemporary student movement that might resist neoliberal reforms. After these remarks, however, the conversation took a turn.

Even if nominally convened to discuss the distributed articles, the seminar participants redirected discussion to personal stories of marketised higher education and anti-neoliberal resistance. One such story elicited laughter, as a young man shared his cynicism about Santander Bank ATM machines that suggested donating a few pesos to education when making a withdrawal. Other storytelling underscored the experience of marketised higher education on the UAM-X campus itself, as when one student responded to another with a rhetorical question about direct and indirect cost of enrolling in school: 'The courses are very expensive, right? [This is] a method of exclusion.'

Through storytelling, participants in the Comité seminar situated their experiences in relation to the student movement histories found in the assigned texts. The 1999 student strike at the National Autonomous University of Mexico (UNAM) stood as an especially notable touchstone for these stories. (The strike was also a key reference point for protest campers in the *Okupa Che*, discussed in the fourth section of this chapter.) But the seminar participants did not refer to the past only to cast the present as the latest in a self-replicating conflict between students and the state. Instead, they drew on the material and symbolic resources of their specific situation to generate and sharpen their collective antagonism towards contemporary injustice. Through storytelling, they tactically engaged with the articles to which they had gained access through the UAM-X, and with student-left discourses sedimented therein, to identify disparate practices and processes through which neoliberal order had been and was being constructed. By denaturalising the present in this way, through personal stories, they facilitated a process of refusal and becoming-other. This *subjectification* was evident when one participant would listen to another and say, 'yes, and,' and then offer their own experience. Here, the participants generated a 'we' feeling and suspended the givenness of social–spatial order; they forged a contingent solidarity around relatable experiences and made their world actionable.

As part of seminar participants' contribution to collective subject formation, they cited ongoing anti-neoliberal student activism elsewhere in the world – in England, Chile, Puerto Rico and Spain. They oriented themselves towards reconfiguring a place of anti-neoliberal student politics that, by virtue of the connections that constitute it, also carries potential to reshuffle social relations in otherwise seemingly far-flung contexts. Here, the storytellers fleetingly articulated shared experiences that demand collective action within and beyond Mexican universities. They decried rising fees and standardised entrance exams (reforms that undermine the socialist legacy of Lázaro Cárdenas in the 1930s and, differently, Luis Echeverría in the early 1970s). And, having temporarily broken consent, they named a subject for anti-neoliberal organising by non-students – for example, participants in the 'movement of the excluded from higher education' (http://aspirantesexcluidos. blogspot. com/) – who, as non-students, nonetheless build power for the pursuit of education as a right and not as a privilege.

The Comité seminar was, however, also shot through with countervailing processes of social reproduction that discouraged the spatialisation of dissensus. These processes stood as variations on an enduring problem for the post-1968 student left: the composition of a politically effective 'we'. Too often, assertions of political identity – for example, 'we are student activists' – configure the field of collective action in such a way as to discourage the formation of horizontal linkages between groups. A mobilisation or an occupation is thereby configured as being 'of the students...our space...our time' (interview with Citlalli Hernández, 3 June 2013, Mexico City). In the Comité seminar, for example, a student visiting from the UNAM expressed a sense of self-enclosed isolation through a sceptical diagnosis of the anti-neoliberal organising that anticipated #YoSoy132 in 2012. Here, resonance around storytelling gave way to a more rigid interpretation. The student asserted that, 'yes', there is a great deal of powerful anti-neoliberal organising going on elsewhere in the world, 'but it's worse out there,' immediately off campus. That is, it's 'worse' in the context of Mexico's student movement than for the movements his peers were celebrating (fieldnotes, 12 July 2011, Mexico City).

Several other seminar participants readily accepted this pessimistic assessment, which echoed a prevalent vision of young people promulgated by mainstream media and experts on youth unemployment – a generational discourse that cast young Mexicans as apathetic in the face of economic constraints. This would receive sustained critique less than a year later, with the rise of #YoSoy132 media alternatives

(Gómez García and Treré, 2014). But, for this student and the young activists who affirmed his diagnosis, would-be political actors beyond the revolutionary student movement were 'ignorant' and irretrievably dominated by the neoliberal state. Students were situated amid a polity incapable of self-emancipation, and they therefore must take a leading role in 'the struggles of our people' (Crane, 2015, 6).

These examples reveal that political education in the *aula provisional* at UAM-X was fraught with tension. On the one hand, young activists engaged in storytelling that facilitated linkages between otherwise individualised experiences. In this way, political education generated a 'we' feeling and exposed an unjust status quo to critique and disruption. On the other hand, young activists sometimes defined the 'we' in such a way as to reify sedimented political identities and foreclose articulation of a solidarity not specifically centred on students. Here, political education did not produce a progressive moment of possibility, but became an inevitable return to an origin. Past movement moments – notably the 1968 massacre – appeared as exemplary to the ways in which young activists can understand the potential for contemporary political struggle. Arguably, a post-1968 student-left discourse channelled young people towards a sedimented repertoire of contention in which students are helpless to do anything but sacrifice themselves.

Protest camps as sites at which lifecourses are given shape

On 17 July 2011, several dozen young activists assembled at the Monument to the Revolution in the financial centre of Mexico City for a march against militarised counternarcotics policing. The activists promoted that day's convergence through social media platforms and by circulating fliers for a '*kaminata* [sic] *por la desmilitarización*' (march for demilitarisation). Several youth and student organisations (for example, the *Coordinadora Metropolitana Contra la Militarización y la Violencia, Contracorriente Estudiantil*) had observably worked to ensure a turnout at the event. Banners and fliers announced their presence at the monument that afternoon. The march would eventually arrive at the *Zócalo*, which was then occupied by SME union activists who were protesting against the privatisation of electricity provision and demanding the restoration of their jobs after a government takeover of generating stations in October 2009.

Before departing for the *Zócalo*, the activists at the monument displayed or collaborated to complete banners and signs. The slogans spoke only indirectly to the drug war, nominally the context for the march; more explicit were assertions of identity and demands addressed to adversaries. One banner read, 'End the criminalisaton of youth!' Another situated the young activists in a wider social field, as *universitarios*: 'Academics for the demilitarisation of Mexico!' Nearby, a group of activists painted a sign that established a link between the university-aligned activists in this march and their union counterparts in the *Zócalo*. These activists cast students and workers as two distinct yet related groups, with the former in a process of becoming the latter: 'Because we students will be workers, worker–student unity!' Still another group of young activists stood by a sign that reiterated the conditions for this unity with an oft-repeated truism, linking the march with a muscular, revolutionary mode of political engagement: 'To be young and not revolutionary is an almost biological contradiction.'

This truism (*ser joven y no ser revolucionario es una contradicción casi biológica*) would notably reappear several months later on the cover of a 1968-themed issue of the free weekly newspaper *MacheteArte*, typically distributed by anarchopunks on busy street corners, at the youth culture street market *El Chopo*, or at demonstrations. Of interest is how an informal mode of political education such as this may undermine the political force of the young activists – how announcing an unquestionable truth, and leveraging the authority of 'biology' to script youthful rebellion along a path of development, may limit what it means for young people to be political.

An imaginary of young people's politics as essentially revolutionary is pervasive in the student-left discourse sedimented in places of ritualised activism in Mexico City. Contributions to this student-left discourse – the sign at the monument and the cover of *MacheteArte* – maintain what McAdam et al (2005) would call a 'stylised image' of a post-1968 'movement family'. Conditions for 1968 and revolutionary activity in the five decades since have, of course, been constituted by dispersed acts, demands and justice claims – from the victories of the women's suffrage movement in the 1950s to the agitation for union democracy in the 1960s, to urban guerrilla movements and peasant organising in the 1970s, to articulations of indigeneity and autonomy in the 1990s and 2000s. But contributions to post-1968 student-left discourse such as these confine multiplicity to an undifferentiated and naturalised opposition defined by age.

In 2013, after months of activism under the sign of #YoSoy132, I interviewed the historian Alberto del Castillo Troncoso. The author of a book on popular memory of 1968 (del Castillo Troncoso, 2012), he provocatively suggested that, 'some 95 percent of the memory [of 1968] is of 2 October', the day of the famous massacre in Tlatelolco (interview with Alberto del Castillo Troncoso, 4 February 2013, Mexico City). The popular memory he had in mind casts this encounter with repression as a horrifying rite of passage. Young people can accordingly experience frontal confrontation with the state as the transition by which to be 'promoted to the rank of revolutionary veteran', here echoing Roberto Bolaño in his novella on 1968 in Mexico City (2006, 77). After Tlatelolco, young people must be recognisably, even self-sacrificially, revolutionary to be political.

Geographers of young people would recognise in this truism a locally meaningful construction of a necessary intermediate stage in the passage to fully realised adulthood (Evans, 2008, 1663–1664; Holt and Holloway, 2006; Valentine, 2003). Casting rebellion as a necessary lifecourse stage arguably depoliticises practices that might otherwise be seen to disrupt the status quo according to which young people's lives are made governable. Naturalising this passage assigns to would-be 'subjects of action' a *revoltoso* or 'rebel' identity that can only be properly performed within narrowly defined limits (May, 2009, 115; Pensado, 2013, 9). Written into the claim of 'biological contradiction' is therefore a homogenising definition of youth as a stage in transition from frivolity to responsibility. But written out are heterogeneous ways of growing up that exceed assumptions about the proper course of maturation. Written out, among other things, is a capacity for world-making that people may realise as protest campers regardless of their age, and not necessarily as adults-in-waiting.

Practices of political education would disrupt such lifecourse scripts by revealing them as constructed and contingent, not natural or inevitable. For example, the invocation of a biological contradiction in non-revolutionary young people was notably appropriate to the place in which the young activists converged for the *kaminata*. They came together that afternoon to prepare and display signs and banners on the plaza above a mausoleum for Mexico's mythologised revolutionary heroes (Pancho Villa, Francisco I Madero, Lázaro Cárdenas and others). Here, the truism – 'To be young and not revolutionary is an almost biological contradiction' – suggests that young people belong in this place only if they perform the *revoltoso* identity that would apparently situate young people as inheritors of the heroism commemorated at the monument. These myths of heroism are, however, fully compatible with the status quo. Indeed, it is through reference to these myths that political parties like the PRI have long made claims to legitimacy (Knight, 2010). In this context, disrupting an unjust social–spatial order would demand refusing the convenient fiction of uninterrupted filiation.

The ambivalence of another sign displayed at the monument that day is therefore revealing. 'Because we students will be workers, worker–student unity!' Suspending for a moment the assumption that students will become workers only when they cease to be students (that is, upon becoming adults), the sign put these social categories – student and worker – under pressure. This assertion that, as students, we will be ('*seremos*') workers is consistent with a class politics that does not take for granted the social group upon which it stakes its claims, but instead intervenes in the composition of that class. This is not a class politics of solidarity around a pre-given likeness. Rather, it is class politics as subjectification – the cultivation of a solidarity that does not yet have a voice, and which is not anticipated within the 'seemingly natural order of things' (Dikeç, 2007, 18). As a pedagogical device, this sign called forth a solidarity by which young people might refuse the roles given by depoliticising scripts of their lifecourse (compare Brown, 2013, 427). As student activists, they will now be workers. Here, political education promises to facilitate forms of political action that exceed given social roles; it does not adhere to the identities and vocabularies sedimented in this place so much as it generates new ways of being together that may more thoroughly disrupt state power.

Protest camps as sites in which to generate solidarity

Michel Foucault (2000) famously argued that 'traditional history' reflects the historian's faith in the development of a social formation from a unitary necessity. This is history written as a tale of 'descent' that moves from a social formation's penultimate expression of development to its ostensible origin. Foucault was not, of course, explicitly addressing himself to activism, much less protest camping. But his argument carries lessons for how to understand or otherwise engage with protest camping. To '[analyse] an event according to the multiple processes that constitute it' arguably would release that event (for example, the protest camp) from 'the sign of a unitary necessity' (Foucault, 2000, 227–229). In post-1968 Mexico City, this would relieve young activists and protest campers from an apparently natural tendency to repeat Tlatelolco. A protest camp could instead be understood and practiced as a singular effect of a solidarity that draws momentum from its constituents' strategic linkage with people heretofore un-integrated with social justice activism. In the words of political theorist Benjamin Arditi, a camp might usefully be understood and practised as an effect of articulation – a '*convocatoría*' into which people converge to speak (personal communication, 6 February 2013,

Mexico City) (see also Chapter Twelve by Barker and Ross in this volume). This notion of solidarity allows that potential constituents might introduce their specificity into a 'we' that challenges closure around narratives of the movement's past as a measure of what can be done in the future. This is not the solidarity imagined by advocates for the position of an established central actor. This latter notion of solidarity was implicit in some commentary on the anti-PRI post-electoral activism of 2012, which cast the 2012 activists as 'direct descendants' of past agitation, particularly the student movement of 1968. In part as an effect of student-left discourse promulgated by the activists themselves, in popular commentary on this protest wave, the centrality of the student was rarely in question. Indeed, the centrality was, if anything, repeatedly inscribed through assertions of continuity in the student movement's traditional adversary. Non-students involved in the mobilisations under the sign of #YoSoy132 were frequently cast as citizens sympathetic to the students' cause, but they were not admitted as protagonists themselves (Gómez, 2012, 19).

Political education in this context carried with it countervailing tendencies – on the one hand, towards social reproduction that stabilises the status quo, and on the other, towards an articulation of spatially and temporally dispersed agitation that might reorient people towards world-making not previously imagined possible. For Rossana Reguillo (2013), placing an emphasis on the latter tendency, #YoSoy132 was a process of subjectification irreconcilable with the past understood as a blueprint for the present. One must recognise, therefore, that #YoSoy132 contributed to both tendencies. Notably through pedagogical practices, for which activists established conditions during previous waves of protest, #YoSoy132 assemblies forged solidarities that exceeded self-enclosed identification around the categories of an inherited political framework.

For example, the #YoSoy132 protest camp under the Monument to the Revolution in 2012 – *Acampada Revolución* – was anticipated by the 15 October 2011 global protests in the name of the Arab Spring, Occupy, and the 15M in Spain. Activists in Mexico City announced themselves as '*indignados*' that day, tactically adopting a political vocabulary and facilitating its sedimentation for mobilisations to come in 2012. Of course, the *indignados* in Mexico City were not the same as those of the *Puerta del Sol* in Madrid. The activists who introduced this political vocabulary to Mexico City also nurtured connections between this name and locally meaningful struggles – SME union activists in the *Zócalo, No más sangre* elsewhere in Mexico; they exceeded the partitioned world that their invocation of this identity might otherwise give to perception. Activists would later harness the 'contingent origins' of the 2012 *Acampada Revolución* as a condition for other solidarities (compare Feigenbaum et al, 2013, 38).

Figure 21.2: #YoSoy132 protest camp (the *Acampada Revolución*) at the Monument to the Revolution, October 2012 (photo by the author)

This tension between two treatments of the past and the practical orientations towards solidarity that correspond to those divergent treatments is also exemplified in the *Okupa Che*, a radical social centre on the campus of the UNAM. Participants in the radical or '*ultra*' tendency of the 1999 UNAM student strike occupied the auditorium as well as its adjacent offices and kitchen on 4 September 2000. The squat or '*okupa*' persists today around a schedule of self-organised workshops, vegetarian meals, and an informal daily market or '*tianguis*', where the occupiers sell crafts outside the *okupa*. This relatively predictable schedule is sometimes punctuated by efforts to evict the squatters. Some of the squatters narrate their resistance to eviction (by police, university administration, and – in some cases – dissenting student activist groups) as resistance to a repressive regime little changed since 1968. Since 2000, occupiers and observers alike have identified the site with an '*ultra*' identity, and anti-authoritarianism founded on its adherents' anticipation of repression (Olivares Alonso, 2015). A statement by a squatter at *Okupa Che* must be understood in this context. According to the young man, although the *okupa* is replete with infrastructure for social reproduction (the vegetarian kitchen, a volunteer-run summer school, a library, regularly scheduled workshops, and so on), it is maintained by people who, in order to distinguish allies from adversaries, now 'hope for repression' (interview with an occupant of *Okupa Che*, 8 February 2013, Mexico City). Social reproduction and this investment in antagonism are not, however, contradictory. Indeed, this chapter suggests that it is precisely by mobilising around a rigid antagonism that young activists often adopt for themselves the oppositional place in relation to the status quo that is popularly regarded as a mark of being revolutionary.

Some practices at the *Okupa Che*, however, reflect a more supple relationship to the past and to this 'stylised image' of the post-1968 movement family (McAdam et al, 2005). For example, squatters in the *okupa* sometimes engage in practices of *vinculación* (linkage creation) to forge solidarities during key movement moments, for example, during the summer of 2012, when the *okupa* hosted #YoSoy132 assemblies (Crane, 2015). During such moments, the residents of the *okupa* relate to popular memory of political violence and conflict not as a blueprint for contemporary political engagement but as strategic resource. This reflects an appreciation both for contingent origins and also for unlikely alliances that facilitate the endurance of the *okupa*. That activists have been able to occupy this site for a decade and a half is in large part due to constitutionally protected university autonomy and the permissive social movement discourses sedimented in the UNAM campus. The protest campers at the *okupa* do face threat of eviction. But recognising these permissive conditions clarifies the wisdom of *okupa* protest campers who have created space for meetings that might, at first glance, not meet the '*ultra*' standards of the post-1999 anarchist punks who remain the face of the squat. In effect, openness to linkages not only injects energy into the meeting spaces and labyrinthine hallways of the *okupa*. It also facilitates a politically productive suspension of sedimented political vocabularies on the assumption of which self-certain activists may otherwise discourage the formation of new antagonism. A process of subjectification was made possible by the occupiers' maintenance of space for *vinculación*.

Conclusion

This chapter reveals a tension that runs through political education in protest camps. On the one hand, I show how political education in protest camps promotes and reflects its practitioners' faith in what

Doreen Massey (2005) identifies as the 'loose ends' and unfinishedness of places. Analysis of examples in contemporary Mexico City shows that protest campers draw upon material and symbolic resources that have settled in places and, from those places, stage encounters that enable a politics of emancipation, beyond the status quo. Political education can accordingly intensify and renew political antagonism. Sometimes simultaneously, however, political education in protest camps reifies political identities and vocabularies through which state power is exercised. In these moments, protest campers cooperate in pedagogical practices that maintain the unjust social–spatial order they ostensibly converge to disrupt. By focusing on these countervailing tendencies, this chapter extends an emphasis in protest camps scholarship on what Sam Halvorsen (2015) identifies as a tension between 'moments of rupture' and 'everyday life' (see also Chapter Ten by Halvorsen, in this volume). I agree with Halvorsen, that ruptures should not be thought apart from the reproduction of everyday life, and that privileging rupture risks feeding an exclusionary form of activist-ism (Halvorsen, 2015, 403). This chapter shows that ignoring the productive tension between innovation and reification also risks missing how processes of subjectification heralded by disruptive protest camping are contingent upon the meanings and materiality sedimented, through practices of social reproduction, in the places they may reconfigure.

My analysis of several examples from my fieldwork in Mexico City suggests that political education expresses both of the tendencies that Halvorsen recognises in protest camping more generally. Young people in post-1968 Mexico City are constrained by sedimented ways of knowing and practising politics, and are channelled along locally meaningful trajectories towards adulthood. Their practices of political education reflect these constraints. But they also articulate solidarities through which young activists may be capable of a more enduring disruption of state power.

References
Bolaño, R. (2006) *Amulet*. New York, NY: New Directions.
Brown, G. (2013) 'The revolt of aspirations: contesting neoliberal social hope', *ACME: An International E-Journal for Critical Geographies*, 12, 419–430.
Chatterton, P. (2005) 'Making autonomous geographies: Argentina's popular uprising and the "Movimiento de Trabajadores Desocupados" (Unemployed Workers Movement)', *Geoforum*, 36, 545–561.

Crane, N. J. (2015) 'Politics squeezed through a police state: policing and *vinculación* in post-1968 Mexico City', *Political Geography*, 47, 1–10.

Crossa, V. (2009) 'Resisting the entrepreneurial city: street vendors' struggle in Mexico City's historic center', *International Journal of Urban and Regional Research*, 33, 43–63.

Crossa, V. (2013) 'Play for protest, protest for play: artisan and vendors' resistance to displacement in Mexico City', *Antipode*, 45, 826–843.

Debroise, O. and Medina, C. (2014) *La era de la discrepancia: Arte y cultura visual en México 1968–1997* [The Age of Discrepancies: Art and Visual Culture in Mexico 1968–1997]. Mexico City: Museo Universitario de Ciencias y Arte.

del Castillo Troncoso, A. (2012) *Ensayo sobre el movimiento estudiantil de 1968: La fotografía y la construcción de un imaginario* [Essay on the student movement of 1968: Photography and the construction of an imaginary]. Mexico City: Editorial Mora.

Dikeç, M. (2007) *Badlands of the Republic: Space, Politics, and Urban Policy*. Malden, MA: Blackwell Publishing.

Evans, B. (2008) 'Geographies of youth/young people', *Geography Compass*, 2, 1659–1680.

Feigenbaum, A., Frenzel, F. and McCurdy, P. (2013) *Protest Camps*. New York, NY: Zed.

Foucault, M. (2000) 'Questions of method', in J. D. Faubion (ed) *Power*. New York, NY: The New Press, pp 223–238.

Gómez García, R. and Treré, E. (2014) 'The #YoSoy132 movement and the struggle for media democratization in Mexico', *Convergence: The International Journal of Research into New Media Technologies*, 20, 496–510.

Gómez, L. (2012) '#YoSoy132', *NACLA Report on the Americas*, Fall, 17–20.

Halvorsen, S. (2015) 'Taking space: moments of rupture and everyday life in Occupy London', *Antipode*, 47(2), 401–417.

Holt, L. and Holloway, S. L. (2006) 'Editorial: theorizing other childhoods in a globalized world', *Children's Geographies*, 4, 135–142.

Knight, A. (2010) 'The myth of the Mexican revolution', *Past and Present*, 209, 223–273.

McAdam, D., Sampson, R. J., Weffer-Elizondo, S. and MacIndoe, H. (2005) '"There will be fighting in the streets": The distorting lens of social movement theory', *Mobilization*, 10, 1–18.

Massey, D. (1994) 'A global sense of place', in D. Massey, *Space, Place, and Gender*. Minneapolis, MN: University of Minnesota Press, pp 146–156.

Massey, D. (2005) *For Space*. Thousand Oaks, CA: Sage Publications.

May, T. (2009) 'Rancière in South Carolina', in G. Rockhill and P. Watts (eds) *History, Politics, Aesthetics: Jacques Rancière*. Durham, NC: Duke University Press, pp 105–119.

Mills, S. (2016) 'Geographies of education, volunteering and the lifecourse: the Woodcraft Folk in Britain (1925–75)', *Cultural Geographies*, 23, 103–119.

Nelson, L. (2003) 'Decentering the movement: collective action, place, and the "sedimentation" of radical political discourses', *Environment and Planning D: Society and Space*, 21, 559–581.

Olivares Alonso, E. (2015) 'Recuperar el *Che Guevara*, demanda añeja en la UNAM' ['Recovering the Che Guevara, an old demand at the UNAM'], *La Jornada*, 23 November, 44.

Pensado, J. (2013) *Rebel Mexico: Student Unrest and Authoritarian Political Culture During the Long Sixties*. Stanford, CA: Stanford University Press.

Rancière, J. (1999) *Dis-agreement: Politics and Philosophy*. Minneapolis, MN: University of Minnesota Press.

Reguillo, R. (2013) 'Disidencia: Frente al Desorden de las Cajas Abiertas – México, Breve y Precario Mapa de lo Imposible', *e-misférica*, 10, http://hemisphericinstitute.org/hemi/es/e-misferica-102/reguillo.

Taylor, V. (1989) 'Social movement continuity: the women's movement in abeyance', *American Sociological Review*, 54, 761–775.

Valentine, G. (2003) 'Boundary crossings: transitions from childhood to adulthood', *Children's Geographies*, 1, 37–52.

Part Four
Conclusion

TWENTY-TWO

Future tents: protest camps and social movement organisation

*Fabian Frenzel, Gavin Brown, Anna Feigenbaum
and Patrick McCurdy*

Introduction

This book has taken a journey through sites of protest across the world, attempting to understand better the place-based politics expressed in protest camps and related forms of occupation-based politics. The case studies in this book were organised into three sections that allowed exploration of some of the differing processes through which it is possible to discuss protest camps and their infrastructures. Through the three sections of the book, several connecting themes have been identified and the purpose of this conclusion is to draw these themes together, both to highlight the contribution this volume makes, and also to identify the places where future research efforts need to be directed.

Diversity and locality

A key insight from this volume is indeed the diversity of the protest camp as a form of social movement tactic. While deployed as a tactic across the globe, protest camping and the use of place-based actions differ significantly. The difference is represented first of all in the protests themselves: ranging from specific campaigns and educational functions (see Chapter Twenty-one by Crane) to broad social upheaval with revolutionary aspirations or character and consequences (see Shevtsova (Chapter Fourteen); Yaka and Karakayali (Chapter Four); and Wang et al (Chapter Seven)), tackling issues ranging from environmental protests (see Russell et al (Chapter Nine)), to housing (see Gordon (Chapter Thirteen); Arruda (Chapter Eighteen); Rollmann and Frenzel (Chapter Nineteen)), austerity (see Kavada and Dimitriou (Chapter Five); Halvorsen (Chapter Ten); and Gerbaudo (Chapter Six)), indigenous rights (see Barker and Ross (Chapter Twelve); and

Thompson (Chapter Eleven)), refugee rights (see English (Chapter Twenty); Pascucci (Chapter Seventeen); and Rubing (Chapter Three)) and corruption (see Davies (Chapter Fifteen)). While prior scholarship has often focused on protest camps within the domain of environmental politics, as this volume makes clear, the tactic of protest camp has been, and continues to be, deployed across a range of issues and political ideologies.

Diversity is further reflected in how protest camps are developed; how and where they are deployed; and, how they react to and incorporate their social, political, cultural and material environment(s). While protest camps often bring very different protesters together and allow them to converge, the chapters have shown that camps look different in different countries, and mobilise different cultural and political symbols. In this way camps always also reflect the political culture of their environment, often the nation-state in which they occur (Frenzel, 2010). The environment in which camps take place is not just a matter of political culture but also country specific laws and regulations that govern public conduct and political activism. The chapters furthermore show the centrality of locality and its specific opportunity structures, availability of resources, meanings and histories.

Finally, diversity is represented in the academic disciplines interested in protest camps and represented in this book. The researchers who contributed chapters to this book come from Anthropology and Area Studies (Pascucci and Shevtsova), Architecture (Arruda and Rubing), Geography (Barker and Ross, Crane, Davies, Halvorsen and Russell et al), Media Studies (Gerbaudo and Kavada and Dimitriou), Organisation Studies (Rollmann and Frenzel), Political Science (Gordon and Thompson) and Sociology (English, Yaka and Karakayali and Wang et al). This shows not only the multiplicity of ways in which protest camps matter, but also the broad interest that exists in this expanding form of protest. With the diversity of disciplines, this book also presented a variety of methodological approaches, ranging from interview-based empirical social research to ethnographic and militant research-based approaches to documentary analysis and historical and philosophical reflection. Most of the chapters have taken an empirical approach, but broader reflections in more theoretical terms also speak from the volume, in particular regarding questions of political theory and philosophy.

Travelling infrastructures

We opened this book by highlighting our focus on infrastructures and materiality as dimensions that evidently cut across the diverse sets and settings discussed here. Based on our prior research (Feigenbaum et al, 2013; Brown and Yaffe, 2014), our approach to protest camps is grounded in the view that the materiality of the camp, as a site of protest and of daily life, gives rise to particular infrastructures and practices that can be traced across protest camps over time and geographic location. The political articulation and shared sociality of protest camps likewise serves to ground a comparative investigation. Our approach is one which uses the concept of 'infrastructures' as a thread to follow through and across protest camps. As a conceptual tool, following infrastructures and their related processes and practices, offers a means to consider similarities and divergences across different forms of contention. In many cases the chapters provided insight into the ways in which protest camps are built, organised and structured, how they speak, what techniques of decision-making are employed and how social reproduction is secured.

Media infrastructures

The centrality of communication within and without protest camps cannot be overstated. In the chapters presented we found continuities between diverse camps in the ways in which they approached the necessity to speak to the outside and communicate internally (see Gerbaudo (Chapter Six); Kavada and Dimitriou (Chapter Five)). While all protest movements speak and communicate, protest camps seem to be specific in their function as communication hubs. The concentration of people in one place over time produces unique communication cultures, often infused with affective connectivity. Affective connectivity is produced out of the physical proximity of people with shared concerns and is at once the source of political power and productive of collective creativity. It is no surprise, then, that many protest camps become media hubs, places of training in media technologies. They often start to install libraries and radio stations, and print their own newspapers. The arrival of social media has brought with it the acceleration and intensification of past media practices and the creation of new ones to deal with the changing information and material environments (see chapters by Gerbaudo (Chapter Six); Kavada and Dimitriou (Chapter Five); and Wang et al (Chapter Seven)). Through technologies, both recent and ancient, from smart phones to hand signals, the production of a collective voice in the camp and the facilitation of multiple voices engaged with the camp, constitutes one of the central shared characteristics of protest camps.

Action infrastructures

The ability of protest camps to enable numbers of people to act in common is perhaps the most obvious political reason for protest camps to emerge and for them to be feared and repressed by governments. Political action is comprised of a number of activities, such as demonstrations, blockades, sit-ins or pickets. What is specific about the cases of political action that constitute and emanate from protest camps, is – in the first instance – their temporality. In the chapters discussed in this book (Russell et al (Chapter Nine); Shevtsova (Chapter Fourteen); Thompson (Chapter Eleven); Wang et al (Chapter Seven)), we see how political action in camps is sustained over time. Unlike a circle march where campaigners disperse after walking through city streets or having posed for a staged photograph, the protest camp is characterised by its construction of a home-place as a site of contention. While the protest camp is neither indestructible nor permanent, the act of protest camping is intentionally designed as a visible antagonism through its constant presence. The endurance and continuity of protest camps allows for individual protesters to join for some time and return later, while the protest itself is maintained. The tactic thus enables different groups of people to participate in different ways, from passers-by to live-in protesters, and this frequently serves to amplify the resources available to protest movements. Protest camps and other place-based protests also enable the preparation for action, for example in training sessions and through reflecting on action with other participants. Particular techniques of protest can be taught, and experiences of protest can be discussed, creating the basis for the creation of more substantial protest communities. Training, skill-sharing, and informal popular education, post-action care and support all form domains of action infrastructures in the case studies discussed in this book (see Crane (Chapter Twenty-one); English (Chapter Twenty); and Russell et al (Chapter Nine)).

Governance infrastructures

The act of protest camping requires political organisation. While camps may be organised in either more hierarchical (see Davies (Chapter Fifteen); Gordon (Chapter Thirteen); and Shevtsova (Chapter

Fourteen)), or more horizontal ways (see Halvorsen (Chapter Ten); and Russell et al (Chapter Nine)), there is a tendency in many protest camps towards a directly democratic or horizontal political articulation. The proximity and affectivity of the protest camp space seems to create such tendency. It is represented in the formation of broad forums of articulation, sometimes in general assemblies, sometimes simply in daily interactions between participants. Even if more hierarchical structures exist, the bearers of leadership can be shown to be responsive to the horizontalist and radically democratic sentiment the camp produces (see Davies (Chapter Fifteen); Gordon (Chapter Thirteen); and Shevtsova (Chapter Fourteen)). In some cases, this might take a populist turn of the politics of the camp (see Shevtsova), but in other cases, a mismatch between leadership and the people of the camp may lead to a disintegration of the movement (see Gordon). Managing and organising the people power of a camp is thus one of the most significant challenges for protest camps. The chapters here point to the creativity with which forms of governance are invented, tested and implemented in camps. Often such forms are learned and have travelled as more experienced protest campers bring ideas with them to new camps. Recent social movement scholarship has pointed to a crisis of representation as a uniting element of protest movements across the world (Sitrin and Azzellini, 2014). Unsurprisingly, these movements often choose protest forms such as the camp, in which new forms of governance and organisation can be tested for a future day, when they could replace representational politics and political elites.

Re-creation infrastructures

Across the cases discussed in this book, we find protesters busying themselves with the provision of shelter, food, entertainment and care. Very often these practices take up large parts of the activities pursued in the protest camp. The organisation of infrastructures for social reproduction take on many forms, but are often based on gifting economies, donations and the free labour of participants. The provision of these services poses the question of resources, and thus competes with other activities, such as the more classical political activities formulating demands, pursuing political action or even banner making. Many of the chapters presented here suggest that the politics of social reproduction is considered to be increasingly central to what protesters see as the priorities in protest camps (see Arruda (Chapter Eighteen); Pascucci (Chapter Seventeen); and Rollmann and Frenzel (Chapter Nineteen)). This may be read, we contend, as a reflection of the increasing crisis of social reproduction, following decades of neoliberalism and the pursuit of austerity since the financial and economic crisis of 2007/2008 (while also building on longer trajectories of social movement concerns with social reproduction, especially influenced by some strands of feminism). The net effect of these policies has been a broad retrenchment of the state from the provision of social reproduction and the increase of global inequality. Many of the camps discussed in the volume have formed in direct and indirect response to the crisis of social reproduction. This concerns in particular the housing protests (see Arruda (Chapter Eighteen); Gordon (Chpater Thirteen); Rollmann and Frenzel (Chapter Nineteen)), the protest camps against corruption (see Davies (Chapter Fifteen) and failed political elites and leadership (see Halvorsen (Chapter Ten); Shevtsova (Chapter Fourteen); and Thompson (Chapter Eleven)). It is of little surprise that the form of the protest camp, which is uniquely geared to addressing social re-production and to producing alternatives, becomes an increasingly visible tactic of protest in this environment.

The challenges of providing social reproduction in camps however remain significant and many of the chapters in this collection have highlighted the limits that protest camps face in this task. At the same time, it has become clear that protest camps provide moments of inspiration and indeed political ideas towards new approaches to care, solidarity economics and mutual aid, unparalleled in other protest forms. The perhaps most lasting impact of protest camps resides in formation of political subjectivities with lived experiences of social reproduction in non-capitalist forms.

Critical reflections on the protest camp form

Reflecting on these shared infrastructures of protest camps, we also want to highlight some of the criticisms of the protest camp form that emerge from the three parts of this volume. In the first part, we collected chapters that speak particularly to the material ways in which protest camps emerge. Rubing investigated protest camp architectures, drawing attention to textiles, while Kavada and Dimitriou examined points of convergence and divergence between mediated and material space. When infrastructures are assembled it makes sense to consider the levels of planning and spontaneity in this process, as Yaka and Karakayali show. Moreover, the objects themselves and the way they are used matter, whether these are kitchen utensils, umbrellas or mobile phones. Reflections by Gerbaudo on the role of ICTs, and by Wang et al on the use of diverse symbols highlight the centrality that materials have in the assembling of people. The materiality of protest camps is a strong focus of our research trajectory, but it also needs to be critically questioned. What is, for example, specifically useful in understanding that protest camps often use tents and do so across different movements? Materiality is imbued with specific agency in the sense that tents offer light, provisional and flexible architecture, which can be likened to a flexible and democratic form of politics (Feigenbaum et al, 2013). But we also want to warn against overlooking the different political contexts in which tents, to stay with this example, can be used. Materiality provides important insight into protest camps as a global phenomenon, but cannot replace an analysis of the specific politics pursued in a camp.

Chapters in Part Two are broadly concerned with the spatial practice of protest camps and the consequences of moving people and infrastructures into place. The occupation of land, of specific localities, is often considered a daring act, subversive to the extent that hegemonic readings of space are undermined. However, territorially based protests also need to reflect self-critically on the practice of taking space. Shevtsova and Thompson show the immense power in capturing and occupying symbolic spaces, underlining that many protest camps strive to create an antagonistic challenge to the status of quo that is expressed in spatial practice. However, Shevtsova warns of the sometimes unsavoury political tendencies that might emerge in such a positioning when it is expressed in overt nationalism. For Barker and Ross the notion of occupation needs to be reflected also in relation to the historical experience of (settler) colonialism. All too often protest camps might assume a spatial *tabula rasa* onto which political projects can be projected, in danger of erasing the histories that particular places carry. Gordon, reflecting on the Israeli housing protests of 2012, shows that the protest functions of social reproduction and contestation can develop conflicting trajectories when leaders emerge that detach themselves from the camp structures. Another danger of the territorial politics of camps is highlighted in the notions of fetishism discussed by Halvorsen and of refrain as Russell et al elaborate. Both chapters are concerned with the limitations of a protest form that focuses on place specifically, particular when the material and spatial practices work to undermine a more flexible response to political opportunities.

The setting up of infrastructures in place and the construction of alternative worlds in protest camps is broadly the topic of chapters assembled in Part Three of the book. The chapters consider the specific power of social reproduction as a domain of struggle. Camps and other place-based protests often become homes to participants, in the sense that protesters here find shelter, food and care. This practice is powerful and at the same time resource intensive. It enables the creation of broad coalitions of protesters, but it also results in tension as boundaries between what is normally rendered private becomes politicised in public debate. All chapters show the immense power of social reproduction, but they also discuss the problems that come to the surface in this form of action. Pascucci highlights how coalitions can form between protesters and outside supporters delivering crucial infrastructures. She discusses in particular how transnational governance may create spaces for refugee action that otherwise might be foreclosed in specific national settings. Three chapters deal particularly with housing protests, a key domain of social reproduction. Arruda shows that protest movements, at times, aim specifically at the provision of housing. She observes how notions of broader alternatives falter as housing is achieved and the participants settle in for more regular lives and routines. Rollmann and Frenzel explain how protest camps can be overstretched when attempting to provide housing while also maintaining political contestation. Crane highlights how the focus of social reproduction can wholly de-radicalise protest camps. When immediate contestation is suspended, social reproduction can become the dominant focus of the protest camps. In other cases, social reproduction can come to dominate when a protest camp becomes an ad-hoc homeless shelter and site for social care for those with mental health or drug problems. In these cases, protesters often feel their limits stretched, untrained in social work and without the resources to provide wellbeing, and plan political action.

Trajectories for future research

This volume has attempted to provide a broad discussion and case study based approach to the study of protest camps. As editors we are also aware of its limits. These limitations suggest a number of areas where future research should focus. As the form of protest camping seems so dominant and present today, it is easy to forget its histories. Few chapters in this volume have approached, with historical detail, camps and camp-related forms in the past. While the book does examine protest camps from around the world, the chapters that specifically address protests from recent history tend not to explore examples of historical protest camps outside Europe and the US. More research needs to be done to trace and analyse the historical experiences of protest camping around the world and map how their trajectories of resistance shape and influence contemporary practice. Other protest camps of significance not examined in this book include, the Aborigine Tent Embassy, Women Peace Camps that followed the Greenham Common protest, the Bonus Army Camp and the Hoovervilles, land occupations in Latin America, South African township housing protests, Japanese anti-globalisation camps like the Anti-G8 camps in 2008, urban land occupations in Berlin, Detroit, London and many other cities, the ZAD in Western France, the No Tav camps in Northern Italy, to name but a few.

The lens we choose to take, by focusing on protest camps, also creates limitations by excluding related forms of protest. While we have expanded the boundaries of what is defined as a protest camp, by deliberately including other forms of protest that feature the infrastructural set we use, this project might be usefully expanded to investigate the many overlaps that exists between protest camps and other spatially and temporarily bound autonomous zones (Bey, 1991). This includes, but is not limited to, the study of squats, urban and rural communes, neighborhood groups and collectives. Tent cities and squats mentioned briefly in our volume, form a particularly crucial link to protest camps, in that questions of social reproduction, and in particular shelter, move to the forefront of these protest forms. In the current, increasingly global crisis of housing, the need to shelter and house refugees and the retrenchment of the state from the provision of social housing, can camps, tent cities and squats provide examples of more autonomous forms of new common housing? Future research should address such questions.

The political orientation of protest camps has also been diverse and yet, following an extended discussion among the editors, we deliberately excluded right-wing camps (for example, the January 2016 armed occupation by right-wing militia men of Malheur National Wildlife Refuge, in Burns Oregon). But our focus on what we would consider progressive social movements did sometimes betray our specific view of left- and right-wing politics. In the context of the protest camps discussed in India or the Ukraine, for example, right-wing politics was explicitly present as a factor in the politics of these camps. Future research might consider right-wing camps more specifically.

The broad appeal of the protest camp form, sometimes cutting across ideological boundaries, points to further structural and geopolitical trajectories for future research. With the retrenchment of the state that is both a result of globalisation and neoliberal policy, the nation-state remains a contested form of political organisation. Many protest camps, in their quest for autonomy from the status quo, also question the legitimacy of the nation-state as the main locus of collective political organisation. We observe the renewed questioning of the territorial boundaries of the nation-state in resurgent regionalisms in Europe, in the autonomous communities of indigenous groups in Mexico, or in the political project of autonomous regions pursued by Kurds. Those projects scale-up significantly the experiences made in many camps, and can be investigated in relation to them.

Conclusion

This volume has thus assembled 17 unique case studies that reflect on the protest camp as a form of political and social action. We think that this is a further step towards understanding this specific form of protest, making connections to others and drawing out lines and inspiration for future research. Overall, protest camps remain a thoroughly understudied, but immensely interesting field for social movement research. We expect protest camps to grow in significance over the next decades – linking different struggles, forming collective imaginaries, and providing an experience of politics unparalleled in representational forms of decision-making, while responding uniquely to new forms of mediatisation. As this volume shows, there is much that critical research can contribute to a better understanding of this form of protest, not just for academic reflection, but also for those who use camps to protest against injustices and create alternative worlds. Moreover, examining the protest camp can often reveal to us the failures of the nation-state to properly care for people. From broken forms of representational governance, to manufactured housing shortages, the nation-state's inability to fulfill its social contract is often what is amplified, contested and problem-solved in the space of protest camps. As such, the protest camp – in both its successes and shortcomings – is an exemplary site of democratic renewal.

References

Bey, H. (1991) *T.A.Z.: The Temporary Autonomous Zone, Ontological Anarchy, Poetic Terrorism*. Brooklyn, NY: Autonomedia.

Brown, G. and Yaffe, H. (2014) 'Practices of solidarity: opposing apartheid in the centre of London', *Antipode*, 46(1), 34–52.

Feigenbaum, A., Frenzel, F. and McCurdy, P. (2013) *Protest Camps*. London: Zed.

Frenzel, F. (2010) *Politics in Motion: The Mobilities of Political Tourists*, PhD thesis, Leeds: Leeds Metropolitan University.

Sitrin, M. and Azzellini, D. (2014) *They Can't Represent Us!: Reinventing Democracy From Greece To Occupy*. London and Brooklyn, NY: Verso.

Index

References to photographs are in *italics*

A

Aboriginal Tent Embassy 5, 43
action infrastructures 13–14, 396
Activism Festivals (Israel) 225–6
actor network theory 209
Adbusters 169
affective connectivity 395
Afghani refugees 45–6
Ahmed, S. 359
Albers, A. 37, 39
Alcatraz, occupation of 192–5
alcohol in camps 251, 360–1
Althusser, L. 61–2
Alÿs, Francis 374
Anderson, B. 57
Anishnaabe community, Canada
    203–4, 209–10
antagonistic form of camp 175
anti-apartheid activists 6–7
anti-colonialism
  Alcatraz, occupation of 192–5
  in Canada 199–214
  Columbia University, occupation of
    186–92
  critique of 182–6
anti-corruption *see* Hazare, Anna
anti-logging blockades 203–4, 208,
    209–10, 211–13
anti-nuclear movement 5–6
anti-road protests 94
anti-summit protests 8–9, 149, 151–2,
    157
architecture *see* textiles
Arditi, B. 383
asylum seekers 45–8
  see also refugees
Athens *see* Indignant movement,
    Syntagma Square
Australia
  Aboriginal Tent Embassy 5, 43
  Occupy Melbourne 26–8
autogestion 164–5, 167

B

Bakhtin, M. 182
Banerjee, S. 269–70
Barry, K. 190
Bastéa, E. 76
Beissinger M.R. 246–7, 255
Benjamin, W. 66, 179
Bennett, W.L. 118
Berlin-Kreuzberg *see* Free Cuvry camp,
    Germany
bodies and protest 38–40, 49
Bonus Army 3–4
Bradley, S.M. 187
Brazil
  Intercontinental Youth Camp, Brazil
    7
  see also Marconi occupation, Brazil
Britain
  Greenham Common 5–6, 94–5
  HoriZone camp 8–9, 149
  South African embassy, London 6–7
  see also Camp for Climate Action,
    Britain; Occupy London
Brown, H. Rap 191
Bruyneel, K. 207
Bryce, C. 210
Butler, J. 38, 39, 48, 49

C

Cairo *see* Mustapha Mahmoud refugee
    camp
Calais Migrant Solidarity/No Border
    camps
  background to 356
  Feminist Security Group 357–9
  research methodology 354
  safer spaces policies at 355–7
  safety considerations at 359–67
Camp for Climate Action, Britain
  background to 147–8
  and camping as political refrain
    155–8

characteristics of 152–3
context of 149–53
demise of 158–9
legacy of 149
and political tensions 153–5
Canada *see* indigenous groups, Canada
Canberra 5, 43
Castells, M. 124, 126
Chalozin-Dovrat, L. 231
Chatterjee, P. 268–9, 270
Chatterton, P. 315, 376
church asylum, Norway 47–8, 49
Churchill, W. 195
Civic Square, Hong Kong 110–11,
113–15, *118*
civil society, India 268–73
climate action camps *see* Camp for
Climate Action, Britain
clothing 39
colonialism *see* anti-colonialism
Columbia Daily Spectator, The 187–92
Columbia University, occupation of
186–92
Comité de Lucha UAM-X 377–80
communications infrastructures *see*
media and communications
conceptual frameworks of camps 10–16
Connolly, W. 323
contentious politics, and space 73–5,
82–6
Contes, Regev 224, 237
Coulthard, G. 199, 201
Cowan, G. 43, 48
Cresswell, T. 321
Crossa, V. 373–4

D

Daphi, P. 73
del Castillo Troncoso, A. 381–2
Deleuze, G. 156
democratic deficit *see* Israeli tent
protest movement
Dikeç, M. 383
diversity of camps 393–4
Dobbs, H. 193
Drax power station, Yorkshire 151

E

Earth First! 8
education
Camp for Climate Change, Britain
151, 152
political education 371–87

Egypt *see* Mustapha Mahmoud refugee
camp
Ehrenreich, B. 297–8
Engels, F. 312–13
Ethiopian refugees 46, 303
Euromaidan, Kiev *250, 253*
background to 243–4, 247–8
compared with Orange Maidan
(2004) 248–52, 255–6
decision-making in 253–5, 256–7
infrastructures 248–51
and political parties 252
representational space 251–2
research methodology 244
right-wing groups 254–5
social media 249
state response to 248, 252–3
transformation to *sich* 252–4

F

Facebook 80, 81, 82, 102, 119, 129,
223–4, 377
Fanon, F. 185–6
fasting *see* Hazare, Anna (India)
feeds *see* live feeds
Feigenbaum, A. 10–11, 53, 65, 74, 82,
94, 175, 206, 209, 246, 266, 322,
333, 376
Feminist Security Group 357–8
fetishism
antagonistic form of camp 175
and autogestion 164–5, 167
and 'cracks' 165–6
and Occupy London 168–75
FMRS (Forced Migration and Refugee
Studies) 294, 295, 297, 299, 300,
301
Foley, G. 5
Fortunate Eagle, A. 192, 193, 194
Foucault, M. 313, 383
France *see* Calais Migrant Solidarity/
No Border camps
Franco, Edinalva 314
Free Cuvry camp, Germany *331, 337,
343*
achievements of 348
background to 329–30
context of 335–6
dual character of 346–8
emergence of 337–40
eviction of 338–9, 342, 344–6, *345*
governance infrastructures of 342–4,
347
location of 335–6, 337

research methodology 331–2
and social reproduction 340–2, 346–8
voluntary and involuntary occupants
346–7
'free' spaces 74
Freeman, J. 222, 234–6
Frenzel, F. 53, 82, 206, 209, 316,
333–4
future research 400–2

G

G8 summit 8–9, 149
G20 summit 151–2
Gamson, W.A. 322
Gandhi, Mahatma 42, 266–7
gender see women
gentrification see Free Cuvry camp,
Germany
Germany see Free Cuvry camp,
Germany
Gezi Park, Istanbul
context of 54–5
emergence of the camp 56
nature of the camp 57, 58–60, 64–5
participants in 58–9
radical infrastructures of 60–6
relation with Taksim Square 57
state response to 54, 55, 59, 64
and teargas 64
Gibson-Graham, J.K. 319, 323
governance/organisational
infrastructures 10, 14–15, 396–7
Grassy Narrows, Canada 203–4, 208,
209–10, 211–13
Greece see Indignant movement,
Syntagma Square
Green Action, Israel 225
Greenham Common, England 5–6,
94–5
Guattari, F. 155–6
Guggenheim Lab 338
Gül, M. 54

H

Haiven, M. 214
Halvorsen, S. 334
Harindranath, R. 270
Harvey, D. 309, 315
Hazare, Anna (India)
and civil society 268–3
fast as political practice 265–8
importance of the site 267
infrastructures 264

and Jan Lokpal campaign 262–5
and the media 265–8, 273
summary of 261–2
and tensions 264
Heathrow airport camp 151, 154
'HeHe' culture 119–20
heterotopias 62, 65, 313, 321, 325
history of camps 3–9
Hofstadter, Noam 226, 232, 236–7
Holloway, J. 164, 165–6, 170, 175, 311
Hong Kong Federation of Students
(HKFS) 110–11, 113–14
Hong Kong Umbrella Movement see
Umbrella Movement, Hong Kong
hooks, bell 313–14
HoriZone camp, Scotland 8–9, 149
Hosey, L. 42–3, 48
housing see Free Cuvry camp,
Germany; Israeli tent protest
movement; Marconi occupation,
Brazil
Huber, Mor 228, 231
Hundertwasser, F. 39

I

India see Hazare, Anna (India)
Indians of All Tribes 192–5
indigenous groups
Aboriginal Tent Embassy 5, 43
Alcatraz, occupation of 192–5
and anti-colonial critique 182–6
see also indigenous protest camps,
Canada
indigenous protest camps, Canada
activists and solidarity 211–13
background 199–202
Grassy Narrows 203–4, 208, 209–10,
211–13
identity and the land 208–11
Oka Crisis 202–3, 208, 211, 213
and outsiders 211–13
and responsibility 213–14
resurgence of 207–8
social media 206
state response to 200, 202, 208
Unist'ot'en 205–6, 208, 210–13
Indignados movement, Spain 91, 97–8,
101–2, 104
Indignant movement, Syntagma Square
aftermath of 87–8
as centre of mediation 82–6
eviction of camp 87
group splitting 77–82
online presence of 80–2

research methodology 75
state response to 79, 85, 87
symbolic significance of 76–7
infrastructures (general) 10–16, 395–8, 399–400
  see also individual camps, action infrastructures, communications infrastructures, governance/ organisational infrastructures, radical infrastructures, re-creation infrastructures
institutionalisation 165–8, 171, 175
Intercontinental Youth Camp, Brazil 7
internet see media and communications
Iplikci, M. 63
Ir Lekulanu 226–7
Israel, Silwan tent protest 43–5, 44, 49
Israeli tent protest movement
  aftermath of 233–4
  author's involvement in 229–34
  current literature 221–2
  and decision-making 229–34
  demise of 233
  early tensions within 226–8
  failure of 229–8
  and formal structures 234–8
  and the media 224–5
  mobilisation of 223–6
  research methodology 223
  Rothschild camp 224–5, 226, 227
Istanbul see Gezi Park, Istanbul

J

Jackson, Jesse 4
Jan Lokpal campaign see Hazare, Anna (India)
Jasiewicz, E. 154
Jerusalem
  Silwan protest tent 43–5, 44, 49
  see also Israeli tent protest movement
Johnson, T.R. 194–5
Jones, J. 210
Jordan, J. 316–17
Juris, J.S. 316

K

Kaika, M. 74, 78
Karaliotas, L. 74, 78
Kaye/Kantrowitz, M. 185
Kejriwal, Arvind 271
Kerrison, Sara Louise 26–7
Khasnabish, A. 214
Khorana, S. 270

Kiev see Euromaidan, Kiev
King, H. 210
King, Martin Luther 4
Klein, N. 182
Kokot, A. 191
Koolhaas, R. 321
Kousis, M. 85, 87
Krischer, O. 117

L

learning in protests camps see education
Leef, Daphni 223–4, 227–8, 231, 233
Lefebvre, H. 72, 73, 164–5, 166, 245–6
Lewis, A. 213
LGBTI community 120, 126, 130, 254
Little Bear, L. 209
live feeds
  audiences of 101–4
  and double nature of protest camps 93–6
  importance of 91–3, 95–6, 99, 103–4, 105
  and Indignados 97–8, 101–2, 104
  meaning of 97
  Occupy Wall Street 97, 98–9, 102–3, 104
  research methodology 96
  risks of 100–1, 105
  and self-representation of protest space 104–5
  and transparency 99–101
London
  South African embassy 6–7
  see also Occupy London
Los Angeles, Occupy 40–1, 42

M

Madrid, Indignados movement 91, 97–8, 101–2, 104
Maidan camps, Kiev see Euromaidan, Kiev
Marconi occupation, Brazil 312, 314
  action infrastructures 317–20
  background to 309–15
  common life and social reproduction 322–4
  communications infrastructures 316–17
  crisis of social reproduction 324–5
  domestic infrastructure 321–2, 322
  governance infrastructures 320–1, 320

infrastructures of 316–22
research methodology 315
as urban camp 315–22
Marx, K. 61
Massey, D. 373
materialism 61–2
McCurdy, P. 53, 82, 94, 95, 206, 209
McGuire, M. 184
McNevin, A. 298
media and communications
bias of 97
at Euromaidan 249
and Hazare, Anna 265–8, 273
at HoriZone camp 9
and Indignant movement, Syntagma
Square 80–5, 87
infrastructures of 12–13, 395–6
and Israeli tent protest movement
223–5
at Marconi occupation, Brazil
316–17
and representation of camps 94–6
and space 72–3
and transparency of camps 99–101
and Umbrella Movement, Hong
Kong 127–30
see also live feeds
Mexico City camps
infrastructures 374–5, 375
locations of camps 372–5
and political education 374–83, 375
and shaping lifecourses 380–3
as sites of learning 376–80
and solidarity 383–6
and subjectification 373, 378
as youth activism 371–2
Meyrowitz, J. 72
Mezirow, J. 319
migrants
NOII movement (No One is Illegal)
212–13
see also Calais Migrant Solidarity/No
Border camps; Mustapha Mahmoud
refugee camp
Milgrom, R. 245–6
MMPT (Movement for Housing for
All) see Marconi occupation, Brazil
Mohawk nation 202–3
Monbiot, G. 154
Monterescu, D. 222
Morgensen, S. 208
Moulin, C. 291, 298, 301–2
Movimento dos Trabalhadores Rurais
Sem Terra (MST) 311

Movimiento de Liberación National
(MLN) 372–6
Muda 315, 318, 319
Mueller, Clayton Thomas 184
Mustapha Mahmoud refugee camp,
Egypt
background to 289–90, 292–4
eviction of camp 300–2
infrastructures of care 296–300
legacy of 302–3
location of 295–6
material support 296
research methodology 290
security at 299
state response to 300–2
and Sudanese diaspora 292–4

N

Nasha Ukrayina 247, 248–9
Native Americans 192–5
Nelson, L. 373
Netanyahu, Benjamin 226
New York, Occupy Wall Street 98–9,
102–3, 104, 181, 181
No Border camps see Calais Migrant
Solidarity/No Border camps
NOII movement (No One is Illegal)
212–13
Non-Stop Picket, London 6–7
Norway 45–8
Nyers, P. 291, 298, 301–2

O

Occupy Central with Love and Peace
(OCLP) 110
Occupy LA 40–1, 42
Occupy London
and antagonism 175
court case 172–3
eviction of camp 172–3
fetishising of 168–75
locations of camps 163
research methodology 164
tactic of 167–8
Occupy Melbourne 26–8
Occupy movement, US
Alcatraz, occupation of 192–5
anti-colonial critique 182–6
Columbia University, occupation of
186–92
reflections on 179–82
see also other Occupy camps

Occupy Wall Street 98–9, 102–3, 104, 181, *181*
occupying, ways of 137–40
Oka Crisis, Canada 202–3, 208, 211, 213
Okupa Che 385–6
online presence *see* media and communications
Orange Revolution, Kiev 247, 248–9, 252, 255, 256
Orvano, Rona 229, 230
Oslo 45–8, 49
Osterweil, M. 309

P

Palestinian protesters
  in Oslo, Norway 45–9
  in Silwan, Jerusalem 43–5, *44*, 49
Park, R. 309
Parubiy, Andriy 251
Peres, Shimon 228
Perry, A. 358
Pickerill, J. 315
pipelines, Unist'ot'en, Canada 205–6, 208, 210–13
plasticity politics 48–9
political education *see* Mexico City camps
political plastic 41–2, 49
Polletta, F. 74
power, and space 75, 87
Price, S. 153
protest camps (general)
  conceptual frameworks of 10–16
  history of 3–9
Puerta del Sol, Indignados movement 91, 97–8, 101–2, 104

R

radical infrastructures 60–5
Rajagopal, A. 268
Rambam, Yigal 224, 226
Ramdev, Baba 263
re-creation infrastructures *see* social reproduction
Reäuberläb 338–9
reclamation sites *see* indigenous protest camps, Canada
Reed, C.T. 181–2, 192
refrains 155–8
Refugee Voice 293, 294
refugees

NOII movement (No One is Illegal) 212–13
Palestinian 45–8
see also Calais Migrant Solidarity/No Border camps; Mustapha Mahmoud refugee camp, Egypt
Reguillo, R. 384
reoccupation sites *see* indigenous protest camps, Canada
representation of space 245, 246–8
representational space 245, 251–2
Resurrection City, Washington 4–5, 42–3
rhizomatic form of movement 124, 126
Roestone Collective 361, 363, 364
Rogers, J. 199
Rosenhek, Z. 221
Routledge, P. 211, 318
Roy, Arundhati 264–5
Rygiel, K. 271, 304

S

Saco, D. 72–3
safety *see* Calais Migrant Solidarity/No Border camps
São Paulo *see* Marconi occupation, Brazil
Saunders, C. 153
Scannell, P. 72
Schein, R. 342, 346
Schmitt, C. 193
Segerberg, A. 118
Semper, G. 37, 48
Sewel, W.H. Jr 73–4, 55
Shachaf, Sharon 226, 236–7
Shafir, Stav 228, 231, 233, 234
Shaindlinger, N. 222
Shakuf baOhel 227–8
Shalev, M. 221
Shmuli, Itzik 224, 226, 228, 233, 234
Shoshan, A. 227
Silwan, Jerusalem 43–5, *44*, 49
Simmel, G. 58
Simone, A. 291
Sitapati, V. 264
Sobolev, Egor 248
social media 395–6
  Euromaidan 249
  Facebook 80, 81, 82, 102, 119, 129, 223–4, 377
  Indignant movement 80–2, 206
  Twitter 95, 96, 97, 98, 206

Umbrella Movement, Hong Kong
127–30
see also live feeds
social reproduction (concept of) 10–11,
15–16, 280–2, 397–8, 399–400
and clashes with political action
333–5, 346–7
see also Free Cuvry camp, Germany;
Marconi occupation, Brazil;
Mustapha Mahmoud refugee camp,
Egypt
Solomon, Victor 187, 191
Sol.tv 98
South African embassy, London 6–7
space/spaces
as centre of mediation 82–7
and contentious politics 73–5, 86
cyberspace 72–3, 80–2, 101–2
defining 71–3
free spaces 4
heterotopias 62, 65, 313, 321, 325
homeplace 314
and power 75, 87
and protest camps 11–12, 74–5
representation of space 245, 246–8
representational space 245, 251–2
safer spaces policies 355–67
spatial agency 75
spatial practices 245–6, 248–51
Spain, Indignados movement 91, 97–8,
101–2, 104
Spence, L. 184
squats *see* Marconi occupation, Brazil
Stern, M. 188
Strasburg 7–8
students
Euromaidan 247, 250
Columbia University occupation
186–92
Umbrella Movement, Hong Kong
110–11, 113–14, 119–20, 123, 125
see also Mexico City camps
Stulberg, R. 189, 190–1
subjectification 373, 378
Sudanese refugees *see* Mustapha
Mahmoud refugee camp
Sullivan, S. 271–2
Susen, S. 311
Swidler, A. 115
Syntagma Square *see* Indignant
movement, Syntagma Square

T

Taksim Solidarity 55, 56
Taksim Square, Istanbul 54–5, 57
Taylor, E. 319
Tennis Court Oath *181*
Tent Monsters 26–8
tents *see* textiles
textiles
and architecture 37–41
and bodies 38–40
in Norway 45–8, *46*
and Occupy LA 40–1, 42
plasticity politics 48–9
and political plastic 41–2, 49
as politics 42–8
and private/public separation 37–8
as protection 37–8
in Silwan, Jerusalem 43–5, *44*, 49
and urbanism 40–1
Tilly, C. 74
Toledano, M. 206
transparency of camps 99–101, 104
Turkey *see* Gezi Park, Istanbul
Twitter 95, 96, 97, 98, 206

U

UAM-X, Mexico City 377–80
Ukraine *see* Euromaidan, Kiev
Umbrella Movement, Hong Kong
anti-Umbrella Movement 129–30
background to 110–12
banners 125–6, *127*
bodies and protest 119–20
and colour yellow 116–18
communications 127–30
demonstrations outside of camp
125–6
embracing dissent 124–7
everyday living in the camps 120–4
gender perspective 124
HeHe culture 119–20
Lion Rock 125, *127*
reasons for support 113–16
rhizomatic form of movement 126
role of universities 125–6
sexual violence 119, 130
significance of umbrellas *115*, 115–16
state response to 111, 112, 113–14,
115, 127–8, 129
as student movement 123
summary of 130–1
symbols of 115–20, *120*

Unist'ot'en, Canada 205–6, 208,
    210–13
United Kingdom *see* Britain
United Nations High Commissioner
    for Refugees (UNHCR) 290,
    292–6, 298, 300, 302, 303
United Progressive Alliance (UPA),
    India 261, 263, 264, 265
United States
  Bonus Army 3–4
  Occupy LA 40–1, 42
  Occupy Wall Street 98–9, 102–3,
    104, 181, *181*
  Resurrection City 4–5, 42–3
  see also Occupy movement, US

V

van Duppen, J. 332, 337–8

W

Washington 3–4, 42–3, 194
Watts, V. 208–9
websites
  Indignant movement 80–2, 83
  and live streaming 95, 98
Weizman, E. 41–2, 43, 45, 49
Whitebear, Bernie 194
Willow, A.J. 203, 204, 209–10, 211
Wilson, A. 249, 251
Wolfsfeld, G. 322
women
  and colonial discourse 358
  Feminist Security Group 357–8
  at Gezi Park, Istanbul 59–60
  Greenham Common 5–6, 94–5
  safety in camps 355–67
  and social reproduction 280–1
  Umbrella Movement, Hong Kong
    124, 130

Y

Yanukovych, Viktor 247
Yee, J. 182–3, 185
yellow, as symbol in Hong Kong
    117–18, *118*, 129–30
#YoSoy132 camp 377, 379, 381, 384,
    385
Yushchenko, Viktor 246–7, 248–9,
    251–2